Richard Whately Cooke-Taylor

Introduction to a History of the Factory System

Richard Whately Cooke-Taylor

Introduction to a History of the Factory System

ISBN/EAN: 9783337338763

Printed in Europe, USA, Canada, Australia, Japan

Cover: Foto ©ninafisch / pixelio.de

More available books at **www.hansebooks.com**

INTRODUCTION

TO A

HISTORY OF THE FACTORY

SYSTEM

BY

R. WHATELY COOKE-TAYLOR

LONDON

RICHARD BENTLEY & SON, NEW BURLINGTON STREET

1886

Printed by R. & R. CLARK, *Edinburgh*.

PREFACE

I HAD aspired to write the *History of the Factory System.*
In collecting materials for doing so two difficulties continually confronted me. The first was the great mass of
detail that would need to be presented to the reader should
the work attempt in even a moderate degree to justify its
title. The second was the lack of material of prime
importance on which such a history could be based. The
factory system of the far past has left no records behind;
that remains still a subject of inquiry and speculation.
The history of the modern factory system is almost equally
difficult of access. It is to be found only in the few, and
generally vague, allusions of very various writers; and in
official documents and departmental reports of this and
other countries. There is absolutely no independent source
of information in English literature, that I know of, dealing
with the whole of this subject. I have preferred instead
then, greatly to limit the scope of my original design, and to
confine it to an Introduction only, and that in outline, to
such a history, arranged in what I consider would be
something like the proper form for a work of the kind to
assume. There should be comparatively little difficulty
hereafter in filling in that outline, and continuing the
narrative down to the present day, were any fairly com-

petent person to undertake the task. Where the real
difficulty lies is in grouping together in an orderly succession
the various impulses, historical and economical, that have
been concerned about the evolution of this particular method
of production; of tracing a continuity, and exhibiting the
points of contact among them; and of suggesting the right
moral throughout. This has been my endeavour here.

It is little less than a scandal to our industrial literature
that the effort was not made before. It is a truly extraordinary omission from it that this most portentous and
characteristic feature of our national economy still awaits
systematic investigation. Foreigners have not been quite
so backward in the matter. In several noteworthy books
abroad, the philosophy and history of the factory system
are dealt with in a capable and thoughtful manner; though
more usually in the interests of some special school of
economic teaching than solely for themselves.[1] But here,
in the land of its fullest adoption; in (as it were) its own
peculiar home; no such philosophical analyses; nothing
indeed but the most meagre treatises exist; those mostly
of a controversial kind; and scarcely any even of them
within the last forty years.[2] It is not that the subject

---

[1] The allusion is to the socialistic economists of Germany, France, and
Italy. It is unnecessary to instance the works of any of these as they have
in no case been made use of in the composition of this volume.

[2] It is worthy of note that none of the English Encyclopædias, nor
other great works of reference, have anything approaching to an adequate
article on the factory system. Many of them have no article on it at all, and
those that have nearly universally confine themselves to a brief summary
of the Factory Acts. Even the *Penny Cyclopædia* cannot be excepted from
this category, though it is perhaps the least culpably negligent in the matter.
In *Great Industries of Great Britain*, published by Messrs. Cassell, there is
a clear statement of modern English legislation; but this is all.

itself is repellent, or of limited interest. A history of the
most productive form of industrial organisation ever known,
of its methods and vicissitudes, should surely be one of
surpassing interest to the statesman and jurist; equally with
the economist and employer of labour; but most of all to
the persons employed. Nor need it be much less so to
every other member of the body politic. That history,
properly told, would be full, in its earlier stages, of quaint
contrasts and still more significant harmonies between the
social conditions of the past and present; of strange survivals
and long neglected facts; of the records of achievements
of high, often of most romantic interest; of unremitting
human interest throughout. Something of this even the
present Introduction may disclose. But how much would
the interest be deepened when the story came to tell of
quite recent times. The history of that revolution in
industry, and consequently all social life, that is the fruit
of the modern factory system, would have to speak of the
most sudden and amazing transformation in human affairs
that mankind has yet witnessed. In the course of little
more than a century the industrial framework of the whole
civilised world has been radically reconstructed, and more
changes have occurred in consequence, even more obvious
and tangible changes—changes conspicuous upon the very
face and features of the country itself—than for certainly
the whole of a previous 1300 years.[1] How that new

[1] An article in the *Fortnightly Review* for April 1882 has the following
remarks on this subject :—"The last hundred years have seen in England the
most sudden change in our material life that is perhaps recorded in history. . . .
The use of steam in manufactures, and locomotion by sea and land, the textile
revolution, the factory system, the enormous growth of population, the change
from a rural to a town life, the portentous growth of the empire, the vast expan-

system of industry arose and spread; what it succeeded; whence it came; whither it tends; to what extent and in what directions it has affected and is likely to affect our destinies :—these are some of the considerations which such a history would deal with, and they are not anywhere, one would say, to be excelled in interest. Least of all, one should surely say, in England, whose prosperity, whose existence almost : whose existence certainly as a great

sion of sea power, of commerce, of manufactures, of wealth, of intercommunication, of the post; then the use of gas, electricity, telegraphs, telephones, steam-presses, sewing-machines, air-engines, gas-engines, electric-engines, photographs, tunnels, ship canals, and all the rest. Early in the last century England was one of the lesser kingdoms in Europe, but one-third in size and numbers of France and Germany; now it is in size twenty times—twenty times—as big as either, and six or seven times as populous as either. London was then only one of a dozen cities in Europe, hardly of the area of Manchester or Leeds; it is now the biggest and most populous city in recorded history, nearly equal, I suppose, in size and population to all the capitals of Europe put together. . . . For 4000 years we know, and probably for 40,000 years, man has travelled over land as fast as his own legs, or men's legs, or horses' legs, could carry him, but no faster; over sea as fast as sails or oars could carry him. Now he goes by steam over both, at least at three times the pace. In previous ages, possibly for twenty centuries, about 100 miles a day was the outside limit of any long continuous journey; now we can go 4000 miles by sea in fourteen days, and by land in five days. . . . The whole surface of our planet has only been known about 100 years. . . . For 20,000 years every fabric in use has been twisted into thread by human fingers and woven into stuff by the human hand. Machines and steam-engines now make 10,000 shirts in the time that was formerly occupied in making one. For 20,000 years man had got no better light than was given by pitch, tallow, or oil; he now has gas and electricity, each light of which is equal to hundreds and thousands of candles. Where there used to be a few hundred books there are now 100,000; and the London newspapers of a single year consume, I daresay, more type and paper than the printing-presses of the whole world produced from the days of Gutenberg to the French Revolution. . . . Take it all in all, the merely material, physical, and mechanical change in human life in the hundred years from the days of Watt and Arkwright to our own is greater than occurred in the thousand years that preceded, perhaps even in 2000 or 20,000 years."

removed; its faults, that closer study might have remedied. But the moment is critical; time is precious; and if the facts thus loosely grouped together should assist, though ever so little, in instructing public opinion upon the matter about which they are concerned, I shall be satisfied that I have acted for the best.

WHATELY COOKE TAYLOR.

May 26, 1886.

CONTENTS

CHAPTER I.

THE FACTORY SYSTEM

CHAPTER II.

OTHER FORMS OF LABOUR ORGANISATION

CHAPTER III.

MANUFACTURING INDUSTRY IN ANCIENT TIMES
(TEXTILE INDUSTRIES)

CHAPTER IV.

MANUFACTURING INDUSTRIES IN ANCIENT TIMES
(MISCELLANEOUS INDUSTRIES)

CHAPTER V.

ANCIENT AND MEDIÆVAL COMMERCE

CHAPTER VI.

MEDIÆVAL MANUFACTURES

CHAPTER VII.

ENGLAND BEFORE THE FACTORY SYSTEM—TO THE REIGN OF EDWARD III.

CHAPTER VIII.

ENGLAND BEFORE THE FACTORY SYSTEM—FROM EDWARD III. TO WILLIAM III.

CHAPTER IX. ✦

THE MODERN FACTORY SYSTEM

CHAPTER X.

THE GREAT MECHANICAL INVENTIONS

INTRODUCTION

TO A

HISTORY OF THE FACTORY SYSTEM

CHAPTER I.

THE FACTORY SYSTEM

Factory—Statutory Definitions—Mill—Manufacture—Manufacture and Mart
—Trade — Handicraft — Art and Manufacture — Agriculture — Laws of
Agricultural and Manufacturing Industry—Machinery—Division and
Combination of Labour—The Factory System—Extractive Industries—
Transport and Building—Services and Commodities—Immaterial Pro-
ducts—Plan of this Work.

THE word "factory" is one that has greatly altered in meaning
within recent times. Its earlier signification
was that of a trading establishment, usually   FACTORY.
in a distant country, with which were associated in idea
the settlements and surroundings appertaining. It is so
defined primarily even yet in most modern dictionaries.
Thus, "a house or place where factors reside to transact
business" (Wright and Webster), and, "the collective body
of such factors ;"—"a house or district inhabited by traders
in a distant country" (Johnson and Lathom).[1] Commercial

---

[1] In Knight's *Cyclopædia of the Industry of all Nations* (1851) it is given
thus: "An establishment of merchants and factors resident in foreign countries
who were governed by certain regulations adopted for their mutual support
and assistance against the undue encroachment or interference of the government of the countries in which they resided." See also Notcutt's *Factory and
Workshops Acts*, Introduction, note (*a*).

1

countries discovering, or bringing into subjection, favourable tracts of foreign territory have commonly established "factories," *i.e.* buildings and bodies of traders there, or frequently these have been planted in the dominions of countries well acquainted and at amity, for purposes of mutual convenience. Occasionally this earlier meaning of the word is found adhering to it still. It is not unusual even now to read of *factories* which civilised countries possess, or desire to possess, in remote places ; establishments, that is, not for the production of commodities but for their exchange. A factory in this sense differed from a colony or other territorial settlement in being established, nominally at all events, for purposes exclusively commercial, and with the consent, obtained or implied, of the inhabitants of the district where it was placed. It has sometimes happened that this consent was assumed too hastily, or has been withdrawn, and that the people in whose territory the factory was situated have attacked it, its defence leading to the acquisition of further portions of that territory, or perhaps even of the whole. It has also happened that the interests of rival factories established perhaps in the same country have come into collision, their disagreements leading to internecine conflicts, or even to wars between parent States. Sometimes neighbouring native communities have voluntarily placed themselves under the rule of the residents at a factory, and so thrust sovereignty upon them. Sometimes they have come gradually under their dominion. An extraordinary instance of great results proceeding from causes such as these is afforded by the spectacle of the foreign possessions of England at the present day, especially in India. The British East India Company, from having been the proprietors of a few "factories" on the coast of Hindostan, came at length, through the operation of certain of them, and by making a bold and dexterous use of the opportunities thus created, to exercise sovereign power over the greater part of that immense peninsula; and to transfer that sovereignty in time to the British crown. It is not beyond the bounds of possibility that, but for the folly of an obstinate king, and the fatuity of an incompetent minister, the whole great continent of North America might now, from the operation of like causes, have been equally a portion of this empire.

At what period precisely the term "factory" lost its primary and acquired its present meaning, is uncertain. Dr. Aikin in a *History of Manchester*, published in 1793, uses the words "mills" and "factories" indiscriminately; while Mr. Baines, in his *History of the Cotton Manufacture* (1835), refers to the use of the latter term for designating a place of production as a modern innovation. Ure's *Dictionary of Arts and Manufactures* has no article on the word "factory." In the last edition (1880) of M'Culloch's *Commercial Dictionary* it is merely described as an abbreviation of "manufactory;" and in Dodd's *Dictionary of Manufactures, etc.* (1876), no allusion to the modern altered meaning is made. The change began to take place apparently towards the end of the last century,[1] and the substitution was a gradual one. Nor is it probable, though it might appear so, that that change was then, or at any time, brought about by a process of etymological reasoning. Ample justification for the present use of the word is to be found of course in its derivation (from Latin "facio"), but for ages *factor* had been rendered *agent*, and all compound derivatives, as *factorise, factorage, factorship,* had had to do with agentship. The explanation therefore must be sought elsewhere. The altered meaning was coincident with the first application on a large scale of foreign motive powers in textile industry, and appears to have had a close relationship to that event.

[1] See *Penny Cyclopædia*, Article "Factory."

What is certain is that, as early at all events as the
year 1802, this word was interpreted in a
STATUTORY modern sense by the legislature. In that
DEFINITIONS. year the first Factory Act (42° Geo. III.
Cap. 73) was passed, being entitled " An Act for the
Preservation of the Health and Morals of Apprentices
employed in Cotton and other Mills, and in Cotton and
other Factories," where the words *mill* and *factory* seem to
be used as complementary or exchangeable terms, but are
nowhere defined, while the older signification at all events
is abandoned. In a succeeding statute (3° and 4° Will. IV.
Cap. 103)—in which the area of restrictive legislation was
considerably enlarged—*mills* and *factories* are again found
coupled together as terms descriptive of places where certain
productive operations are performed, and still as yet with no
separate distinctive meanings attached to them. It was
not until a much later statute (7° and 8° Vic. Cap. 15)
that this deficiency was made good, and the title "factory"
fixed by law. The seventy-third section of that Act recites,
that *factory* " shall be taken to mean all buildings and
premises situate within any part of the United Kingdom of
Great Britain and Ireland wherein, or within the close or
curtilage of which, steam, water, or any other mechanical
power, shall be used to move or work any machinery
employed in preparing, manufacturing, or finishing, or in
any process incident to the manufacture of cotton, wool,
hair, silk, flax, hemp, jute, or tow, either separately or mixed
together, or mixed with any other material, or any fabric
made thereof;" and the term "mill" is not employed,
except in connection with "mill-gearing," between which
and "machinery" some nice distinctions are drawn, which
have a history of their own. At this time, therefore
(1844), the expression "factory" meant generally any place
devoted to spinning or weaving fabrics by power, and

specifically the fabrics formed of the materials named; that is, it nearly fulfilled the still ordinary conception of the term. In 1860 bleach and dye works, and in 1861 lace-works, were added to the other protected places,[1] and in 1864 an entirely new departure was made in the inclusion of a number of miscellaneous industries in no way connected with textile manufacture, nor necessarily with machinery moved by power. This necessitated the definition of "factory" being extended accordingly. In 1867 a large number more was added,—the definition thus requiring still further, and some very remarkable extensions; and an Act was now passed for the first time for the regulation of workshops. Under one or other of these Acts all the manufacturing industry of the country was, or was intended to be, included. The term "factory" by this time had come to mean an extraordinary variety of things. It meant not only every place wherein power other than manual was in use in any process connected with the production of textile fabrics (together with bleach, dye, and print works, etc.) and a great variety of other works, specially named under the Act of 1864, as well; but also (30° and 31° Vic. Cap. 103, Sec. 3) "*Any premises*, whether adjoining or separate, in the same occupation, situate in the same city, town, parish, or place, and consti-tuting one trade establishment, in, on, or within the precincts of which *fifty or more persons* are employed in any manufac-turing process;" thus therefore, amongst other changes, re-introducing the criterion of number (familiar in another form in the very first statute) into the consideration of what did and did not fulfil the definition of a factory within the meaning of the law;—and so the matter remained until the enactment of the Factory and Workshops Act 1878 (41° Vic. Cap. 16), which is still in force.

[1] Printworks had been similarly legislated for as early as 1845 (8° and 9° Vic. Cap. 29). In this Act, for the first time, a purely manual process was protected.

Under that Act we obtain the present statutory definition of a factory, while by the same instrument all previous Factory and Workshop Acts are repealed and the entire body of legislation relating to these two classes of places is incorporated. Factories are divided by its provisions into two kinds, Textile and Non-Textile Factories ; and any place where a manufacturing process is carried on that is not included in either of these divisions is called a Workshop. Textile Factories mean for the most part what they did under the Act of 1844 (already quoted), but the title Non-Textile Factory has several significations attached to it. First, it means every place where a mechanical power is made use of in manufacture (or in aid of it) that is not a Textile Factory. Next, it includes places where certain selected industries are practised, and where only manual power is employed—defined, for various reasons, as factories under previous statutes. Then some special industrial processes [1] are for the first time classified in this way ; and lastly, some other special processes, treated as appertaining to Textile, are nevertheless classed as being carried on in Non-Textile Factories. [2] The principle of making number a test of whether a place is legally a factory or not is again abolished, and the new principle of distinction fixed (with the exceptions noted) in the circumstance of whether manual or other motive power is employed. Speaking generally, therefore—and it is obviously impossible to speak at once precisely and briefly in a matter so complicated—the present conception of a factory in English law is : Any premises wherein a foreign motive power is employed in a manufacturing process;—and all other such places where only manual power is used, are (with certain exceptions) workshops.

---

[1] For instance quarrying, and the labour on "pit-banks."

[2] Printworks, and bleaching and dyeing works (41° Vic. Cap. 16, Sec. 40).

The confusions in classification and terminology thus displayed may be traced, like many similar ambiguities, partly to a historical source.

They will be often found to have arisen from the changes that have occurred in the essential qualities and utilities of mills and manufactories from time to time, for which no corresponding changes either in ordinary or exact language have been provided. Mill is a very ancient word, having an unusually uniform sound and spelling in a great variety of languages. In Old English, it is *miln*; in Icelandic, *mylna*; in Danish, *mölle*; in Dutch, *molen*; in various dialects of German, *mulin, muli, mül, mühl*; in Latin, *mola, molinâ, molinus*; Greek, μύλη μύλος; Welsh, *melin*; French, *moulin*; Spanish, *molino*; Italian, *mulino*, etc. etc.[1] Its primary meaning is "An engine or machine for grinding or comminuting any substance" (Webster). Some such contrivance has been in use from time immemorial (Exod. xi. 5); at first in the form of the ancient quern or hand mill, for grinding corn; an implement still to be met with in the East, and even as much nearer home as in the far north of Scotland and the adjacent islands. In its original simplicity, this elementary piece of mechanism is thus described by Mr. Tylor (*Anthropology*, chap. viii.): "The quern or hand mill of the ancient world in its simple form consisted of two circular flat mill stones, the upper being turned by a handle, while the grain was poured in through a hole in the centre, and came out as meal all round the edge. . . . If the reader will notice the construction of a modern flour mill, it will be seen that the neatly faced and grooved mill stones are now of great weight, and the upper one balanced on the pivot which gives it rapid rotation from below by means of water or steam power, but notwithstanding these mechanical improvements the essential

[1] On the word Mill, see Max Müller's *Oxford Essays*, p. 27 (1856).

principle of the primitive hand mill is still there."[1] The
same author relates, in a brief and singularly interesting
manner, the early steps by which this useful appliance
passed out of the domain of hand labour into that in which
other natural motive powers are made subservient to the
purposes of industry. "In the period of ancient civilisation," he remarks (pp. 203, 204), "there appear the beginnings
of that immense change which is remodelling modern life by
inventions which set the forces of nature to do man's heavy
work for him. This great change seems to have been
especially brought on by contrivances to save the heavy toil
of watering the fields. A simple hand labour contrivance
of this kind is the *shadoof* of the Nile valley, where a long
pole with a counterpoise at one end is supported on posts,
and carries a bucket hanging from the longer end to dip up
water from below. It was mechanically an improvement on
this to set a gang of slaves to turn a great wheel with
buckets or earthen jars at its circumference, which rose full
from the water below, and as they turned emptied themselves into a trough at a high level.[2] But when such a
wheel was built to dip in a running stream, then the current
itself would turn the wheel, and thus would come into existence the Noria, or irrigating water-wheel, often mentioned
in ancient literature, and to be seen still at work both in
the East and in Europe. By these or similar steps of
invention, the water-wheel was made a source of power for
doing other work, such as grinding corn, instead of the
women at the quern, or the slaves at the treadmill, or the
mill horse in his everlasting round." Mr. Tylor further
asserts that such machinery was not only "early applied to
grinding corn" but "afterwards to other manufactures." It

---

[1] *Anthropology: An Introduction to the Study of Man and Civilisation*, by
Edward B. Tylor, D.C.L., F.R.S., p. 201 (Macmillan and Co., 1881).
[2] Like the modern dredger.

is probable that these processes were always of the same kind however, *i.e.* of the nature of "grinding or comminuting," until comparatively recent times. Throughout antiquity, and the earlier classical era, mills of the larger kind were usually turned by oxen,[1] and of the smaller sort by slaves, principally women.[2] This was the practice with the ordinary domestic grinding mill attached to the houses of the wealthier classes, a machine worked either by the hands or feet, and which in the latter case must have borne an unpleasant resemblance to the treadmill still occasionally to be seen in our prisons, and even sometimes employed on just the same work. Anderson (*History of Commerce*, vol. i.)[3] quotes a story from Pancirollus to the effect that water mills for grinding corn were introduced at Rome by Belisarius (555 A.D.), and conjectures that he must have meant "reintroduced," for that they were known there, according to Pliny,[4] long before. They certainly were so, as the following graceful effusion, attributed to Antipater (supposed to have been a contemporary of Cicero), abundantly shows: "Cease your work ye maids who laboured at the mills, sleep and let the birds sing to the returning dawn, for Demeter has bidden the water nymphs to do your tasks; obedient to her call they throw themselves on the wheel, and turn the axle and the heavy mill." Beckman, from whose well-known work[5] the above quotation is taken, has a very elaborate article on classical mills. He plausibly explains by the cheapness and abundance of slave labour the small estimation in which water-driven mills seem anciently to have

[1] For Egyptian mills, which were similar, see Wilkinson's *Ancient Egyptians*, chap. v.

[2] *The Life of the Greeks and Romans*, by Guhl and Koner, p. 183.

[3] *An Historical and Chronological Deduction of the Origin of Commerce from the Earliest Accounts*, by Adam Anderson (London, 1801).

[4] *Lib.* xviii. Cap. 10.

[5] *History of Inventions, Discoveries, and Origins*, by John Beckman (Bohn's Edition, 1877), vol. i., Articles, "Corn Mills," "Saw Mills."

been held, an indifference indicated alike by the clumsiness
of their construction and by the rare mention of them in
contemporary literature.   He instances cases of the existence of such mills in Germany and France as early as the
fourth and sixth centuries respectively.   Mention is made
by him of a German water-mill for the sawing of timber,
also in operation in the fourth century, and he expresses the
belief that mills for cutting stone, similarly driven, were in
use there even earlier.   He relates a story of the ill success
attending the enterprise of a Dutchman who, in 1663, erected
in London a windmill for sawing timber.   He was compelled to abandon his attempt in consequence of the ignorant
opposition of his competitors in trade ; and a similar fate
overtook the experiment of another foreigner who erected
one in the same place more than a hundred years after, that
is to say within little more than a century from the present
time.   Windmills are said to have been introduced into
Europe from the East about the time of the Crusades.
Beckman further alludes to ancient mills for grinding the
materials used in making colours ; but of mills applied to
any process connected with textile industry he makes no
mention.

Water-driven corn mills were probably introduced into
Britain by the Romans, and were certainly in use there
during the Roman occupation.   Throughout the period of
the Saxon epoch, and during the greater part of the Middle
Ages, these were commonly attached to the houses of the
great nobility and clergy ; and among the obligations of a
vassal was that of having his corn ground at the lord's
mill.   Such mills were regarded as essentially appertaining
to the land,[1] and being in fact implements of agriculture

---

[1] See description, in "an anonymous work bearing the title of *Fleta*," of a
Manor in the time of Edward I. (quoted from *The English Village Community*, by Frederick Seebohm, p. 46 (Longmans, 1883), where "mills belonging to the land and having a monopoly of grinding for the tenants at fixed

rather than of manufacture. How soon, either here or elsewhere, they were applied to other and to what purposes, is
a matter involved in great obscurity. As early as 1313, at
all events, we have certain information of "A mill for the
dyers on the banks of the Irk,"[1] and a few years later (in
1322) of "a fulling mill" turned by the same river. But
water mills for *fulling*, that is *pounding* cloth, were certainly
in existence here before that time, as mention is made of
them in charters of an earlier date. Now it is almost
certainly in connection with this latter process that we
should look for the germ of that enlarged signification which
in later times pertained to the term mill. The operation of
fulling bore a sufficiently near resemblance to the earlier
and proper processes of mill work not to appear utterly
foreign from the older conception of a mill, and was in
fact sometimes also called "milling," in obvious accord with
this view. Soon, however, the term began to include
other processes more remote. In 1551 complaint is made
to Parliament of the establishment of "gigge mills," contrivances that is for raising a *pile* or *nap* on cloth, a process
therefore wherein little trace of the original meaning of the
word "mill" remains, and at length *winding, spinning,* and
a variety of operations dealing with the treatment of fibrous
material are found spoken of as performed in mills ; operations wherein the original technical signification is altogether
lost. Its close connection with the term "factory" now
commences, the explanation seeming to be, that when the
novel edifice which we now know by that name appeared in

charges" are mentioned. Mills and millers are also mentioned in the Liber
Albus of Peterboro' Abbey (*idem*, p. 73). In Green's *Conquest of England*
(Macmillan, 1883), water mills are spoken of as common before the Danes
(p. 7) ; and in a note the author says, "No Manor was complete without its
mill, and Domesday gives 272 mills in Dorset, some simply *winter* (? mills),
some on streamlets that have wholly vanished."

[1] *History of the Cotton Manufacture in Great Britain*, by Edward Baines
jun. p. 90 (London : Fisher and Jackson).

England first, the corn and fulling mills were the buildings
most nearly analogous to it in popular experience, and that
thus the names as well as the functions of these places got
mingled. Afterwards when steam power succeeded water
power as a motor, and the public became familiar with the
new method of production, the analogy was no longer so
obvious, and the terms tended to separation.   Ultimately
" factory " was defined by statute, and there has ensued the
remarkable result that corn mills themselves are now
factories under the latest principal Factory Act.[1]

A transformation similar in kind to this, and, if possible,
even greater in degree, has occurred in the
use of the kindred word manufacture.
"Manufacture," says Dr. Ure (*Philosophy of Manufactures*,
Book I. chap. i.), " is a word which in the vicissitudes of
language has come to signify the *reverse* of its intrinsic
meaning, for it now denotes every extensive product of art
which is made by machinery with little or no aid from the
human hand, so that the most perfect manufacture is that
which dispenses entirely with manual labour."   This is
certainly a very remarkable perversion from a very obvious
derivation,[2] though it may be doubted whether it has in
reality taken place to quite the extent that is here suggested.
It was not exactly true then,[3] nor is it exactly true now,
that either in technical or popular parlance the word manufacture invariably connotes the idea of machinery.   Some
very humble manual operations were, and are still, often
dignified with that title, as one may at any time observe in
passing through the streets of a country village and reading
descriptions outside the shops and workshops of the industries

MANUFACTURE.

---

[1] Factory and Workshops Act 1878. See *ante*, p. 6.

[2] *Manus*, a hand, and *facio*, I make.

[3] Dr. Ure's *Philosophy of Manufactures* was first published in 1835. A
third edition, continued down to 1861, and edited by Mr. P. L. Simmonds,
F.S.S., is in Bohn's Scientific Library.

pursued there. Still less is this connection between manufacture and machinery necessarily and invariably inferred
by statute. The Factory Acts Extension Act 1867, contained a definition of "manufacturing process" as "any
manual labour exercised by way of trade, or for purposes of
gain," in or "incidental to the making of any article," and
although that Act is now repealed, it does not appear that
the legal conception of manufacture embodied in it has
therefore been abrogated. On the contrary, it has in certain
cases been deliberately retained, and incorporated into subsequent legislation. In the Factory and Workshops Act
1878, for instance, "manufacturing process" is not defined
at all, but, from the retention of some purely manual industries in the class of Non-Textile Factories,[1] it is clear that the
distinction made by Dr. Ure is not (in its integrity at all
events) adopted by the current law. It is, however, also
clear that some approach is made towards it. Though
manufacture itself is not defined, commodities are in a
general way held to be either *made* or *manufactured* according as the process of producing them is carried on in a
factory or workshop ; that is to say, by hand only, or by the
aid of foreign motive power : certain industries not thus
regarded being reckoned as exceptions. While Dr. Ure has
done good service then in directing attention to the remarkable change that has occurred in the technical meaning of
this word, it is undesirable, in the interests of a proper
apprehension of the subject, to allow that, either in its
ordinary or statutory use, manufacture has come to signify
" the *reverse* of its intrinsic meaning." Mr. Babbage [2] makes
the distinction here under discussion in quite another way.

---

[1] Bookbinding, fustian-cutting, letterpress printing by hand, etc. See
ante, p. 6.

[2] *Economy of Machinery and Manufacture*, by Charles Babbage, chap. xiii.
(London : Murray, 1846).

"A considerable difference exists," he says, "between the terms *making* and *manufacturing*. The former refers to the production of a small, the latter to that of a large number of individuals," and this also is a distinction that has been known to factory legislation, though not sanctioned by the statute now in operation. The first Factory Act ever passed, as well as the Factory Act of 1867, contained (we have seen) numerical qualifications for the definition of "factory," and incidentally also of "manufacture;" and some memory of these still haunts our ordinary thought and language. The only difference between (let us say) a shoemaker's shop and a shoe factory, or a manufactory of earthenware and the more humbly named *pottery*, is in popular apprehension still the number of persons employed in those places; and so all through the round of other industrial operations. Mr. Babbage's conception of the matter, whether legal or logical, must be allowed then to be general, and is one that cannot ever perhaps be wholly dispensed with. It remains to notice a still more special and technical application of the words mill and manufacture, principally confined to what are usually called distinctively the factory (*i.e.* textile factory) districts. According to this one, *manufacture* is held to signify in a special sense *weaving*, as particularly distinguished from spinning, and from the other preparatory processes to which the raw material of textile fabrics are subjected; and thus in an establishment where spinning and weaving were both carried on, the spinning department would be specially called the *mill*, and the weaving department the *factory*, and weaving, among all the processes performed there, would be alone spoken of as "manufacturing." To what extent, and over what area, this last nomenclature prevails, and how far it is traceable to earlier distinctions in kind, and to their historic developments, might furnish further interesting matter of reflection to the etymologist and antiquarian, but must not detain us here.

There is a further signification of the term "manufacture," however, on which a few words are necessary. It is that signification of it where   MANUFACTURE AND MART.
it stands as a common noun, expressing
the circumstance of an existing industry at any time or place; the sense in which we speak of "a manufacture" *being established*, or *having arisen*. In this case the use of the word has clearly a direct relation to magnitude. It is not until an industry has attained a certain and very considerable importance that it is usual to speak of it as a manufacture. Other facts are also generally implied when the word is thus used. It is implied that the production of goods is capable of supplying more than local needs, or supplying, at all events, local needs of a very extensive character; that many persons are employed in it; and that it is an important feature in the social condition of the country where it is extant. Thus we speak of the woollen "manufacture" being established in England only after a certain period, when it began to be carried on upon a larger and more systematic scale—though woollen goods had been made here long before. We say that a linen manufacture existed in Egypt, and a cotton manufacture in India, from very early times, because linen and cotton goods were produced there and then in great quantities. The word manufacture is in this sense a noun of multitude, and its primary meaning is undoubtedly the making upon a very large scale. Indeed the more we regard it the more difficulty do we find in getting rid of this implication in the word, and that in spite both of derivative inaccuracy and the vacillations of statutory treatment. Mr. Fox Bourne, however, seems inclined to substitute the term "mart;" that is to say, he would call the great centres of production as well

as the great centres of sale in early times, "marts." "There were marts but apparently no great factories in the ancient world," says that pleasant writer,[1] and a country or place which was a great producer by hand labour would therefore, if we understand him rightly, be most properly termed a mart. We cannot agree in this designation. A mart is exclusively a place of sale, where no production need necessarily be carried on, and where in fact it often is not carried on; and a place which is a great producer of commodities is a place which has "a manufacture" of those commodities, whether they be made by machinery or by hand.

Other distinctions between making and manufacturing

TRADE.

have been suggested. For instance, that the one (making) is production for use, the other (manufacturing) production for profit;[2] and that *making* properly relates to producing for home consumption only, and *manufacturing* for trade. The former definition hardly seems a tenable one, inasmuch as it is philosophically impossible to separate the idea of profit from use, though the conception undoubtedly includes a valuable and very suggestive thought. The latter is equally untenable as a comprehensive definition, but is of great practical importance in directing attention to the inevitable association of trade with manufacture. So close is this association indeed, that it may be assumed as a general truth that the two things are mutually dependent. Not until production has developed on a very large scale, that is, until at all events the principal requirements of the producing place are first fully satisfied, does trade originate. But then it usually does so. Equally; not until a very great impetus is given to produc-

---

[1] *The Romance of Trade*, by H. R. Fox Bourne, chap. ix. p. 213 (London: Cassell and Co.)

[2] This is the view of the modern Socialists.

tion by the possibility of trade is a manufacture likely to
arise. Thus regarded, manufacture is the making commodities
in excess of local needs, and trade is their organised dispersion;
and in pursuing the history of the one we shall generally
find ourselves on the track of the other.

The legal distinction between manual and machine labour is
sought to be fixed at present, however, in still
another direction, namely, to be made to rest   HANDICRAFT.
between manufacture and handicraft, originally, as is evident,
synonymous terms. The ninety-fourth section of the Factory
and Workshops Act now in force reads as follows :—" A
child, young person, or woman, who works in a factory or
workshop, whether for wages or not, either in a manufacturing process or handicraft, etc. "—wherein these two methods
of production (by handicraft and manufacture) are treated
as convertible ; the place where the work is done deciding
under which of the two designations it is to be classed.
This latest effort after precision is not a very happy one.
The essential difference between manufacture and handicraft
is not at all the one that is thus implied, nor is it desirable
that the latter designation should, like the former one,
acquire a perverted meaning. Handicraft is a word with a
very noble significance and history of its own. In the
economy of ancient and mediæval industry all skilled trades
were viewed as *crafts* and *mysteries*, the professors of which
crafts and exponents of which mysteries were " handicraftsmen," a different class, in all respects that are pertinent to
the present subject, from mere labouring men, either in the
factory or the field. Their position social, political, and
economical was dissimilar. It is so still wherever the same
class exists—not having been crushed out of being by the
competition of the factory system—that is to say over even
now a great part of the world. The proper conception of
handicraft is then nearly the *opposite* of the modern concep-

tion of manufacture, and the two terms cannot be regarded as convertible without a distinct loss to economic nomenclature. The one (handicraft) is the system of isolated individual effort; as opposed to the other, the system of combined, and generally mechanically aided, production; and it is very desirable in spite of all difficulties to retain and fix these terms in those meanings. The drafters of Factory Acts have been too often negligent in their phraseology, and students of the factory system are bound of course to borrow the phraseology they have employed, but the rescue of this particular term from the fate that evidently impends over it would be a distinct gain to industrial technology.

This conspicuous negligence in definition will cause less astonishment if one recalls the inherent difficulties of the subject, and they are especially apparent in relation to the occasionally cognate sphere of Art. Even philosophers of eminent distinction have been unsuccessful in assigning quite satisfactory limits to the respective spheres of art and manufacture, and when ordinary technologists have taken the difficulty in hand they have usually ended by enormously increasing it. The subdivisions that have been made or suggested, for instance, into "industrial arts" and "fine arts;" into "useful arts," "art manufactures," "manufacturing arts," and so forth; though sometimes sufficiently well defined for practical purposes, are, when submitted to the test of logic, wholly misleading. When experts have failed then in drawing such nice distinctions with precision, it is not wonderful that legislators should have gone widely astray. The only distinction in ultimate analysis is between Science and Art; that is to say, between the way of knowing a thing, and the way of doing it. All kinds of arts, fine or coarse, industrial or imaginative, are equally arts, though of different kinds, some being pursued principally by means of the hand, others

ART AND MANUFACTURE.

principally by means of the head, but all having connection with both hand and head at last. Their classification is simply a matter of convenience, often of merely temporary convenience, and, as has been seen already in the case of *manufacture*, that classification for convenience is often very perplexing in its results. What is wanted is an altogether other principle, having reference to an altogether different, a consistent, and a truly distinctive body of facts.

There is one art at all events, which has ever been considered apart from manufacture; which cannot, on the other hand, claim a place
AGRICULTURE.
among the fine arts, and which occupies itself with perhaps the most important of all productive processes. This is the art of husbandry, of tillage, of agriculture—the sowing of seeds, the preparing the ground for their reception, and the gathering in of the results. The position of agriculture in respect to the factory system is isolated and singular. Alone among directly productive processes it is under no state supervision. Yet it has not been for the want of strong efforts to include it, that the conduct of even this art has escaped being swept into the comprehensive net of factory legislation. There was for several years a project before Parliament for legislating for fields in the same way as for factories, and an Act was subsequently passed under the title of "The Agricultural Children Act," promulgating in fact a like system of regulation.[1] There was even a doubt expressed at one time, and on good technical grounds, whether fields were not already, if not actually factories, then at least workshops within the meaning of existing statutes.[2] In

---

[1] 36° and 37° Vic. Cap. 67.

[2] See evidence of Mr. Inspector Bignold in Report of the Royal Commission on Factories and Workshops (1876), vol. i. Appendix C. p. 24. The argument was this : By Section IV. of the Workshop Regulations Act a workshop was defined "any room or *place whatever*, in the open air, or under cover, in which any handicraft is carried on by any child, young person, or women ;"

consequence, however, of the different manner in which the Act at present in force is drawn, this nice legal point is now set at rest. The Agricultural Children Act was a failure, owing to no proper machinery having been provided for putting it in force; but it was foredoomed in any case, not only because of the inherent defects of construction with which it abounded, but, more obviously still, on account of the fundamental and radical differences which exist, and must continue to exist, in spite of any legal enactment to the contrary, between a factory and a field. It is instructive to note how little consideration was given to these essential differences at the time of its promulgation : how the reformers were prepared to ignore alike the history, nature, and methods of legislative restrictions on manufacture in their anxiety to extend them to agriculture. Yet the organic difference between the two—between procuring the beneficent gifts of Nature, and transforming them into materials of commerce—should hardly need to be insisted on ; and the practical differences are evident as soon as stated. It is obvious that the business man who can indefinitely extend his operations by indefinitely increasing the capital employed in them, and who can turn over that capital several times perhaps in one year, is in quite a different position from that of the farmer, who can, under no circumstances, reap his harvest more than once within the same period, and who is absolutely dependent even then, both for its quantity and its quality, on influences outside all human control. Of late years, no doubt, farm-industry has tended more and more to resemble factory industry, owing to the employment of machinery in many

and by the same section "handicraft" was defined to mean "any manual labour exercised by way of trade or for purposes of gain in or incidental to adapting for sale any article." It was argued that "a boy hoeing turnips in a field" is exercising manual labour for purposes of gain in adapting for sale an article, to wit a turnip. Is he not therefore employed in a workshop ?

of the processes of agriculture. The use of the steam-plough and steam-thrashing machine is a portent of no ordinary kind. Similarly, the employment of gangs of persons associated for certain purposes at certain seasons of the year (as for instance for the hop-picking in the Southern Counties) is a method of production that so far resembles factory labour as to have developed some of the evils by which that system in its earlier days was notoriously disgraced. Properly considered, however, there are few points of real likeness among these apparent analogies. The improved machines are only complicated developments of the simple tools that have long been in use; and the mysterious power by which they are set in motion is but another added to the still more mysterious forces with which the farmer has been from the first familiar, in the growth of his crops and the generation of his live-stock. As for agricultural gangs, they do no more than manifest the ordinary conditions of an un-organised crowd under circumstances somewhat favourable to disorder; and they have moreover been provided for by a special Act of Parliament.[1] The fundamental differences between production by agriculture and manufacture lie much deeper than any such superficial coincidences, and, as a proper comprehension of this department of the subject is of supreme importance in the survey we are about to enter on, it will be well to re-state here the terms of what are commonly called the "laws" of manufacturing and agricultural industry—the formulas, that is to say, that have latterly been devised to describe their inevitable operation and incidence.

Economists[2] divide all production of material wealth

---

[1] The Agricultural Gangs Act 1867.

[2] The current political economy of the last half century is what is made use of here. Until that has been superseded by a systematic body of doctrine of equal worth and scope it cannot be regarded as displaced by new views, which, upon some important points, are at issue with it.

into two kinds: (1) the production direct from the soil

LAWS OF AGRICULTURAL AND MANUFACTURING INDUSTRY. by the application to it of human effort; (2) the shaping of the material thus produced into forms fit for human use. The first of these they consider to be the act of Agriculture, the second the act of Manufacture.

Primarily, of course, all production is from the earth, which, including all the facilities that are active or dormant in it, is the elementary source of wealth; as of the material being of man himself. From it he springs, to it he returns, the whole and sole part that he plays in the productive act being that of disengaging the materials of wealth from their natural surroundings, and re-arranging and combining them for use. In other words, his is the part of adaptation, of *contrivance*,[1] to use the well-chosen expression of the Duke of Argyll. He contrives to drive or drag through the ground a plough which he has previously contrived to fashion; and into the furrow thus made he contrives to drop a seed; and, if all has been contrived happily, a plant will in due time be the result. He gathers the fruit of this plant (which has arrived at maturity by means of principles and influences unknown to him), and, by a variety of further contrivances, he makes of it bread to eat, wine to drink, or clothing to wear. All that he himself has accomplished throughout is intelligently to adapt to his wants the spontaneous gifts and energies about him. Similarly in the training of animals as beasts of burden; and in the utilising of all other forces over which he may obtain dominion: he adds nothing to their native qualities, he merely adapts them to his needs.[2] Thus far, then, the act of production in agri-

[1] *Reign of Law*, by the Duke of Argyll. People's Edition (Strahan and Co., 1871).

[2] *Principles of Political Economy, with some of their Applications to Social Philosophy*, by J. S. Mill, Book I. chap. viii. Seventh edition (Longmans, 1871). *Principles of Political Economy*, J. R. M'Culloch, p.

culture and in manufacture is the same: an act, that is to say, not of creation but of contrivance; and the limits of both are defined by that distinction. But the next step in their progress develops a difference. "After a certain, and not very advanced, stage in the progress of agriculture, it is the law of production from the land that, in any given state of agricultural skill and knowledge, by increasing the labour the progress is not increased in an equal degree; doubling the labour does not double the produce; or, to express the same thing in other words, every increase of produce is obtained by a more than proportional increase of the application of labour to the land."[1] In manufacture, on the contrary, the law of the increase of production is the direct reverse of this; that is to say, an increase of effort is rewarded by a more than proportionate return, and doubling the labour more than doubles the produce. The reason is that, while the land is limited both in extent and in fertility, there is no calculable limit to the increase of population and of capital, which are the only other instruments of production. Given abundant material, under conditions not otherwise unfavourable,—and let the element of restricted territory be eliminated,—and then wealth and population might go on increasing (say the economists) to any conceivable or inconceivable extent; or would be checked, if at all, only by circumstances outside the range of economic phenomena. In the words of Mr. Senior, "If 300,000 families are now employed in Great Britain to manufacture and transport 240,000,000 of pounds of cotton, it is absolutely certain that 600,000 families could manufacture and transport 480,000,000 of pounds of cotton. It is in fact certain that

84 (Alexander Murray, 1870). *Political Economy*, by Nassau W. Senior, reprinted from the *Encyclopædia Metropolitana* (1850). *Manual of Political Economy*, Henry Fawcett, M.P. Book I. chap. v. Last edition, 1883 (Macmillan).

[1] *Principles of Political Economy*, by J. S. Mill, Book I. chap. xii.

they would do much more. It is not improbable that they
could manufacture and transport 720,000,000. The only
check[1] by which we can predict that the progress of our
manufactures will, in time, be retarded, is the increasing
difficulty of importing materials and food. If the importation
of our raw produce could keep pace with the power of
working it up, there would be no limit to the increase of
wealth and population." "In other words," says the same
author,[2] "the powers of labour and of the other instruments
which produce wealth (other than land) may be indefinitely
increased by using their products as the means of further
production."

The principal means by which this high degree of productiveness in manufacture is attained is by
the use of tools and machinery. These are
also, and have been of course for long, employed in the
cultivation of land; but they have not produced, and in
that sphere of action can never produce results similarly
great. For, granting that their use might, for a time, and
under exceptional circumstances, double, or even quadruple
production over a certain area ; it certainly could not increase
such production an hundred, twenty, or probably ten-fold ;
nor could it, for any length of time, increase it at all without
greatly exhausting the soil. Yet it is equally certain that
the use of tools and machinery in manufacture *can* increase
production in these high ratios, not only without exhausting
any of the means and possibilities of continued productive-

MACHINERY.

---

[1] Mr. Senior speaks here only of purely economic checks, and of the
possibility of predicting them. Checks arising from physical or political
causes, *e.g.* earthquakes, floods, wars, and revolutions, might of course at any
time (not only retard but positively) annihilate the prosperity of a nation.
There are possibly also some other statements in the above passage which the
author might have been inclined to modify had he been revising his work at
the present day. As an illustration, however, the quotation is none the less
adapted to our purposes.

[2] *Political Economy*, by Nassau W. Senior, p. 86.

ness but even by increasing them all the while. An instrument, whether a simple chisel or a complicated form of steam-engine, may assist in making many more instruments of the same kind, and these again in making an almost infinitely greater number still. What fails at length, is not the capacity of new machines to make an ever-increasing number of newer ones, but either the demand for those newer machines to be made, or the material wherewith to make them. The possibility of their continued production remains. This is, moreover, but one of the many wonderful qualities they possess. Babbage sums up the advantages derived from the use of machinery under three principal heads, which are, however, far from exhausting them: (1) the addition which they make to human power; (2) the economy they produce of human time; (3) the conversion of substances, apparently worthless, into valuable products.[1] The various instances cited by him in illustration of these several advantages, and of the way in which they work, are tolerably well known, but may be mentioned. One whole chapter (much commended by Mr. J. S. Mill) treats of the benefits arising from machinery in "exerting forces too great for human power, and executing operations too delicate for human touch." Other chapters treat of the "accumulating and regulating" powers of machinery, and of the ease with which they are brought under human control; and others again of other excellent qualities inherent in them. These need not be dwelt upon. Neither Mr. Babbage, however, nor Mr. Mill, nor indeed any of the economists, enter into the considerations adverse to machinery; as to its deteriorating effect, for instance, on the artistic faculty of the workman, and its vulgarising and stultifying influence on human life and conduct. Such considerations are not the concern of economic science they say; the proper subject

[1] *Economy of Machinery and Manufactures,* chap. i.

of which is wealth, not ethics or culture. They constitute
an aspect of the labour question, nevertheless, which cannot
legitimately be ignored in any philosophical analysis of it
as a whole ; and which should never be left out of account
in viewing labour from any but the purely economic stand-
point.

The next principal means by which the efficiency of manu-

DIVISION AND facturing industry is so greatly enhanced
COMBINATION OF consists in the division, combination, and
LABOUR. adaptation of labour, devices which can be
carried in it to such extraordinary lengths. Adam Smith
was the first modern writer of eminence who laid great
stress on the extreme importance of this element in manufacturing production. The first three chapters of the *Wealth
of Nations*, in which he did so, were hailed by the majority
of contemporary readers almost in the light of a revelation.
Yet, of these celebrated chapters, it is hardly too much to
say, that they are scarcely more remarkable for what they
include than for what they omit. From the most rudimentary beginnings of society there must evidently have existed
some divisions of labour which differ chiefly in degree from
much to which Adam Smith so strongly called attention.
This great thinker wrote, moreover, before the development
of the factory system,[1] and therefore before the general
introduction of foreign motive powers into manufacture, and
the rearrangement of industrial processes that has resulted
therefrom. Had this been otherwise, he would certainly have
perceived more fully than he ever seems to have done that
it is co-operation rather than division of labour that constitutes the essential principle, and that, while the former
includes the latter, the latter does not by any means necessarily include the former. He would probably have substituted some such expression as specialisation or organisation

[1] *The Wealth of Nations* was published in 1776.

for division of labour; and would have known, as at that period he had no opportunity of knowing, how impotent in itself is the most perfect form of such a force in comparison with the new motive powers that were just then coming into use. The expression *division of labour* has, however, become so thoroughly naturalised in the language and literature of economic science, that it would be a matter of some difficulty to displace it now; and it is better therefore retained, in spite of its insufficiency, though always with these necessary explanations and reservations.

The chief ways in which division of labour is said to benefit production are the following:—(1) in the increased speed and dexterity that is likely to accrue to the workman from having his attention and skill concentrated on one manufacturing operation; (2) in the saving of his time, effected by his not having to pass repeatedly from one process to another; (3) in the stimulus that he is likely to receive towards the invention of labour-saving machinery. It will be gathered from what was said under the last heading that the third of these supposed advantages is open to some doubt in practice. The habit of continually repeating the same operation is quite as likely to blind a workman to other possible methods of performing it as it is to suggest such new methods to his mind. In point of fact, many of the inventors and perfecters of labour-saving machines (*e.g.* Arkwright, Cartwright, Lee) have not themselves been mechanics; nor do craftsmen who have acquired great dexterity look necessarily to increased quantity of work as their ideal, but sometimes, happily, to improved quality. It is only when division of labour is found in union with a general employment of machinery that the impulse is inevitably towards increased production, but it does seem to be so then. The use of automatic machinery in the place of manual labour has the effect of greatly increasing competition, and production tends

to be pushed to its extreme capacity regardless of everything
besides; which is the position of much modern manufacture.
To the three assumed advantages of the division of labour,
thus formulated, Dr. Ure, Mr. Babbage, Mr. Mill, and most
succeeding economists, have been in the habit of adding
another, which is defined by the last-named writer as " The
more economical distribution of labour by classing the work-
people according to their capacity,"[1] and to this further
element of efficiency, which is in reality the original one, is
attributed the separation of the sexes, and the employment
of young children in many branches of industrial production.
The separation of the sexes in any occupation is generally a
natural division; but the employment of children in manufacturing operations too delicate or too unremunerative for
adults to perform, is greatly induced by the use of machinery.
That particular incentive to child-labour was a very potent
one in the earlier days of the modern factory system. It was
not, of course, either then or ever, the only one, for the lower
wages at which such labour can be obtained was, and must
always be, a powerful motive for employing it as well.
But it was just then the characteristic inducement; and
it undoubtedly was the abuse of this particular result of
the division of labour that first drew public attention
strongly to the dangers and evils of the new regime, and
initiated those reforms in the legislative treatment of
it which give to this subject its particular and pressing
interest now.

The most conspicuous instance ever known of the advan-
THE FACTORY   tages and disadvantages alike, which arise
SYSTEM.   from the division of employment and the
use of implements combined, is found in that organisation of
labour known to modern times as specifically The Factory
System. The Factory System, in technology, " designates,"

[1] *Principles of Political Economy*, Book I. chap. viii.

says Dr. Ure,[1] "the combined operation of many orders of work-people, adult and young, in tending with assiduous skill a series of productive machines, continually impelled by a central power;" and this definition sums up with much neatness many of the essential features and early characteristics of this method of production, while at the same time it fails to exhaust, or even to indicate, much of what is now embraced within the phrase. It includes " such organisations as cotton, flax, silk, and wool mills, and also certain engineering works," but it excludes "those in which the mechanisms do not form a connective series, and are not dependent on one prime mover " . . . such as " iron-works, dye-works, soap-works, brass-foundries, etc." " Some authors indeed," Dr. Ure continues, "have comprehended under the title factory all extensive establishments wherein a number of people co-operate towards a common purpose of art, and would therefore rank breweries, distilleries, as well as the workshops of carpenters, turners, coopers, etc., under the factory system. But I conceive that this title in its strictest sense involves the idea of a vast automaton, composed of various mechanical and intellectual organs, acting, in uninterrupted concert, for the production of a common object; all of them being subordinated to a self-regulated moving force." " If," he concludes, " the marshalling of human beings in systematic order, for any technical enterprise, were allowed to constitute a factory, this term might embrace every department of civil and military engineering—a latitude of application quite inadmissible." It has already been shown that most of the work-places here enumerated by Dr. Ure as being " quite inadmissible " have, nevertheless, been since included in the statutory definition of the term " factory," and many more in that of the cognate term " workshop." Moreover his own definition is so ponderous

[1] *Philosophy of Manufactures*, pp. 13, 14.

as to be almost incomprehensible, and is far too recondite
for ordinary use. " An automaton composed of various
mechanical and intellectual organs, acting in uninterrupted
concert," is a definition of the factory system which, even if
technically correct, would be of little practical usefulness ;
and as for the danger that the terms " factory " and " factory
system" will ever be so expanded as to embrace civil and
military engineering, it is one of which all fear may safely
be dismissed. It is of the essential nature of a factory and
of the factory system, under whatever guise, that their
purpose is invariably production, while the eventual purpose
of military labour is always destruction. Even when
military engineering is devoted, as it sometimes is, to productive purposes, as in the making of roads or of railways,
such constructions are instruments not so much of production
as of transport, and in as far as they are used for non-military
purposes they become in their nature industrial, and must
be viewed and classed accordingly. Next, the notion that
the terms " factory " and " factory system " might come to
be so widely conceived of as to embrace the works of civil
engineering, is a notion only a little less absurd than the
last. The operations of civil engineering like those of
agriculture, are operations performed on the surface of the
earth itself, and not on products raised from the earth.
They are operations extending over areas of indefinite
extent, instead of being comprised within establishments of
definite bounds ; and lastly, they are concerned in the
production of utilities and facilities of various kinds, and
not of commodities at all ; or, to use an economic phraseology more strictly technical, their products are instruments
of wealth rather than wealth itself. The truth is that Dr.
Ure, like others among his contemporaries, never did or
could quite understand the full nature and significance of
the organisation he was at such pains to describe. He

knew the factory system only in its infancy. Neither history nor philosophy afforded him any quite satisfactory analogy to it. What wonder therefore that he judged it partially? We, who live more than a century later, and who have witnessed its astonishing expansion since his time, are still wondering what is to be its ultimate form; still blundering through the mazes of philosophy and technology for final conceptions and definitions of it, and of the now familiar things with which it deals: and we are still a long way from having arrived at these.

A good illustration of this confusion, which prevails alike in the minds of legislators and of writers on the factory system, is furnished in the recent inclusion of quarries and "pit-banks" in the number of places classed as factories or workshops by law.[1] Mining is a process of industry conducted on a system similar to the factory system; it is performed by a body of congregated labourers assembled for the purpose in a place of definite bounds. But mines are not so included, and justly not so, because they appertain to the soil, which is not one of the materials of wealth, but one of its sources; the source, in fact, from which all materials spring.[2] They are provided for by special enactments. Should not the same principle apply to quarries? There exists between the two this difference; that the work in a quarry is not invariably confined to the mere extraction of material, but extends often to the shaping of it; which latter process is legally and naturally a process of manufacture;[3] and that the quarry differs from the

EXTRACTIVE INDUSTRIES.

[1] 41° Vic. Cap. 16, Sec. 93 ; and Sched. iv. part ii.

[2] *Principles of Political Economy*, by J. S. Mill, Book I. chaps. i. and ii. See also *ante* AGRICULTURE, p. 19.

[3] M. de Laveleye points out how "the manufacturing industries receive from the extractive and agricultural their raw materials and give them the final form demanded by consumption."—*Elements of Political Economy*, p. 3 (Chapman and Hall, 1884).

mine in that the work in it is generally open to view, and
is not therefore carried on subject to the very difficult
and special conditions that must naturally attend underground labour. Where this is not the case, as in some
slate quarries where the slate is procured by underground
borings, the quarry is in fact considered a mine, and labour
therein is regulated by the Metalliferous Mines Act.[1] But
there are many quarries where the process is simply that of
hewing out blocks of stone and sending them away to be
cut and employed elsewhere, and it is not easy to see how
that operation differs much from mining; unless indeed it
be to more resemble *digging.* Yet the place where this is
done becomes by law a factory or workshop, while a mine
or a field can in no case be either. With labour on the
surface of a coal mine, on what are called pit-banks, the
circumstances are again somewhat different. The processes
pursued there are not those of extracting material, but of
sifting and arranging it, in other words of *altering* and *adapting* it for manufacture and sale, and these are "manufacturing processes" by statute.[2] But what is singular is, that
this very simple and primitive kind of occupation is more
strictly legislated for as regards juvenile labour than the
severer and more abnormal labour underground. The
interior of a coal mine is the subject of one set of legal
restrictions, and the exterior of the same coal mine of two
sets; and a child may be employed below under easier
conditions than above, and a woman above ground under
either of the two sets: which are not in harmony.[3]

Many other inconsistencies in the public comprehension
and present classification of productive employments might be pointed out, but a couple
more will suffice. The great department of

TRANSPORT AND
BUILDING.

[1] 35° and 36° Vic. Cap. 77.   [2] 41° Vic. Cap. 16, Sec. 93.
[3] Coal Mines Regulation Act 1872 (35° and 36° Vic. Cap. 76).

industry that is concerned with transport is unrecognised as being related to manufacture, and is therefore unprotected; though the bringing commodities to market is economically considered a part of their "production," and the need of exterior control is certainly as obvious here as anywhere. The Merchant Shipping Acts indeed have done something for sailors, and the Canal Boats Acts (1884) something for canal children; but for persons engaged about land carriage nothing has been done. The occupation of ship-building again is under strict statutory regulation,[1] while the occupation of housebuilding is not, and in this case it is not easy to discover either logic or utility in the distinction. A carpenter's apprentice working in his master's shop again is under the protection of the Factory Act, but working away from it he is not so. A bookbinding room is a factory; but a dressmaking room is a workshop. Such are some types of these cases.

A still wider practical and philosophical question is opened when we come to consider the quondam economic classification of labour into commodities and services. The day has SERVICES AND COMMODITIES. probably gone by when this classification could be seriously proposed as a basis of practical action; when the labour of any human creature, that is, would be regarded as a commodity and nothing more, but the distinction between the two forms of labour nevertheless is, and must continue, a very real one. The contract between any two persons under which the one agrees to serve the other *generally*, for a stated reward, is of a clearly different kind from that under which a specific service is arranged for. On the other hand, it is often diffi-cult to decide, either in law or economics, where operative labour justly ends and service begins. In the language of economists, production only ceases as consumption supervenes;

---

[1] 41° Vic. Cap. 16, Sec. 93; and Sched. iv. part ii.

in other words, not until the finished product is placed in the hands of the consumer can its " production " be properly said to be completed.[1] How then does it come about that persons engaged in placing the product in the consumers' hands are regarded as unconnected with its manufacture ? Why is it, for instance, that women engaged in making articles for sale at the back of a shop are subject to the regulations of the Factory Act, whilst those engaged in disposing of them at the front of the shop are not ? And how is it that another woman may be brought within the protection of that Act by her master doing no more than offering for sale any portion of pastry that she has baked in his oven?[2] How is her contract of service with him affected by such an act ? How does her labour thereby approximate more nearly to the factory system ? It was at one time seriously proposed that there should be a so-called Factory Act for domestic service,[3] and this last quoted instance shows how nearly such an ideal, then generally considered ridiculous, has been actually approached. The comments on it at the time showed how little what was really faulty in the proposal was understood.

No less difficult and complicated is the question of the position that should be assigned to what IMMATERIAL PRODUCTS.[4] are called "immaterial products" in any scientifically constructed scheme for the protection and supervision of human labour. Should there be a Factory Act for those who labour with their brains as well as those who labour with their hands ? It may be replied that there is no *factory system* in connection with this kind of labour, and therefore nothing neces-

[1] *Principles of Political Economy*, J. S. Mill, Book I. chap. ii. par. 6.
[2] Baking for sale is a process under the protection of the Factory Act (46° and 47° Vic. Cap. 53).
[3] At Trades Union Congresses in Liverpool and Dundee.
[4] On immaterial products of labour and their relation to wealth, see J. S. Mill, Book I. chap. iii.

sitating special legislation; but the principle of the Factory
Acts has long since been extended to occupations where no
factory system prevailed. It may be imagined again that
there is no class of persons, the producers of immaterial
commodities, of the sex, age, and condition of protected
classes. But this depends upon what we understand by
that phrase. There are many children employed about
theatres and shows, and of course many women; and these
are producers of immaterial commodities under almost any
conception of the term.[1] The large class of clerks again, in
both public and private offices, in warehouses, shops, etc., and
teachers, would seem to come properly under the designation
of persons whose work results in immaterial products; for
if not so, under what designation should they be classed?
They are not servants; nor are they producers of material
commodities. These persons have never had any place
assigned to them under the modern factory system, yet the
scale upon which the work that they perform is in many
cases done, and the methods, and often even the appliances
for doing it, are such as are very analogous to much factory
labour.[2]

The difficulties, equivocations, inconsistencies, and con-
tradictions, both in word and deed, that have thus been
passed in review, make up a remarkable spectacle of our
attitude as an industrial people towards the factory system.
What they primarily show is, a want of general comprehension and of definite public action in relation to this matter.
What they specifically show is, a most extraordinary jumble
of principles, practices, efforts, and intentions in our dealing

[1] The principle of protecting occupations of this kind was recognised by
an Act passed in 1879 called "The Children's Dangerous Performance Act;"
but there was no proper provision made for putting that Act in force.

[2] What is the essential difference, for instance, between letterpress printing and type writing? Yet the former process is strictly supervised by the
Factory Acts, and the latter is not.

with it.   There is absolutely no guiding principle of action
throughout.   A new set of definitions, and a body of
rules founded upon it, is promulgated, legalised, and
abandoned.   An entirely new system supplants it, or a
portion of the former is tacked on to, or slipped in with,
the latter.   Presently a fresh one supervenes.   All are
excogitated piece by piece, and with no reference at all to
the whole field to be covered, or to a proper knowledge of
the nature of the enterprise thus entered on.   But they
teach also how superficially as yet the nation has laid to
heart the full meaning and bearings of that new system of
production itself, which within little more than a century
has nearly ousted all others from its midst; how partially
heretofore it has conceived the new obligations that have
been thus cast upon it.   When its course is still more
fully run, the obligations in question will doubtless be
made clearer, and will be faced then, it may be hoped, in
a philosophic and systematic spirit.   When the whole labour
question is comprehensively re-studied, as it should be, in
the light which the factory system sheds upon it, the inconsistencies adverted to may be removed.   In the meanwhile
it appears to the present writer that it is in tracing the
influences that have gone to the formation and development
of that system, and by contrasting it with other industrial
systems, that we may most hopefully approach this task.

On such an enterprise then we are about to enter, and
an obvious preliminary is, to state in what
PLAN OF THIS WORK.
sense will be used throughout this work
the expressions *factory, factory system, mill, and manufacture,*
about which so much has been already said; and in what
order, and to what end, the subsequent recital will be made.
The word "factory," then, will be used all through these
pages in its popular rather than its historical or legal sense
up to the period of its being defined by statute.   The early

signification of a trading establishment will be altogether and everywhere excluded, and the later meaning, of a place of production, will be at first, and everywhere, understood. It will be held to be *any* such place of production ; that is, any *definite place* where *associated industrial production* is carried on, *by whatever means.*[1] This definition of it will postulate its close connection with the term "manufactory," and that word and factory will be regarded as practically synonymous up to the time of statutory definition. The *verb* Manufacture will signify in all cases to make any commodities on a large scale, especially for exportation, and the *noun of multitude* Manufacture will mean the sum of the commodities produced in that way. ·Where A Manufacture (noun of multitude) is referred to, it will be understood that there must be, of course, a system of manufacture to have produced it, but not necessarily *manufactories*, for a manufactory is a place of definite bounds, but manufacture is a term far more indefinite. Thus a district may possess a great handicraft manufacture but have no manufactories. Such is, for instance, the case with India, and is and has been with other places. It is the case in several districts of England now, where cottage industries prevail. From the time of special statutory enactment the meanings of these words vary with the vicissitudes of statutory definition, and they will be employed accordingly. The word *mill*, however, will be kept

---

[1] One of the best definitions of a factory yet offered is in a *Report on the Factory System of the United States*, by Carroll D. Wright, Washington, 1884 :—" A factory is an *establishment* where several workmen are collected for the purpose of obtaining greater and cheaper conveniences of labour than they could procure individually in their homes ; for producing results by their combined efforts which they could not accomplish separately, and for preventing the loss occasioned by carrying articles from place to place during the several processes necessary to complete their manufacture." This is too far removed, however, from our modern English definitions to be made practical use of here.

as nearly as possible to its proper signification throughout, namely, that of a place in which a certain class of operations, usually of the nature of reducing a greater bulk to a less, is carried on.

With respect to the term *factory system* a somewhat lengthier exposition is requisite. From the dawn of history there are occasional indications of factory systems of some kind existing ; that is to say of combined labour in establishments of definite bounds being employed for purposes of industrial production. This Introduction will commence its survey with those early types. In some primeval countries they remain indications only, or the traces fade away when subjected to closer examination. In others, no traces of the kind exist at all—there was apparently no production beyond the supply of immediate wants, and no trade. In a few they assume large and shadowy proportions, which pique while they fail to satisfy curiosity. It is chiefly in the world of remote antiquity that remains of this latter kind are found —remains of a great factory system which prevailed over certain parts of it, and supplied millions of customers with products. The enormous populousness of the ancient world at various epochs [1] seems to have necessitated some such system of production, which accordingly sprang into being at those times and places to meet those wants, even as it has done at various epochs of later times under a like compulsion. In Egypt, in Assyria, in Phœnicia, and elsewhere, such an organisation of labour seems to have prevailed. In India, in China perhaps, and in some other places, the manufacturing organisation was dissimilar :—labour was not conducted on the factory system. As history proceeds, the

---

[1] See Wilkinson's *Ancient Egyptians*, chap. v., where the suggestion is made that the world may have been at many other epochs as populous as it is now. See also for the classical period Hume's well-known essay, "Of the Populousness of Ancient Nations," vol. i. p. 411, edition of 1767.

memory of those old times, and of their political and industrial conditions grows faint, and classical civilisation coming to the front for a while dominates mankind. There is little about the factory system to be noted then, except its bare existence, the circumstance that as society became again more highly organised, and the necessity for making provision for its wants again more pressing, a more highly organised labour system came necessarily into vogue, a circumstance common alike to the later civilisations of Greece and Rome; and which will be noted accordingly. Then follows the rush of the barbarians upon the western world, and all familiar forms of social life go down before it. No great manufacture is traceable in the west during the Dark Ages, but in the south-east of Europe it still maintains its place, transmitting its traditions, and a method modified by new conditions, by the familiar, but at that time almost imperceptible channel of trade. Then emerges an order of things, in many respects resembling, yet in some so unlike, the ancient order. An immense stimulus is given to industry, partly by a great increase of population and greater facilities for trade, but also by novel contrivances in the physical and mechanical worlds, having production for their end. New political and economical conditions accompany these changes, and at length the modern factory system fully fledged takes its place among the great labour systems of the world.

The materials that are accessible for ever so superficial a review of the tendencies and events thus indicated are extremely meagre. Many of the great nations of antiquity, and still more of the classic ages, had an inveterate scorn of trade and industry, things which they regarded as in their nature mean and sordid, beneath the dignity of high-spirited and enlightened men. They have left accordingly scarcely any trustworthy accounts of such matters, and

those which we possess are to be found elsewhere than
in their formal writings. They are to be found in the
chance allusions of their poets and sacred writers, in their
descriptions of the manners and customs of other races;
and in the results of modern antiquarian and anthropological
research. Similarly, the writers of the Middle Ages had
other and very different preoccupations. During the early
part of that period they were engaged in almost constant
controversies among themselves, they were entangled in the
toils of the scholastic philosophy, and their thought was
of almost anything but industry and social organisation.
There was in fact very little industry to write about, and
very little organisation at all, except of the religious kind.
Then followed the Renaissance, where all the prejudices of
the ancient world were revived with the ancient learning,
and the vices of classicism imitated with even a greater
success than were its virtues. The writers of those times
adopted, with their models, a tone of contempt towards
industry, which the military spirit of the day tended to foster
and perpetuate; and the tone thus begotten of classicism and
nurtured by feudalism has continued, with rare exceptions,
until within about a century of the present day, since when
the industrial and democratic spirit has been superseding it.
It will be our own endeavour to exhibit this progression, so
far as it relates to the subject under review, in an orderly
succession, though necessarily in the briefest manner. This
Introduction does not pretend to be in any proper sense a
history of manufacture, of commerce, or of trade; of the
organisation of labour—further than of the particular form
of organisation with which it is specifically concerned—of
processes, inventions, or usages. These things are to be
found treated of elsewhere, with a fulness proper to their
importance, and a special knowledge to which the present
writer does not by any means lay claim. It will suffice for

him if the gleam of light he is enabled to shed on this comparatively untravelled path, though in truth no better than a glimmer, be yet strong enough to mark the way for others, who may hereafter, with greater qualifications, be induced to tread it.

CHAPTER II.

Prehistoric Times—The Patriarchal Age—Village Communities—Despotism
—The Tribal System—Slavery—Serfdom—Hereditary Trades—Caste—
Guilds—The Municipal System—The Manorial System—The Feudal
System—Free Industry—Competition—Capital and Labour.

LESS than fifty years ago the inhabitants of the civilised world believed, and were satisfied with the belief, that mankind's genealogy on earth did not extend further back than six thousand years or thereabouts. Since then a complete revolution has occurred in all educated conceptions of this matter. An extraordinary series of successful investigations has revealed the existence of an older world, inhabited by now extinct races of men, the remains of whose handiwork are found alike in the soil we till, and under the sites of the cities we people. It has been proved, as certainly as anything can be proved, that ages before the earliest light that history sheds upon the past, men and women, in all material respects similar to ourselves, occupied the countries we now occupy—lived, died, were buried and left descendants, where we live, love, and die to-day. No direct knowledge of these former races reaches us from the oldest traditions of the earliest time. They have left no voluntary records of themselves. All our knowledge of them is derived from their skeletons and tools, and the bones of animals on which they fed, relics that are occasionally discovered in the caves that were used as places of refuge, and under the gravels and clays that now cover their hunting and fishing resorts. The antiquity of some of these remains cannot be less than fifty thousand years, and is probably often much greater.[1] The fashioning of the rude flint and bone implements thus discovered was presumably the earliest manufacture in the world. Of the system of industry which produced them it is impossible of course to give any accurate description. With the aid of analogy, however, and by the light of the most recent discoveries in anthropology a fair conception of it may be formed. The earliest condition of man is now generally believed to have been, not one of savage isolation, as has been often assumed;[2] still less of innately acquired civilisation afterwards tending to decay, as has also been contended;[3] but of gradual evolution from very variously constituted family groups. "Mankind," says Mr. Tylor, "can never have lived as a mere struggling crowd, each for himself;"[4] and equally certain it is that no member of the human family has ever appeared on earth clothed in the full panoply of letters, arts, and language—like Minerva springing from the brain of Jupiter. Population must at all times have been first made up of family groups or households, consisting at the least of a single pair and their descendants; but also more usually perhaps being of some more complicated structure. Such family groups in an almost endless variety of structural complication are still found all over the world. Into most of them the conception of property sooner or later forces itself, whether property in chattels, cattle, or land; whether

---

[1] *The Great Ice Age*, by James Geikie, F.R.S., second edition, revised 1877, p. 436 (Ed. Stanford). *Primitive Man*, by Louis Figuier, Introduction. (Chatto and Windus, 1876). *The Human Species*, by A. De Quatrefages; International Scientific Series, third edition, chaps. xii. and xiii.

[2] By Rousseau, for instance, and his school.

[3] By the school of which Dr. Whately was perhaps the best known disciple.   [4] *Anthropology*, p. 402.

of a personal or family kind; and this is the first step towards industrialism. The next is when barter is developed. The members of the group learn to exchange their superfluities with one another for other objects which they desire to possess. This step is one that man only among animals is known to take. An extended system of exchange leads to trade, which presupposes manufacture; and the considerable organisation of labour that this implies has been generally held to portend a much advanced stage of human development. Sir Charles Lyell, however (*Antiquity of Man*), believed himself to have discovered the undoubted traces of a "manufactory" of stone implements near Berne in Switzerland;[1] and if the reality of that discovery be allowed, we see in how primitive a stage of progress organised production may occur. We can thus picture to ourselves the prehistoric conditions of human labour. Family groups roam over the surface of the earth in search of food, sheltering themselves as best they can in some cave or fissure; and here and there these groups gather together into communities more or less organised; even at length so highly organised as to own property, and carry on a primordial trade and manufacture.

Anthropologists divide the earliest industrial epoch, which they call the Stone Age, into two periods, the Palæolithic and Neolithic, or the eras of rough and polished stone implements. Such eras are of course not epochs of history, but of progress. To these succeed in their classification the Bronze and Iron Ages respectively: in the former of which we first make historic acquaintance with the Greeks, who are just emerging from it in Homeric times. At some period during the Stone Age the manufacture of earthenware, they say, began; and at a later date

---

[1] See also *Primitive Man*, chap. vi. Regular workshops of primitive stone implements have likewise been lately found in Brittany.

in the same epoch the arts of spinning and weaving were discovered.

When men began to gather together into larger groups these were at first still formed upon the model of the family. The earliest system THE PATRIARCHAL AGE. of organised civil society was the patriarchal.[1] Upon this point Sir Henry Maine speaks in unequivocal terms.[2] "The effect of the evidence derived from comparative jurisprudence," he says, "is to establish that view of the primeval condition of the human race which is known as the Patriarchal Theory." This theory "was originally based on the Scripture history of the Hebrew patriarchs in Lower Asia:" and that connection, he thinks, "has rather militated against its reception as a complete theory." Quite independent investigations have, however, conducted him "inevitably to the same conclusion," till, "the difficulty at the present stage of the inquiry is to know where to stop, to say of what race it is *not* allowable to lay down that the society in which they are united was originally organised on the patriarchal model." The "chief lineaments" of such a society are therefore, as the same writer observes, familiar to most of us from childhood. "The points which lie on the surface are these: The eldest male parent—the eldest descendant—is absolutely supreme in his household. His dominion extends to life and death, and is as unqualified over his children and their houses as over his slaves; indeed the relations of sonship

[1] This is disputed. Many recent writers of eminence (the brothers M'Lennan, Bachofen, and Morgan, for instance) believe that a communal state of all relations generally preceded the institution of the family. The questions of precedence is not pertinent here, nor is it properly within our province to discuss what constitutes *organised civil society*. It is sufficient for the purpose in view to sketch the main outlines of the communal and patriarchal systems in their industrial connections. See on this subject Sir J. Lubbock's *Origin of Civilisation*, fourth edition, pp. 98, 99.

[2] *Ancient Law*, eighth edition, p. 122 *et seq.* (Murray, 1880).

and serfdom appear to differ in little beyond the higher capacity which the child in blood possesses of becoming one day the head of a family himself." The industrial organisation is necessarily the counterpart of the political. "The flocks and herds of the children are the flocks and herds of the father," who directs all industrial operations, and claims their fruits as his. Primitive society "laboured under an incapacity" to imagine any bond, or principle of subordination, other than the family principle. When the reality of this failed, it was even found easier to "feign a relationship" than to substitute another form of union. Under this system labour and its results were the property not of the labourer, nor of the family or tribe, but of the head of the tribe. Individualism was wholly merged in the governing unit. There was no contract nor competition. The nature of the rule was that of a voluntary despotism under a despot exacting his utmost rights.

Such a constitution of society is connected historically with the circumstance of a migratory life,
VILLAGE COM- the stage of development in which history
MUNITIES. first reveals man to us. In point of fact the organisation just described would seem to be one best suited to a nomad community. But as tribes and families settle upon the soil new motives of conduct are evolved, when either of two alternative courses, we are told[1] is likely to be pursued. The bond of union being then fixed less in kinship than in occupation of land, the head of the family group will either cease to be a patriarch and become a sovereign, or will be dispensed with altogether. In the first case kingship supplants kinship as the supreme power; in the second case communism supplants both. It was long supposed that the former course was the natural, or

---

[1] *Village Communities in the East and West*, by Sir Henry Maine, *passim*. See also, by the same author, *The Early History of Institutions*, p. 72 *et seq.*

even inevitable one; the analogy of those nations of whose affairs we have written records being exclusively, and not always very intelligently, followed; but more recent and very careful researches into the sociology both of historic and prehistoric peoples have established directly contrary conclusions. The collective ownership of the land at one time or another by groups of cultivators, either united in fact by blood relationship, or believing or pretending to believe themselves so united, is now entitled to take rank as "an ascertained phenomenon of primitive society" in every quarter of the globe.[1] "In *all* primitive society," says M. Emile de Laveleye,[2] "whether in Europe, Asia, and Africa, alike among Indians, Sclavs, and Germans, as even in modern Russia and Java, the soil was the joint property of the tribe, and was subject to periodical distribution among all the families, so that all might live by their labour as nature has ordained." The community that settled upon the land might be variously organised and variously named; but the characteristic feature—that of communal possession—was general. The importance of these deductions to the present subject will be fully perceived only when it is considered how intimately the land tenure of any country is related to its other productive artifices and arrangements.[3] The soil being the ultimate source of wealth, the manner in which it is dealt with is in the long run, and next to labour, the most important of all economical factors. It cannot for long be disassociated from the industrial system that exists beside it; the one is the

---

[1] *Early History of Institutions*, by Sir Henry Maine, Lect. I. (Murray, 1880).

[2] *Primitive Property*, by Emile de Laveleye. Preface to Original Edition (Macmillan, 1878).

[3] "It is certain," says Mr. Thorold Rogers, "that the agriculturist must earn more than is necessary for his own support before any other person can contrive to exist."—*Six Centuries of Work and Wages*, by James E. Thorold Rogers, M.P., p. 159 (Swan, Sonnenschein and Co., 1884).

complement of the other. We must perforce suppose then
that the industrial system in communal times was in all
essential principles the same as the agricultural, for it could
not have substantially differed from it. It was thus a
labour system in which the very mainspring of our present
system, what we call in fact the "law" that regulates it,
i.e. competition, was wholly absent. The remuneration of
labour was not, when thus organised, determined by supply
and demand. It is doubtful indeed if any values were, or
ever could be, so assessed under archaic labour systems.
"What in a primitive society," asks Sir Henry Maine,[1] "is
the measure of Price? It can only be called Custom. . . .
Men united in those groups out of which modern society
has grown, do not trade together on, what I may call for
shortness, commercial principles. The general proposition
which is the basis of political economy made its first
approach to truth under the only circumstances which
admitted of men meeting at arms' length, not as members
of the same group, but as strangers. Gradually the
assumption of the right to get the best price has penetrated
into the interior of these groups, but it is never completely
received so long as the bond of connection between man
and man is assumed to be that of family or clan connection.
The rule only triumphs when the primitive community is
in ruins." The immense significance of these facts cannot
be overrated, nor can it be dwelt on here. It is sufficient
that the facts themselves should be thoroughly recognised
and laid to heart. That much, however, is absolutely
necessary in any, even the most meagre, survey of the
history of labour. Nor are we without the opportunity of
witnessing the spectacle of the typical village community at
the present day even within the dominions of Great Britain.
In India both agricultural and manufacturing industry have

[1] *Village Communities,* pp. 190, 196.

been pursued along communal lines from time immemorial, and although the introduction and progress of other ideas are gradually uprooting this system there, they have not yet quite done so. There, custom, not competition, has for ages been the regulator of price; and tradition, not the ratio between demand and supply, has been the ruler of labour. The same was the case all over ancient Germany, as we learn from Cæsar and Tacitus, and as all modern researches confirm. The village community under the name of the Mark was the universal type of society, and this Mark was a definite area of land farmed by, and redistributed among, all the members of the Mark community according to certain invariable conditions. We shall hereafter see into what later economic forms this germ developed under the influence of novel circumstances; and shall have occasion often to note its incompatibility with the present order of things. In the meanwhile the following vivid and eloquent description of the beauty of the old ideal will scarcely be out of place here, affording, as it does, a contrast, melancholy or inspiriting as we view it, to that widely different system of production with which we are definitely concerned. It is taken from Sir George Birdwood's excellent work on *The Industrial Arts of India*.[1] "Outside the entrance of the single village street, on an exposed rise of ground, the hereditary potter sits by his wheel moulding the swift revolving clay by the natural curves of his hands. At the back of the houses which form the low irregular street, there are two or three looms at work in blue and scarlet and gold, the frames hanging between the acacia trees, the yellow flowers of which drop fast on the webs as they are being woven. In the street the brass and copper smiths are hammering away at their pots and pans; and farther

---

[1] *The Industrial Arts of India*, by Sir George C. M. Birdwood, C.S.I., pp. 135, 136, and 312 (Chapman and Hall, 1880).

down, in the verandah of the rich man's house, is the
jeweller working rupees and gold mohrs into fair jewelry,
gold and silver earrings, and round tires like the moon,
bracelets and tablets and nose rings, and tinkling ornaments
for the feet, taking his designs from the fruits and flowers
around him, or from the traditional forms represented in the
paintings and carvings of the great temple, which rises over
the grove of mangoes and palms at the end of the street
above the lotus-covered village tank.   At half-past three or
four in the afternoon the whole street is lighted up by the
moving robes of the women going down to draw water from
the tank, each with two or three water jars on her head:
and so, while they are going and returning in single file, the
scene glows like Titian's canvas, and moves like the stately
procession of the Panathenaic frieze.   Later the men drive
in the mild gray kine from the moaning plain, the looms
are folded up, the coppersmiths are silent, the elders gather
in the gate, the lights begin to glimmer in the fast falling
darkness, the feasting and the music are heard on every side,
and late into the night the songs are sung from the Ramayana or Mahabharata.   The next morning with sunrise, after
the simple ablutions and adorations performed in the open
air before the houses, the same day begins again. . . . We
cannot overlook the serenity and dignity of his life if we
would rightly understand the Indian handicraftsman's work.
He knows nothing of the desperate struggle for existence
which oppresses the life and crushes the very soul out of
the English working-man.   He has his assured place,
inherited from father to son for a hundred generations,
in the national church and state organisation ; while nature
provides him with everything to his hand, but the little
food and less clothing he needs, and the simple tools of the
trade.   The English working-man must provide for house-
rent, coals, furniture, warm clothing, animal food, and spirits,

and for the education of his children before he can give a
mind free from family anxieties to his work. But the sun
is the Indian workman's co-operative landlord, coal merchant,
upholsterer, tailor, publican, and butcher; the head partner
from whom he gets almost everything he wants, and free of all
cost but his labour contribution towards the trades-union
village co-operation of which he is an indispensable and
essential member. This at once relieves him from an
incalculable dead weight of cares, and enables him to
give to his work, which is also a religious function,
that contentment of mind and leisure, and pride and
pleasure in it for its own sake, which are essential
to all artistic excellence. The cause of all his comfort, of his hereditary skill, and of the religious constitution under which his marvellous craftsmanship has
been perfected is the system of landed tenure which has
prevailed in India, and stereotyped the social condition
and civilisation of the country from the time of the Code
of Manu."

The amazingly stable, general, and efficient system of
labour just referred to is the very opposite
of another system which long dominated
DESPOTISM.
vast regions of the world, and still holds its own in several
of them. The most ancient despotisms of the history of
the Egyptian, Assyrian, Persian, and Arabian governments,
were typical instances of this form of society. These all
took their rise apparently in the patriarchal system, and
developed generally on a theocratic basis. The monarchs
were both priests and kings, or sometimes deified human
beings. The labour system was one of more or less
graduated tyrannical exaction. Other modified despotisms
appear to have taken their rise in the communal system,
and to have preserved some of the communal spirit in their
institutions, and the most remarkable instance of this is found

in what we are told of the ancient government of Peru : the
nature of which was that of a benevolent despotism.   From
Dr. Letourneau's work on Sociology we copy a few interesting
particulars on this head which must suffice :[1]—"The great
mass of the people were governed much in the same way as
a careful cultivator will bring up and look after his domestic
animals.   Every male inherited his father's profession ; he
was not allowed to choose any other employment.   By right
of birth a man was either labourer, miner, artisan, or soldier.
The population, divided into groups of 10, 50, 100, 500,
and 1000 persons, each having its chief, was attached to the
soil.   The government officers treated the people kindly as
though they were a flock of sheep.   Every man had his
task set out for him beforehand ; he was married ; a portion
of ground was given to him for his maintenance.   His
morality was watched ; he was dressed ; and, in case of
need, assistance was given to him.   In the empire of the
Incas, liberty and misery were equally unknown. . . . The
people worked for everybody. . . . All their undertakings
were performed in the same way ; to work the mines, to
graze and look after the numerous flocks of lamas, to shear
them, to weave the stuffs of wool or of cotton, to make the
roads, etc.   But each Peruvian owed to the State only a
certain stated portion of his time.   As soon as his task was
finished, he was replaced by another man ; he was also
maintained by the State as long as the State had need of
him."   Between these extreme forms of personal and communal overlordship were, of course, many other phases of
despotism, as that of the Roman Republic and Empire, of
the Chinese Empire, and of the Vedic Government in India.
Independently of form, however, the spirit of despotism is

[1] *Sociology, based upon Ethnography,* by Dr. Charles Letourneau.
Translated by Henry M. Trollope, pp. 480 and 410 (Chapman and Hall,
1881).

always the same. It is that of the subordination of the individual to the monarch or supreme governing authority. Absolute power is deposited in one or a few. The characteristic feature with respect to labour organisation is, that the labour is not supposed to be undertaken in the interests of one, as under the patriarchal system, or in the interests of all, as under the communal system, but to be a privilege, which the despot farms out to his subjects on his own terms. Labour, in short, is not the property of the labourer but of some other authority. Wherever a government assumes this attitude towards labour—an attitude which is of course quite different from that of demanding to exercise proper control over it—the nature of the relation that is established is despotic.

Different from the three systems already described is the tribal system, though in every case the difference is more one of degree than kind. As the early family group developed often into the patriarchal, and sometimes into the communal group, so did the patriarchal group in later times develop commonly into the clan or tribe. The steps of this progression, the characteristic distinctions between the two forms of organisation, and the relations subsisting among them ending in "the gradual transmutation of the patriarch into the chief," are detailed at length by Sir Henry Maine.[1] Sometimes this "transmutation" comes more rapidly. An individual arises within the tribe more powerful than the rest, and either deliberately alters in his own favour the political constitution of the body, or, becoming known and revered as a prophet, or a leader of successful warfare, has supreme power thrust upon him quite independently of any hereditary claim. The Celtic tribes—Teutonic, Scandinavian, and British—were often led by such elective chieftains, though

THE TRIBAL SYSTEM.

[1] *Early History of Institutions*, pp. 116, 117.

generally with a leaning towards the representatives of one
or a few favoured families.[1] The right to rule in such cases
is founded on personal prowess, not descent, at all events at
first. The chief is but the person held in highest estimation by the tribe. Such a one would not share equally,
as in a true community, in the toil and fruits of labour,
nor, like the patriarch, arrogate to himself its whole proceeds; he would be supported in a position different from
the rest by a portion of the common revenue being set aside
for that purpose at the instance of the other members of the
group. It is in this last circumstance beyond all others that
M. Guizot conceived the radical distinction between the
patriarchal and tribal systems to consist, and his observations
on the whole subject are too valuable to be omitted even in the
little space that we can afford them here. He thus forcibly
dwells upon this difference:—"The patriarch lived in common
with his children, his near relations, the various generations
which united themselves around him, all his kindred, all his
servants; and not only did he live with them all, but he
had the same interests, the same occupations, and he led the
same life." But "another family system presents itself,
namely, the Clan (or tribe), a petty society whose type we
must seek for in Scotland and Ireland. Through this system,
very probably, a large portion of the European family has
passed. This is no longer the patriarchal family. There is
here a great difference between the situations of the chief
and that of the rest of the population. They did not lead
the same life; the greater portion tilled and served; the
chief was idle and warlike. But they had a common origin :
they all bore the same name ; and their relations of kindred,
ancient traditions, the same recollections, the same affections,
established a moral tie, a sort of equality between all the

[1] Compare *The English Village Community*, by Frederick Seebohm, chap.
vii. (Longmans, 1883).

members."[1]   It is easy to see how similar differences distinguish the despotic from the tribal system.   In the former the despot lives upon his people's labour at his own discretion ; in the latter the chief is supported by his people's labour at their discretion, and is, in fact, as much bound to them as they to him.   His revenue is paid as a salary, not possessed as a right.   It is given in return for duties expected from him ; it does not descend as of divine appointment, or as if in the inevitable nature of things. Society in Greece and Italy just before the historic period was probably constituted in this manner.   In Scotland and Ireland it was thus organised until quite recently.   The more highly developed tribes in the south of Africa, the .Zulus, Kaffirs, and others, seem to be so constituted politically now.

In the tribal system labour is more free than in any labour system we have yet examined.   This form is in fact an advanced form of organisation socially considered.   Property is held in possession by the whole tribe, and distributed among its members by common consent, though not necessarily rigidly re-divided, as under the communal arrangement.   From an industrial point of view, however, it is seldom successful.   It does not lead to great accumulation of wealth, for the motives that impel to saving are not sufficiently strong ; the fruit of a labourer's industry is only his own subject to the necessities of others, who may not be —and commonly are not—industrious persons ; and subject also to any call upon it that the chief of the tribe may make for purposes quite the reverse of industrial.   Thus it is a system seldom applicable to settled industry, and particularly unsuitable, therefore, to the civilisation of modern times.

We have hitherto spoken of members of a family, group,

[1] *History of Civilisation*, by F. Guizot.   Bohn's Edition, 1882.   Vol. i. p. 70.

tribe, and nation, in their proper capacities as political factors in those variously organised bodies, and with special reference to the labour question.

We have traced a sort of evolution from the original germ —the ethnical group—onward to the community, the clan, and the despotically governed monarchy—in one or other of which later forms it commonly resulted. This evolution does not, of course, always follow strictly the lines thus marked out, nor always follow even similar ones. Occasionally revolution is substituted for evolution, and in one vast throe the ordinary work of centuries is accomplished. Sometimes degeneration sets in before the work of evolution has proceeded far. Sometimes society appears to remain for long ages stationary. Up to the present, however, we have said nothing of another class of persons outside all these political groups, and only necessarily attached to certain of them— the class of slaves. The origin of slavery must be traced to a time when in warfare defeated adversaries were not invariably massacred—to a time, therefore, of comparatively much progress. That this last circumstance was the principal one in which slavery originated is a belief that is now very generally held. Patriarchs or chieftains employing all their native forces in foreign forays would need to have their material necessities supplied at home meanwhile, and a certain number of captives taken in war were accordingly spared and set apart for that purpose in the absence of the usual labourers. Such persons were the earliest slaves. As social arrangements became more settled their ranks were however also supplied from other sources. Offenders against the wellbeing of the community, to whom some punishment short of death was considered appropriate, had a similar position allotted them; and this is recognised as the next great cause of slavery. The necessity for such arrangements should increase as the chiefs became great sovereigns over vast dominions, and would obviously grow with the power and splendour of the monarchs and the extent and wealth of their territories. As general prosperity increased as well, whether under this or other organisations, members of the dominant classes would often separate themselves from industrial occupations too, even in peaceful times, and give these over to slaves, who would thus at length monopolise them. The history of Greece affords an extremely interesting example of the growth of this latter labour system, and the overthrow of the great Roman dominion was notoriously hastened by its development. With the advance of luxury, personal slavery would follow on industrial—this last the most derogatory though seldom the most distressing form of bondage; while in other countries those changes might not —or might not always in just the same way—occur.

It is clear that, under any system of slavery, the laws of competitive industry can only operate partially; for labour, itself one of the principal subjects of exchange, is not wholly under the control of those laws. Equally it is clear that, where human beings themselves are among the things exchanged, economic formulæ suitable to a free labour-market do not apply. But at the same time it must be remembered that, in so far as labour is viewed as a mere impersonal factor in production, to that extent it is primarily immaterial whether the labour is supplied freely or on compulsion. The same quantity and quality of commodities might be produced equally well by slaves as by free men, though that is, on the whole, unlikely to be the case. It is only when labour ceases to be viewed impersonally, and comes instead to be recognised as embodied in a human creature, that the moral argument against slavery is supplemented by the economic; and then it is equally applicable in economics whatever the enslaving influence may be.

It appears from the foregoing remarks that there were two principal ways in which slavery ori- ginated—the first, the taking of captives in war; the second, the privation of personal liberty as a punishment for misdemeanour. There was also a third very usual way; namely, the general conquest of a whole country. In such a case those inhabitants of the conquered lands who had not been actually engaged in defending them would be reduced to servitude with the rest, but generally to servitude of a modified kind. They would not invariably be disturbed in their possessions, nor set to the performance of menial duties, or of the severer kinds of labour, but be often continued in the occupations in which they were found, especially if the occupation was that of agriculture. Or they would be, if skilled artificers, attached to the retinues of great persons, or perhaps transplanted to other places, there to pursue their avocations for their own or their employers' profit, subject to certain rules. For such persons it is desirable to find another name than slaves, and for their condition another name than slavery.

SERFDOM.

We adopt here the names of serfs and serfdom. It is true that there are objections of an historical kind to such a nomenclature. Both the name and the condition of serf- dom are said to be of comparatively modern origin, and neither the one nor the other to be known to archaic juris- prudence. But this we hold to be an error. Whatever may be the case with the name, we believe the fact of serfdom was a well-recognised condition of society, at least as early as the fact of slavery, and possibly earlier. The agricultural population of all conquered countries were from the first rather serfs than slaves, for they were attached to the conquered land, not to the persons of the conquerors. Such were the Helots of ancient Greece, the Coudras of Hindostan, the Adscriptitii and Coloni of the Romans.

"We are too much in the habit," says M. Guizot,[1] "of attaching to the word *slave* one bare single idea, of connecting with the term one sole condition; this is an entire misconception. . . . Some were domestic slaves, sent to a man's country estate to labour in the fields there instead of working indoors at his town house. Others were regular serfs of the soil, who could not be sold except with the domain itself; others were farmers who cultivated the ground in consideration of receiving half the produce; others farmers of a higher class, who paid regular money rent; others a sort of comparatively free labourers—farm-servants who worked for wages." M. Guizot is speaking here of a particular period of history—that, namely, following the decline of the Roman dominion in the west—but this classification is probably applicable to far anterior times. Alike under the tribal and communal systems of society there were so-called slaves, who really resembled in their social status serfs; they had rights in their labour, though not the full control of it; and we have the authority of Sir Henry Maine that they were not unknown to even the patriarchal family.

The institution of slavery was thus very general.[2] It was, in fact, inherent in most ancient forms of civilisation, though it frequently took the modified form of serfdom. It marked at first a decided advance in human conceptions and actions, and the best minds of many ages were unable to conceive of any form of society from which it should be absent. It is impossible to understand ancient or mediæval history without constantly remembering this fact; and the organisation of all ancient labour systems is incomprehensible without continual reference to it.

[1] *History of Civilisation in France*, p. 309.

[2] "Slavery," says Mr. Freeman, "has been the common law of all times and places till within a few centuries past."—*Comparative Politics*, by Edward A. Freeman, M.A., p. 248 (Macmillan and Co., 1873).

Above the ancient servile classes, though constantly
recruited from their ranks, and generally
HEREDITARY TRADES.
mixed up with them in a manner that is
not always easy to understand, stood the artificers, operatives, and petty traders.

The number and functions of these would naturally
vary with the character and constitution of the community
of which they formed a part. In a nomad community both
number and functions would be few and simple ; in a settled
community more numerous and complex ; and in both those
forms of society in primitive times, crafts and trades appear
to have had a tendency to become hereditary—a tendency
perpetuated in some instances with astonishing persistency.
" In societies of an archaic type," says Sir Henry Maine, " a
particular craft or kind of knowledge becomes in time an
hereditary profession of families, almost as a matter of
course ;[1] and in another place[2] the same author assigns a
reason for this, to the effect that it is the necessary order of
things where status not contract is the regulating impulse.
Now as this relation of status to contract is extremely
pertinent to this subject, perhaps the most pertinent of all
legal relations, it may be well to dwell a little on the nature of
it here before proceeding further with this sketch. By Status
legists mean then immemorial custom, *prescription*, a condition independent of individual preference ; while by Contract
is meant on the contrary a condition altogether brought about
by individual arrangement. The movement of all progressive
societies, says Sir Henry Maine,[3] " has been uniform in one
respect. . . . The individual is steadily substituted for the
family as the unit of which civil laws take account. . . .
Nor is it difficult to see what is the tie between man and

---

[1] *Early History of Institutions*, Lecture VIII.
[2] *Ancient Law*, chap. v. p. 170.
[3] *Idem*, p. 168.

man which replaces by degrees those forms of reciprocity in rights and duties which have their origin in the family. It is contract." Of the history of this substitution of contract for status, which is in fact the keynote of the whole economic history of modern times until quite recently, we are presently to give a summary. We have yet to conclude with primitive types of labour organisation. The existence of hereditary trades in the early commonwealths, whether fixed or migratory, sprang naturally from the ideals with which ancient society was permeated—ideals strangely different from ours. Under the industrial systems that have mostly occupied the world, and which in some quarters still flourish, it would "as little occur to a son that he was not born to follow his father's calling as that he was not to bear his name." Everything in the mind of the primitive man was fixed from the beginning, and change in the obvious order of things was "accident" and "catastrophe." It may also be, as is suggested by Mr. Mill, that there was a utilitarian sanction at the basis of the hereditary trade system, though it scarcely seems necessary to look for it there. His view of the matter is, however, too suggestive and characteristic to be passed over. He says,[1] "The further we look back into history, the more we see all transactions and engagements under the influence of fixed customs. The reason is evident. Custom is the most powerful protector of the weak against the strong: their sole protector when there are no laws or government adequate to the purpose." Mr. Mill was a utilitarian philosopher, and would naturally infer a motive of this kind where another might overlook it. The question belongs in any case rather to philosophy than history.

The substitution of contract for status as the moulding force of industrial organisation; the protection afforded by

---

[1] *Political Economy*, Book II. chap. iii.

good laws well administered ; the restlessness born of modern
facilities of communication, and the great uprising among
men of the principle of unrestrained competition have pretty
nearly abolished the hereditary system in trade, as well as
in some other domains of modern life.   It still lingers only
where those novel influences have not much permeated.
The good and evil qualities of such a system may be briefly
indicated.   On the *credit* side of the account should be put
the superiority in workmanship that is likely to be secured
by the transmission of hereditary attainments—a superiority
possibly incapable of being to the same extent secured in
any other way.   On the *debit* side must be placed the
diversion into a preordained channel of talents conceivably
capable of more productive employment in another sphere.
In favour of the system, might be urged its undoubted influence in the development of native art; against it, the
artificial barriers raised up by it against the introduction of
foreign arts and processes.   The tendency in hereditary
trades must always be towards the perfecting of elder types
rather than to the production of new ones.

Sometimes hereditary customs hardened into law, resulting
in the institution of *Caste.*   This happened
CASTE.
chiefly where the usage was taken under
the protection of religion, to whose sanction it then appealed
as a final arbitrator, and from which it professed in time to
derive its origin.   Such was the course that seems to have
been followed in ancient Egypt and Persia among other
countries, and which has been certainly followed during
vast ages in India.   It has been argued on the other hand
that the origin of caste should be referred to the existence
in the same country of different races ; and so far as the
political divisions into castes are concerned, an original
impulse of this kind may often be traced.   But in the case
of artificers and craftsmen, it is more likely that these were

country : is inevitably bound up with the proper solution of the problems they present. Those problems too are becoming more pressing as time proceeds; as this system strikes its roots deeper, and spreads its branches wider, at the expense of elder and less energetic growths; and this while a dazed legislature is painfully feeling its way among them, with half concessions and temporary expedients, clumsily enough for the most part, while still on the whole faithful to the high responsibilities of its trust.

It is in the light of this last consideration, added to those already stated, that I have resolved to abbreviate the contents and hasten the publication of this book. The expansion of the factory system into nearly all departments of industrial employment in this country has become an already accomplished fact. Commensurate with it, has become the desire among the better minded of the people, including our more thoughtful legislators, to take precautions that the new order of things shall be introduced at the least preventible cost of human health and happiness. It was not so always, but such is the feeling now. But this benevolent intention is at present checked and hampered; is liable to be diverted from its proper course and rendered nugatory, or even injurious, by the amazing ignorance of the history and philosophy of the whole subject that prevails. I am anxious to make a humble beginning towards a better state of things. "The student of social and industrial problems," says a recent writer, "ere he can rightly understand them, and properly estimate their force, must learn something of history, primitive, mediæval, and modern,"[1] and my aim is to supply from those sources a

---

[1] *Distribution Reform*, by Thomas Illingworth (Cassell and Co., 1885).

sketch that might aid such a student in understanding the factory system of to-day. No one can feel more fully than I do how imperfect and inadequate the performance of this attempt is ; how crude, hasty, and fragmentary. Still it is an attempt, as I believe, in the right direction ; and if its only result be to incline more capable minds into the same train of thought it would serve a very useful purpose. If it should itself, however, have the greater result of introducing something like order into popular conceptions of this matter, where nothing but chaos was found before, even though it were only *something like* order, and not the particular order that was expected or is approved, it would then have more than fully achieved its end.

For this book, I must repeat, professes to be no more than an *introduction* to the history of the factory system, not to be that history itself. It proposes to show how such a history might be written ; how I should myself have written it if opportunity, ability, sufficient knowledge, and other circumstances had been in my favour ; and it is intended to suggest the proper moral that ought to pervade such a one. I have commenced, therefore, at the dawn of combined labour: which is the first germ, of course, of a factory system : and roughly sketched some of the labour organisations of very ancient times. Those labour systems differed in several notable respects from ours, and to these differences I have drawn attention ; and they much resembled ours in several more. It is of great importance that the points of resemblance equally with the points of divergence should be recognised. From the most ancient times I have passed to classical antiquity, where the indications of a factory system are fainter than before, but are found nevertheless; and from classical to mediæval times, where the indications are fewer still, but never wholly absent. In the course of this progression I have had occasion to observe that trade and manufacture are inextricably related, and I have added, therefore, a chapter on ancient and mediæval commerce. Where the limits would at all permit, I have said a few words on the social and political, as well as the industrial, conditions of the time dealt with, and of the classes referred to. I wish to make it clear that the modern factory system is so far from being the only conceivable factory system —as is commonly assumed—that it is, in fact, but one of many actual ones which have already had their day; and may be but the precursor of others yet to come; that its essential economy is not, therefore, to be studied in any one particular aspect, but in various aspects, and that consequently all exterior dealing with it, to be successful, must be founded on those wider considerations, historical and economical, that I have endeavoured to bring into view.

In the preparation of a work of this scope my reading has necessarily taken a wide and very various range. Equally, in keeping within the limits that I have imposed upon myself and in accelerating the completion of the undertaking, has that reading been generally compelled to be of a very superficial kind. I may at once allow that much of this book is a compilation from others; and it is so inevitably. No work of precisely the same kind has, so far as I am aware, ever appeared before; and the materials for it (in the spirit in which I have here employed them) are such as do not yield themselves easily to casual research.

Those materials have had accordingly to be sought far and
wide amongst the works of others, generally amongst well-
known works as the most accessible.   I have availed myself
of such assistance as these supply without scruple; and in
some parts of the text the principal labour has been their
proper collation and piecing together.   I have in every
case endeavoured to make acknowledgment of the assistance
thus rendered in the most conspicuous way.   Where a book
is quoted for the first time, I have generally given in the
notes its title, date, edition, and the names of the author
and publisher (where possible) in full.   If cited at second
hand, I have named the intermediate authority.   Where
a quotation is made at length, I have almost invariably
(I have striven to do so invariably) used the author's own
words; and I have preferred to take this course rather than
epitomise, often at very considerable inconvenience to myself.
If occasionally all these precautions have failed me in
making the full acknowledgment that I desire, it is either
an oversight, or because the authority quoted is too well
known, of too ancient date, or too obscure, for the reference
to be useful.

Just at the last, the completion of this book has been
hurried more than I had once expected or intended.   The
great likelihood that the area of factory legislation will soon
be further enlarged, and the unusual interest that the public
is now showing in this and kindred questions, have induced
me to issue it at the very earliest possible opportunity.   It
is not without a pang that I do so, conscious as I am of its
numerous imperfections; its many sins, both of omission and
commission; its crudities, that further revision might have

persons whose occupations in a great lapse of time having become hereditary were, on the accession to supreme authority of some powerful prophet or lawgiver, assigned and fixed to them as their proper portion in the commonwealth, and thenceforth remained so sanctioned. In the instance of India, the country nearest in point of interest to ourselves, and where best in modern times the problem can be studied, Sir George Birdwood clearly thus conceives of the institution. "The arts of India," he says,[1] "are the illustration of the religious life of the kingdom as that life was already organised in full perfection under the Code of Manu, 900-300 B.C." An industrial system to be already "organised in full perfection" evidently implies many previous ages of specialisation, and an evolution probably through many earlier types. But, once so organised on the caste model, its religious character dominated it thenceforth. "Every thought, word, and deed of the Hindus belongs to the world of the unseen as well as of the seen; and nothing shows this more strikingly than the traditionary arts of India. Everything that is made is for direct religious use, or has some religious significance. The materials of which different articles are fashioned, their weight, and the colours in which they are painted, are fixed by religious rule. An obscurer symbolism than of material and colour is to be traced also in the forms of things, even for the meanest domestic uses. Every detail of Indian decoration, Aryan or Turanian, has a religious meaning, and the arts of India will never be rightly understood until there are brought to their study, not only the sensibility which can appreciate them at first sight, but a familiar acquaintance with the character and subjects of the religious poetry, national legends, and mythological scriptures that have always been their inspiration, and of which they are the perfected imagery." How

[1] *The Industrial Arts of India*, part i.

foreign does all this sound to our modern conceptions of the functions and principles of industrial economics! The institution of caste was not nearly so universal in ancient society as that of slavery. It did not exist in Phœnicia and its colonies, nor among the classic nations, except in a political form. The patricians and plebeians of Rome were not members of castes but of classes. The helots of Greece were vassals under the protection of the State. The northern nations of Europe and Asia seem to have been generally unfamiliar with this variety of social organisation; and it is possibly to this circumstance, not the least among many, that the splendid history of the tribes that overran Europe may be attributed. Those barbarians bore within them the germs of progress and infinite adaptability, whilst a people moulded into castes is naturally unable to conform itself to changed circumstances.

Where hereditary handicrafts were not necessarily weighted with religious sanctions, the handicraftsmen sometimes found it desirable to seek for some other bond of union, or principle of exclusion. This want was likely to be more especially felt in countries that had been greatly devastated by war, and where foreign dominion had been imposed upon a population not wholly cowed. It was also naturally more likely to be felt in countries where the advantages of industrial association had become familiar to the people owing to the communal possession of land. The result was the formation of Guilds. Such associations were not always, however, exclusively formed among hereditary craftsmen, nor was the bond of union always necessarily industrial. It might also be judicial, social, or religious, or all these together. With our immediate forefathers of the Teutonic race, among whom guilds first begin to show their most familiar and characteristic features, these several purposes of the guild were in use.

There was first the frith guild, which was a voluntary
association among the humble classes for purposes of mutual
protection in troublesome times. There was next the
religious guild, which was of the nature of a pious confraternity or brotherhood; and there were the later merchant
guilds and craft guilds for purposes connected with trade
and production. The origin of these associations is lost in
antiquity.[1] Among the Romans there existed a similar system
of trade organisation at a very early period of their history;
and traces of a like system are to be discovered in a far
remoter past, in most advanced societies indeed where caste did
not prevail. The most striking differences between the caste
and guild organisations may thus be rapidly summed up.
The caste was essentially a religious institution, whose prime
characteristic was that its constitution was imposed upon it
from without: the guild was an organisation of various form
whose shape and motive power were supplied from within.
The caste was a body necessarily hereditary and unprogressive;
the guild not necessarily either. In political language the
one institution was aristocratic; the other, in the widest
sense of the term, democratic. Mr. George Howell[2] gives
an interesting account of the origin and essence of guilds.
Quoting from the learned work of Dr. Brentano,[3] he patrioti-
cally assigns to England the honour of being their birthplace.
This means probably that they took firm root here earlier
than in any other part of Europe, where they were at first
sternly repressed. The unsettled condition of England from
the fifth to the tenth century may have favoured the
formation of such voluntary associations, and the free

[1] Sir Henry Maine believes guilds to have simply "grown out of the
primitive brotherhoods of co-villagers and kinsmen."—*Early History of Institutions*, p. 233.

[2] *The Conflicts of Capital and Labour*, by George Howell (Chatto and
Windus, 1878).

[3] *The History and Development of Gilds, and the Origin of Trade Unions*,
by Lujo Brentano ('Trübner and Co., 1870).

traditions of the people probably fostered them. At the time of the Norman Conquest there were already several important guilds established in England holding charters from both Saxon and Danish kings, and within the next two centuries similar organisations had spread widely over Europe. Their most usual form at this time was that of the merchant guild, into which the social or frith guilds and the religious guilds had generally merged. M. Lacroix in his splendid work on *Manners, Customs, and Dress during the Middle Ages*,[1] furnishes some very interesting information concerning the continental guild societies. He traces their origin, first, to the Roman *colleges of workmen*, " which were leagues of artisans following the same calling," and next, to certain Scandinavian organisations " whose object was to assimilate the different branches of industry and trade, either of a city or of some particular district." Their northern origin is shown by the derivative meaning of the word guild, or more properly " gild," which in Norse signifies a *feast*—that method of promoting industrial good-will being obviously as popular among our early ancestors as it is still among ourselves. Their descent from the Roman form of association (*collegia opificum*) is exemplified, he considers, in both the constitution and nomenclature of some of the early foreign societies. Brentano, on the other hand, will not admit the connection of guilds with the Roman colleges,[2] and would argue that M. Lacroix's instances related to trade societies rather than guilds, properly so called. But they were to develop into this latter form afterwards, and it is, as we have seen, a question if they had not in some cases been actually preceded by it. It was not indeed until the social system of the Middle Ages had

---

[1] *Manners, Customs, and Dress during the Middle Ages, and during the Renaissance Period*, by Paul Lacroix (London : Bickers and Son).

[2] *The History and Development of Gilds*, part i.

assumed something like a definite shape that the craft guilds and merchant guilds became specialised from amid the general industrial confusion, and forthwith struggled for supremacy, nor until they were thus specialised that the guild became distinctively a form of labour organisation.[1]

The confusion here noticed between early continental trade societies and guilds arose mostly from the circumstance that the guild system was often, in south-western Europe, grafted upon an- THE MUNICIPAL SYSTEM.
other fully-organised labour system which had preceded it in those parts. It is exceedingly difficult to obtain any precise idea of the nature of the trade societies of ancient Rome ; nor, in the absence of that, is it possible to satisfactorily compare this labour system with the one just described, nor to assign a priority in time to either of them. If, as some authorities assure us, the guild was an organisation known to our remotest Aryan forefathers, then any system that even the earliest development of Roman civilisation pro-duced was young in comparison ; while, if its birthplace is to be fixed in England, then the Roman municipal system, itself the successor of the Greek city system, was certainly by a long time its predecessor. There was, however, a clear distinction between them in any case, though they came afterwards to be so closely associated. The guild organisation was far more archaic both in type and essence than any form of the municipal system ever was or could be. The latter was a product of classical civilisation, and its basis was contract not status, its wide distribution over the western world portending, in fact, that change in the social system of those parts (to which allusion has been made) which consisted in law being substituted for custom as the regulating economic force. Under this influence the old ideals with which we have hitherto been concerned are

[1] See p. 258.

found taking a subordinate place, and the destinies of mankind are submitted to a new impulse. Custom and tradition begin to lose their hold, or at all events wax ever weaker. The new influence is contract, the new impulse the superior sanctity of law to natural right. All mediæval society was permeated with this doctrine, and modern society has only recently begun to repudiate it. "This great result proceeded," says M. Guizot, "from the vast and enduring influence of the Roman power. Rome itself was, in its origin, only a municipality—a corporation. The government of Rome was merely the aggregate of the institutions which were suited to a population confined within the walls of a city; these were municipal institutions—that is their distinguishing characteristic."[1] Moreover, "this was not the case with Rome only," but was general throughout the entire West. "There was at this time no country; that is to say, the country was wholly unlike that which at present exists; it was cultivated, as was necessary, but was uninhabited. The proprietors of the lands were the inhabitants of the towns. They went forth to supervise their country properties, and often took with them a certain number of slaves; but that which we at present call the country—that thin population, sometimes in isolated habitations, sometimes in villages, which everywhere covers the soil—was a fact almost unknown." There was no local "manufacture;" operative industry was a domestic profession, carried on by slaves for the benefit of their masters, and every proprietor of slaves had whatever usual productions he required manufactured in his own house. "He had slave blacksmiths, slave shoemakers, slave carpenters, slave ironworkers; and he not only employed them in making things for himself, but he sold the products of their industry to freedmen —his clients and others—who had no slaves of their own."

[1] Compare Freeman, *Comparative Politics*, Lect. III.

As Rome extended her conquests so did this system extend, and long after her empire ceased it remained operative amongst her colonies. In the East it was from the first associated with, and modified by, long-standing customs, which again asserted themselves when the outward pressure was withdrawn, but through Italy, Germany, Spain, Gaul, and Britain, it established itself firmly. There, it was the dominant influence at the time of the revival of letters, arts, and industry; and much of our modern thought, especially in the domain of jurisprudence, is deeply tinged with the municipal spirit. It readily united with the guild system—the guild in many places becoming, in fact, the municipal body—and the two together did good work at first in the cause of freedom and enlightenment. But though in its essence, and especially in its relation to labour, the municipal system was at first liberalising, it was ever tyrannical towards trade, which it overwhelmed with protective regulations; and this was its chief defect. In time it became tyrannical to labour also, and ultimately the rule of the guild was of the nature of a despotism, and its utility was lost. The particular purpose of its industrial organisation was somewhat different from any yet noticed. It was not a system designed to serve the family, the tribe, the community, the monarch, or the state, but the interests only of each several industrial microcosm within the state, over which it shed its influence, and within which it claimed very arbitrary power. Its solvent was citizenship, not family relationship, prescription, or custom. Its motive force was contract, not brotherhood.

Widely as the municipal system extended at the close of the classical era—the period of history at which we may now consider ourselves to have arrived—and unimportant as the country was THE MANORIAL SYSTEM.

in comparison with the town in the view of Roman jurists, yet there was a country, and there were special rural as well as municipal labour organisations, nevertheless, which in some wide regions of the world were even the more important of the two, and long remained so. This was certainly the case over the greater part of the north of Europe,[1] including Britain after the departure of the Romans. So averse at first were the conquerors of that island from the life of towns that for a long while they wholly avoided the great centres of population, and even when they did not wantonly demolish them, still preferred to live outside their walls. The social system that, under these circumstances, sprang up in rural parts is what is known as the manorial system. It was primarily a system founded upon agricultural needs, as was inevitable, but it embraced all industrial concerns. This organisation proceeded directly from the mark organisation, the manor being obviously a development of the mark. Some allusion has already been made to the constitution of the Teutonic mark. It was primarily a village community, holding land in common, and organised politically upon that basis. In process of time members of the mark might acquire private property in land. This acquisition would be forced upon them, for instance, in the case of the conquest of another country. Some development of the mark system would thereupon become a necessity, something that at the least cost of principle would best meet the requirements of the new case; and this development occurred when the northern races overspread Europe. The system of village communism, existing hitherto as the mark, became transformed into the system of the manor.[2] The

---

[1] "Till the reign of Charlemagne there were no towns in Germany, except a few that had been erected on the Rhine and Danube by the Romans."— Hallam's *Middle Ages*, p. 611, Cheap Edition (Ward and Lock).

[2] Mr. Seebohm thus defines a manor : "An estate of a lord or thane with a village community, generally in serfdom, upon it" (*The English Village Community*). A most interesting description of it, and of the process of its

labour arrangements in this organisation may be described thus: The portion of land called by the name of a manor was held by a lord, part as his private domain, part in holdings let to different classes of tenants, and part as common land. The lord's portion was cultivated for him free of cost, but he subsisted those who worked for him whilst they were so employed. At other times they farmed their own holdings. His domestic needs were provided for by the lowest class of dwellers on the manor—the domestic slaves—who lived in his house, or in out-buildings adjacent to it. They could possess no property, and such rude arts and industries as existed were in their hands. The lord of a manor exercised judicial authority, subject to the common law of the country, over the whole group. This system indicates with much distinctness the transition from communism to the private ownership of land, and is principally interesting to us here upon that account. The cultivators of the soil have, we see, still a proprietorship, though a limited one, in it. It also fills up the vacant places in the landscape at those points which the municipal system had not occupied.

The feudal system in so far as we are concerned with it as a system of labour must be regarded as a further development of the manorial system. The manor under other circumstances became a *fief*, and was held by military tenure from the crown, instead of by mere right of private possession: and the principal fief was divided into minor fiefs, which were let to tenants upon similar terms. The obvious economic change here is the further departure from the communal possession of land, and the introduction of a new sanction for private property in it, namely, that of military service. The political

development from the mark, is to be found in *The Growth of English Industry and Commerce*, by W. Cunningham, M.A., pp. 51-55 (Cambridge University Press, 1882). See also *Comparative Politics*, pp. 102, 116.

feature that invites earliest attention is the presence of a
king; not reigning as an absolute monarch, like an oriental
sovereign, or as a military despot, like a Roman emperor, nor
yet by common acclamation as a chief, but as the most
powerful among a number of lesser kings, all bound to him
by well recognised principles of allegiance, with mutually
incumbent rights and duties. The industrial features of
the system are those that have been described under the
last three heads mingled and loosely bound together. This
binding together of incoherent elements is at once the explanation and justification of the feudal system. At first
all is confusion, but presently a decisive tendency is apparent.
" The establishment of the feudal system," says M. Guizot,
" produced one modification of unmistakable importance;
it altered the distribution of the population over the face of
the land. Hitherto the masters of the soil, the sovereign
population, had lived united in more or less numerous
masses of men, whether sedentarily in cities or wandering in
bands through the country. In consequence of the feudal
system these same men lived isolated, each in his own
habitation, and at great distances from one another. You
will immediately perceive how much influence this change
was calculated to exercise upon the character and course of
civilisation. The social preponderance, the government of
society, passed suddenly from the towns to the country;
private property became of more importance than public
property; private life than public life " (Lect. IV.) Individualism is born. The result upon the municipalities is
quickly seen. The feudal sovereign withdrawing himself
more and more from the towns, commutes his claims upon
them for payments in money or kind; and the organised
town societies gladly avail themselves of the opportunities
thus created to purchase immunities from feudal dues.
From purchasing such privileges they soon come to demanding

them as a right; from repudiating the sovereignty of a non-resident feudal lord to establishing a sovereignty of their own. This is a sovereignty based upon individual arrangement; that is, upon contract. The country does not at first participate in those advantages; for status makes its last stand there; but its time is evidently coming.

The feudal system was adverse to industry; its conception of society was fragmentary, and its tendency was towards a personal despotism. It favoured the individualistic spirit, and thus indeed industry grew in spite of it; but it had little sympathy with the associative principle which alone renders great undertakings possible.

In this cursory glance at the various great organisations of labour that have from time to time existed, we have now passed from the FREE INDUSTRY. most primitive types to the threshold of that which has in modern days been hailed as the only natural and proper one. We have wound our way from custom to status, and from status to contract, and have reached at length the system of free industry, that is of its competitive organisation. Confining ourselves to the briefest possible historical summary of this evolution, we have seen how, outside the guild organisations and the municipal institutions of the Middle Ages, the ordinary course of manufacturing industry came to be almost wholly of a domestic character, being carried on in the castles and on the manors of wealthy and powerful proprietors; whilst within those bodies it was organised on a strictly artificial system. There is at this point then no production for profit but what is under a minute local regulation, either corporate or individual: there is scarcely any manufacture. There is restriction of industry on all sides. Whence came the new ideal? It proceeded at last partly from the abuse of those restrictions, and partly from other sources of change. The exactions of the municipal

bodies and trade societies had begun to rival the worst
obstacles that any former labour system had ever put in
the way of industrial progress. Their " privileges," instead
of being incentives, had come to be positive obstacles to
trade : their protection, industrial slavery. It became an
advantage to energetic craftsmen to live outside the towns,
as it had formerly been to live inside them; and gradually
all over Europe the spectacle was witnessed of artificers
transferring their labour to the suburbs of great cities, or to
villages not yet organised on the municipal model. Even
wild and uninhabited districts came to be thus preferred for
the locations of manufacture—a circumstance that explains
the otherwise singular situations in which some great industries have grown up. Removed from all mediæval trammels,
an industry had there some chance to develop in its own way,
for although the raw material and products might still be
subjected to State interference, its instruments and methods
were within its own control. Thus arose a system of free
industrial enterprise in opposition to the corporate industry
of towns, and a contest began between the two which
could have but one issue. In vain did the corporations look
to the State for assistance, in vain impose more strictly
protective regulations on themselves in the hope of holding
their ground against free industry, the whole strength of
the great economic forces of modern life was arrayed on
the other side, and their utmost efforts were condemned to
failure.[1] A like revolution occurred in the relations of the
cultivators to the soil at the same time. The serfs became
free labourers, often small proprietors ; their relation to their
employers and to each other being no longer of a customary

[1] For instances of this kind in English history, see many of the statutes
passed in Tudor times, where the effort was constantly made to limit certain
manufactures to certain towns to which they were especially supposed to
belong, and where the effort was always unsuccessful ; compare chap. viii.
pp. 323-4.

kind, but one of contract. Feudal rights were circumscribed, feudal privileges abolished. A system of industry unlike any other that had yet appeared overspread the civilised world, which began rapidly to show signs of great material prosperity under its influence.

The soul of the new system was competition, alike in labour and the products of labour. Competition of a kind—in skill and endurance COMPETITION. for instance, and even occasionally in productive energy— had always existed, but competition in productive energy had been subject in all the archaic systems of labour to strict limitations, in some almost to the point of extinction. Under the communal, tribal, and patriarchal organisations, for example, there was evidently little inducement to labour very energetically, for in the first and second of these the produce was divided with other persons, with but little reference to the industry of the individual producer; and in the third it all went to the patriarch. The limitation was here in the nature of things. Under despotic governments again, and where the labour system was that of slavery, there was obviously no incentive to industry beyond the point that was absolutely required by the taskmaster; the stimulus was compulsion, and competition had therefore little room for action. Under the system of caste again there was more or less an involuntary limit fixed; and under the guild and municipal systems the members of the corporations voluntarily fixed a limit on themselves. What competition there might be in any of these cases would be likely to be directed then towards the quality not the quantity of the work done; and some of the finest industrial work ever produced we find to have been produced accordingly under the most despotic of labour systems, whether the despotism took the form of a religious, political, or municipal sovereignty. But the main characteristic of the new system was, that the competition was

towards the production of quantity not quality, and that in
this direction there was at length *no* limitation set, either by
usage or by any internal or external law. It was this that
constituted its great novelty as a system of production, as well
as its great power as an economic force. Herein also was
its chief defect, either æsthetically or socially considered.
When there was no external impulse to regulate the manufacture, and the greatest freedom in every other respect was
absolutely assured, the temptation became excessive to make
the competition ever a competition downwards, to sacrifice,
that is, the quality of the product to the quantity. The
number of persons who can judge, or who even profess to be
able to judge, of the intrinsic value, and still more of the
artistic merit, of a manufactured commodity is comparatively
small, but the number who require products of manufacture
is practically illimitable. The great increase of population
at home which accompanied the economic changes that have
been described, and the discovery of new quarters of the globe
having new and vast populations with which trade might be
opened, immensely stimulated, if it had not actually aroused,
this feeling, to which the general political emancipation in
progress both at home and abroad gave new impetus. The
mechanical appliances that were presently invented afforded
the required means to satisfy the increased demand. Unre-
stricted competition, therefore, quite naturally, and as it were
inevitably, set before itself the economic ideal of a great
extension of production, and not of great excellence in it;
and similarly with respect to its social ideal. Free industry
at first felt no need to inquire into the welfare of any of its
agents, for was not every one at liberty to come and go as he
pleased, and did not the competition of the labour market
itself decide who should come and go?—beyond which there
was now to be no acknowledged standard of rectitude. The
forces of production were " natural forces ;" clearly the great

thing then to aim at was that they should be unrestrained
in their movements, so that the compulsion of "Nature" only
should be felt. There was no slavery that it was proper to
provide against but a personally imposed slavery. Such was
the new philosophy and belief.

An incident of this reign of free competitive industry
was the appearance in a new relation of two
clearly specialised classes of persons engaged capital and labour.
about production—capitalists and labourers. Labourers and
capitalists there had of course always been wherever production on a large scale was known, but hitherto they had
stood towards each other in different positions from what were
now impending. A patriarch, a despot, a tribal chief, and a
corporate trade body had far other relations to the operatives
in their employment than those which are embraced in the
payment of wages alone, the distinctive characteristic of
the new system. To those of them who were slaves they paid
of course no wages at all, and such as were not slaves
were still bound to them by well recognised and mutually
incumbent ties of customary or legal obligation. But
in the new form of capital and labour organisation, under
the system of perfectly free industry, there was no personal
tie or mutual obligation recognised. There was simply
an exchange of so much labour on one side for so much
payment on the other, and there all connection between the
contracting parties stopped. There, too, all interest in
each other and in each other's work, so far as the necessary
requirements of the system were concerned, ceased also.
Such a form of labour organisation was new in the world.
It was about equally far from communism and personal
despotism. It had clearly no relation to the guild or tribal
systems. It was the ultimate form of contract under the
unchecked impulse of competition. In the sphere of manufacture its effect soon became manifest in the greater ac-

cumulation and more unequal distribution of wealth; and
in that of agriculture in the aggregation in few hands of
great estates, and the cultivation of them on the large scale.
The owners became less and less occupiers, and the occupiers
ever fewer.   A struggle began between capitalists on one
side and labourers on the other, which tended to greatly
separate them at first, though it may not do so at length,
and the full results of which are not yet seen.

It was during the prevalence of this organisation and
this struggle that the modern factory system appeared.
When it emerged upon the scene the old industrial ideals
had passed away, and competition and capital were masters
of the field.   Upon this form of labour organisation the
factory system was destined to shed important lights, and
under it to obtain its great early triumphs.   At what cost
they were obtained, and whether the factory system is inevitably bound up with such a one is still matter of debate.

CHAPTER III.

TEXTILE fabrics mean properly all things that are woven
(*texere*, to weave), and the expression "textile industries" should accordingly be exclusively limited to the labours of the loom.   In popular
parlance, however, and equally in the language of statutory
enactment, this signification has been much misapplied;
spinning, and nearly all processes of preparing materials
for weaving, being commonly classed as textile processes;
whilst, on the other hand, some woven fabrics are omitted
from the textile category.   In the animal and vegetable kingdoms, it seems generally to be held now that any series of
industrial operations having weaving for their final stage
may be so named; but that in the mineral kingdom this rule
is not to hold good.   An instance may be quoted.   Some
ancient nations probably, and some European nations

TEXTILES.

certainly,[1] had a way of weaving garments of pure gold.
This might still be spoken of popularly as a textile manufacture, especially if it came to be confounded, as it probably would, with the manufacture of what is now called
"cloth of gold;" a composite tissue in which the metal
is laid on to the yarn before this is wrought in the web.
But would the weaving of ordinary wire netting be so
described ? Neither operation is in point of fact thus classed
by statute ; nor assuredly would the preparation of the wire
for the loom be.   Contrariwise, certain manufactures which
very nearly resemble the weaving of animal and vegetable
fibres, are by law arbitrarily included in, or excepted from,
textile work : as netting, lacemaking, embroidery, straw
plaiting, and possibly some more.   It is hopeless to endeavour to reconcile these inconsistencies of nomenclature.
Throughout this chapter we shall in all cases follow what
is the popular, rather than the scientific or statutory conception, arranging the subjects dealt with in an historical
more than technological order, so far as any proper order
is aimed at.

History and tradition, sacred and profane, unite with
the latest discoveries in archæology in
WEAVING.
assigning a very high antiquity to the art
of weaving.[2] If not the very earliest of the great industrial

---

[1] Especially the Venetians. For a full and very interesting account of
this industry, see the article on "Wire Drawing" in Beckman's *History of
Inventions*, vol. i. p. 414, Bohn's Edition.   On ancient weaving of mineral
substances, generally, see *Textrinum Antiquorum*, by James Yates, M.A.,
London, 1843, Book III. ; compare Ps. xiv. ; Acts xii. 21.

[2] The Assyrians attributed its invention to Semiramis ; the Egyptians to
Isis ; the classical nations to Minerva ; the Arabs to a son of Japhet ; the
Chinese to the wife of their Emperor Yao ; the Peruvians to Mamacella, also
a wife of their (first) sovereign Manco-Capac.   "These traditions serve only
to carry the invaluable arts of spinning and weaving to an extremely remote
period, long prior to that of authentic history."—*History of the Cotton
Manufacture*, chap. ii.

arts it was certainly one of the earliest.[1] Prehistoric mounds and burial-places yield continually to industrious explorers woven textures of unknown antiquity ; and the most ancient records in existence of the most ancient countries contain references to the implements and materials used in fashioning textile clothing. In the colder climates the skins of animals were probably first made use of for covering the human body; and vegetable products in the warmer ones ; a probability which, besides the more obvious reasons which it has to recommend it, seems to be confirmed by what is known of the primitive distribution of plants and animals over the surface of the earth. The earliest historical notice relates, however, to the latter kind of clothing. In the story of the expulsion of Adam and Eve from Paradise we read that they "sewed fig leaves together;" and if for *sewed*, which is evidently inaccurate, we substitute some such word as *interlaced* or *fastened*, we perceive at once how a rudimentary kind could have been thus in fact constructed, suitable to their opportunities and surroundings. Experience would in such a case have soon suggested the selection of other leaves better adapted to the purpose, and the longer and slenderer ones, and the larger kinds of grasses, have been increasingly preferred. Thus a rude kind of matting clothing would no doubt be in time produced; and such a kind we know to have been produced in this way elsewhere, and to be even now in use in some islands of the Pacific Ocean, and in portions of the interior of Africa. After a while, and under favourable circumstances, the finer vegetable fibres would be discovered and resorted to; and next, following probably on the accumulation of flocks, and on still advancing knowledge, the turn of the animal staples

[1] Mr. Yates believes that the knowledge of *felting* preceded that of weaving.—*Textrinum Antiquorum*, p. 3.

would come. In this manner the list of materials which experience shows to be suitable would be gradually completed; and in a brief and popular way such may in fact be said to have been the actual course of events.

By this time, too, the art of spinning would have been discovered, and should have been carried to some perfection. The weavers would have

SPINNING.
found that the finer fibres were more easy of manipulation than the coarser ones; made more handsome garments; were pleasanter in wear; and could be made as strong by twisting several together. This experience once gained—in the first instance with those vegetable fibres, with which we have supposed it to originate—would not cease there, but be extended to the similar productions of the animal kingdom too. The fleece and hair of sheep, goats, camels, and creatures of that kind would be experimented upon, and those that were found fitting brought into use. Nor, in the lapse of time, need we suppose the search to end, nor has it, in fact, ended here. Insects, and even marine creatures, have supplied, and do still supply, materials for spinning. The beautiful filament that is produced by the silkworm is familiar to all.[1] The *byssus* of the ancients, while that term seems sometimes to have been used as a generic one applying to various substances, was also the name given to an excretion from the tongue of a shellfish (the Pinna) common along the shores of the Mediterranean Sea. The threadlike tentacles by which this creature adhered to the rock and procured sustenance, were, and occasionally are still, made into small articles—as gloves and stockings.[2]

[1] The process of preparing raw silk for weaving is, however, technically called "throwing," as the filament is already strong enough for use. It is only in the manufacture of waste silk that it is actually spun.

[2] Such articles may be sometimes purchased in Sicily and the south of Italy. On the whole subject of the Pinna, see *Textrinum Antiquorum*, Book I. chap. v.

Even the common house-spider has been laid under contribution to the same end. Those curious insects have
been carefully cultivated and propagated like silkworms in
the hope of obtaining from their labours similar results.[1]
It would be an overwhelming task, in short, to compile,
or attempt to compile, a complete list of the many things
that have at all times and places been spun, or been
attempted to be spun, for industrial purposes. Whatever
has appeared likely to lend itself to that treatment has
probably been tried. The endeavour has, in fact, never
ceased. The earliest implements of spinning too (the distaff
and spindle) have been, from time immemorial, industry's
own chosen symbol; and if, in the origin of both, weaving
· preceded spinning—as seems probable—the latter occupation
has, on the other hand, down almost to quite recent times
been the more popular and better regarded of the two.

The first great country of the world of which we have
anything approaching intimate knowledge,
and where we earliest find a settled political   IN EGYPT.
and social system existing, is Egypt. There, too, have been
found an immense variety of relics, and in many cases full
pictorial representations, of several of the principal processes of art and manufacture; and there, also, is supplied
to history the first type of a country where industry was
a national occupation. Persistent investigations have, moreover, revealed to us the inner life of that extraordinary
people, till we are enabled to contemplate it with almost as
much precision as we can contemplate the social condition of
a contemporary community. We know that nearly 4000

---

[1] For a very interesting account of an experiment of this kind, and its
results, by an ingenious Frenchman, M. Bon, see a *Handbook of Silk, Cotton,
and Woollen Manufactures*, by my father, Dr. Cooke Taylor, published by
Messrs. Bentley in 1843. I may take this opportunity of acknowledging my
great general obligations to this little book, not only in the composition of
the present chapter, but throughout much of this work.

years ago (and how much more we do not know), long ages
before what we are accustomed to regard as the legitimate
dawn of history, a highly organised, complex, and already
venerable civilisation, was established in that narrow strip
of fertile land that borders either bank of the Nile in the
latter part of its course. That there an industrious and
cultivated people existed, and flourished exceedingly; a
people possessed of a high artistic faculty, a copious national
literature; inhabiting many populous cities;[1] exporting
commodities largely to other countries;[2] and in the full
enjoyment, in short, of what even moderns are accustomed
to consider the refinements, elegancies, and active motive
interests of life. In their great mausoleums, and from
among the ruins of their vast buried cities, have been
obtained the earliest examples of primeval manufacture,
examples of work in some respects not inferior to ours,
and the existence of which but for the direct evidence
of our senses we should almost certainly have regarded
as fabulous. With this people then, the inquiry into the
manufacturing industry of the earliest times must necessarily commence. Indications of a still earlier manufacture
may be found, or suspected, elsewhere; obscure references
to an industrial epoch even anterior may be forthcoming;
but the industrial pre-eminence of Egypt at a time when
the vague shapes of the enormously distant past begin first
to assume a form and substance that we recognise as
familiar, is a fact that cannot be disputed, any more than
can be disputed the fact that the scenes depicted on its
monuments are faithful representations of the life of those
times, and that some of the products of them are still with

---

[1] Herodotus affirms that no less than 20,000 "populous cities" existed in
Egypt during the reign of Amasis.—Herod. ii. 177 (quoted in Wilkinson's
Ancient Egyptians).
[2] 1 Kings x. 28; 2 Chron. i. 16.

us.   Of all these sources of information it will be our
duty to avail ourselves here in a way necessarily rapid and
superficial.   We shall first briefly pass in review the
materials, implements, and character, of the textile industries
of the ancient Egyptians, and afterwards strive to form some
estimate of the system of manufacture that prevailed among
them.

It is in connection with this country that distinct reference
to the arts of spinning and weaving is first
found in the Bible,[2] the earliest and most   MATERIALS.[1]
valuable repertory of industrial information we possess.
When thus mentioned, they are seen to be already in an
advanced stage of development, importing many ages of
previous knowledge and gradual improvement.   Seventeen
hundred years before the Christian era, the Hebrew Joseph,
a favourite minister at the Egyptian court, was ordered to be
" arrayed in vestures of fine linen" on the occasion of his
successful interpretation of a dream for the reigning Pharaoh.
This is the earliest certain reference to woven clothing anywhere.   The " coat of many colours," previously presented to
the same personage by his father (Gen. xxxvii. 3), may have
been of any other construction ; but " fine linen " is unequivocal—equally as to the material used and the nature and
quality of the workmanship.   The linen manufacture was,
in fact, at that time the national manufacture of Egypt, and
had been so apparently for an immense number of years.
The country produced the flax plant in great abundance ; as
it does in a less degree to the present day ; and of all
fabrics, linen was accordingly held in most regard.   There
was even a supposed special religious significance attached
to it.   The clothing of the priesthood and upper classes was
almost exclusively made of linen ; and it was in quite exclusive

---

[1] For a full list of the materials used in ancient textile manufacture, see
Textrinum Antiquorum, part i.   [2] Gen. xli. 42.

use for the burial of the dead. Its manipulation was carried to the very highest degree of perfection too, and it probably constituted, in the form of yarn, the principal Egyptian export. Woollen cloth, made there also,[1] was considered a greatly inferior texture, and even unwholesome and unclean. It was principally used for purposes of upholstery, and for the clothing of the lower orders; though occasionally for the outer garments of the upper classes as well.[2] Sometimes wool and flax were mixed together in manufacture, as they very often are still. Mixed fabrics of this kind are several times referred to in Scripture, the reference being generally accompanied by a prohibition against their use. Thus, "Thou shalt not wear a garment of divers sorts, as of woollen and linen together" (Deut. xxii. 11); "She seeketh wool, and flax, and worketh willingly with her hands" (Prov. xxxi. 13); "The garment also that the plague of leprosy is in, whether it be a woollen garment, or a linen garment; whether it be in the warp, or woof; of linen, or of woollen; whether in a skin, or anything made of skin (Lev. xiii. 47, 48); and again (Lev. xix. 19), "neither shall a garment mingled of linen and woollen come upon thee." We learn from these citations that the religious prejudice against woollen clothing extended to the Jews. It has sometimes been doubted whether this was indeed a religious prejudice at all, even in Egypt, and not rather a sanitary precaution; woollen garments, it is averred, being unsuitable to those warm climates. But, in face of the general opinion of modern times in favour of just this kind of clothing for them, the suggestion does not seem a

---

[1] Chemmis, the city of Pan, was particularly renowned for its early manufacture of woollen stuffs, and continued to be so "nearly till the period of the Roman Conquest."— *Ancient Egyptians*, vol. iii. p. 114.

[2] See Wilkinson's *Ancient Egyptians*, vol i. p. 280; vol. iii. p. 114. Mr. A. J. Warden's *The Linen Trade, Ancient and Modern*, pp. 157, 158 (Longmans, 1864).

happy one. Nor can another one, that it was the traditional hatred of the shepherds and all their belongings[1] that inspired the dislike, be reasonably accepted. The Hebrews were a pastoral race, and yet we find them adopting the prejudice. A more probable explanation than either is, that the motive of the prohibition was more political than either sanitary or religious; or, to speak more accurately, that it was an economical motive over which for political reasons the sanctions of religion were thrown. Wool was not a native product of Egypt while flax was, and the acute rulers of that country (who were at once priests and statesmen) may easily have devised these quasi-religious customs for really commercial purposes.[2] The Jews would have carried the prejudice away with them along with the industry, without inquiring too curiously into its origin.[3] With regard to cotton, it has been authoritatively denied, but without sufficient reason, that it was ever used for manufacturing purposes in ancient Egypt. Mr. Baines (*History of the Cotton Manufacture*, vol. i. chap. i.) makes this strange assertion in almost as few words, and assigns

---

[1] "Every shepherd is an abomination unto the Egyptians" (Gen. xlvi. 31).

[2] Compare the policy of the English Parliament in requiring all corpses to be buried in woollen shrouds (30° and 36° Car. ii.) See p. 322.

[3] Mr. Warden in his history of *The Linen Trade* points out that the exclusive wearing of linen cloth in the performance of ceremonial offices was known to the Greeks. "The followers of the Orphic and Bacchic rites," he says, "which were, according to Herodotus, Egyptian, and the Pythagoreans also, were forbidden to enter any sacred edifice, or to bury their dead in woollen vests." He adds, "There is a sacred reason assigned for this, says the old traveller, and *this sacred reason kept him from telling more*" (pp. 158, 159). The last sentence is very pertinent. Was the "sacred reason" the desire simply to sell their linen? and does Mr. Warden hint at this here? But, in fact, the old belief in the greater purity and sanctity of linen compared with other textures has had a far wider range than is thus assigned to it; and it may be doubted if it is even yet quite extinct. It was not unknown in the north from very ancient times; and the lawn sleeves of our own bishops, and the linen surplices of our clergy, seem to continue the tradition.

even a comparatively recent period for its being still unknown there. "It may be concluded," he declares, "with
certainty, that at this time (445 B.C.), the cotton manufacture
prevailed generally in India, and also that it existed in no
other country westward of the Indus." On the other hand,
Sir G. Wilkinson asserts with equal emphasis not only that
"cotton cloth was among the manufactures of Egypt" at a
much more remote time, but even that "cotton garments
supplied by the Government for the use of the temples are distinctly mentioned in the Rosetta Stone" (*Ancient Egyptians*,
vol. iii. chap. ix.) Dr. Cooke Taylor, going still further
(*Student's Manual of Ancient History*, chap i. sec. 5),[1] claims
the plant as in fact indigenous to the country, like flax, and
its manufacture usual there; and Mr. Warden quotes with
approval the authority of Pliny, that "even the priests
sometimes wore and were partial to cotton garments"[2]—that
is when off duty we must suppose. The same fact is vouched
for by Julius Pollux, who (as quoted by Wilkinson) "after
describing the cotton plant as an Egyptian production, and
stating that the cloth was manufactured of the 'wool of its
nut,' adds, that 'they sometimes make the woof of it and
the warp of linen:'"— a very common practice indeed in
modern manufacture. On the whole then, the general concurrence of skilled opinion, both ancient and modern, is largely
in favour of the view that cotton goods were known and
manufactured in Egypt from very ancient times. It is
otherwise with respect to silk. It is almost certain that it
was not manufactured nor even known in Egypt previous to
the Ptolemies. It is even doubtful if it has ever been
manufactured there at all. If it has, the manufacture has
certainly been always of a very unimportant character.

[1] Second edition, 1839 (J. W. Parker).
[2] *The Linen Trade, Ancient and Modern*, by Alex. J. Warden, chap. ii.
sec. 2, "Egyptian Linen" (Longmans, 1864).

But it is ever to be remembered in discussing the nature of ancient textile fabrics, that the accounts of them, and the materials of their construction, that have descended to us from contemporary observers are invariably untechnical, and that our conclusions from those authorities should be drawn with caution. Those accounts were mostly written by warriors, geographers, and poets, and their descriptions are at least as wanting in accuracy as the records of authorities so unqualified to judge in the matter were primarily likely to be.

From delineations on the monuments we obtain a very good notion of the implements used by the ancient Egyptians in their textile manufac- WEAVING IMPLEMENTS. ture. They employed both the horizontal and upright looms, and the former seems to have been generally worked by men. It may have been this circumstance that led Herodotus astray into making the astounding assertion that weaving was in Egypt an exclusively masculine occupation. This was so far from being the case, that many paintings not only distinctly show women weaving, but are in such excellent preservation as to enable us to follow every step in the process. The loom in these representations consists generally of a simple cross-bar, over which the warp is passed, the weft being introduced by what is apparently a thin metal instrument with a hook at the end, and forced into its place by another somewhat similar one. The woof is pressed *down*, not *up;* which we learn from Herodotus was contrary to the usual practice. Two women are usually depicted as employed,[1] one to pull the weft through the warp, the other to drive it home into the web. The cloth is wound off from the bottom of the frame. There is also extant, however, the picture of another loom showing a man weaving,[2] and the weft pushed upwards;

[1] See Fig. 382, Wilkinson's *Ancient Egyptians.*
[2] See Fig. 384, *Ancient Egyptians.*

so that the Egyptians knew of both ways. In these looms
it is supposed that the finer fabrics were woven, and the
coarser ones in the horizontal loom, which did not admit of
such delicate manipulation of the yarns. Of the latter
kind of loom the following is a good description : " The
framework is held fast by four blocks securely embedded in
the ground; the workman sits upon that part of the web
already finished, which is in the original painting a small
delicately chequered pattern of yellow and green; the
materials spread around prove that the yarn was dyed in
the wool before it was placed in the hands of the weaver.
The horizontal loom was obviously derived from the more
ancient process of mat weaving; it appears to have been
chiefly applied to the manufacture of plaids or checks, the
patterns for which were most likely suggested by the inter-
lacing of barks or of broad-leaved plants."[1] It is easy to
imagine how laborious such a process of weaving as any one
of these, but especially the last, would be. The ancient
Egyptians do not seem to have been acquainted with any
instrument analogous to the shuttle, but either drew the
weft through with their fingers, or used such a tool as has
been described. The marvel is therefore all the greater at
the wonderful results achieved. How vast, we are called
upon to reflect, must have been the number of persons
employed in this industry to have produced so largely with
such poor appliances.

The art of weaving in Egypt is so closely connected in
the records that have come down to us with
NETTING AND EMBROIDERY. the arts of netting and embroidery that they
may well be considered together. Isaiah
so coupled them, and, in denouncing vengeance against that

---

[1] *Silk, Cotton, and Woollen Manufactures,"* p. 6. Wilkinson appears to be
doubtful whether in this instance it is a mat or a piece of cloth that is being
woven, but from this description it should be more probably a carpet or rug.

country, foretells how " they that work in fine linen, and they *that weave networks*, shall be confounded" (Isa. xix. 9); and "broidered work from Egypt" is several times alluded to in Scripture. What was this "netting" and this "broidered work?" Netting appears to have been a process analogous to our lace making; and to have been carried to great perfection. Every writer on Egyptian antiquities alludes to this texture, and to the garments of extreme fineness made of the net; "so delicate were some of them," says Pliny, "that they could pass through a man's ring, and a single person could carry a sufficient number of them to surround a whole forest."[1] They were chiefly (we may suppose) of the nature of shawls, scarfs, and such like articles of apparel, worn round the neck and upper portion of the person; and are so figured on many of the monuments. What is known by the name of "embroidery" and "embroidered work" may have been either or both of two things. It was either needlework sewn on to the cloth by hand, like the mediæval embroidery, or fancy designs woven in the web, or sometimes one and sometimes the other. It is clear, indeed, that the Egyptians had from a very early time the secret of weaving patterns, and practised the art with great dexterity. How early this dexterity was acquired, as well as to what great perfection the work was carried, and how highly valued, we may gather from the fact that the Jews carried the art away with them from their captivity in Egypt (1500 B.C.), and made use of it for the most sacred purposes, in the embellishment of the tabernacle, for instance, and for the dresses of their priests.[2] Aaron not only had a highly ornamental coat of this character, but his girdle was "of fine twined linen, and blue, and purple, and scarlet, of needlework" (Exod. xxxix. 28, 29). Somewhat later, on the occasion, namely, when Deborah

---

[1] Pliny, xix. 1.   [2] Exod. xxvi. 36 ; xxxvi. 37 ; xxxviii. 18.

celebrates the success of the Jewish arms in a hymn of
triumph, we find an extraordinarily high value set on vestments thus adorned.   We read (Judg. v. 28-30) how, "The
mother of Sisera looked out at a window, and cried through
the lattice, Why is his chariot so long in coming? why
tarry the wheels of his chariots?   Her wise ladies answered
her, yea, they returned answer to herself.   Have they not
sped? have they not divided the prey; to every man a
damsel or two ; to Sisera a prey of divers colours of needlework, of divers colours of needlework on both sides, meet
for the necks of them that take the spoil?"   A "damsel or
two" ranks as but an insignificant "prey" in this division
of spoil compared with one of "divers colours of needlework," especially if wrought "on both sides !"[1]   Sometimes
gold was interwoven with the more precious cloths, and we
are indebted to Moses for a very careful and accurate
description of the process: "they did beat the gold," he
writes (Exod. xxxix. 3), "into thin plates, and cut it into
wires, to work it in the blue, and in the purple, and in the
scarlet, and in the fine linen, with cunning work."   According to Pliny,[2] to weave cloth with gold was the invention of
the Asiatic King Attalus, and the Babylonians were the most
celebrated in that kind of manufacture ; but this is obviously
an error.   Doubtless the Babylonians attained great distinction in it, but the process was known in Egypt before the
time of Attalus, as early, Wilkinson thinks,[3] as Osirtasen
the First, i.c. about 1700 B.C.

The "fine linen" was, however, the *speciality*, the

FINE LINEN.
"staple commodity," of Egyptian textile
manufacture.   It was sometimes of astonishing fineness, even when judged by modern criterions
of excellence.   A piece of linen cloth was found near

---

[1] For the comparative value set upon woven patterned garments and slaves
at another epoch, compare Virgil, *Æneid*, v. 284, 285.

[2] Pliny, viii. 48.   [3] *Ancient Egyptians*, vol. ii. p. 129.

Memphis, concerning which Wilkinson writes,[1] that "some idea may be given of its texture from the number of threads in the inch, which is 540 (or 270 double threads) in the warp, and the limited number of 110 in the woof;" and he further quotes the testimony of both Pliny and Herodotus to the same end.   It is not necessary to go into any technicalities on this subject.   It is sufficient to know that all modern researches conspire with the oldest and most trustworthy traditions to show that the Egyptians had reached a degree of perfection in the manufacture of linen some 4000 years ago, such as we have only attained here, if we have ever attained it at all, within the last century.

That yarn so fine as was used in some of these fabrics could be spun by hand is certainly an extra- SPINNING
ordinary circumstance, and would be well- IMPLEMENTS.
nigh incredible had we not the parallel instance of the handicraft cotton manufacture of India, still in operation, to compare with this one.   Nor is the wonder at all diminished when we come to contemplate the simple tools employed.   These were in spinning practically confined to the two implements, the distaff and spindle, immemorially in use, and which may be sometimes seen in use even in Europe still.   Several of these spindles have been discovered entire and are preserved.   They are thus described by Sir G. Wilkinson : "The spindles were generally small, being about one foot three inches in length, and several, found at Thebes, are now in the museums of Europe.   They were generally of wood, and, in order to increase their impetus in turning, the circular head was occasionally of gypsum or composition ; some, however, were of a light plaited work, made of rushes or palm leaves, stained of various colours, and furnished with a loop of the same materials for securing the twine after it was wound."   Spinning among the

[1] *Ancient Egyptians*, vol. iii. chap. ix.

Egyptians was often a domestic occupation, in which females of all ranks engaged, and in which men also were occasionally employed, but it is difficult to believe that it was exclusively so. Among pictures found on the ancient monuments are those illustrating the private life of some great Egyptian lady spinning in the midst of her domestics and superintending their labour, as was the custom in the classical age, and in our own country in Saxon times, and in a less degree later ; but domestic spinning in the humbler ranks is not shown. The mistress is distinguished from her servants not more by her more elaborate dress than by the more elaborate ornamentation of her spindle, and the rich vase in which the material for spinning is contained. In *Ancient Egyptians,* chap. ix., the figures of some spindles found at Thebes are given. The following is a catalogue of them :—Fig. 1 " is a sort of cane, split at the top to give it a globular shape ;" Fig. 2 " has the head of gypsum ;" Fig. 3 is " entirely of wood ;" Fig. 4 " of plaited or basket work." There is also shown " the loop to put over the twine," and a "ring of wood for securing the twine," *i.e.* yarn. Other implements that have been found there and elsewhere in Egypt, connected with textile manufacture, are combs for carding the raw material, and flat wooden planes and rods for smoothing and calendering the cloth.

Though spinning and weaving were practised as domestic operations in Egypt, as has been said, it is EGYPTIAN TEXTILE MANUFACTORIES. difficult not to believe that there were establishments for producing on a large scale as well, similar in several essential conditions to our modern factories, and owned both by private persons and the State. In no other way can the vast quantity of linen yarn exported be accounted for ; a quantity so great as to be the principal source of supply for the other great nations of antiquity, not to mention the " fine linen," of

which so much has been already said. Dr. Cooke Taylor,
indeed, and Mr. Warden, both assert such to have been the
case, and though they furnish no actual evidence of the fact
their authority is of great weight. Thus, treating of " recent
discoveries in Egyptian antiquities," the first writer distinctly
says, "we find from them that the Pharaohs had very large
spinning establishments, such as we should in the present
day call factories, so that there was not only enough of yarn
left for home consumption in the valley of the Nile but also
for exportation" (*Silk, Cotton, and Woollen Manufactures*, p. 5);
and elsewhere (p. 23), in connection with another branch of
the subject, he speaks of great *weaving establishments*, " as in
Egypt." In still another place (*Student's Manual of Ancient
History*, second edition, p. 42)[1] the same author writes of
" stuffs woven in large manufactories under the superintendence of the priests," who, he adds, " had a monopoly of all
the cloths used for sacred purposes, especially for the
mummies." Mr. Warden's testimony is more guarded.
He says,[2]—" The manufacture of linen in Egypt in very
early times formed one of the principal branches of industry to the inhabitants, very many of whom were engaged in its production. The city of Thebes was early
celebrated for its linens, and it is very probable from the
immense quantity that must have been made that there
may have existed distinct establishments for its manufacture
in various parts of the kingdom, of a kindred nature to the
hand-loom weaving-shops not yet extinct in this country "
(Scotland, 1864). Sir G. Wilkinson does not express any
opinion on this subject, nor, so far as we are aware, have
other Egyptologists ; a fact strikingly characteristic of the
extraordinary inattention bestowed on such matters by even
eminent men. He reproduces, of course,[3] in common with

[1] J. W. Parker, 1839.　　[2] *Linen Trade, Ancient and Modern*, p. 151.
[3] Vol. iii. p. 138.

other historians, the celebrated picture from Beni Hassan
representing the various processes to which flax was subjected—from the steeping it in its natural state to its
manufacture into rope and cloth[1]—but this may evidently
be a series of operations grouped together for purely pictorial
purposes, and not necessarily all carried on together in an
establishment of definite bounds. It is true that the presence of a superintendent over the whole work might lead
one to make the required inference, but that inference would
still be a wide one, nor even then would the series of operations portrayed answer in any considerable degree to the
modern conception of work in a textile factory. The
absence of an unequivocal representation of such a place is
the more unfortunate that the same want is not found in
the pictorial representations of other undertakings. In
many of these, industrial co-operation is distinctly and
often vigorously portrayed, but in textile manufacture *never*.
The omission is indubitable. We are, therefore, dependent
altogether on probabilities, and on authority, for the belief
that great textile establishments did exist in ancient Egypt.
But this need not daunt us. The probabilities in favour of
that belief amount almost to certainties. Even leaving out
of account, for the moment, the initial question of how else
could all the linen and linen yarn have been produced, the
least consideration shows how completely consonant such a
system of production would be with what is known of other
facts connected with the labour organisation of this strange
people.[2] The prodigious works they undertook and accomplished in mining, building, and engineering; in the manu-

---

[1] Fig. 386.

[2] In reference to some of these Sir G. Wilkinson says emphatically, "The
distribution of labour seems to have been as well understood by the Egyptians
as in modern times." On the cognate subject of the similarity of their land
system to ours, see *Egypt of the Pharaohs and of the Khedive*, by F. Barham
Zincke, chap. 32 ; (Smith and Elder, 1873). Compare p. 47.

facture of metals and earthenware; not to speak of minor industries (such as tanning), imply an acquaintance with the utility of the combination and organisation of labour, which it is surely most unlikely would have just stopped short at being applied to the staple industry of the country. Nor need we be surprised at the absence of any mention, or representation, of definite textile establishments, nor dubious of their existence merely because these have not been found. It was never the custom until quite lately to take formal notice of such things. History, as we have elsewhere observed, was of too stately and aristocratic a complexion to concern itself with them, and art did not acknowledge them to be within her sphere. We may assume it as almost certain, ·then, in the opinion of the present writer, notwithstanding the absence of direct evidence, that great industrial establishments devoted to textile industry did exist in Egypt, on a scale proportionate to the other great industrial enterprises in which the people of that country engaged. But in what sense, we must next ask, were these places "factories"? and in endeavouring to answer that question, and to realise them to ourselves, two essential circumstances are to be borne in mind. First, that the labour was all manual; and next, that it was seldom, if ever, free.[1] With those two essential circumstances realised, however, we may allow a free scope to fancy in picturing the doubtless gigantic proportions of such places, and the numerous swarms of human beings that would be congregated therein for work. Applying to them our knowledge of the way the Egyptians conducted other operations of public profit and usefulness, and, acting on the hint of Mr. Warden, it would be easy to imagine,

---

[1] In *Ancient Egyptians*, vol. ii. p. 60, there is a picture from Beni Hassan of women weaving and spinning under the direction of an overlooker. This is the nearest approach to the representation of a factory we possess. Two of the spinsters have their legs bound together, apparently to imply that they are slaves.

7

for instance, immense hand-loom weaving buildings, or
adjoining tenements, situated in the poorer quarters of the
large towns, in the mountains, on the edge of the desert, or
wherever land not required for agriculture or for other
edifices was available.   And, following up the fancy, might
not the " treasure cities," which the Israelites were employed
to build (Exod. i. 11), have been places of this kind ?   If
not, what then ?   Mere granaries for food stuffs or for storing
the spoils of war (the common interpretation) would hardly
have been named *cities ;* but the great centres of the national
manufacture of Egypt, with the abounding population that
we know from our own experience grows up about such
places, more fully than anything else would deserve that
title.   The notion may not be wholly fanciful.   It might
seem more difficult at first to imagine the " spinning establishments " spoken of with such confidence by Dr. Cooke
Taylor, for these we cannot at all picture independently
of modern models, since previous to the modern factory
system all spinning was with us a domestic occupation.   It
may aid us in doing so, however, if we cease to combine
with the idea of congregated factory labour that of buildings
and machinery, so closely associated by experience in our
minds with it.   In the rainless climate of Egypt, buildings
would be a superfluity, either for spinning or weaving,
both of which operations could be just as efficiently carried
on in the open air; while of machinery there would, of
course, be none.   Have we here possibly the key to the
whole mystery ?   Might not the great Egyptian textile manufacture have been chiefly an open-air occupation—as in India
—and the spinning, if not also the weaving establishments,
great camps or villages, not necessarily enclosed, and when
enclosed called *cities ?*   Such an explanation would well
account for the absence on the monuments of the likeness
of any place similar to the modern factory; and would

equally accord with all we know of Eastern customs. The city or camp would not, indeed, then answer to " our modern conception of a factory," but would not differ very widely from our statutory definition of one. In what legal requirement, it may be asked, would such a place differ from a large pottery for instance, where no foreign motive power is employed, or a village of small pottery works ?—all of which are now classed as factories by our law.[1] There would be no necessary difference at all. There remains the final essential circumstance to remember, that the labour would be supplied principally, perhaps exclusively, by slaves ; and in all probability by slaves taken in warfare. This, too, would agree with the universally lugubrious appearance the weavers present on the monuments—an appearance which is quite a marked characteristic of them. So, too, might these last considerations assist us in understanding how so great a production of textile commodities could ever have taken place in Egypt at all. Material was practically unlimited, and so we now perceive was labour ; for it was limited only by the lives of slave labourers, which were absolutely of no account ; there was practically no *plant*, no premises, no wages, and no fuel, so that preliminary expenditure would be at a minimum. The capitalist supplied raw material and supervision, together with bare subsistence, and no more. The capital employed, such as it was, seems to have been found both by the State and by individuals ; certainly by corporations as well as by the State. Wilkinson speaks of " cotton garments supplied by the Government for the use of the temple ;" Dr. Cooke Taylor of the priests holding " a monopoly of all the (flax) cloths used for sacred purposes ;" and we know that Solomon entered into relations with the contemporary government of Egypt (2 Chron. i. 16)

---

[1] Any place where the manufacture of earthenware is carried on is a "factory," under the Factory Act of 1864, and subsequent Acts.

to supply him with linen yarn. Thus is proved, at least, a corporate as well as a State occupation of textile factories, and we have much reason to suppose, though we have no actual proof of it, that there were individual master manufacturers as well.

We conclude then that there was a great organised factory system in ancient Egypt applied to OTHER ANCIENT the production of textile fabrics, and that COUNTRIES. that system was both national and individual—that is, that the State owned factories but was not the exclusive owner. The further characteristics of that labour organisation were, that it was a system of slavery, and that all production was manual. We shall find the same to have been the case in some other ancient countries, and may suspect it in many more, where like conditions prevailed. In dealing with these other countries, however, we must still more abbreviate our method of treatment. We shall simply take those whose names are prominent in ancient history, and note any circumstances that connect them with textile industry, especially when carried on upon a large scale.

The first after Egypt that compels attention is Ethiopia. The mists of antiquity hang heavily over ETHIOPIA. that mysterious land, and are penetrated only by an occasional ray of the light of modern research, or even of ancient tradition. What we know of it is, that at a very remote age a very powerful nation was established there on the upper waters of the Nile—a nation so eminent and so powerful that it has been questioned if it did not precede Egypt itself in civilisation, and it is certain that some of its monarchs reigned there. A thousand years before the Christian era it was already despatching great armies to such distant countries as Assyria,[1] and

[1] Rawlinson even thinks that Assyria, or at all events Chaldea, may have been originally colonised from Ethiopia (or Cush).—*Five Great Monarchies,*

Judea,[1] and had for long been carrying on (it is supposed) a large and lucrative trade with India. It is this last circumstance that brings it into prominence in connection with the present subject. It cannot be even guessed to what extent the manufacture of textile fabrics was carried on at Meröe, its principal city (or possibly district),[2] but great interest attaches to this place from the belief that if not largely engaged in the cotton manufacture itself, it was the great mart for the productions of India, coming by way either of Abyssinia or Arabia on their way to the Egyptian market. It has from the same circumstance been supposed to have been the gate through which the cotton manufacture first made its way into Egypt at all. Its interest for us therefore is indirect. It cannot well be left out in any survey of ancient manufacturing countries, nor can it with any certainty be included as one of them.

It is otherwise with Idumea—Edom—or "the land of Uz," famed in Scripture history. This is the country wherein is generally acknow-

ledged to be laid the scene of the beautiful poem called "The Book of Job," and in that most ancient record there is one allusion made by the patriarch which it is impossible to pass unnoticed even in so superficial a survey of ancient textile industry as this. It is where the writer is found complaining of the rapid passage of time, in words that must ever wake an echo in the hearts of many readers. "My days are swifter than the weaver's shuttle," he says, "and are spent without hope" (Job vii. 6). This is the version

by George Rawlinson, M.A., chap. i., fourth edition (Murray, 1879). Compare Gen. x. 8-10.

[1] Chron. xiv. 29. The Ethiopian army was "a thousand thousand, and three hundred chariots," on this occasion.

[2] Meröe was in that part of Africa which we now call the Soudan. Its principal town was on the upper Nile, about 120 miles below Khartoum.

in the Vulgate, but it is not the only or the best one.   In
Wemyss' translation it is rendered thus [1]—

> "My days are slighter than the weaver's yarn,
> They are finished like the breaking of a thread."

Two considerations of great interest arise out of this
quotation.   The first is as to the use of the word "shuttle"
in the ordinary version.   Was there really such an implement in use in Idumea at so early a date?   The second is
as to the antiquity of the poem wherein the allusion itself
occurs.   It is unnecessary to state here more than the bare
results of the considerable controversy that has gathered
about these two points.   It is now generally admitted that
the word translated shuttle is mistranslated, and should
rather be rendered *yarn* or some equivalent (as in Wemyss'
version): perhaps "weft" would be the nearest term in
correct technology.   No implement of the nature of a shuttle
is known to have been used till long after this time.   We
have already seen that a very different one was certainly in
use in Egypt.   As to the antiquity of the Book of Job
itself, that is still a matter of keen research.   It is complicated, it seems, with the further difficulty of whether the
book was composed "by Job himself, by Moses, or by a
later writer," beyond which we should imagine complication
cannot further go.   But by whomsoever composed, it is
generally conceded now that the condition of things described
there was extremely ancient, "at least as old as Moses." [2]
Independently then of the introduction of the questionable
expression "shuttle," it is thus at all events proved that the
art of weaving had already been long known and practised
in Idumea at an immensely remote time: so well known

---

[1] *Job and His Times* (Jackson and Walford, 1839).
[2] *Notes on the Old Testament*, by Alfred Barnes; *The Book of Job*,
Introduction, xii. (Blackie and Son).

there, and so long practised, as to have even furnished the
material for a popular poetic figure.

Southwards from Idumea stretches the great peninsula
of Arabia.   From this prolific land in long
intervals of history have issued hordes of   ARABIA.
warriors who have more than once changed the destinies
of mankind.   When its inhabitants first emerge into the
qualified light of traditionary record, they are recognised as
wandering (often predatory) traders, but not as manufacturers;
and this character they have practically retained throughout.   In connection with the present branch of our subject
they appear as carriers between the great countries of Egypt,
India, Phœnicia, and Assyria; the principal manufacturing
centres of ancient times.   But they appear also in industrial
history, then and after, as the progenitors of great races, who
have often borrowed and adopted foreign arts and industries,
and actively aided in their progress and dissemination.

Next in interest, historical and industrial, to ancient
Egypt—even if it be not allowed to be in
actual rivalry with it—is ancient Assyria,   ASSYRIA AND
and especially that part of it more particu-   BABYLONIA.
larly pertaining to its later capital, Babylon.   Here the
cotton and woollen manufactures were early prosecuted on
a very large scale.[1]   They appear to have been particularly directed to the production of costly dresses, and of
carpets and shawls; the last named always an object of great
luxury in the East.   On these shawls were woven or
embroidered, "often in gold, the figures of fabulous animals—
the dragon, the griffin, and other unnatural combinations of
form, probably originating in India" . . . and "it was by
means of the Babylonian manufactures that the knowledge
of these fanciful and imaginary beings was conveyed to the

[1] Rawlinson's *Ancient Monarchies*, vol. ii. p. 570. See also, by the same
author, *Egypt and Babylon*, chap. viii. (Hodder and Stoughton, 1885).

western world, and from them they were transferred to the
Greek vases."[1]   The historical books of the Bible contain
many allusions to the splendour of these fabrics.   Thus
from the Book of Joshua (vii. 21) we learn that a " Baby-
lonish garment" formed a much treasured portion of the
spoil which Achan treacherously concealed in his tent after
the capture of Jericho; and other references will quickly
occur to biblical scholars.   The classical writers make
frequent mention of them and their magnificence.   Pliny
remarks that among all nations " the Babylonians were most
noted for their skill in weaving cloths of various colours ;"
Publius Syrus compared a " peacock's tail to a figured
Babylonian mantle enriched with gold ;" and " it was always
deemed to be one of the most singular displays of asceticism
in the elder Cato that he immediately gave away a splendid
Babylonian shawl which some foreign potentate had be-
queathed to him as a remuneration for political services."[2]
Unhappily, of all these splendid robes no actual specimen
is preserved, " the delicate texture of such fabrics has pre-
vented them from descending to us even in the most tattered
condition."   We can judge of them only by the pictures on
the monuments.   What these show, besides the shape of
the dress (which was generally more flowing than that of
Egypt) is, that " robes and draperies of all kinds were
always more or less patterned, and this patterning, which is
generally of an extremely elaborate kind, it is reasonable to
conclude " (says Rawlinson) " was the work of the needle."[3]
It is further " remarkable that the earliest representations
exhibit the most elaborate types of all, after which a reaction
seems to set in—simplicity is affected, which, however, is
gradually trenched upon, until at last a magnificence is
reached little short of that which prevailed in the age of

[1] *Silk, Cotton, and Woollen Manufactures*, p. 16.   [2] *Idem*, p. 18.
[3] Rawlinson's *Ancient Monarchies*, vol. i. pp. 396, 397.

the first monuments."[1] So that we have here a proof of
an ebb and flow of fashion in those remote ages similar to
what is now experienced among the most polished nations
of the present day. Of the nature of their textures called
Sindones, so often mentioned by classical writers, there exists
much difference of opinion. Whether these stuffs were of
cotton, flax, or silk, is the matter in dispute—the old dispute
in fact with regard to so many ancient textures. On the
whole the preponderance of skilled opinion now is in favour
of their having been of cotton woven very fine. Mr. Rawlinson expresses a particularly high opinion of the quality of
these cotton textures. " Next to their carpets," he says, " the
highest character was borne by their muslins. Formed of
the finest cotton, and dyed of the most brilliant colour, they
seemed to the Oriental the very best possible material for
dress. The Persian kings preferred them for their own
wear, and they had an early fame in foreign countries at
a considerable distance from Babylonia " (*Five Ancient
Monarchies*, vol. ii. p. 570). Besides woollen and cotton
fabrics, the Babylonians manufactured a good deal of
linen cloth, the principal seat of the manufacture being
Borsippa. This was produced, says Mr. Rawlinson, " chiefly
for home consumption, long linen robes being generally worn
by the people."[2] Some of the Sindones may have been
of flax;[3] but the probabilities are strong against silk having
been manufactured in Assyria previous at all events to
the Persian Conquest. Subsequently, there was a very

[1] Rawlinson's *Ancient Monarchies*, vol. i. p. 397.

[2] *Five Great Monarchies*, vol. ii. p. 571.

[3] Compare Robertson's "Disquisition concerning Ancient India," *The
Works of William Robertson, D.D.*, 2 vols. Appendix, p. 66 (Edinburgh: Nelson,
1839), where the name *Sindon* is derived from that of the river Indus or Sindus,
in the neighbourhood of which it is conjectured that flax was manufactured
and "wrought in the highest perfection." Compare also Sir William Jones's
Third Discourse, p. 428, quoted there.

large manufacture of silk, and it long continued to reside there. Bonomi says of it,[1] "the silken robes of Assyria, the produce chiefly of the looms of Babylon, were renowned long after the fall of the Assyrian empire ;" and the same information reaches us from other quarters. But whether silk came earlier or later into use, and whether Sindones were exclusively cotton goods or not, undoubtedly the most characteristic fabric of the Assyrians in very ancient times was their woollen stuffs. It was from them that the Persians learned to make the carpets which bear their name at the present day ; and most neighbouring nations of antiquity made use of Babylonian rugs for decorating their palaces and harems. Unhappily, the policy of those Persian conquerors did not tend towards the encouragement of this or any other industry, and from the time that Babylon finally fell under the yoke of Cyrus (538 B.C.) its prosperity declined. Alexander the Great had designed to restore its industrial supremacy, but died before giving the experiment a trial.

What has been said of the textile manufactories and manufacturing system of Egypt is applicable ASSYRIAN MANU-FACTORIES. with but little variation to Assyria and Babylonia where the conditions of life were in many respects so similar. There also industrial production was upon a large scale, and carried on under a system of combined slave labour. Semiramis, who is credited with the introduction of the cotton manufacture into the country, is also credited with the introduction of the factory system there. She is "stated *by many writers of antiquity*," says Bonomi,[2] " to have founded large weaving establishments along the banks of the Tigris and Euphrates." Now this is directer

---

[1] *Nineveh and its Palaces*, p. 449 (Bohn's Edition).

[2] *Idem*, by Joseph Bonomi, F.R.S.L., third edition, p. 449 (G. Bell and Sons, 1875).

testimony to the existence of ancient textile factories than any that we have with regard to Egypt, or any other ancient country, and should finally set at rest the question as to the existence of such establishments in ancient times at all. The chief classical authority upon whom Bonomi relies, we suppose, is Strabo, and it is an authority that cannot be questioned, but it certainly is unfortunate that he does not state who are the others.

The Phœnicians were the most celebrated among the people of antiquity, after the Babylonians and Egyptians, for the manufactures of textile fabrics, and, like the Egyptians, they were a people who held industry in honour. As the speciality of the latter was their fine linen, and of the former their gorgeous woollen goods, so the purple dyed cloth of Tyre was un-equalled. Like the Babylonians they imported cotton and linen yarn from India and Egypt respectively; and the principal seat of their weaving trade seems to have been at Sidon, where also their great glass-works were situated. To what perfection the weaving of their fine goods was carried may be incidently learned from Homer, who makes Hecuba choose " a veil " of Sidonian manufacture in prefer-ence to all others, as an offering to Minerva. This curious reference is thus given in Pope's translation—

PHŒNICIA.

> " The Phrygian queen to her rich wardrobe went
> Where treasured odours breathed a costly scent ;
> There lay the vestures of no vulgar art—
> Sidonian maids embroidered every part,
> Whom from soft Sidon youthful Paris bore
> With Helen touching on the Tyrian shore.
> Here as the queen revolved with careful eyes
> The various textures and the various dyes,
> She chose a veil that shone superior far
> And glowed refulgent as the morning star."
>
> (*Iliad*, VI.)

Elsewhere (*Odyssey*, XV.) the same distinguished authority
tells us of Phœnician women being sometimes captured by
the pirates of the Levant, and sold into slavery in the Greek
islands, because of their notorious skill in weaving. Both
linens and calicoes were apparently manufactured in Phœnicia,
and were exported probably to very distant places. But
their greatest success must have been with their woollens, as
it was in the dyeing of woollen stuffs that the Tyrian purple
attained its great celebrity. Like the Assyrians, they could
obtain the raw material for this manufacture in inexhaustible
quantities from the neighbouring mountain ranges, for it is
of these mountain ranges that Cuvier declared the sheep to
have been originally a native. Great factories of various
kinds no doubt existed here : dye-houses, glass-houses,
foundries, and textile factories.

Of the colonies planted by this adventurous people,
CARTHAGE.
Carthage was the most celebrated, both in
general history and for its manufacturing
industry. It was especially distinguished for its shawls.
An entire and considerable book was written by one Polemo,
Concerning the Shawls of Carthage. This was in the
days of its earlier prosperity, when the area of the city was
no less than twenty-nine miles round, and the people were
peaceable and industrious. In later times the industrial
was exchanged for a military spirit, and by the end of the
Punic Wars but little remnant of its industry or prosperity
was left.

The history of the Jews, as found in the Bible, is full of
PALESTINE.
references to the manufacturing prosperity
of Tyre, Egypt, and Babylon, and is invaluable to the student of industrial history on that account
alone. The Jews themselves, however, were not an industrial, but a pastoral and agricultural people, though there is
certainly one allusion (in 1 Chron. iv. 21) to manufacturing

operations of the textile kind conducted by them upon a large scale,[1] and they were well acquainted with the principle of division and combination of labour. Vainly did their prophets and kings from time to time strive to arouse in them a different spirit. In vain had Moses long before especially commended spinning to them as an occupation highly useful and honourable (Exod. xxxv. 25, 26); seven hundred years later we have already found Solomon entering into a commercial treaty with Egypt to supply his people with yarn.[2] The national character appears to have been consistently averse in ancient times from both commerce and manufacture, and ever tending to revert to its original, the nomad and predatory type. Their value to industrial history is thus rather in what they tell of others than in what we learn of themselves.

A very general consensus of authority points to India as the birthplace of the cotton manufacture. The cotton plant is certainly indigenous INDIA. there; but so it is elsewhere; in America, for instance, the inhabitants of which country were found clothed in cottons by the earliest explorers. This circumstance is not therefore of itself conclusive evidence of the belief implied, though it may be allowed to be valuable contributory evidence. There is, however, a great body of other testimony of a very vague and various, and some of a fairly precise description, tending in the same direction. There is first the general tradition on the subject, and next the statements of the early geographers and historians. There is also written evidence. In the Vedas, which are the sacred writings of the Hindoos (about 1200-1000 B.C.), weaving is frequently alluded to, and Sir George Birdwood believes that even at

[1] The passage is translated "the families, or perhaps the partnerships of the manufactory of byssus."—See *Textrinum Antiquorum*, p. 282, note.
[2] P. 99.

that remote time the industries of the country had reached
their zenith, or even perhaps passed it; and he especially
commends for excellence the "gold brocades and filmy
muslins" already then produced.[1] There is next the derivation of the word.   In the English translation of the
Bible the word cotton is nowhere used, though a passage
in the Book of Esther (i. 6) is believed to refer to it.
The doubtful word in this passage translated "green," is
according to Sir George Birdwood, *karpas*, the Sanscrit
karpasa, and Hindoo, *kapas*—that is, "cotton (in the pod),
an aboriginal Indian production." Herodotus is the first
author who not only mentions, but actually describes the
cotton plant, which he undoubtedly considered peculiar to
India.   The "father of history" (writing about the year
445 B.C.), in detailing the many wonders which he had
heard of that country, thus expresses himself on this point
(*Herod.* Book III. chap. cvi.): "They possess likewise a kind
of plant which, instead of fruit, produces wool of a finer and
better quality than that of sheep : of this the Indians make
their clothes;"[2] and Nearchus, the admiral whom Alexander
employed to descend the Indus (327 B.C.), also mentions
garments of "something much whiter and finer than flax
. . . growing upon trees," which he found the natives of
those regions wearing.   Strabo repeats and adopts these
statements.   Commenting upon them, Sir E. Baines observes
(*History of the Cotton Manufacture*, chap. ii.) that, if "at
that period cottons were the common clothing of the people,
it may with strong probability be inferred that they had
been so for centuries;" an expression of opinion that fairly

[1] *The Industrial Arts of India*, by Sir George C. M. Birdwood (Chapman and Hall, 1880).

[2] A more literal translation of this passage is: "And the wild shrubs there bear as crop wool, in beauty and excellence surpassing that from sheep, and the Indians provide themselves raiment from these trees."

represents the prevailing one upon the subject.[1] But the same distinguished authority, going also beyond this, contends that, while it is proved that at the time of Herodotus the cotton manufacture prevailed generally in India, it is equally certain "that it existed in no other country westward of the Indus;"[2] and Dr. Ure,[3] another great authority, considers this "insulation of the cotton manufacture in India . . . one of the most singular phenomena in the history of man." A most singular phenomenon it would undoubtedly have been had it had any existence at all. But we know that it had not; that on the contrary cotton textures were manufactured in all the great Eastern countries ages before this; and possibly far away in the north and west as well. Though the cotton manufacture therefore may have indeed originated in India, it had a far wider range in primeval times than even the extensive boundaries of that peninsula. This error has for its complement another one, namely, that the ancient Indian manufacture was *confined* to cottons. So far is this from being the case, that from the earliest information we have of any materials manufactured there at all, they appear to have included all the principal ones now in use, even silk. Sir George Birdwood, an unimpeachable authority on the subject, writes thus in unequivocal terms of this branch of it, " No information is given in the Rig Veda of the materials of which clothes are made ; but in the time of the Ramayana and Mahabharata, cotton, silken, and woollen stuffs are constantly mentioned. In the Ramayana the nuptial presents to Sita, the bride of Rama, from her father, consisted of woollen stuffs, furs, precious stones, fine silken vestments of divers colours, and princely ornaments and sumptuous carriages. The

[1] Compare Robertson's *Disquisition concerning India*, sec. 1, "the manners, the customs, and the dress of the people are almost as permanent and invariable as the face of nature itself." [2] *History of the Cotton Manufacture*, p. 18.
[3] *The Cotton Manufacture of Great Britain*, by Andrew Ure, M.D., F.R.S. Book I. p. 3 (Charles Knight, 1836).

Ramayana gives no names of places where particular articles of clothing were made; but in the Mahabharata, in the enumeration of the presents which the feudatory princes brought to Yudhisthiva, as their lord paramount, mention is made of furs from the Hindoo-Kush, of woollen shawls from Abhiras from Gujarat, and of clothes of the wool of sheep and goats, and of thread spun by worms, and of plant fibre (hemp), woven by the tribes of the north-western Himalayas, of elephant housings presented by the princes of eastern Hindostan, and of pure linen (muslin), the gift of the people of the Gangaw, the Carnatic, and Mysore." It would not be easy to extend this list.

With respect to the implements of manufacture used in India, it would appear that the native loom was somewhat different from that of ancient Egypt, already described, and therefore different from that in use in Greece (which was borrowed from Egypt), and generally throughout the west until recent times. It more nearly approached in make the modern hand-loom. The principal differences were in the make and use of the shuttle, and in the general rudeness of the parts. It is thus described in Mill's *History of India :*[1] "The loom consists merely of two bamboo rollers, one for the warp and the other for the web, and a pair of gear. The shuttle performs the double office of shuttle and batten, and for this purpose is made like a large netting needle, and of a length somewhat exceeding the breadth of the piece. This apparatus the weaver carries to a tree under which he digs a hole large enough to contain his legs and the lower parts of the gear. He then stretches his warp by fastening his bamboo rollers at a due distance from each other on the turf by wooden pins. The balances of the gear he fastens to some convenient branch of the tree over his head; two loops underneath the gear in which he inserts his great

[1] *History of British India*, by James Mill, Book II. chap. 8, 1820.

toes serve as treadles, and his long shuttle, which also performs the office of batten, draws the weft through the warp and afterwards strikes it up close to the web." Women were occasionally employed in weaving as well as men. Spinning was generally performed here as elsewhere with the distaff and spindle, but the thread wheel was also known. Probably the former method was used for the finer, and the latter for the coarser yarns.

We have already described in some detail a few leading features of the industrial system of ancient India.[1] That system was one conterminous INDIAN MANUFAC-TURING SYSTEM. with the system of land tenure, which was that of the village community. After the Persian Conquest a sort of modified feudal system was introduced, and it spread over portions of the country, though by no means over all of it. Under this system some of the best handicraftsmen were often taken up and attached to the suites of the ruling chieftains, as in Europe during the Middle Ages. They were highly valued and well treated, and produced excellent work. But a great part of the country still continued to live in a state of industrial communalism, and, under every variety of rulers, has continued to do so to the present day. Under that method of production there was, of course, no room for a factory system in our modern sense, though, in the wider sense of the expression which we have in part adopted, this was, in fact, *their* factory system. It was a system of free manual labour, in which there was no division of employment, and no active competition, preserved from the fate which overtook a similar system in so many other countries by the institution of caste.

There is reason to believe that the ancient inhabitants of Persia and India were of the same race, but the traditions on the subject are too obscure, THE MEDES AND PERSIANS. and the authenticated facts too few, to entitle the supposition to the place of an historical fact. The Medes

[1] Chap. ii. pp. 49-51, 63.

were a cognate race, and both Media and Persia were provinces of the great Assyrian empire at the time that it was at the height of its power.   Afterwards (700 - 500 B.C.) they revolted and became after two centuries the conquerors in their turn, subsequent to which their general history is but a history of decaying prosperity disguised for a while by astonishing military prowess.   The industrial history of the Medes and Persians is, therefore, included in the industrial history of the provinces which they annexed,[1] especially in that of Assyria, of whose noble products they have sometimes been given the original credit.   Their arts and manufactures were but what they inherited from their former masters, and on these they never afterwards improved.

Among the countries conquered by Persia was Lydia, which previous to that time had been an important manufacturing centre.   At Sardis, its capital, the arts of weaving and dyeing had early been carried to great perfection, and it was already a celebrated commercial emporium for the trade of Asia Minor.   After its conquest the industrious inhabitants settled elsewhere, principally in the Ionian cities along the coast, and especially at Miletus, which thenceforward became highly celebrated for its woollen manufactures.   In Lydia and at Miletus manufacture was clearly carried on under the ancient factory system, as in Phœnicia and elsewhere.

LYDIA.

Phrygia, also situated in Asia Minor, was another country long and early celebrated for its manufacturing eminence.   It fell successively under the dominion of the Lydians, Persians, and Romans, but maintained its character for industry to the last.   The Phrygian mantle was greatly esteemed as a fashionable garment in Rome up to the period of its fall.   This was probably as much on account of its purple colour as its

PHRYGIA.

[1] Rawlinson, vol. iii. p. 345.

shape and quality. The Phrygian "cap" had also a reputation of its own familiar to classical scholars. Both Lydia
and Phrygia were further particularly celebrated for their
splendid embroideries.

If native Chinese historians were to be fully credited,
what we have hitherto been satisfied to call
antiquity should be relegated to quite a   CHINA.
recent period in the history of mankind, in face of the claims
which they advance. Their first man or "oldest inhabitant,"
one Pwan Khoo, dates back no less than 96,000,000 of
years before the Christian era! We shall possibly be excused by our readers if we do not attempt to commence our
inquiries into Chinese manufacturing industries at that date,
and the more willingly, as we shall have to do so in any
case at the already stupendously early one of 2700 B.C.
At that time (if any reliance at all is to be placed upon
their chronicles, which have all the internal marks of
accuracy) the Chinese were already a civilised people, in
possession of a settled government, under the conduct of a
monarch of distinguished ability, one Hoangti. The wife of
this enlightened ruler seems to have been no less distinguished
than himself. Tradition assigns to her many excellences,
and amongst others that of having been the earliest dis-
coverer and intelligent appreciator of the useful qualities of
the silk worm. She first, it is alleged, taught how to cultivate and employ this insect for the purposes of industry.
It is impossible to test the truth of this story by any
external evidence that we possess. The nations inhabiting
the east of Asia had not the advantage of those that inhabited
the west, of coming into contact with races like the Jews
and Greeks, who constituted themselves the historians of
their times, and we know accordingly scarcely anything of
them from this source. Neither have those countries been
very fully explored by industrious antiquaries in recent times,

as has been the case with Syria, with Asia Minor, and, in a less degree, even with Hindostan. Records of their own of great authority and antiquity they possess, but these are generally as little known to scholars as is their language to philologists, or the topography of their country to travellers. We may be satisfied then with taking this story and all the earlier part of their history on trust, and we shall go back for facts no further than to Confucius (551 B.C.), from which time we have certain evidence of the silk manufacture having been for long a flourishing industry in China. Of the extent of its diffusion over the ancient world there are still great differences of opinion; and, with respect to the Chinese system of production, the same remark applies. It must, however, from the very nature of silk culture and manufacture, have been always conducted on a highly organised scale, if not actually in manufactories of definite bounds. There were, we know, districts where silk manufacture was exclusively pursued, as the porcelain manufacture was in others, by a sort of communistic village co-operation; and there were, in the latter case at all events, imperial factories as well. There were probably also silk weaving districts in most of the great cities, whose products were bought up for sale by capitalist traders, as is still the case; and there were the houses where the silk worms were reared, which must have often been on a large scale. It is believed by some that the Chinese were acquainted with the cotton manufacture too, as early, or even earlier, than that of silk, and that the cotton tree was indigenous; but this is mere speculation. No cotton is known to have been manufactured there before the eleventh century, and the cotton plant was not cultivated for certain till the thirteenth, when it was introduced into that country at the time of its conquest by the Mongol Tartars in 1280.[1] It is unlikely that they have ever

_____
[1] _Encyclopædia Britannica._ Ninth edition. Article "Cotton."

manufactured wool. In later years a very considerable linen manufacture has sprung up, but it is unknown at what time it took its rise.

The early history of Greece is enveloped in great obscurity, and when at length it begins to emerge into light it is so surrounded by GREECE. tradition as to be almost valueless in precise narrative, though one would not willingly exchange those beautiful traditions for a far more consistent story. It seems to have been a country much given to textile manufacture from a very early time. In that celebrated 27th chapter of Ezekiel —invaluable in the history of ancient commerce—mention is made among the various commodities imported at Tyre, of "blue and purple (stuffs) from the isles of Elishah," and Elishah is believed to have been a name given to the islands and southern peninsula of Greece, a name afterwards continued to the mainland in the form of Elis. The primitive inhabitants of these and neighbouring parts were notorious adepts in the arts of spinning and weaving flax and wool, both in the heroic and classic ages. Their poets sang the praises of their industry with almost as much fervour as of their beauty and strength. Homer and Theocritus are about equally eloquent on this theme, and in the case too of no less celebrated a person than the fair and frail Helen of Troy. The former describes the Egyptian Queen Alcandra presenting this familiar heroine with a golden distaff, in token of her supremacy in spinning; whilst the latter, in a fit of genuine enthusiasm as to her weaving capabilities, exclaims—

> " None in her creel winds such a thread as she,
> Nor on the cunning loom more skilfully
> With *weaving-comb* [1] the warp and woof can wed,
> And cut the cloth from beams high overhead."

The same poet (Theocritus), and with him Horace and Virgil

[1] *i.e.* what is now technically called the "reed."

have not disdained to eloquently sing the praises also of the
fine woollen cloths of Miletus ; and Horace, Tibullus, and
others have for ever celebrated the " silken " robes of Cos.
Of these last vestures, so famous for their transparency, it is
necessary to say a few words.   They might have been taken
for certain for a sort of netting, like that in use among the
fashionable ladies of ancient Egypt, but for the great
authority of Aristotle, who unequivocally records that from
a very early period silk was both woven and spun at Cos ;
and for the constant tradition that they were really silken
robes.   Pliny says on this matter : " The Grecian women
unravel the silks imported from Asia, and then weave them
anew ; whence that fine tissue of which frequent mention is
made in the Roman poets under the name of *Coan rests*."
The learned Salmasius has shown, however, says Dr. Cooke
Taylor, " that Pliny in this passage misunderstood the passage
of Aristotle's Natural History to which he referred.   The
Greek means nothing more than ' females wind off the web
of the silk worm, and then weave the thread,' not as Pliny
would interpret it, 'unravel the texture of the dress, and then
weave it over again.' "[1]   This explanation would restore
their manufacture to them, and is at all events more likely
than the other.   Even with so great a concurrence of
authority, however, it has never been finally allowed that
silk was actually the material meant after all, and that the
product was not perhaps a fine muslin, or something else.
In Greece, weaving was often a distinct trade, carried on by
a separate class of persons, but in addition every considerable
domestic establishment, especially in the country, contained
the necessary apparatus for making cloth.   The spinning of
yarn was at first the characteristic employment of women ;
and " the most noble in the land did not think it beneath
them to join in this labour ;" the production being for home

[1] *Silk, Cotton, and Woollen Manufactures*, p. 27.

consumption only; and "the work principally carried on by female slaves, under the superintendence of the mistress of the house" (Warden, p. 186). After the heroic age, however, the national character underwent an alteration and was less disposed towards industry. It became usual then to encourage operatives and artisans from foreign countries to settle in Athens and the other large towns,[1] as was so much the case in Rome; and manufacturing for trade became usual. Establishments of the character, if not upon the scale, of the great ancient factories (from which they were manifestly copied), were then introduced, and among places specially named for these are Megara and Miletus: the former celebrated for its coarse, the latter for its fine woollen cloths. Another centre of industry particularly mentioned by Pliny is the Achæan city of Patræ: "where the women being twice as numerous as the men, would alone appear to have worked in the factories" (Warden, p. 192). The work of the factories was performed by slaves, the spinning usually by females, and the weaving by males.[2] Blankets and the coarser kinds of fabrics for clothing the working-classes were the usual productions of these establishments. We have no hint that any power other than manual was employed in them.

The principal Greek colonies, besides those in Asia Minor and Italy, that attained to high manufacturing eminence were Colchis and GREEK COLONIES. Rhodes. The former was a fertile country on the Black Sea, the scene of the celebrated search for the "golden fleece," said to have been undertaken by Greek explorers in the thirteenth century B.C. What the "golden fleece" really was is a matter that has never been properly ascertained.

---

[1] *Social Life in Greece*, by Rev. J. P. Mahaffy, F.T.C.D., fifth edition, pp. 310-402 et seq. (Macmillan, 1883).

[2] *Silk, Cotton, and Woollen Manufactures*, p. 30.

The strangest suggestions have been made concerning it;
not the least strange, nor yet the most unlikely, being that it
was really a skein of yellow silk that had found its way
from the mysterious Serica (Eastern China), where the silk
manufacture was already in existence.   Others imagine it
but an ordinary wool-fell dyed yellow.[1]   Gibbon mentions a
custom in that country of using the fleeces of sheep for strain-
ing " water impregnated with particles of gold," and believes
that that might be the origin of the legend.   This would
imply a great abundance of gold there, an implication which
modern research does not justify.[2]   What Colchis was really
celebrated for in ancient times was its linen manufacture;
and it is even possible that the fabulous voyage might have
been undertaken to study this, though it is difficult to see
why it should not in that case have been made in prefer-
ence to Egypt, whence the Colchians are believed to have
originally come.   Rhodes, like Cos, was colonised by the
Dorians, and, like it, was celebrated for its industry.   It
developed in time into so rich and powerful a state that the
Rhodian commercial code was adopted as the basis of maritime law on all the coasts of the Mediterranean.   Its
principal manufactures were woollen and cotton cloths.
Cyprus was also partially colonised by industrious Greeks;
as were also Corcyra, Ægina, and many of the other islands.
Among the lesser of these celebrated for their manufactures
were Scyros and Lesbos.   It was in the former that the great
Achilles concealed himself, disguised in female attire, and thus
agreeably occupied his time; the rendering is by a friend—

> " Only Achilles of them all, amid
> King Lycomedes' daughters lying hid,

---

[1] The word Colchis means "saffron," which is a plant yielding a yellow
dye.   The fable is that Medea disclosed the nature of this dye to Jason, the
leader of the expedition.

[2] *The History of the Decline and Fall of the Roman Empire*, by Edward
Gibbon, Esq., Variorum Edition, vol. iv. p. 478, 1854.

Learned wools, not weapons ; and with hand milkwhite
Wrought maiden's work, and was a maid to sight.
For, just like them, woman he seemed to grow,
Just such a rose blushed on his cheeks of snow ;
Whene'er he stepped, his step was as a girl's,
And a girl's veil he wound about his curls.
But a man's love in his man's heart did bide,
And so, from dawn of day till eventide,
He lingered at Deïdameia's side,
Oft kissed her hand, oft her gay web would raise,
And warp and woof alike, as sweet, would praise.

BION (Idyll, VII.)

The domestic manufacture of the island seems in this
instance to have been turned to rather dangerous account.

The history of Italian textile industry resembles in most
respects that of Grecian.   The later Romans,
like the later Greeks, parted in the course   ITALY.
of national development with much of their early simplicity
of character, and permitted the home manufactures for which
they were formerly famous to fall into desuetude or devolve
upon slaves, while they imported all that was costly and
curious of the fabrics of other nations.   Yet there was a time
when the Roman matron, like the Greek matron, was proud
of her proficiency in spinning, and when poets and historians
alike held it in honour, as we have found the Greek poets
also doing.   It will be remembered that when Collatinus
paid his ill-omened midnight visit to the beautiful Lucrece,
she was found spinning among her maids, an old-world type
of how the good wife should under such circumstances be
found.   There was in every considerable Roman country
house an apartment too (the "textrinum"), as in Greece,
specially reserved for textile manufacture, and fitted up
with all the requisites of spinning and weaving.   Equally,
as we know from Virgil, was textile industry a usual occupation in the cottage.   In the following vivid little sketch

of an interior, we have the whole scene brought before us as
it might be witnessed in those primitive times :—

> " At eve by lamplight in the winter time,
> One, a late worker, with his sharp knife shapes
> Torches, like ears of corn ; while crooning song
> To cheer her never-ending toil, his wife
> Deftly with finest comb plies warp and woof."
>
> *(Georg.* I.)

The condition of manufacture in earlier Greece and Rome
thus resembled very much that of the greater part of modern
Europe up to the dawn of the new factory system.   The production was for home consumption, and principally domestic ;
the superior goods being at first brought always from a
distance.   There, as here, the clothing of the commonalty was
" homespun ;" and there, as here, there was a distinct class of
hand-loom weavers, who received their yarn from the spinners
to make into cloth,[1] as until lately was the practice in English
manufacturing districts.   The very same difficulty beset
them too at length that beset our hand-loom weavers about
a century and a half ago, the difficulty, namely, of obtaining
adequate supplies of yarn.   The home trade was much
hampered on this account, and yarn was for some time,
after corn, the commodity imported most into ancient Italy.
But even this resource was not sufficient to meet the continually increasing requirements of the population, and in
later times we read : " Rome was full of manufactories, where
paid workmen shared with slaves consigned to the rudest
tasks the fatigues, though not the profits, of manufacture."[2]
The Romans were nevertheless even less than the Greeks
naturally a manufacturing people at home.   They encouraged
rather production on a large scale in their colonies and

[1] *The Life of the Greeks and Romans*, by E. Guhl and W. Koner, p. 519
(Chatto and Windus).

[2] *History of Political Economy in Europe*, p. 54, by Jérôme Adolphe Blanqui
(George Bell and Sons, 1880).   See also Guhl and Koner, p. 186.

dependencies. It was their habit to collect together from all sources the best artificers and makers of textile and other fabrics, and form them into *colleges*, with certain privileges and under strict imperial control; and these they established out of Italy, in large manufactories, where were made the clothing and accoutrements for the troops, and other commodities in most demand in Rome.

Of the methods of spinning and weaving adopted by the classical nations, the following account may be accepted as authentic :—" The material prepared for spinning was wrapped loosely round the distaff, the wool being previously combed, or the flax heckled by processes not very dissimilar to those used at the present day. The ball thus formed on the distaff required to be arranged with some neatness and skill in order that the fibres should be sufficiently loose to be drawn out by the hand of the spinner. . . . The distaff was generally about a yard in length, commonly a stick or reed with an expanse near the top for holding the ball. It was sometimes composed of richer materials. . . . The distaff was usually held under the left arm, and the fibres were drawn out from the projecting ball, being at the same time spirally twisted by the forefinger and thumb of the right hand. The thread so produced was wound upon the spindle until the quantity was as great as it would carry. The spindle was made of some light wood, or reed, and was generally from eight to twelve inches in length. At the top of it was a slit or catch to which the thread was fixed, so that the weight of the spindle might carry the thread down to the ground as fast as it was finished. Its lower extremity was inserted into a whorl or wheel made of stone, metal, or some heavy material which both served to keep it steady and to promote its rotation. The spinner who, as we said before, was usually a female, every now and then gave the spindle a fresh gyration by a gentle touch, so as to increase the torsion or twist of the thread. Whenever the spindle touched the ground a length was spun ; the thread was then taken out of the slit, or clasp, and the thread just finished wound upon the spindle ; the clasp was then closed again, and the spinning of a new thread commenced." [1] The weaving was performed in the upright loom, similar to that in use in Egypt, from which country, in all probability, the Greeks obtained it. We take a brief description of this loom from *The History and Principles of Weaving*, by Alfred Barlow : [2] " The warp is suspended from the top beam of the loom, and the lower ends are tied up in separate portions, which are weighted to keep the threads in tension. The cloth was woven *upwards*. Before the reed was invented the weft thread is said to have been combed evenly into its place by means of a comb adapted for the purpose, and the blow was given to drive them together by the use of a flat sword-shaped piece of wood which was introduced into the shed for the purpose. This latter instrument was called the Spatha. . . . Such an instrument is still used in some kinds of mat making."

We must hasten to the conclusion of this chapter. Little at all is known of the textile industries of ancient Gaul and Germany, but they were evidently widely spread there in remote times. When the Gauls first made their appearance in Italy in the earlier days of the Republic they were already a clothed race, and their garments were of the textile kind. Similarly, the Germanic nations which bordered the Roman dominions wore textile fabrics, and it was only when the Roman's arms advanced far into the interior that they found a people clothed in skins. The writings of Cæsar and Tacitus are

GAUL AND GERMANY.

---

[1] *Silk, Cotton, and Woollen Manufactures*, p. 31.
[2] Sampson Low & Co., 1878.

the chief authorities we possess on these subjects, and unfortunately they treat little, if at all, of manufacture.   Some
indirect allusions, indeed, occur throughout their writings,
but the references are not sufficiently pertinent to quote
here.   From other sources, however, we have undoubted
and more direct evidence of a textile manufacture of extreme
antiquity in these countries.   In various parts of them, and
particularly in what we now call Switzerland, scraps of textile
clothing have been found, and are preserved, belonging to
the Neolithic or later Stone Age.[1]   Along with them have
been found too even the actual implements used in their
manufacture, and fragments of fishing-nets constructed with
great skill.[2]   At what period the Stone Age may be placed
in those countries we cannot for certain say, but, considering
the early diffusion of a knowledge of metals there, it should
be at a very remote time indeed.

A vast tract of country lying north of the Caspian and
Euxine Seas, and of uncertain bounds east
and west, was anciently inhabited by wild   SCYTHIA AND
SARMATIA.
tribes known to the countries around the
Mediterranean under the dreaded names of Scythians and
Sarmatians.   These tribes did not wear textile clothing but
furs, procured, it is supposed, from the regions of higher
latitude which they adjoined.[3]

In Scandinavia the case seems to have been otherwise.
Fragments of textile fabrics of great anti-
quity have been found there, but so decayed   SCANDINAVIA.
as to be scarcely of any use to the antiquary in judging their
quality and period of production.   It is certain, however,

---

[1] *Primitive Man*, p. 261 *et seq.*

[2] *Idem*, p. 135.   See also Tylor's *Anthropology*, chap. x. ; Keller's *Lake
Dwellings of Switzerland*, translated by Dr. J. E. Lee, p. 323.

[3] Compare Tacitus, *Germania*, 46 ; Claudian, *De Bello Getico*, 481 ; Duncker's
History of Antiquity, chap. viii. pp. 229-235 ; Herod. iv. ; Justin. lxi.
cap. 88.

that both linen and woollen stuffs were worn; the latter as
early as in the Bronze Age,[1] and probably long before.

A mere glance at the New World must suffice. When
the Spaniards discovered and conquered
MEXICO.
Mexico they found established there a civilisation far older than their own, and manufactures already
arrived at a higher degree of perfection than anything that
had been known in Europe for a thousand years. In
Prescott's *History of the Conquest of Mexico* the amazing
story is told, with characteristic eloquence and fulness of
detail, and a single quotation from that easily accessible
book is all we can afford. It is a list of the products of the
country which seem most to have struck the historian's fancy,
and which assuredly imply not only an immense technical
knowledge and skill, but an industrial past of vast antiquity.
"There were cotton dresses and mantles of feather work,"
he says, "exquisitely made; ornamented armour; vases and
plates of gold; gold dust, bands, and bracelets; crystal, gilt,
and varnished jars and goblets; bells, arms, and utensils of
copper; reams of paper; grain, fruits, copal, amber, cochineal,
cocoa; wild animals and birds; timber, lime, and mats."[2]
Add to this list that they were acquainted with and in
possession of silk; that they manufactured both linen and
woollen as well as cotton goods, and had apparently done
so from time immemorial, and were well acquainted with
metals, and some notion of the industrial eminence of the
ancient Mexicans may be formed. Their system of possession and production was something like that of India.

The Peruvians had arrived at about an equal degree of
perfection in manufacture about the same
PERU.
time; and apparently without any inter-

[1] *Scandinavian Arts*, by Hans Hildebrand, in South Kensington Museum
Art Handbooks.
[2] *History of the Conquest of Mexico*, by William H. Prescott, vol. i. p. 36
(Bentley, 1843).

course between these two countries. How long they had been at that high point of elevation, and through what prodigiously long rounds of centuries they had been attaining to it, who can say? but the probability is that both nations were already in their decadence when they became known to the modern world. They were more a pastoral people than the Aztecs, and the nature of their fabrics followed this national bent. They chiefly manufactured robes, shawls, carpets, and hangings for their palaces and temples (like the Persians), made of the fine wool of the llama, and of the huanacos and vicunas—species of sheep native to their country. Their cloth, we are specially told, was " finished on both sides alike." Their system of industry was almost certainly wholly domestic, but under strict government supervision. " The fleeces were deposited in public magazines after shearing time, whence they were served out to separate families in such quantity as they required. . . . The stuffs were fabricated by the women, who understood perfectly well the art of spinning and weaving. With these stuffs the families used first to clothe themselves, and the over abundant matter was put into the stores of the Inca. Men were employed to watch over the distribution of the goods, and also over the execution of the work."[1] In this case there is a factory system and a manufacture, but not manufactories ; the system is a communal not a competitive one, and no power other than manual is employed.

[1] *Sociology*, p. 411.

CHAPTER IV.

MANUFACTURING INDUSTRIES IN ANCIENT TIMES
(MISCELLANEOUS INDUSTRIES)

Dyeing and Printing—Colours known to the Ancients—Tyrian Purple—
Ancient Dyers and Dye-houses— Bleaching—Fulling—Metallurgy—
Tubal Cain—Metals known to the Ancients—Gold—Silver—Brass—Iron
—Copper—Tin—Lead—Mercury—Metal Manufacture—Founding, Cast-
ing, and Refining—Earthenware—Bricks—Pottery—Porcelain—Glass—
Paper—Leather.

VERY closely connected with the early history of the textile
arts, is the early history of the art of dye-
ing, so closely connected with it, indeed, as
to have given rise to quite a little controversy among biblical scholars as to which art preceded the
other. The focus round which this rather trivial argument
has raged, is that so celebrated garment which Jacob gave
to his youngest son Joseph, the "coat of many colours," to
which reference has already been made.[1] Was this vest-
ment a textile fabric at all? and if so, was it of the nature
of a plaid, or check, or formed of pieces of variously coloured
cloth stitched together? Or was it the dyed skin or fleece
of an animal, or made of coloured grasses, or what?

It is unnecessary to enter deeply into this controversy.
If it were not woven and dyed in the usual way by Jacob,
or the members of his household, it may very easily have
been procured from somewhere else; and, indeed, the great

DYEING AND
PRINTING.

---

[1] *Ante*, chap. iii. p. 85.

value set upon it would seem to imply that such had been the case. The gift of a coloured garment has ever been esteemed one of the greatest marks of favour in the East, and the favour would be obviously increased were the garment one of rare and foreign workmanship. But it may have been of native manufacture as well. It is true that textile clothing is not mentioned as being known in Canaan before the time of Joseph, and that "skins of beasts" are; but what of that? Dyeing is not mentioned either. Those who would argue from such slender facts to the exclusion of a knowledge of woven clothing at that epoch forget the great lapse of time, the *many centuries*, that intervened between these two casual notices, nor even with all those expunged would be any nearer to proving their case.

It will be desirable to turn from these barren surmises to such facts as may be rapidly grouped together in connection with ancient dyeing. Our sources of direct information are as usual all but non-existent; but by continuing the course of historical and deductive investigation hitherto pursued, it is possible to arrive at some interesting results. We know, for instance, that the art of staining skins was one practised from very remote times in ancient Egypt, and that the Hebrews carried away a knowledge of it with them from thence, and greatly valued it, for "rams skins dyed red" were among the various offerings made to the tabernacle when Moses had led the children of Israel into the wilderness (Exod. xxv. 5). We know, further, that other fabrics were about the same time subjected to a like process, for the words "blue, and purple, and scarlet," so often found in Scripture, are universally understood now as implying the *material* dyed, as well as the colour, and that material as being cloth, or yarn, or both. We further find this art by no means confined to Egypt, and after-

9

wards to Palestine, but early carried to great perfection
in other very ancient countries, particularly Assyria,
Phœnicia, and Persia. In India, also, coloured garments
are amongst the earliest mentioned.[1] Later, we notice the
extraordinary value set on some of these dyed stuffs. One
pound of wool dyed of the Tyrian purple colour cost in
the time of Augustus £32 of our money, and under some
of the later emperors the wearing of purple by any one not
a member of the royal family was a crime punishable with
death. But for any details of the processes, or of the
agents employed, we look through ancient authors in vain.
Pliny, indeed, to whom one would naturally turn for information on the subject, especially repudiates any concern with it; "I should have described the art of dyeing,"
he says, "had it been included among the number of the
liberal arts;" as a mere industrial process he obviously
considered it quite beneath his notice. Nevertheless, the
same author does in a well-known passage afford a glimpse
into the system pursued in Egypt at his time, which is
worth noting for more reasons than one. "There exists
in Egypt," he writes, "a wondrous method of dyeing. The
white cloth is stained in various places, not with dye-stuffs,
but with substances which have naturally the property of
absorbing (i.e. fixing) colours. These applications are not
visible on the cloth, but when the pieces are dipped into a
hot caldron containing the dye, they are in an instant
after drawn out dyed. The remarkable circumstance is,
that though there be only one dye in the caldron, yet
different colours appear on the cloth, nor can the colours
be afterwards removed" (Hist. Nat. xxxv.) It will be
perceived by those versed in such matters that the description thus given is nearly as applicable to printing as
dyeing, and might be taken as a very fair account of one

[1] Ante, chap. iii. p. 109 et seq.

portion of the former process. It is, in fact, certain that both processes were well known long before Pliny wrote, and also that he was unacquainted with the technique of the whole subject. His well affected scorn of dyeing may in this light be viewed as a convenient mask assumed to hide his ignorance. The secrets of such operations were, in fact, very closely kept. They were often confined, not only to certain classes of the community, but even to certain families. It has further been suggested that the art of dyeing was already in its decadence in Pliny's time, which is likewise probable; for it does not seem that the classical nations were at all as skilful dyers as the people of a remoter past; and it is certain that whatever skill they had they derived from them: they did not develop it of their own initiative, as they did their excellence in other departments ; in the Fine Arts, for instance, painting, sculpture, and the manufacture of earthenware. These considerations lend too a particular interest to the inquiry what agents the earlier dyers had at their disposal; and upon that point we shall avail ourselves of what appears to be a very carefully wrought out summary contained in a useful little work by Mr. James Napier, entitled *Manufacturing Arts of Ancient Times*.[1] The following is the list suggested :—

"*Colouring Matters.*—Kermes, indigo, woad, madder, archil, safflower, alkanet, henna, broom, galls, berries, walnut, pomegranate seeds, Egyptian acacia, and shellfish."

"*Salts.*—Sulphate of iron (copperas), sulphate of copper, (bluestone), acetate of copper (verdigris), acetate of iron (iron liquor), alum, alkaline carbonates, lime, and soap."

The power of making useful application of such agents as are named here, " indicates,"—says Mr. Napier,—" a considerable knowledge of practical chemistry, although they

[1] Paisley (Alexander Gardner), 1879.

(the ancients) may not have known anything of chemistry as a science." " A modern dyer confined to this list would," he thinks, " find it very difficult to produce to satisfaction all the colours the ancients possessed ;" but they may have been acquainted with methods of employing them of which we know nothing. Whether those methods might have been discovered fortuitously however, and traditionally preserved, or that they had an art of chemistry of their own, since lost, is unknown.[1]

We gather from sacred and profane history that nearly all the principal colours with which we are acquainted were known in the ancient world, and we infer, therefore, that many of the intermediate tints were known also.   In Scripture mention is made of *white, blue, red, crimson, scarlet, and purple,* but neither yellow nor green, and *black* only indirectly.   With the exact distinctions between some of these colours, as, *e.g.* red, crimson, scarlet, and purple, we are unacquainted ; the difficulty residing not only in our dependence on a right translation of the foreign equivalents, but also in the fact (before mentioned) of materials as well as colours being often indicated by these terms.   Taking *crimson* and *scarlet* together, and reserving *purple* for further consideration, we gather from Scripture some curious facts concerning them. Scarlet is the colour first mentioned (Gen. xxxviii. 28), and by the familiar way in which it is then spoken of, it would appear that that dye, and that dyeing, were already well known.   Afterwards this colour is found generally

COLOURS KNOWN TO THE ANCIENTS.

---

[1] Herodotus (Book I. chap. cciii.) tells the following story of a certain tribe of the Caspian, worth noting in this connection :—" In these forests certain trees are said to grow ; from the leaves of which—pounded and mixed with water—the inhabitants make a dye, wherewith they paint upon their clothes the figures of animals, and the figures so impressed never wash out, but last, as if they had been inwoven in the cloth from the first, and wear as long as the garment." This reads like the chance discovery of some very powerful vegetable dye.

associated with red; "red and scarlet" is a not unusual form. Sometimes with crimson, as in Isaiah's beautiful figure, "Though your sins be as scarlet, they shall be as white as snow; though they be red like crimson, they shall be as wool." Crimson was selected, along with blue and purple, as one of the three colours for the veil of Solomon's temple. Blue seems to have been a very favourite colour in Assyria; Ezekiel writes, "She doted on her lovers, on the Assyrians her neighbours, who were clothed with blue, captains and rulers." It was also very anciently celebrated as a dye in Greece. The same writer tells of "blue and purple from the isles of Elishah."[1] "Fine linen" was probably white, as it is often found mentioned in opposition to other fabrics dyed variously. Whether it were a bleached white we cannot say. Yellow was, and still is, a favourite colour of the Chinese. It was also very highly esteemed in Persia. Mr. Napier suggests that this was probably because the Persians "had a proper yellow dye." "Among some other ancient nations of the East"—the same author writes—"yellow was a symbol of subjection . . . exclusively worn by women." Green does not seem to have been much worn in ancient times, and black (for wearing apparel) appears to have waited until quite recently to achieve the melancholy predominance that it now obtains.

The most interesting of all ancient dyes was purple, and especially the far-famed purple of Tyre. TYRIAN PURPLE. The ingenuity of numberless commentators has been exercised upon the question of what this celebrated colour was, and how produced. Some have affected to deny altogether the popular account of its production, and supposed the story invented to conceal the circumstance of its extraction from a less rare and costly source; whilst others have pointed out the improbability of

[1] Ezek. xxvii. 7, *ante*, p. 117.

the source indicated having been under any circumstances
ever capable of supplying the requisite quantity of material.
The value of these arguments can be better gauged presently when we have described the source in question;
and, as the matter is of exceptional interest, we may perhaps
be excused, even in an untechnical work like this, for doing
so at some length.   For that purpose we will avail ourselves
of a very vivid and careful description of the whole process
taken from Swinburne's "Travels in the Two Sicilies," quoted
in Bischoff's *Woollen and Worsted Manufactures*, p. 20,[1]
which is probably the best account extant.   It is as follows :—" Purple was produced from two sorts of shellfish,
the murex and the purpura, both belonging to the tes-
taceous, or third order of Linnæus' sixth class.   From the
former a dark blue colour was obtained ; the latter gave a
bright tint approaching to scarlet.   The body of the animal
that inhabits these shells consists of three parts ; the lowest,
containing the bowels, remains fixed in the twisted screws
at the bottom, for the purpose of performing the digestive
functions ; it is fleshy and tinged with the colour of the
food ; the middle division is of a callous substance and full
of liquor, which, if let out of its bag, will stain the whole
animal and its habitation ; the third and upper part is made
up of the members necessary for procuring food and pro-
pagating the race.   The murex generally remains fastened
to rocks and stones ; the purpura, being a fish of prey, is
by nature a rover, and one of the most voracious animals of
the deep ; the proper season for dragging for this shellfish
was in autumn and winter.   To come at the liquor, the
shell was broken with one smart blow, and the pouch
extracted with the greatest nicety by means of a hook.   If
the shells were of small size they were thrown by heaps

[1] *A Comprehensive History of the Woollen and Worsted Manufactures*, by
James Bischoff, Esq. (Smith, Elder, and Co., 1842).

into the mill and pounded. The veins were laid in a cistern, salt was strewed over them, to cause them to purge and keep sweet, in the proportion of 20 ounces of salt to 100 lbs. of fish. They were thus macerated for three days, after which the mucilage was drawn off into a leaden caldron, in order that the colours (by being heated therein) might acquire additional lustre and vivacity, as all marine colours do by mixture with that metal. To keep the vessel from melting, 18 lbs. of water were added to 150 lbs. of purple, and the heat given horizontally to the bottom by means of a flue brought from a furnace. By this process fleshy particles were carried off, and the liquor left pure after about ten days' settling. The dye was tried by dipping locks of wool in it till they had imbibed a dark blue colour. As the colour of the murex would not stand alone, the dyer always mixed a proportion of purpura juice with it. They steeped the wool for five hours, then shook, dried, and carded it; dipped it again and again, till it was saturated with the dye. The preparation requisite for staining 50 lbs. of wools with the finest deep amethyst colour was 20 lbs. murex to 110 lbs. of purpura. To produce the Tyrian purple which resembles the colour of coagulated blood, it was necessary first to steep the wool in pure unboiled purpura juice, and then let it lie and simmer with that of the murex. By different mixtures of these two dyes, varieties were obtained according to the changes of fashion, which ran into violet until the reign of Augustus, when it inclined to the Tarentine scarlet, and this soon after made way for the Dyabasa Tyrica, the most extravagant dye of all the tints. We read of fleeces being dyed upon the backs of sheep, but remain in the dark as to the method and advantage of that process. The Greeks, who were never at a loss for an ingenious fable to cover their ignorance of origin and causes, attributed the discovery of purple to the dog

Hercules, which, in a range along the shore, met with a shellfish and greedily crushed it between its teeth; instantly
an indelible purple stained its muzzle, and by this accident
was suggested the first idea of dyeing cloth. The art was
most undoubtedly practised in times of very great antiquity."
It is clear that the process here described was for the purpose of production on a large scale, and that ancient dyeing
was carried on under that system. Respecting the cost of
the dye and the dyed stuffs thus produced, we have the
most astonishing statements. From Mr. Napier's *Manufacturing Arts of Ancient Times*, pp. 289-291, we take the
following:—"It is related that Alexander the Great found
in the treasury of the Persian monarch 50,000 quintals of
Hermione purple of great beauty and 180 years old, and
that it was worth £25 of our money *per pound weight*."
The same writer points out, however, that this does not
agree with other estimates of the value of this dye: "Indeed," he adds, "so much confusion exists in the statements
concerning the Tyrian purple, that not a few have considered the whole matter of the shellfish dye a sort of
myth; not that there was no truth in the shellfish producing a sort of dye, that cannot be gainsaid, but that the
many wonderful stories told about it in ancient times were
used as a blind to cover and conceal the knowledge of
cochineal and a tin mordant, which it is maintained the
Tyrians possessed." "We think," he continues, "the error
lies in confounding all purple colours with the Tyrian or
shellfish dye, which seems to have been rare and costly at
all times, and necessarily so."[1]

[1] Compare Kenrick's *Phœnicia*, p. 238 : "It was only on the rocky part of
the coast from the Tyrian climax to Haifa that they (the shellfish) were found
in perfection." Hence the extreme rarity of the real dye. But Duncker
points out that elsewhere, for instance in the bays of many of the Grecian
islands, they were "found in extraordinary quantities," p. 71. Perhaps an
inferior kind.

This explanation seems the most likely one, and is that now generally adopted. There were many kinds of purple— even several kinds of Tyrian purple—differing in quality ; the inferior being made to resemble as nearly as possible the superior kinds ; but still only one genuine Tyrian dye, properly so named. Modern artifices of trade could afford many a parallel to such a condition of things. As for the actual colour, the very finest tint was of a *violet* or amethyst hue, but there were at least two others.[1]

There is a curious legend extant which lends a certain sacred interest to the occupation of the ancient dyer. It is thus given by Mr. Napier : " Persia was much famed for dye- ing at a very early period, and dyeing is still held in great esteem in that country. Persian dyers have chosen Christ as their patron ; and Bischoff says that they at present call a dye-house Christ's workshop ; from a tradition they have that He was of that profession. They have a legend—probably founded on what Pliny tells of the Egyptian dyers— that Christ being put apprentice to a dyer, His master required Him to dye some pieces of cloth of different colours, He put them all into a boiler, and when the dyer took them out he was terribly frightened on finding that each had its proper colour." This, or a similar legend, also occurs in the apocryphal book, entitled *The First Gospel of the Infancy of Jesus Christ*. The following is the passage :— " On a certain day, also, when the Lord Jesus was playing with the boys, and running about, He passed by a dyer's shop whose name was Salem, and there were in his shop many pieces of cloth belonging to the people of that city, which they designed to dye of several colours. Then the Lord Jesus, going into the dyer's shop, took all the cloths

ANCIENT DYERS AND DYE-HOUSES.

---

[1] See Kenrick's *Phœnicia*, chap. viii. ; Duncker's *History of Antiquity*, p. 287 ; Birdwood's *Industrial Arts of India*, pp. 237, 238, etc.

and threw them into the furnace. When Salem came home
and saw the cloth spoiled, he began to make a great noise,
and to chide the Lord Jesus, saying, ' What hast Thou
done unto me, oh, Thou Son of Mary ?   Thou hast injured
both me and my neighbours; they all desired their cloths of
a proper colour, but Thou hast come and spoiled them all!'
The Lord replied, ' I will change the colour of every cloth
to what colour thou desirest !' and then He presently began
to take the cloths out of the furnace; and they were all
dyed of those same colours which the dyer desired.   And
when the Jews saw this surprising miracle they praised
God."   We are not acquainted with the origin of this
legend.

   Dyeing, both among the classical and more ancient
nations, was a strictly hereditary occupation.   In Rome a
separate quarter of the city was set apart for the habitations
and dye-houses of the craft; and the same was the case in
Jerusalem, and generally throughout the East.   It is stated
by Bischoff, *Woollen and Worsted Manufactures*, that,
" In every province, and particularly in Phœnicia, there
were certain houses for dyeing purple, belonging to the
emperors, and each of these was under the inspection of an
overseer, whose chief business was to take care that the
articles were well dyed.   These overseers and their work
were again under the inspection of a higher functionary."
That is to say, that the dye-houses were in our sense
factories, and the property of the State.   In Kenrick's
Phœnicia, we read that " the superintendents of these dye-
houses are mentioned in a law of the year 372,"[1] and that
" after the conquest of Syria in the seventh century, the
imperial dye-house was established in Constantinople."[2]
Thus was the factory system of ancient times continued
into the dark ages.

         [1] P. 443.   [2] P. 14.

Previous to the very recent discovery of the powder called "Bleaching Powder," or chloride of lime, the sun was the great bleaching agent in use. Cloth, required to be white, was first thoroughly washed, and then exposed for a lengthened time to the influence of the sun and air. The ancients had a special way of preparing it for this final part of the treatment :—" In some way or other," says the Rev. Samuel Martin,[1] " a certain degree of putrid fermentation was observed to carry off the colouring matter from vegetable fibres. The practice must therefore have arisen of macerating cloth in water mixed with putrescent animal matter, which has continued to the present day from the earliest times. The secret was also found out by many nations of antiquity, that *natron*, the *nitre* of Scripture, combined with and carried off the colouring matter with which cloth is stained, and the substance is still used for the same purpose. According to Pliny, the ancient Gauls knew the use of a lixivium formed from the ashes of burnt vegetables as a detergent, and also to combine it with oil so as to form a soap." In one of the tombs of Egypt we have a representation, as the hieroglyphic denotes, of the washing or whitening of cloth. One man is seen rubbing the fabric in a vessel containing liquid, and another is shaking it out preparatory to the next process, which consisted of its being wrung, stretched lengthwise, and fully exposed to the air.

It is probable that ancient bleaching was always of this primitive kind.

The above process is applicable to the treatment of vegetable fibres. For the whitening of woollen, sulphur has long been in use. In paintings found at Pompeii, fullers and scourers are seen

[1] *The Useful Arts* (James Nisbet and Co., 1851). See also *The Life of the Greeks and Romans* (Guhl and Koner), pp. 487, 488, where illustrations of scouring cloth are given.

at work preparing woollen cloth in much the same way as described above, to be dealt with afterwards perhaps by this agent.[1] The actual *fulling* was done by treading with the feet. At how early a period the valuable properties of the kind of clay called "Fuller's Earth" was known is not certain, but it is difficult to imagine an adequate substitute for it now.

Of the manufacture of metals on a large scale in ancient times we know little or nothing, and even the little that we fancy we know has been inferentially acquired. That various metals were very largely manufactured we do indeed know, for we read of the infinite number of shapes that they assumed under the artificers' hands, and may even see and handle some of these products at the present day. But we know for certain little more, and may not here concern ourselves with learned speculations. What little is accessible to the unlearned we shall strive to fit into a connected tale.

METALLURGY.

Scarcely had the progeny born of our first parents multiplied beyond the extent of an ordinary patriarchal family, when we read in the Bible of their being in full possession of the knowledge of metals, and the art of working in them. Tubal Cain, who was but the great-great-grandson of Adam and Eve, was, we are told, "an instructor of every artificer in brass and iron" (Gen. iv. 22).[2] It is obvious that there is a difficulty about accepting this statement literally. In the first place, the metal which we know by the name of brass is of

TUBAL CAIN.

---

[1] See also a plate in Wilkinson's *Ancient Egyptians* (No. 393), where a male and female scourer are at work preparing cloth.

[2] Mr. Kenrick points out, "An Essay on Primeval History," p. 82, how Etymology often shows that the supposed name of an inventor is "only a personal expression of the fact of the invention;" and thus that Tubal Cain may *mean* a worker in metal merely, and is not necessarily a proper name (B. Fellowes, London, 1846).

comparatively recent discovery; and if we supply its place with bronze, that is an amalgam of copper and tin, and tin, at all events, could not have been known under the circumstances supposed. Copper, it is conceivable, might have been found, for it was native in that country; but even then it is scarcely credible that those earliest inhabitants of the earth would be already acquainted with the difficult process of smelting it from its ores, and all that that knowledge and process implies. As for iron, all the difficulties that confront us with respect to copper confront us with respect to it—and many more besides. We are reduced thus to one of two suppositions in the matter. Either that the statement is not to be taken in its natural sense, or that the knowledge alluded to was miraculously conferred. Into an investigation of the comparative value of those suppositions we obviously cannot enter. That investigation belongs either to the sphere of the supernatural, with which we are not concerned, or is otherwise the affair of the biblical commentator and historian.

Proceeding onwards instead—from antediluvian times and the vague misty ages that succeed them—the first gleam of steady light METALS KNOWN TO THE ANCIENTS. shines once again on Egypt, and those old wandering Arab tribes that early made their way there. From Egyptian tombs have been recovered gold and silver ornaments, and bronze and copper implements, dating back as far, at all events, as the fourth dynasty—that is some 4000 years ago; or to about the time of Abraham's visit to the country. But gold and silver were already in extensive use in Canaan too at that period—in such common use, indeed, as to be even made into articles of *jewellery* (Gen. xxiv. 47, 48). If such refinements of metal work as "earrings" and "bracelets" had already found their way into the wardrobe of a rude pastoral sheik, we may imagine then, but can scarcely realise, the already vast antiquity of metal manufacture. It is not for some centuries after, however, that we meet with anything like a list of metals. This is at length furnished by Moses, and in a very complete form. The occasion is the spoiling of the Midianites (Num. xxxi. 22), and we read of "the gold, and the silver, the brass, the iron, and the tin, and the lead," captured on that occasion. This is the earliest enumeration of metals on record. Following the order of the list, we shall say a few words upon each of them separately.

Not only on account of its position in this enumeration, but for other cogent reasons, gold has an undoubted right to be considered first.

GOLD.

From time immemorial it has been generally, though not universally, accepted as the prime representative of wealth, and the symbol of temporal dignity and power. Its splendour and beauty have always been recognised, while its purity, ductility, and power of resisting decay, could not long fail to be noticed, and are unequalled among metals. As to its claim to a high antiquity, that must also be allowed to be beyond cavil, especially if we allow, as some believe, that it is mentioned among the products of the Garden of Eden itself! The passage where this mention occurs is in any case so curious, and of so high an interest, that it will be well to give it in full. The words of Scripture are these: "And a river went out of Eden to water the garden; and from thence it was parted, and became into four heads. The name of the first is Pison: that is it which compasseth the whole land of Havilah, where there is gold; and the gold of that land is good" [1] (Gen. ii. 10-12). The implication in this passage of the situation in which the gold was found accords with the way in which its presence ordinarily

[1] It is to be noted, however, that Moses only actually says that there was gold there *in his time.*

becomes known over the earth's surface still. It is in just
such situations as those described that gold is discovered in
new countries now—first in the bed of a stream, and afterwards in the rocks from whose exposed surfaces the action
of the water has washed it. Another noteworthy circumstance is the remark that "the gold of that land was good."
This would seem to imply that the gold was found in a
pure or nearly pure state, as gold often is ; and even possibly
that an impurer kind was known.

Profane history corroborates in a remarkable manner the
evidence afforded by sacred history of the great antiquity of
gold. It was almost certainly known to the great nations
of antiquity earlier than any of the other metals—perhaps,
in some cases, excepting silver. In ancient Ethiopia, and
in Egypt and Arabia, there were large gold mines, and the
Egyptians and Ethiopians used both gold and silver pro-
fusely, not only for ornament, but for much more homely
purposes. The great profusion of gold in remote antiquity
is indeed one of the continual marvels and mysteries of
ancient history.[1] The Assyrians were perhaps the most
extravagant of ancient peoples in their employment of it.
Not only was it used for domestic purposes of various kinds
by them:—for works of art, of course—and for personal adornment—but even for the outer decoration of their buildings—
the very roofs of their houses being adorned with gold and
silver. As for the interiors of those palaces, the descriptions
of them are too wearisome to quote, owing to the exceeding
costliness of decoration told of ; and it will suffice to say
that it is computed, in Kitto's *Cyclopædia of Biblical Literature*,
that the total value of the precious articles and treasures con-

[1] In such profusion was gold formerly found in some parts of Africa, particularly in Ethiopia, that even the fetters for binding captives were said (by
Herodotus) to have been made of it. This may or may not have been one of
the exaggerations of ancient writers, but it is certain that quite common
utensils were made of gold. Compare *Ancient Egyptians*, chap. viii.

tained in the temple of Belus at Babylon, exceeded one hundred and twenty millions pounds sterling![1] Both the Jews and Phœnicians were also great accumulators and users of gold. It has often been calculated what was spent on the decoration of Solomon's temple, but the result appears merely fabulous.[2] The Medes and Persians were similarly lavish. A writer in the *Encyclopædia Metropolitana* states that the palace of Ecbatana was "nearly a mile in circumference; the roof was covered with tiles of silver, and the beams, ceilings, and pillars, all covered with scales of silver and gold." Similarly astonishing things are told of Nineveh, Persepolis, and other great cities.

Passing from these Oriental nations to Greece and Italy, we find gold much in use for the adornment of chariots and armour in the age of Homer, and for personal and house decoration. Some centuries after, its manufacture in Greece attained the greatest excellence. In the time of Phidias and the great sculptors, the goldsmith's art is said to have reached the highest degree of perfection.[3] Most of the finest works then produced are lost, but a few of the less ambitious ones have been preserved in ancient tombs, especially in Etruria, where recent excavations have brought them to light. These objects have excited alike the admiration and the envy of modern experts. It is the opinion of Signor Castellani, "whose judgment on the point is practical as well

[1] Compare Rawlinson, vol. ii. chap. iv. p. 514 *et seq.*

[2] The following is Mr. Napier's calculation. Supposing the talent of gold worth £5475, the talent being 125 lbs. in weight, it will make the value of the gold about 73s. per ounce. The talent of silver is valued at £342 : 3 : 9, or 4s. 4½d. per ounce ; so that the gross value of all the sums known to have been given would be :—Sum accumulated and in the public treasury—gold, £547,500,000 ; silver, £342,187,500. Contributed by David from his private resources—gold, £16,425,000 ; silver, £2,395,312. Contributed by the people —gold, £28,000,000 ; silver, £3,421,875—Total, £939,929,687.

[3] *The Industrial Arts*, p. 5, published for the Committee of Council on Education (Chapman and Hall, 1876).

as sound," that we have obtained from the cemeteries of Etruria objects in gold of a workmanship so perfect that "it is difficult to imitate, *or to explain*, the process of execution;" and further, that "he has never seen a single work in gold of after times, including even the most artistic periods, which can be compared for elegance of form, or skill of handicraft, with the archaic productions of Greek or Etruscan art."[1]

The subject of silver in primitive metallurgy is very closely connected with that of gold, with which metal silver was often found mixed.

SILVER.

It is probable that gold was the first discovery, as tradition alleges, and that that discovery led to the extraction of silver from its mineral surroundings afterwards. This probability is increased by the fact that in Egypt silver was known by the name of "white gold," and the further curious circumstance, of the comparatively little use to which in the remotest times it seems to have been put. After the Phœnicians conquered Spain, however, its valuable qualities became better understood. In such enormous quantities did those enterprising navigators find it there that they are said to have used it for making their anchors as a cheap substitute for any other material.[2] Silver was plentifully found in Asia too; as it has been also in America. It is a metal very generally diffused. It was probably the first one coined into money; and still remains the one most universally coined.[3] Like copper, it is too soft for most purposes of mere utility except when mixed with an alloy; and unlike copper it does not seem to have been very

---

[1] *The Industrial Arts*, p. 5.

[2] Aristotle, *De Mirab*, cap. 147. But another interpretation is that *fish-hooks* not anchors are really meant.

[3] Wilkinson points out that "The word silver is commonly used in Hebrew to signify money, as *argent* is in French."—*Ancient Egyptians*, vol. iii. p. 237.

10

greatly used in this way till lately. Comparatively little esteemed at first, it has been increasing in favour continuously to the present time.

What we now call brass is a mixture of copper and

BRASS.

zinc; what is called brass in ancient writings was almost certainly bronze, a mixture of copper and tin. Of those two metals we shall come to treat presently. Zinc is not believed to have been discovered previous to the sixteenth century of our era.[1]

There is no metal so generally diffused over the surface

IRON.

of the earth as iron; and none of which such various and important use is made. Speaking either in ordinary or anthropologic language, the whole civilised world is, and has long been, in "The Iron Age," and possibly is not far from having reached its climax in it. But if this metal is ever to be displaced from the position of eminence that it now enjoys, imagination fails to conceive anything that would adequately supply its place. We need but to reflect for ever so brief a time to assure ourselves how intimately our whole present system of life and civilisation is bound up with iron. Yet in the great civilisations of the long past this metal was comparatively little used, and that notwithstanding that it seems to have been well known.[2] Whether its valuable properties were not fully realised, or that it was imagined to be scarcer than it really was, or that its extraction was too difficult a process for the early metallurgists, or what the cause was, we cannot say, but the fact remains, that a far inferior metallic compound (bronze) was long used for purposes to which iron was much better adapted for many ages after the latter

---

[1] Beckman's *History of Inventions*, vol. ii., article "Zinc."

[2] This statement is of course opposed to the belief that used to prevail (see, for instance, Jacob on *The Precious Metals*), but it is in full accordance with the most recent discoveries. See Wilkinson, vol. iii. chap. vii.; Tylor's *Anthropology*, p. 278, etc. etc.

was known.[1] In the enumeration of metals by Moses, we find it placed (of the pure metals) third, and it is quite possible, notwithstanding all difficulties, that this may actually be its proper chronological position in regard to discovery. We have learned that Tubal Cain was acquainted with iron, and Palestine was described long afterwards (Deut. viii. 9) as "a land whose stones are *iron*, and out of whose hills thou mayest dig brass." We incidentally read too of many familiar uses to which it was put in that and adjoining countries. The bedstead of Og, the King of Bashan, was of iron (Deut. iii. 2) ; and iron tools were forbidden to be used in building the altar of stones in Mount Ebal (Deut. xxvii, 4, 5). Of another time and place we learn, that the chariots of the Philistines were of iron (Judg. i. 19); and in David's hymn of victory after triumphing over his numerous enemies (2 Sam. xxii. 35) mention is even made of a bow of *steel*. But long before this both iron and steel were well known in Egypt. In the tombs at Memphis are to be seen pictures of ancient Egyptian butchers, "Sharpening their knives on a round bar of metal attached to their aprons, which from its blue colour can only be steel; and the distinction between the bronze and iron weapons in the tomb of Rameses III., one painted red, the other blue, leaves no doubt of both having been used."[2] In Ethiopia also iron was in use at a very remote time ; and a great antiquity is claimed for its manufacture in China. Pliny the elder, writing in the first century of the Christian era, even speaks of Chinese steel being unequalled for goodness ; and places the Parthian iron next to it.

When the Greeks appear in history they are just passing from the Bronze to the Iron Age, and Homer as also

[1] Homer mentions iron weapons being in use at the siege of Troy ; but those of the great chieftains were of bronze.

[2] *Ancient Egyptians*, vol. iii. p. 247.

Hesiod mention both iron and steel; the latter averring that
" brass " preceded the former in the operations of husbandry,
as it appears to have likewise done in the operations of war.

Among the Romans iron was known from the first,
though it was for a long while unaccountably scarce.
Polybius, the earliest historian of Rome, notices its military
use. It appears from him that the helmets and breast-
plates of the Roman soldiery were of bronze, but the shield
had a boss and outer border of iron. The sword was " a
strong cut-and-thrust blade, of Spanish steel, and the spear
was pointed with iron."[1] Diodorus Siculus, and Pliny
the elder are among the earliest writers on its manufacture; and the latter thus quaintly and comprehensively
describes some of its uses in his day, by which time it is
evident that its value had become better known. It is, he
tell us, " A metal which we may well say is both the best
and the worst implement used now in the world, for with
the help of iron we break up and tear the ground, we
plant and plot out groves, we set our port yards, and
range our fruitful trees in rows, we prune our vines, and
by cutting off the superfluous branches and dead wood,
we make them every year to look fresh and young again.
By the means of iron and steel we build houses, hew
quarries, and cut in stone; yea! in one word, we use it
to all necessary uses of this life. Contrariwise, the same
iron serveth for wars, murders, and robberies; not only to
offend and strike therewith in hand, but also to reach and
kill afar off, with divers sorts of darts and shot, one whiles
discharged, and sent out of engines, and another while
launched, and flung by the force of the arm, yea, and
sometimes let fly with wings. This I take to be the
wickedest invention that ever was devised by the head of

---

[1] *Useful Arts and Manufacture,* published by the Society for Promoting
Christian Knowledge, p. 8.

man; for to the end that death may speed away faster to a man, and surprise him more suddenly, we make it to fly as a bird in the air, and to the arrow, headed at one end with deadly iron, we set feathers at the other, whereby it is evident that the mischief proceeding from iron is not to be imputed to the nature of it, but to the unhappy wit of men."[1] Iron was largely manufactured in several provinces of the Roman Empire, especially in Spain and Britain.

Notwithstanding the above very full summary of the uses of iron in Pliny's time, which sounds almost like a catalogue of its capabilities at the COPPER. present day, it appears from the excavations at Pompeii and Herculaneum, as well as from the writings of the Latin poets, that great quantities of articles, even tools and weapons of war, were at the same time still made of bronze, that is of copper mixed with tin. We have here a voluntary preference for the softer metal in typically crucial cases. This mystery, which is common to all the metallurgy of the remote past, has never been quite satisfactorily explained. How could that compound metal be made of sufficient hardness for the purposes demanded of it; of so fine a temper, in fact, as to be actually preferred to iron and steel? Even chisels for engraving stones were apparently thus made; and it is still an open question if the sculptures on the granite monuments of Egypt, which have defied the power of forty centuries to obliterate, were not cut with bronze tools. Nor is this the strangest thing about it. It was not only in the east, but in the far north, and the extreme west, that the same, or nearly the same, compound metal was so employed; and this quite independently of whether iron was procured in those countries or not.[2] Bronze implements have been found in

---

[1] *Useful Arts*, p. 9.

[2] Sir G. Wilkinson gives the following analysis of a bronze chisel which he himself found at Thebes :—Of 100 parts there were 94·0 of copper, 5·9 of tin,

mines as far north as Siberia, as far south as Nubia, they have been found alike in Scandinavia and India. Nor is this yet all : "When Brazil was first discovered by the Portuguese, the rude inhabitants used fish-hooks of gold, but had no iron, though their soil abounded in that metal ; and the people in Hispaniola and Mexico were in like manner unacquainted with iron when first visited by the Spaniards though they had both ornaments and implements of gold, and weapons of copper, which latter, as we learn from the analysis of Humboldt, they had acquired the art of hardening by some alloy of tin, or, in other words, of converting copper into bronze." These are cases in which nations apparently did not use iron, although they had plenty of it ; and then we have the other cases in which they used it very sparingly, or deliberately preferred bronze, having a knowledge of the capabilities of both.

The mystery as to the general use of bronze in antiquity is ever so much deepened when we come to the consideration of the subject of Tin.

TIN.

Copper was a metal very generally found in the East, but tin was rare. Whence came this latter metal, of which such immense quantities were used, and on which so high a value was set ? This inquiry, besides its intrinsic interest, has a special one for us, as the sequel will show.

In the list of metals given by Moses, tin stood fifth, and no mention was made of copper, which was doubtless included in the term " brass." For purposes of convenience we have

0·1 of iron. "Its point is instantly turned by striking it against the very stone it was once used to cut, and yet when found, the summit was turned over by the blows it had received from the mallet, while the point was intact, as if it had recently left the hands of the smith who made it." Mr. Napier (*Manufacturing Arts of Ancient Times*) quotes a large number of analyses of bronze made from objects found in various places—as Egypt, Assyria, Greece, Gaul, Britain, and even Peru—all of which show comparatively trifling variations in their constituent parts.

preferred to consider copper in close succession to iron, and to advance iron to the third place.

The first difficulty with respect to tin is, as to its Eastern name. That by which it is known in Scripture is *bedil*, but among the Greek writers *kassiteros*. Are these two names identical in meaning? further, do they represent this metal at all, or something else? Beckman enters very fully into this question, and into the whole subject of tin. He is not quite sure, nevertheless, whether *bedil* means tin, or lead, or another metal, *stannum*, and the article is generally unsatisfactory. His conclusion is, after an elaborate investigation, "that it is probable, but by no means certain, that the ancients *were* acquainted with our tin."[1] This is rather a qualified conclusion after so learned a dissertation, to which the reader is referred for further particulars, and we must venture to go somewhat beyond it.

It is acknowledged on all hands, by Beckman himself amongst others, that bronze was widely used in ancient times, and as it has never been suggested that bronze can be made without tin, it seems to us that the greater must include the less. But after having thus assumed to override the difficulty of tin being very anciently in use at all, we are only then on the threshold of others scarcely less serious. Whence did it come?[2] Beckman declares it to be "one of those minerals which have been found in quantity only in a few countries, none of which ever belonged to the Greeks or the Romans, or were visited at an early period by their merchants." This again we shall have to dispute presently. But in the meanwhile, what is the absolutely earliest information on the subject? It is supplied by

[1] *History of Inventions*, vol. ii. p. 206.
[2] Mr. Tylor, *Anthropology*, p. 279, speaks of tin mines in "Georgia, Khorassan, and elsewhere in inner Asia where, perhaps, the discovery was made of using it to harden copper into bronze." This suggestion, if authenticated, would go a long way towards solving some of the difficulties of the problem.

Ezekiel. Amongst the commodities which the Tyrians are said (Ezek. xxvii. 12) to have imported, are "silver, iron, copper, and *bedil* from Tarshish." But where was Tarshish? The answer to this long-debated question is, that Tarshish was undoubtedly Tartessus, a district in the south-west of Spain, conterminous with the modern Andalusian coast.[1] From this district, therefore, the Tyrians obtained tin. But did they obtain it from nowhere else, and from whence did the rest of the world obtain it ? On this point Mr. Elton, in a recent work, *Origins of English History*, propounds a novel theory, which we will briefly state.

It must be remembered that Ezekiel's writings do not date back further than to about 600 years B.C., and that for more than double that time previously tin had apparently been very generally in use. Now Tarshish is first mentioned in Scripture shortly after the flood (Gen. xi. 4) as one of the settlements of the sons of Japhet ; but it can hardly be supposed that it had much commerce at that time. Was there then no other great source of supply farther east ? One known to other nations besides the Phœnicians ? The Greek name for tin (*kassiteros*) now comes to our assistance. This name, it appears, is derived from "kastira, the Sanscrit name for the metal," and there was an island, Cassitira, in the straits of Malacca, or at all events somewhere in the neighbourhood of the Malay peninsula. "It is from this last-named place," says Mr. Elton, "that our supply of tin even at the present day is principally derived, and whence it was also principally derived in the far past." Here, then, we seem to approach something definite. The name of the district which in southern seas had long supplied the metal, became, in the mouths of Greek historians, the name of

[1] See Elton's *Origins of English History*, p. 8 (Quarritch, 1883). Kenrick's *Phœnicia*, chap iii. ; Wilkinson's *Ancient Egyptians*, chap. ix. ; Duncker's *History of Antiquity*, p. 85, etc. etc.

the metal itself, and was applied afterwards to other islands
in the western seas from which it also reached them. But
where were these other Cassiterides? A very general consensus of opinion places them off the south coast of Britain.
Cornwall and the adjacent islands were the Western Cassiterides.[1] That opinion also has been challenged by Mr.
Elton, who believes the Western Cassiterides were islands
lying closer to the coast of Spain. This further difference
of location is, however, comparatively unimportant. The
bedil that was brought from Tarshish then, 600 B.C., and of
course earlier, came first from islands off the Spanish coast
to be there transhipped; that *bedil* became in Greek mouths
kassiteros; this was the name given to tin brought first
·from eastern seas; the Greek writers applied the name to
all tin; and the Romans did the same. Tin is still found
largely in Cornwall, where also primeval workings have
been discovered, and not in any other islands that are
known near the western coast of Spain. It is also still
found in the Malay peninsula. Now it is a characteristic
of tin that where it abounds it generally persists; and
that where found at all, it is usually found in very large
quantity. The likelihood is then that there were at least
two great ancient centres of the tin trade, these two, and
the probability is that there were more; that tin was
supplied to the ancient world first from the East, but
afterwards also from the West, the principal source of
tin supply in the latter region being Britain,[2] which un-

---

[1] It is unnecessary to quote the great mass of easily accessible authority in
favour of this very general opinion. The ancient testimonies on the subject
are well summarised in Macpherson's *Annals of Commerce*, under date
"524 B.C."

[2] In Dr. Smith's *Cassiterides* this argument is concisely summed up as
follows :—"We recall attention to the simple fact that tin was an article of
ancient commerce, at least as early as 1200 B.C., on the eastern shores of the
Mediterranean. This is an established truth. It is certain that tin was used
and sold at Sidon and Tyre at this early date. Whence then did it come? The

doubtedly had also a tin trade with Greek and Roman merchants both before and after it was a province of the Roman Empire.

Lead was known as early as the time of Moses (as we have seen), and it was in very familiar use in the time of Job (whether earlier or later than Moses we cannot say), for we find that remarkable person thus expressing himself towards it: "Oh that my words were now written! oh that they were engraved on a tablet! That with an iron graver and with *lead* they were engraven upon a rock for ever!" (Job xix. 23, 24). "This reference," says Mr. Napier, "is considered to refer to an inscription first engraved on stone, and afterwards filled in with lead, a beautiful application for the preservation of writing;" and this is a clear and happy explanation of a passage that might otherwise have seemed obscure. It is probable that lead was originally found in conjunction with silver, for they usually exist together. It was well known in ancient Egypt, where among other uses it was employed for *soldering*,[1] as with us. This must have been after the discovery of tin, for, as Pliny observes, "Lead can only be united by the addition of tin" (Pliny, xxxiv. 16). It existed very anciently in Britain, and was probably mined previous

LEAD.

universal testimony of all history and tradition answers from Britain. This testimony has been received, and the British origin of the tin supplied as an article of commerce in the earliest times, has been believed by great numbers of learned men in different ages and countries. Having carefully studied the subject, they have been fully convinced that the ancient Phœnicians traded with Britain for this metal, and regularly took it from the coast of this island, in Phœnician ships, to Tyre and Sidon. The names of those who have entertained this opinion would, if collected, exhibit a body as numerous, as intelligent, and as entitled to deference and respect as could be found supporting almost any historical truth." It is worth consideration, too, if the mystery about the sources of tin production was not a purposely designed one, first, on the part of the Phœnicians, and then of the Carthaginians, to keep the monopoly of this most valuable traffic in their own hands. Compare chap. v. p. 189.   [1] *Ancient Egyptians*, vol. iii. p. 259.

to the Roman occupation, but certainly very extensively afterwards. It is a very widely diffused metal, and its principal characteristics—weight and softness—are noticed by many ancient writers.

There is reason to believe that mercury, or quicksilver, was also known at a very early time, but whether as a metal apart from its ores is MERCURY. uncertain. It seems to be alluded to in places as a purifier of other metals—one of its natural properties—but this subject, like most other subjects in ancient metallurgy, is involved in great mystery. It was long the fashion to hold this mysterious tone about this subject, indeed until comparatively recent times. As a pigment (vermilion) ·it was in use among the Romans, and probably much earlier.

We have next to consider the system and methods of manufacture pursued with respect to these METAL MANUFACTURE. several metals. Unhappily we are almost wholly without information on this head. Some descriptions of ancient mining we possess, borrowed both from writings of contemporaries and the observations and conclusions of modern archæologists and travellers; but of anything direct on the subject of ancient metal manufacture there is as nearly as possible an entire absence of information. Particularly is this the case with smelting, or the procuring the metals from their ores by fusion—the manufacture proper— as distinguished from the handicraft industries of founding, casting, forging, and refining. We know scarcely anything of it.[1] That they were so procured, we know, of course; for in the first place they (except those that were found

---

[1] Wilkinson says on this point that on some of the monuments of Egypt the "processes of washing the ore, smelting or fusing the metal with the help of the blowpipe, and fashioning it for ornamental purposes, are represented; but, as might be supposed, these subjects merely suffice as they were intended to give a general indication of the goldsmith's trade."

pure) could be procured in no other way. And in the second place we have, or can have, ocular demonstration of it, for in the neighbourhood of ancient mines that have been explored, and in other places, have been found the obvious remains of large smelting operations. Great heaps of "slag" encumber the ground, what is left after the metal is extracted. But no records or representations of these operations remain. Reduced to surmise on that omission, might it not be because the metal works and mines alike were supplied by slave labour? We have had to notice a similar oversight, for a similar supposed reason, in respect to textile factories. The labours of the unhappy persons working at those great places of production were not generally considered worthy of commemoration; even as the processes themselves were viewed as rude and base. Thus they escaped alike the notice of the historian and the sympathy of the artist. Such quasi-descriptions of ancient smelting operations as can be traced anywhere are ever bound up intimately with descriptions of mining operations, and one very beautiful description of mining in the far past we do indeed possess, the allusions in which to the manufacture (as well as extraction) of metals, give us an opportunity, of which we gladly avail ourselves, of quoting it here in full. It is taken from Job xxviii. 1, 2, slightly altered.

> " Truly there is a vein for silver,
> And a place for gold where they refine it.
> Iron is obtained from the earth,
> And ore is fused into copper.
> Man putteth an end to darkness,
> And completely searcheth everything :
> The rocks, the thick darkness, and the shadow of death.
> He sinks a shaft far from a human dwelling ;
> They, unsupported by the feet, hang suspended :
> Far from men they swing to and fro.

> The earth, out of it cometh bread,
> And when turned up beneath it resembles fire.
> It's stones are the places of sapphires,
> And gold-dust pertains to it.
> The path thereto no bird knoweth,
> And the vulture's eye hath not seen it,
> And the lion hath not walked over it.
> Man layeth his hand upon the flinty rock ;
> He overturneth mountains from their foundations.
> He cutteth out canals among the rocks;
> And his eye seeth every precious thing.
> He restraineth the streams from trickling down ;
> And bringeth hidden things to light."

The mechanical devices for preserving and working the mine here described are such as might be employed now. But of even greater interest to us are the allusions to the several metals. "There is a vein for silver;" that is, as it is otherwise rendered (Coverdale), "There are places where silver is molten;" and "a place for gold," *i.e.* as Barnes says,[1] "A workshop, or laboratory, for working the precious metals." "Iron is obtained from the earth, and ore is fused into copper," or, in the Vulgate, "iron is taken out of the earth, and brass, or copper, is molten out of stone." The distinction made here as to the extraction of the different ores of copper and iron could not be surpassed : the form in which iron is generally found is that of an earth, while copper is never found in that form, but as a hard mineral substance, from which the metal is procured by fusion. It is impossible not to be convinced from this extract that whenever Job wrote metallurgy must have been in a very advanced condition; and that, wherever the country lay of which he wrote, it was rich in mineral wealth. It would occupy too much space to quote, even briefly, the testimony of numerous travellers who have visited the remains of some of the prodigious mining and smelting works of a long by-

[1] The *Book of Job*, vol. ii. p. 60.

gone age, and whose narratives are more or less pertinent to our subject. A single one must suffice. This, however, we shall quote in full, containing, as it does, a most vividly picturesque description of the system of labour at those places, and of the methods of workmanship applied to the metals there. It is taken from Bonomi's account of the mines which he visited in the Bisharee desert, and is quoted in Wilkinson's *Ancient Egyptians*, and elsewhere. It is as follows :—

" In the valley, near the most accessible part of the excavation, are several huts, built of the unhewn fragments of the surrounding hills, their walls not more than breast high, perhaps the houses of the excavators or guardians of the mine ; and separated from them by the ravine or course of the torrent is a group of houses about 300 in number, laid out very regularly in straight lines. In those nearest the mines lived the workmen who were employed to break the quartz into small fragments, the size of a bean, from whose hands the pounded stone passed to the persons who ground it in hand-mills, similar to those now used for corn in the valley of the Nile, made of a granitic stone, one of which is to be found in almost every house at these mines, either entire or broken. The Kings of Egypt condemned to the mines notorious criminals, prisoners of war, persons convicted by false accusations, or the victims of resentment. And not only the individuals themselves, but sometimes even their whole families are doomed to this labour, with the view of punishing the guilty and profiting by their toil. The vast numbers employed in these mines were bound in fetters, and compelled to work day and night without intermission, and without the least hope of escape ; for they set over them barbarian soldiers, who speak a foreign language, so that there is no possibility of conciliating them by persuasion, or the kind feelings which result from familiar converse.

When the earth containing the gold is hard, they soften it by the application of fire, and when it has been reduced to such a state that it yields to moderate labour several thousands (myriads) of these unfortunate people break it up with iron picks. Over the whole work presides an engineer who views and selects the stone and points it out to the labourers. The strongest of them provided with iron chisels, cleave the marble shining rock by mere force without any attempt at skill; and in excavating the shaft below ground, they follow the direction of the shining stratum without keeping to a straight line. In order to see in these dark windings, they fasten lamps to their foreheads, having their bodies painted sometimes of one and sometimes of another colour, according to the nature of the rock; and as they cut the stone it falls in masses on the floor, the overseers urging them to the work with commands and blows. They are followed by little boys who take away the fragments as they fall, and carry them out into the open air. Those who are above thirty years of age are employed to pound pieces of the stone, of certain dimensions, with iron pestles in stone mortars, until reduced to the size of a lentil. The whole is then transferred to women and old men, who put it into mills arranged in a long row, two or three persons being employed at the same mill; and it is ground until reduced to a fine powder. No attention is paid to their persons: they have not even a piece of rag to cover themselves; and so wretched is their condition that every one who witnesses it deplores the excessive misery they endure. No rest, no intermission from toil, are given either to the sick or maimed; neither the weakness of age nor women's infirmities are regarded; all are driven to their work with the lash, till at last, overcome with the intolerable weight of their afflictions, they die in the midst of their toil. So that these unhappy creatures always expect worse to come than what they

endure at the present, and long for death as far preferable
to life. At length the masters take the stone thus ground
to powder and carry it away to undergo the final process.
They spread it upon a table a little inclined, and pouring
water upon it, rub the pulverised stone until all the earthy
matter is separated, which, flowing away with the water,
leaves the heavier particles behind on the board. This
operation is often repeated, the stone being rubbed lightly
with the hand; they then draw up the useless and earthy
substance with fine sponges, gently applied, until the gold
comes out quite pure. Other workmen then take it away
by weight and measure, and putting it with a fixed proportion of lead, salt, a little tin, and barley bran, into earthen
crucibles well closed with clay, leave it in a furnace for five
successive days and nights, after which it is suffered to cool.
The crucibles are then opened, and nothing is found in them
but the pure gold, a little diminished in quantity."

What horrors are here disclosed! Little wonder, indeed,
that those who sculptured the ancient monuments had no
desire to transmit pictures of this kind to posterity; that
historians have not been anxious to preserve for our execra-
tion the records of a system of manufacture carried out in
this wise.[1]

There was an ancient Greek tradition that the art of
casting metal was first practised at Samos,
FOUNDING, CASTING, not more than six or seven hundred years
AND REFINING.[2]
before Christ, but this is easily shown to be
a fable, as are other stories on the same subject promulgated
by Pliny and Pausanias respectively, and copied by other
writers from them. The arts of founding and casting

---

[1] The Athenians, as is well known, had mines, the property of the State but
farmed to private individuals, which were worked on a system similar to this.

[2] Places where the founding or casting of metals is carried on are
"Factories," under the Factory Extension Act 1867.

metals were known in Egypt many centuries before the earliest of the dates given by those writers, and probably known too in most of the other great Eastern countries. It is sufficient to cite a single instance in proof of this: the "molten calf" which the Israelites set up as an idol during their wanderings in the wilderness. This image must clearly have been "cast." The process of refining is also very often alluded to in Scripture. It supplies many beautiful similes to the poets and prophetical writers. A few may be given: "when he hath tried me, I shall come forth as gold" (Job xxiii. 10); "thou hast tried me, as silver is tried" (Ps. lxvi. 10); "I will bring the third part through the fire, and will refine them as silver is refined, and will try them as gold is tried" (Zech. xiii. 9); "I will purify thy dross, and take away all thy tin" (Isa. i. 25). Many more are to be found. Mr. Napier has some very careful and ingenious remarks upon the process of refining, or "cupelling," which he supposes to have been practised in these cases. It very much resembled, he concludes, what would be practised now where operations on a small scale are conducted. Wilkinson gives two well-known pictures from the Egyptian monuments relating to such refining, or small smelting operations. In the one case, a man is sitting over a fireplace closed in on three sides, and is blowing through a blowpipe on to a mass of metal disclosed by an opening on the fourth side (Fig. 405). In the other, "the furnace seems only a heap of fire upon the surface of the earth, and the bellows are two large bags filled with air, upon which a man is standing with a foot upon each bag, the aperture of the bag being connected with a pipe leading into the fire. While the man is seen putting all his weight upon one bag to compress out the air into the fire, he is also seen lifting up his foot, and, at the same time, the

11

upper fold of the other bag, by a string in his hand, by which the bag is being again filled with air." These methods, primitive as they are, imply at all events a very proper appreciation of the most effective means of securing the end desired. The metal when run into a liquid state was ready for casting if necessary. Moulds in which ancient castings have been taken are not uncommon prizes of the archæologist. Specimens of them, both of bronze and stone, have been discovered in almost all quarters of the world.

EARTHENWARE.

Next in interest and importance to the art of the metallurgist—that of extracting metals from the earth—is that of the worker in the earth itself. The shaping of clay into vessels is probably one of the earliest efforts of human ingenuity ; and the baking them so as to be fitted for utensils, or as building material, represents a great subsequent advance.

BRICKS.

Whether in history the art of brick-making preceded or followed the art of pottery, we have no certain means of ascertaining, but the earliest information we possess of either manufacture is of bricks, for they were used by the immediate descendants of Noah in building the " Tower of Babel." The Chaldean artificers said one to another, " Go to, let us make bricks, *and burn them thoroughly.* And they had brick for stone, and slime had they for mortar " (Gen. xi. 3). Of bricks then that most famous edifice was built—bricks obviously too of a very superior kind. This was (according to conventional chronology) about 2200 B.C., and before that time there must evidently have been for long a manufacture of inferior bricks for the art to have been so far advanced. On this subject Mr. Rawlinson speaks with exceptional authority ; and from his celebrated work, *The Five Great Monarchies of the Ancient Eastern World,* we extract one or two passages about ancient brickmaking in Chaldea and Babylonia. Thus[1]—

"The earliest traditions and existing remains of the earliest building alike inform us that the material used was brick. The earliest brick hitherto discovered in Chaldea is eleven and a quarter inches square, by two and a half inches thick; the baked brick of later date is longer, being thirteen inches square by three inches thick. The sun-dried brick was laid in mud as a mortar, for the kiln-dried bitumen was used." Of bricks of the period of Nimrod and Urukh, he says: "Not only are his bricks found in a lower position than any others, at the very foundation of buildings, but they are of a rude and coarse make, and the inscriptions upon them contrast most remarkably in the simplicity, in the style of writing used, and in their general archaic type, with the elaborate and often complicated symbols of the later monarchs. The style of Urukh's building is also primitive and simple in the extreme. His bricks are of many sizes and ill-fitted together, he belongs to a time when even the baking of brick seems to have been comparatively rare, and he is altogether unacquainted with the use of lime mortar, for which he substitutes moist mud or bitumen; his age is as early as 2326 B.C., possibly a century earlier."

Great interest attaches to the manufacture of bricks in ancient Egypt owing to its connection with the history of the Jews. Like other manufactures there, it appears to have been principally, though not exclusively, a government monopoly;[2] the bricks being universally stamped, either separately or in series, with the name of the king, or some other privileged person in whose time they were made. Slaves, especially captives, were most commonly employed at this labour, and it has been proved that the

[1] Vol. i. chap. v.   [2] Compare chap. iii. p. 100.

bricks were made both with and without straw to bind them. Those formed from the Nile mud required that strengthening, and some found in Upper Egypt had reeds and even sticks introduced into them for this purpose; while others formed of the clay on the edge of the desert did not require it, but held together of their own consistence. The Jews, it will be remembered, were in captivity in Lower Egypt.

Ancient nations, where stone was plentiful, naturally used few bricks, and this manufacture was not, therefore, a considerable one among them. The Phœnicians and Carthaginians built with stone. So did the Greeks. The Romans used both stone and brick, and in later times arrived at great perfection in the manufacture of the latter. In India and China bricks were ordinarily used; but the temples were of stone or hewn out of the solid rock. At Sardis, and elsewhere in Asia Minor, some of the great palaces were of brick. In various parts of America the remains of great edifices of an unknown age built of brick have been discovered. In northern Europe bricks were not made till much later.

There is nothing found more universally (considering its brittleness), among ancient relics of all times, than a rough kind of hand-made pottery.

POTTERY.

Indeed, wherever there is the material, there are certain sooner or later to be earthen vessels, for the most unobservant savage cannot for long handle clay without imposing on it a deflected surface, and recognising uses to which this may be put, and the progress from that recognition of a great possible utility to the most perfect manufactures of Etruscan or Greek art is, in its essence, but a question of degree. It is evident from numerous references in the Bible that the art of potting was not only practised in Palestine, but that there were large manufactures of pottery there. We know also that there was a distinct class or caste of potters; and that they had a "pottery district," as we have. In 1 Chronicles (iv. 23) we read of "the potters, and those that dwelt among plants and hedges: there they dwelt with the king for his work." It was probably a manufacture for which the Jews had an aptitude. In Egypt all the process of potting, from the mixing the clay to the turning out the finished work, is represented in the tombs of Thebes and Beni Hassan, with perfect fidelity and distinctness. The Egyptians, however, did not ever arrive at the same perfection in this manufacture that they did in their treatment of vegetable fibres and metals. Possibly the clay of the country was not of the quality to permit of their doing so, and, at all events, they were left far behind in it by other nations who in the first instance were indebted to them for the knowledge of the art; and beyond all others by the Greeks. The perfection which earthen manufacture attained in the hands of that artistic people is too wide a subject to enter on here; it will be sufficient to recall the fact that the constant effort of succeeding peoples has been directed to emulating its excellence.

The early Assyrians were not greatly distinguished in potting, notwithstanding the rich deposits of clay they possessed. Few relics of their pottery have been found at Nineveh, and those usually of an inferior kind.[1] At Babylon,[2] on the other hand, the manufacture was of "excellent quality,"[3] but does not appear to have been pursued so successfully as some other industries; while in Phœnicia, the pottery manufacture was quite overshadowed by the great fame of the glass-work. In Italy excellent ware was produced very early. That mysterious people, the

[1] Bonomi's *Nineveh*, p. 438.
[2] *Five Ancient Monarchies*, vol. i. p. 405.
[3] *Idem*, vol. ii. p. 568 ; Duncker's *History of Antiquity*, vol. i. p. 303.

Etruscans, manufactured a beautiful and singular kind of
earthenware, fragments of which still remain, and which in
several respects does not resemble any other that is known.
After contact with Greece, however, Greek art rapidly supplanted ancient Tuscan, and it is not always easy now to say
which is native art and which imported.

In India very fine pottery was early produced, and its
manufacture was general. We have elsewhere cited[1] a
passage from Sir George Birdwood, who, in a work from
which we have several times quoted, selected this as one of
the most typical of the "Industrial Arts of India," and
eloquently celebrates its antiquity and other virtues. In
Germany and Scandinavia there was no early artistic pottery.
China demands a paragraph to itself.

The highest possible antiquity is claimed for the glazed
pottery or porcelain manufacture of China;
PORCELAIN.
which country has by a curious freak of
fortune imposed its name (in our language) on that product
itself. The difference between pottery and porcelain may
be shortly expressed thus :—the one is not glazed, and the
other is, though there are many minor differences and
resemblances as well, which have, moreover, a tendency to
increase as new compositions are invented and imitated.
A more technical (and precise) way of putting the same fact
would be to say, that porcelain is distinguished from earthenware by being a partially vitrified compound. The most
perfectly *vitrified* compound is glass, from which the name,
vitrify, is derived (*vitrum*, glass). Porcelain then is a substance, as it were midway between pottery and glass. It
is necessary to insist on this distinction, as ignorance of
it has led to many historical misapprehensions on this
subject.

Careful researches have failed to show that porcelain

[1] Page 49.

proper was known at all among the great prehistoric nations ; nor to the Greeks or Romans. It seems undoubtedly to have originated in China, *when* cannot even be guessed. "The most that is known on this head," says the writer on the "Manufacture of Porcelain and Glass," in Lardner's *Cabinet Cyclopædia*, p. 104, "is gathered from the written annals of Feon-Leang, a city belonging to the same ditrict of the Empire as King-te-Ching, wherein it is recorded that, from the time answering to the year 442 of the Christian era, the last-mentioned place has enjoyed the honour of supplying the Imperial Court with porcelain, and that one or two mandarins have usually been deputed from Pekin to inspect this part of the workmen's labours." "The invention of the art," he adds, "would assuredly date from a much earlier period," and "it is a very common opinion in China that the porcelain ware made by their ancestors was superior in quality to any more recently manufactured."

In the first century of the Christian era a ware long supposed to be the real China porcelain was known in Europe, and Pliny relates of it that pieces were first brought to Rome from Pontus in Asia by the army of Pompey, 64 B.C.[1] Later researches have gone to show however that this was not porcelain at all; but that the "Vasa Murrhina" (which is the ware alluded to), were "formed out of a transparent stone dug from the earth in some of the eastern provinces of Asia."[2] A similar explanation may probably also apply to the story of Propertius, that at a very remote date this art was commonly practised in Persia, for the only other nation that is undoubtedly known to have had a very ancient manufacture of porcelain is Japan ;[3] and this may

[1] *Natural History*, Lib. XXXVII.

[2] "Porcelain and Glass," Lardner's *Cabinet Cyclopædia*, p. 7. Compare *Ancient Egyptians*, chap. vii. p. 71.

[3] See Sir Rutherford Alcock's *Art and Art Industries in Japan*, p. 193 ; also p. 190.

easily have been imported from the neighbouring continent. The Chinese porcelain is made of a clay called Kaolin, of a similar kind to some that is now found in Cornwall; and named after it China clay (used also for adding weight to cotton goods); and near Limoges in France. Its production is carried on upon a vast scale, and under the strictest regulations for ensuring secrecy. The writer on this subject in Lardner's *Cabinet Cyclopædia*, whom we have more than once quoted, thus described the establishments where porcelain is manufactured: " The factories employed at King-te-Ching for the porcelain manufactures are of great extent. They are walled round and contain sheds under which the processes are carried on, as well as dwellings for the work-men. The number of people employed in one of these factories is very great, as must appear when it is considered that almost every piece of porcelain produced, however small, passes through more than sixty different hands before it reaches a state of perfectness." In China everything is stationary, and this system of factory labour has probably been as long in existence there as the great national industries themselves. It is difficult not to infer then that the same system has been applied to those other industries, though we have not the same undoubted proof of it.

Glass is not mentioned in the Old Testament, and for GLASS. a long time it was believed to be a comparatively modern invention. Its original discovery has been variously imagined. The best known account is that of Pliny,[1] who attributes it to a fortunate accident, which may be thus described. Some sailors who had kindled a fire on the sea-coast of Phœnicia, near the mouth of the river Belus, happened to let fall into it certain bags of nitre which formed a portion of their ship's cargo. The fire fusing together the nitre and sand produced *glass*,

[1] *Hist. Nat.* XXXVI. chap. xxvi.

and the sailors, delighted with the beauty of the substance, showed it to the Sidonians inhabiting the neighbourhood, who quickly turned the discovery to advantage, and in process of time carried the art of glass-making to great perfection, transmitting the knowledge of it eventually to other nations. Unfortunately for the credit of this story, the substance in question was well known and in full use long before the supposed date of this event; and most other stories of a similar kind respecting it may be dismissed equally summarily. It is now all but universally admitted that the origin of the discovery is to be looked for in the smelting of metals; the refuse of which operation gives a kind of glass, more or less perfect according to circumstances. The story is as good as another (especially as another of Pliny's), but it is no better. The Greeks could never quite rid themselves of the belief that things quite old in the world, but new to them, were in fact discovered by them; or that at all events it was incumbent on them to invent some account of the discovery. Possibly we moderns are not wholly exempt from the same weakness. The germ of truth probably is the fact of the Sidonians having been the first, or among the first, of ancient peoples to attain proficiency in glass manufacture; and there certainly seems to be a very strong consensus of opinion in their favour on that head. But the acceptance of even this modicum of fact in the fable leads to some startling conclusions. Wilkinson distinctly asserts, and *proves*, that "as early as the reign of the first Osirtasen, *more than* 3500 *years ago at least*, the use of glass was well known to the Egyptians, and that the process of glass-blowing is represented during that monarch's reign, in the paintings of Beni Hassan, in the same manner as it is on later monuments in different parts of Egypt, to the time of the Persian Conquest."[1] It would thus seem

[1] *Ancient Egyptians*, vol. iii. p. 88.

that, unless the discovery of the art were independently
made in both places, the Egyptians must have derived it
from the Sidonians about 2000 years before the Christian
era, or not long after Nimrod is said to have established the
first stable monarchy on earth.   Nor is this all; Wilkinson
further mentions (and gives woodcuts of) glass bottles, "met
with on monuments of the fourth dynasty, dating *long before
the Osirtasens*, the representation showing the transparent
substance and the contained wine," and this kind of bottle
is found likewise figuring among the offerings to the gods;
and at the *fêtes* of individuals, alike from the earliest to
the latest times.   If then the supposed secret of the
Sidonians was already known to the Egyptians long before
4000 years ago, to what an astonishing height of antiquity
must we mount for the discovery itself in Phœnicia, and
for its communication thence!   It is on the whole easier
perhaps to believe in a separate discovery.[1]   The form of
the blowpipe, and of the bottle indicated in the pictures
referred to have a very great resemblance to those in use
now; the bottle being not perhaps quite so ugly as ours
are usually.   The fused material at the end of the tube is
coloured green to make the artist's intention unmistakable,
but the glass objects made by the Egyptians and Phœnicians
were of a great variety of colours.   They excelled especially
in the manufacture of coloured beads, and both nations carried
the imitation of precious stones to a perfection that might well
excite the envy of a Parisian (or of a Birmingham) jeweller.
It is not doubted now that many of the huge jewels
mentioned in the Bible and other ancient books were in
reality but imitations made of glass.   Some of their processes
seem to have been extremely difficult and beautiful.   They
"had the secret of introducing gold between two surfaces of

[1] Duncker says that "the making of glass was undoubtedly older in
Egypt than in Phœnicia."—*History of Antiquity*, p. 286.

glass; and in their bottles a gold band often alternates with blue, green, and other colours." Another process common in Egypt more than 3000 years ago was but lately attempted at Venice, whereby "the pattern on the surface was made to pass in right lines directly through the substance, so that if any number of horizontal sections were made through it, each one would have the same device on its upper and under surface. The skill required in this exquisite work is not only shown by the art, but the fineness of the design, for some of the feathers of birds, and other details are only to be made out with a lens, which means of magnifying was evidently used in Egypt—where this mosaic glass was made." "Indeed," say Wilkinson, "Winckelmann is of opinion that the ancients carried the art of glass-making to a higher degree of perfection than ourselves, though this may appear a paradox to those who have not seen their work in this material;" and they certainly, he adds, "used it for more purposes."[1] In Assyria, glass of a very superior kind was also produced in great quantity, but it did not equal in fame the Phœnician and Egyptian ware. Layard declares that travellers can scarcely walk any distance in the neighbourhood of where Nineveh and Babylon are supposed to have stood without stepping upon glass fragments.

The principal seat of glass-making was in later times Alexandria. The Romans, about the time of Nero, established a coarse manufacture of glass-drinking vessels at Rome, but the art made slow progress there, and ultimately perished. In the reign of Tiberius, the secret of rendering glass malleable is said to have been discovered by a Roman architect who had been banished from the city. Confiding in the importance of his discovery to procure his pardon, he returned; but the emperor taking quite a different view of

[1] For instance, for coffins! On the other hand not for windows ever, for the Egyptian houses had none.

the matter, and considering only the effect which such a
discovery would have in depreciating the value of other kinds
of glass, ordered him to be beheaded, and his secret perished
with him.   This story is somewhat differently told by Pliny,
who relates it of an artist upon whom the populace engaged
in glass-making, not the emperor, wreaked vengeance—
from, however, the same motive.

Paper proper appears undoubtedly to have been a
Chinese invention, and but comparatively
lately introduced into Europe from there.[1]
PAPER.
It will therefore more fitly form a subject for discussion
elsewhere.   But of the many substitutes in use for paper in
ancient times, this is the place to say a few words.   The
earliest mode of recording events was by carving their
history on the bare rock itself (Job. xix. 23, 24).   Afterwards on detached portions of the rock, smoothed and
shaped for the purpose.   Afterwards other hard substances
were used.   The Decalogue we know was engraved on
stone, and the ancient Egyptians and Assyrians wrote on
bricks and terra-cotta cylinders.   They also sometimes used
copper, lead, and wood.   So did the Jews, ancient Greeks,
and Persians.   The works of Hesiod, for instance, were
cut on lead; the laws of Solon on wood.   The early Arabs
used the skins and shoulder-bones of sheep; the Romans
wax tablets; and many of these methods of preserving
records and communicating ideas continued to be employed
after better substitutes were known.   The cumbrousness
of most of them would, however, obviously be a great objec-
tion always, and human ingenuity must have been very early
stimulated to supply their places with something better and
more transferable.   From the animal and mineral to the

---

[1] Casiri, in his first *Bibliotheca Arabico-Hispana*, states that paper was
first brought to Mecca in the year 88 of the Hegira (710 A.D.)   From thence
it spread to Europe.

vegetable kingdom is a natural progression, and in this domain, consequently, the next great advance was made. "Of vegetable substances," says Mr. Aikin,[1] "the first chosen would be those which Nature presents in a state fit for immediate use ; such are all those kinds of leaves which with a sufficient size possess also a certain firmness of texture to enable them to bear the action of the *style*, or other sharp-pointed instrument, by which the forms of the letters or characters are traced. In many parts of tropical Asia the leaves of various kinds of palm-trees have been used from the remotest antiquity to the present time as the common material for writing on, and the memory of this material lingers with us still in the use of the word *leaves* applied to sheets of paper when folded up in the book form. But the word "book" itself equally directs our attention to another one. The barks of certain trees were used as well as the leaves for writing on. Now the word which we pronounce "beech" was called by our Teutonic ancestors "bock," and still retains nearly the same sound in the dialects of Germany, Holland, Denmark, and Norway. Hence is derived the English word "book."[2] Similarly, the Latin word "liber," from which we derive our term "library," means the inner bark of a tree. So far, these are raw materials, but the Egyptians, with their accustomed ingenuity, very early manufactured a substance far superior to any unmanufactured one. In the swamps of Lower Egypt grew a plant which Herodotus called *biblos*, but the Latin writers *papyrus*, from which Latin form our word *paper* is derived. This plant " has a woody matted root two feet or more in thickness, from which arises a tuft of simple narrow sharp-pointed leaves, from among these push up a few upright

[1] *Arts and Manufactures*, p. 348 (Van Boorst).
[2] *Idem*, p. 350. The Greek form of book is *biblion*, from which our word Bible comes.

triangular stems, from ten to fourteen feet high, crowned by a nodding tassel of green filaments, at the base of which are the chaffy, rush-like flowers. These stems are tough, like those of the water-rush of this country, of which the bottoms of chairs are made; and in the time of Herodotus were twisted into cables for ships, and were also made into matting of which were formed the sails of vessels navigating the Nile." From this plant the material was obtained.

The mode of manufacturing the papyrus paper is thus described:—" If we cut a stem of papyrus across we shall find that the exterior green bark, which is very thin, encloses a white cellular pith containing a few longitudinal woody fibres; a texture, one would think, as ill adapted to be written on as could well be chosen among all the varieties of vegetable organisation; and, in truth, the paper made of this substance had always great defects, though for some centuries it was almost the only article employed for this use in the Roman Empire. The rolls of manuscript found at Herculaneum appear to be all of papyrus, and from Pliny and other classical writers it is clear that the manufacture of paper was one of the most important of those carried on in Egypt and Rome. The following was the process : The fresh stem being cut into pieces about a foot or a little more in length was stripped of its bark, which, as I know from experiment on a stem of papyrus grown in a stove in England, peels off very easily. The pith was then cut down longitudinally into sometimes fewer, but never more than twenty slices; of these the middle ones, as being the widest, were reserved for the best paper, and the others were formed into three or four sorts according to their width. A table was wetted with the muddy, glutinous water of the Nile, and a row of slices was laid down on it, each slice touching, probably a little overlapping, the adjacent ones. This first layer was then crossed by a second one of inferior quality, and the leaf thus formed was put under a press in order to consolidate and dry all the parts; finally, it was dried in the sunshine. As the papyrus could not be sliced except when fresh cut, the Roman paper-makers, of whom one Fannius in the reign of Augustus was the most celebrated, confined their attention to the remanufacture of the paper as imported from Alexandria. Paper of the fourth quality (called Amphitheatrica) was preferred for this purpose. It was in the first place entirely taken to pieces, and then put together again with a looser texture, flour paste with a little vinegar being the cement most generally employed, but for the very finest sort boiling water was poured on crumb of bread and strained from it when cold. The leaf was then beaten carefully with a mallet in order to extend all the slices evenly, and to bring them in contact, it was then a second time brushed over with size, and a second time beaten, after which it was pressed and dried; lastly, it was polished by rubbing with a dog's tooth or smooth shell."[1]

Varro, quoted by Pliny (*Hist. Nat.* XIII. xxii.), considers the use of papyrus as a material for writing on not to have commenced till after the time of Alexander the Great; but Wilkinson asserts, on the contrary, that "Papyri written upon were common in the age of Suphis or Cheops, the builder of the Great Pyramid,"[2] *i.e.* about 2000 years before Alexander's time. The later writer is far more likely to be right. We also gather from the same eminent authority that its manufacture was a special government monopoly, and that consequently its price was very high. It was only used for documents of great importance. For ordinary purposes, earthenware, stone, wood, leather, etc., continued to be employed. Parchment, long supposed to have been invented by Eumenes, King of Pergamos (250

---

[1] *Arts and Manufactures*, p. 357 *et seq.*   [2] Vol. ii. p. 98.

B.C.) is also proved now to have been in use centuries
before his time; certainly in Egypt, and probably in Assyria.
The last-named material (parchment) should be more
properly included among animal substances,
LEATHER.   in the treatment of which the great nations
of antiquity were so highly skilled. The dressing of skins
was naturally and necessarily one of the earliest manufactures in the world. It was also one of those that was
early carried to the greatest perfection. It may be doubted
if we have in subsequent times ever reached the degree of
excellence in the treatment of leather that was reached by
the great nations of antiquity. Their system of manufacture, too, and their appliances, were in this case nearly
exactly the same as ours. On the monuments of Egypt
every process of tanning and leather-making is represented
with perfect distinctness, and "the tanner may be seen
sitting amid his pits, surrounded by tools much as they are
still used at the present day" (*Industrial Curiosities*, by A.
H. Japp, LL.D.,[1] chap. "Leather"). Nor can his work have
been wanting in that best quality of workmanship—per-
manence: "In the British Museum real tanned sandals are
to be seen, such as are known from paintings and sculptures
to have been worn in Egypt 3000 years ago."

The Israelites carried away a knowledge of the leather
manufacture with them in their flight from Egypt (2 Kings
i. 8); and the classical nations were very familiar with it.
It was one, indeed, very widely spread. It is curious to
note, then, that it seems always to have suffered under a
sort of stigma. The tanners in Thebes were confined to a
particular part of the city; those in Jerusalem were not
allowed to carry on their occupation within its precincts;
and in both Greek and Roman cities special quarters were
assigned to the followers of this trade. Whether the reason

[1] Fisher Unwin, 1882.

for this stigma was of a supposed sanitary kind, or of a religious kind, we do not know, but it was probably of either. An important result was, that this industry does not appear to have been carried on in government establishments, like so many others, but to have been always in the hands of individuals; and it is said to have been the one in which workmen, associated together in trade societies, were first employed. Now these must have been free workmen. It follows, then, that ancient tanyards — perhaps the tanyards even of ancient Egypt—were conducted upon a principle *in all respects* similar to the modern factory system [1] —that is, by associated free labour in establishments of definite bounds.

[1] Tanyards are classed as factories or workshops by our present statute law according as to whether manual only or other motive power is employed in the manufacture; and in either case they are subject to our factory system of regulation.

12

CHAPTER V.

THE portion of history commonly called the Middle Ages embraces a period of about a thousand years, between the fifth and the fifteenth centuries, or from the subversion of the western Roman Empire (476 A.D.) to the discovery of America (1492 A.D.)[1] It is a period of great gloom and stagnation so far as those countries are concerned in whose history and prosperity we are at the present time most interested, and especially in relation to the subject-matter of this work. The great nations of early antiquity and of the classical age, and the stupendous political and social systems that they had inaugurated and maintained, had then passed away, and their places were occupied by unknown hordes of rude conquerors issuing from unexplored regions of the North, and by a complete confusion of all relations—social, political, and industrial. The arts and manufactures which had been so highly prized by them, and in their hands brought to such perfection, were scornfully ignored or recklessly contemned by these invaders; they either perished

THE MIDDLE AGES.

[1] From "the invasion of France by Clovis to that of Naples by Charles VIII.," according to Hallam (*Middle Ages*, chap. ix. part i.)

wholly, or where they survived at all, did so fitfully, at long intervals of time and place, and under altered conditions of production and exchange. A new deluge, but this time confined to the social order, overflowed the civilised world, and once again everything was in confusion, and once again a new start had to be made. The Middle Ages supplied the period of incubation that was necessary to this new start. It was requisite, first, that the disintegrating processes in past systems should be carried to their ultimate developments ; and next, that the germs of future systems should be set. For such a purpose the interval of a thousand years' duration, more or less, need not seem an unreasonably long one in view of the prodigious past that was done with, and the portentous future that was in store. Accordingly, within that time, the change from ancient to modern history ran its course ; and it is ordinarily remarked of the Middle Ages that, for about one-half its span—say to the tenth or eleventh century—the industrial tendency was ever downwards, and that from about then symptoms of the new birth were seen. The sixth, seventh, and eighth centuries witnessed, perhaps, the lowest depth of this declension; and the next three—including, as they did, the establishment of the Saracen power in Europe, the Crusades, the foundation of the commercial greatness of the Italian republics, and the remarkable development of trade and industry in north-western Europe which eventuated in the establishment of the Hanse League—first began to set a term to it.

For a better comprehension of these and earlier industrial changes we propose to consider very briefly in this place the principal routes taken by commerce whilst they were in progress.

MOVEMENTS OF COMMERCE.

The direction of commercial routes determines very largely the localisation of industry, as the localisation of industries determines very largely the direction of commercial routes.

Those causes act and react upon each other in a way it is not
difficult to point out, and are themselves the results of several
other causes whose influences, though more remote, are very
familiar factors in human things. From among the latter
set of causes that greatly influence the progress of industry
or commerce, three principal ones may be isolated as specially
operative. The first is a settled and free government; the
second a convenient maritime situation; the third the
possession of appropriate raw material for trade and manufacture. We shall have occasion to refer to these severally
as we trace the main routes of commerce at various times.
We shall find that, though often in union, and indeed inextricably intermixed, they are sometimes found separate, and
that their separate operation is usually most efficient at very
different epochs. In the infancy of society, for instance, while
navigation is yet an unfamiliar art, it is the third, modified
by obvious topographical considerations, that commonly counts
for most; and thus fertile valleys—both on account of the
material they provide for sustenance and trade, and the ready
ingress and egress they allow—are naturally the first centres of
industry, and the easiest paths leading between them are the
first highways of commerce. The most ancient commerce
on record was conducted accordingly from such centres and
along such routes; the most practicable routes, namely, that
led to the three great valleys of the Euphrates, Nile, and
Indus. Afterwards, however, when the superior highway of
the sea becomes available, internal trade is increasingly
abandoned, and the movements of commerce, and, therefore,
the localising of industry, are more affected by the greater or
less proximity to a seaboard. Thus, in the classical age, the
industrious nations are found clustering round the shores of
the Mediterranean; and we may afterwards note prosperity
following pretty generally the coast-line all over the world.
Ultimately, with land and sea both fully available, the char-

acters of the traders themselves, and of their institutions, are the matters of greatest moment; which is the condition at the present day over a great part of the world.

If we choose for purposes of convenience to consider ancient Babylon ("a land of traffick . . . a city of merchants," Ezek. xvii. 4) as the commercial centre for the post-diluvian pre-historic period, we can easily trace two great principal caravan routes leading eastward and westward from it which practically traversed all the then known world, and along which manufacturing industry spread itself.[1] The first led through Persia to India, by way of Balk, Kashmir, Kandahar, and the country now called Afghanistan, to the valley of the Indus; and how much farther southward is unknown, but possibly to the farthest point of the peninsula. It gave off a branch eastwards towards China on the way, by Bokara and northern Thibet, or met other caravan routes from those countries somewhere near there. The geographical considerations that would approve such a route are as obvious now as formerly; for the physical formation of the country remains the same; and of the industrial ones it may be enough to say, that even after this immense lapse of time some remnants of old trade still cling to the same mountain passes. The merchandise that passed along them in those days would be costly and various. " From Kandahar and Kashmir fine wool, and the shawls which are still so highly valued . . . emeralds, jaspers, and other precious stones from the desert of Bactria . . . cochineal, or rather the Indian lac . . . gold and gold-dust;"[2] cotton and perhaps silk; and in return, from Babylon, " articles of luxury, such as perfumed waters, carved walking canes, engraved stones, seal rings," and the like—special Babylonian manufactures,—

---

[1] A much fuller list of caravan routes is given by Mr. Rawlinson in *Egypt and Babylon*, p. 138.   [2] *Student's Manual of Ancient History*, p. 71.

besides, no doubt, textile fabrics and the materials for their
manufacture from Egypt or Assyria; food stuffs from various
parts; and glass from the Phœnician manufactories.   The
western route is no less easy to identify.   It took first a
northerly direction to Tauris (Tabreez), dividing afterwards
into two branches, one entering Syria, the other passing
through Armenia and Asia Minor to Scythia, Sarmatia,
and the distant countries beyond.   The Syrian road again
divided.   One branch led to the great maritime industrial
cities of Phœnicia (Tyre, Sidon, Sarepta, etc.), from whence
there was communication by water to all the countries
round the Mediterranean; the other passed by the north
of Arabia to Egypt, through Idumea (or Edom), by its
celebrated commercial capital Petra.   It was to divert some
part of this traffic from that route and secure it for Palestine
that Solomon caused the splendid cities of Baalbec and
Palmyra (the ruins of which still remain) to be built in the
midst of the Syrian desert.   In Petra there would be
accumulated for exchange the rich produce of southern
Arabia, before this came to be despatched to Europe and the
East, as in later times, by the Red Sea and Persian Gulf.
This ancient Arabian trade, so interesting in all its associations,
has been thus happily described:[1]—"From Yemen, called
Arabia the Happy, the southern division of the Arabian
peninsula, caravans brought through the desert frankincense,
myrrh, cassia, gold, and precious stones, the gold being
probably obtained from the opposite shores of Africa.   But
before the Phœnicians had a port on the Red Sea they
obtained also through Asia the produce of southern India
and Africa, more especially cinnamon, ivory, and ebony."
This trade is also alluded to by Ezekiel;[2] and "it will be

---

[1] The modern authority on this subject is generally Heeren.   *A Manual
of Ancient History*, by A. H. L. Heeren (Oxford, 1829); *Historical Researches*,
etc.   The quotations here are mostly from the *Student's Manual of Ancient
History*, which adopts generally Heeren's views.   [2] xxvii. 19-23.

seen that some of the trading cities mentioned retain their
names at the present day." Thus[1] "Wedan and Javan
(probably cities near the straits of Bab-el-Mandeb) brought
thee from Uzal (the district of Sanaa) wrought iron, cassia,
and cinnamon, in exchange for thy wares. Dedan (one of
the Baharein islands in the Persian Gulf) was thy merchant
in precious clothes for chariots. Arabia and all the princes
of Kedar (the nomad tribes of northern Arabia) were the
merchants of thy land in lambs, and rams, and goats: in
these were thy merchants. The merchants of Sheba (Saba
or Mariaba) and Raamah (an Arabian city on the Persian
Gulf), they were thy merchants; they occupied in thy fairs
with chief of all spices, and with all precious stones and
gold. Haran and the merchants of Asshur and Chilmad
(Arabian tribes) were thy traffickers. These were thy merchants in all sorts of things, in blue clothes, and broidered
work, and in chests of rich apparel, bound with cords, and
made of cedar, among thy merchandise." Passing westwards
from Idumea, the southern route next lay through Sinai
into Lower Egypt, and thence through Middle Egypt to
Thebes. Here it met the great African caravan routes from
the east, south, and west, and at this vast emporium the
treasures of Asia and Africa would be exchanged. The
produce of this trade is pretty well known to us from the
paintings on the ancient Egyptian monuments, and through
many references in the Bible. It included gold, iron, ebony,
ivory, and skins; slaves from Ethiopia and the negro countries;
corn, flax, linen, and leather goods from Egypt itself; perhaps
cotton from India (by way of Abyssinia and Meröe); glass
and dyed woollen stuffs from Sidon and Tyre; and horses,
mules, and furs from the countries north of the Caspian.

The prime requisites of this caravan traffic were:—in the
mountains, a road to travel along; in the desert, water; and

---

[1] *Student's Manual of Ancient History*, p. 86.

in both cases occasional halting-places (called caravansaries). These halting-places would be formed at suitable points, generally where several roads converged, and here, while the beasts were resting, portions of their burdens might often be unpacked and exchanged for other merchandise, likewise brought from a distance, and such caravansaries come thus in time to develop into places of considerable trade, some-times into important villages, and even into important towns. They would become "marts."[1] A resident population would after a while grow up in them, whose function, at first only to provide accommodation for the incoming caravans, might develop at length into negotiating the exchanges, and transacting the business of the travellers. Occasion-ally the population thus gathered together would in the intervals between the arrivals of their customers take to industrial work themselves, and the place would become a manufacturing as well as a trading centre. At other times its greatness would remain wholly dependent on the carrying trade, and an alteration of trade routes would ruin its pros-perity at once. The situation and vicissitudes of some great cities of antiquity, often seemingly inexplicable, are easily accounted for in this way, and we have a near parallel in our own times since the introduction of the railway system, prin-cipally applicable, indeed, in new countries, but often visible in England too. Places which a short time since were railway junctions and nothing more, may often be noted rising now into quite considerable towns, from the same circumstance of their favourable situation as centres for converging routes.

Quite other determining influences are brought into play where commerce is by sea, and in the most ancient history that is familiar to us the change from land to sea traffic was first made at the instance of the Phœnicians. Neither the

ANCIENT MARITIME COMMERCE.

[1] See p. 15.

ancient Egyptians nor Babylonians were addicted to the sea, nor had ever for any lengthened period of their history much native commerce that way. When, occasionally, in the dim and confused records of their early trade, we meet with what appear to be spasmodic exceptions to this rule, we usually find also that they come as the result of an impulse from without, and that the traffic itself was in the hands of strangers. Even in their later history the same peculiarity continues noticeable. The palmy days of maritime commerce in the later history of both those great countries— the days of the Ptolemies in Egypt, and of the Caliphs in Bagdad—occurred under the rule of aliens. Many reasons might be assigned for this fact, among them those already ·instanced as so much determining the normal direction of commerce and industry, *i.e.* the natural productions and geographical situations of the countries, and the national character and institutions of their inhabitants. The great despotisms of Egypt and Assyria were unfavourable to individual enterprise, which is the soul of maritime adventure ; and the enormously fertile valleys in which those old civilisations were established, supplying as they did all chief requisites for the satisfaction of human wants, removed from their occupants any great incentive to external trade. In India, where the early conformation of society was more democratic, the case should have been different, but unfortunately we know absolutely nothing of ancient Indian commerce. In China the position was much the same as in Egypt, as it remains to the present day. With respect to the Hebrew race again; with whose early history we are the most familiar ; they do not appear to have taken more kindly to maritime adventure than to manufacture.[1] Not the utmost efforts of their greatest rulers, David and Solomon, could make them a sea-loving people ; and they have retained

[1] Compare chap. iii. p. 109.

even to the present day this characteristic, through every change of destiny. During one brief and brilliant epoch of their history we do indeed find them engaged in a lucrative and extensive trade, and as this is the very earliest maritime commerce of which any accounts, however insufficient, exist, we shall examine what is known of it in some detail.

David was the first to begin, or at all events to largely develop, this commerce, B.C. 1040. Having about that time subdued the Edomites (2 Sam. viii. 14), he came into possession of two important seaports on the Red Sea, Elath and Eziongeber, which had been previously in their possession. From these the trade was carried on. It was principally, we shall here consider it exclusively, that mysterious one with Ophir and Tarshish, of which we are told so much in Scripture, and the localising of which has so sorely exercised the minds of Scripture commentators for so many centuries. The identity of these two places has never been quite satisfactorily settled. In a former chapter (chap. iv.) we have assigned Tarshish to Spain, and this is now the all but universal opinion about it; but where was Ophir? and how were both it and Tarshish approached from the Red Sea? Where was Ophir? An almost infinite variety of answers has been given to this question. Ophir was in Arabia, was on the east coast of Africa, on the west coast of Africa, was on the coast of India, was one of the East Indian islands, was the Malay Peninsula, was the island of Madagascar, was the island of Ceylon: these are but a few specimens of such replies. But Ophir is found constantly united in trade enterprises with Tarshish, which is in precisely the opposite direction from any of these places, and they are spoken of as if they were both accessible in one voyage. How can that be? The way to Tarshish was by the Mediterranean,

(margin note: HEBREW COMMERCE: OPHIR.)

not by the Red Sea; the way to Ophir (on almost any hypothesis) was by the Red Sea, not by the Mediterranean. There is only one way in which in a single sea voyage they could both be visited, namely, by circumnavigating Africa. Must we believe then that in those extremely early times that great feat was actually accomplished? There is not in the whole history of ancient commerce any problem of greater fascination or of superior interest to this one. The subject may be found very fully discussed in Bell's [1] edition of Rollin's *Ancient History*, and later writers have added very little indeed to the authorities and facts that are there accumulated. One notable suggestion is, that the name Ophir was a generic one, applying rather to a particular ·trade than to a particular place;[2] and others scarcely less ingenious are hazarded. It is clearly impossible for us here to take any considerable part in this great argument. Wherever Ophir was, or whether there were but one Ophir, or several, or that the name was but a corrupted one of the similarly sounding name Africa, or whatever the true explanation may be, it is clear that this trade was both extensive and lucrative in no ordinary degree; for it was a prime factor in procuring for Solomon that vast wealth for which he was then and ever after so celebrated. Had his degenerate successors retained it, their subsequent history, and that of the ancient world, might have been very different.

---

[1] That writer concludes unmistakably that the fleets of David and Solomon, manned by Phœnician sailors, lent by Hiram, King of Tyre, did circumnavigate Africa a thousand years before the Christian era; 400 years before it was also circumnavigated by Egyptian vessels, again manned by Phœnician sailors under Pharaoh Necho; and about 2500 years before the passage round was rediscovered by Vasco de Gama (1498 A.D.) The time taken was three years (2 Chron. ix. 21), and the ships that went by the Red Sea returned by the Mediterranean, and *vice versâ*.

[2] This is the opinion of the learned Bochart. See Rollin's *Ancient History*, with Notes and Supplements by James Bell, vol. iii. p. 75 (Glasgow: Blackie and Co., 1828).

But they had not the spirit or energy to do so; and after Solomon's time it passed through various hands and suffered much decay, being now in possession again of the Edomites; now again for a short time of the Jews; then for a little while of the Syrians; till at length the Phœnicians, who had after all the best right, succeeded in engrossing to themselves what remained of it for many years. In later times, under the Ptolemies, rival ports were built upon the Red Sea, and much of this trade was diverted to Egypt, while the remainder (after the destruction of Tyre) gravitated principally to Ephesus, Alexandria, and Constantinople respectively, where it rested until the Saracens forced it into a new channel, of which Bagdad and its port Bussora were the principal emporiums. How ultimately, in the hands of Portuguese, it re-entered its old channels, and passed from them to the Dutch, and from the Dutch to us, belongs to the history of modern commerce.

The Hebrew ships engaged in the trade with Ophir were manned then by Phœnician navigators (1 THE PHŒNICIANS. Kings ix. 27; 2 Chron. viii. 18), and the Phœnicians succeeded to it themselves at length. In the meanwhile they were pursuing a similarly adventurous career towards the west and north. Commencing with the nearer shores and islands of the Mediterranean and gradually working their way westwards, their ships early (how early it is even difficult to guess)[1] passed the pillars of Hercules and steered out into the Atlantic Ocean. On their way they left colonies, and founded important industries wherever they went; and some of these colonies became nations, and some of those industries have not even now quite deserted the localities where prehistoric judgment placed them.

[1] Duncker (*History of Antiquity*) places it "at least 1100 B.C.;" Bell (Rollin's *Ancient History*) even earlier, namely, 1240 B.C.

Cyprus was one of the earliest of these colonies ; Carthage was the most important. They had important settlements from a very early date also at Crete, Sicily, and Sardinia ; at several places on the coast of Italy, and at Gades (Cadiz) in Spain. From Spain they made their way to the coasts of Gaul and Britain,[1] and probably, though not certainly, as far north as those of Prussia and Denmark. From these latter countries they obtained, either directly or through intermediaries, amber ; from Britain tin ;[2] productions on which an enormous value was set in those times ; and in return they taught the wild natives of those rugged coasts some of the arts of civilised life. From Spain they appear to have procured immense riches ; the mineral resources of that country being then, as now, extraordinarily great. These they shipped eastwards, where the demand for metals has been unremitting at all times, and procured in return an abundance of the necessaries and luxuries of life, which their own limited and more sterile climate yielded only in small quantity. It was characteristic of the Phœnicians, as of their immediate descendants the Carthaginians, to be very jealous traders, and to guard with infinite care the secrets of where were situated those distant countries to which they resorted. Instances are recorded of their trading ships courting imminent peril rather than a rival should follow them,[3] and the utmost caution was exercised always in this respect. It is certain too that they purposely spread false descriptions and reports of places frequented by their merchants in order to mislead others ; and it is probably to this cause more than any other that we should attribute the mystery in which all their western commerce is shrouded. That mystery was designed, and it is almost beyond hope now to ever fully pierce it.

[1] Strabo, Lib. III.   [2] Compare chap. iv. p. 150.
[3] A story of this kind is told by Strabo.

The Carthaginians were the legitimate successors of the
Phœnicians in the maritime supremacy of
THE CARTHAGINIANS.
the ancient world ; and they emulated them
alike in their commercial virtues and vices. They were
equally enterprising, jealous, and ruthless. They are said
to have put to death all strangers who wandered into those
possessions of theirs which they wished kept to themselves ;
and they pirated the goods, and even persons, of others, as
the Phœnicians had done from time immemorial, and as
the Greeks indeed were doing with little less avidity much
about the same time. They were adepts at driving a hard
bargain ; but, if we are to believe their enemies (from whom
alone our knowledge of them is drawn), not very scrupulous
in adhering to one. The imputation of " punic faith " in a
derogatory sense became proverbial. No more is known for
certain of their general commerce than of that of the
Phœnicians ; but fragmentary notices of the voyages of two
celebrated Carthaginian navigators, Himilco and Hanno, have
been preserved,[1] which throw some light on it. The former
of these seems to have rediscovered Britain ; the latter
sailed southward along the African coast and explored great
portions of it, returning the same way. The dates of those
voyages are unknown, but they were certainly undertaken
before the Carthaginians came into conflict with the Romans.
The new markets for their goods thus opened greatly
increased their prosperity and power, to the extent that
they even bade fair at one time to become masters of
the civilised world. But a new state across the Mediterranean was now aspiring to that position, and the inevitable
conflict which came at last resulted in their complete overthrow. That conflict was with Rome. The Carthaginians
were dependent in it upon foreign mercenaries, and, though
these were splendidly led, they failed against the troops of a

[1] By Polybius, Festus Avienus, and others.

people that scorned alike trade and leisure, and took to war as a profession and a pastime. After a prolonged agony Carthage was razed to the ground, and so completely destroyed that scarcely a vestige of it now remains. Its glory, commerce, and industry passed away from it not to return again.

We may take the era of Carthaginian maritime supremacy as the most proper one to consider ancient commerce as decisively tending to be diverted from the old overland caravan routes into the wider channel of maritime trade ; and as that wherein manufacturing industry, following in its steps, began definitely to desert the great inland valleys for countries with a convenient seaboard.

The commerce of classical times is a matter exceedingly difficult to deal with. The maritime commerce of the Greeks and Romans was principally confined to the eastern Mediterranean CLASSICAL COMMERCE. and Black Seas, though the Romans during their later history benefited by a far wider one in the hands of colonies and dependencies. That which the Greeks as a people possessed, again, they enjoyed less in their corporate capacity than as an assemblage of petty states, each carrying on an independent traffic of its own. The bond of union in this confederacy was politically weak, however strong commercially, and was liable at all times to violent disruptions, with their usual concomitants of sudden antagonisms and indiscriminate reprisals. Greek commerce thus early acquired, and long retained, a rather evil reputation, the imputation of piracy clinging to it with suspicious tenacity for many centuries. The principal commercial cities of Greece proper were Athens and Corinth ; the first being the most powerful, especially after the completion of the long walls uniting the adjoining seaport (Piræus) with the city, which were built at the instigation of Themistocles. Its principal trade was in grain,

which came in great quantities from Egypt, Palestine, and
the countries round the Black Sea, to supplement a native
growth insufficient for the support of an abounding population. Corinth ranked next to Athens, though indeed it
enjoyed at one time for a brief space a period of perhaps
even greater prosperity. Situated on the isthmus of the
same name, with harbours both on the Saronic and Corinthian
Gulfs, facing that is both east and west, it commanded two
seas, and was the connecting link between them. Thus
advantageously placed it became, after the fall of Tyre, the
chief emporium where the products of the East and West
were exchanged; and manufacture following as usual in the
steps of commerce, it was quickly advanced to the position
of the greatest industrial centre in Europe. It was greatly
renowned in ancient times for the production of a peculiar
kind of bronze (" Corinthian brass "), but was also then, and
for long afterwards, largely engaged in textile industry.
It fell the same year as Carthage (146 B.C.), being
then utterly ruined by the Roman general Mummius;
from which date what Grecian commerce remained is to be
found among the settlements of the various branches of
the Greek people. The principal of these settlements
were: Miletus, Phocæa, Ephesus, and Smyrna, in Asia
Minor; and elsewhere in the Mediterranean, Syracuse and
Marseilles. There were, however, many more. If Macedonia
is to be reckoned in this connection as a part of Greece,
we must at all events include Alexandria. The history
of Greece is not a commercial history; but wherever its
commerce penetrated, it brought a civilising and refining
spirit with it, and spread a love of knowledge and freedom;
and its eminence in manufacture long remained. The
Romans, who succeeded to its power, were not a commercial
people either. In their earlier history they took, indeed,
scarcely any part in commerce; and it was only when, in

their ever-increasing round of conquests, great commercial
States were brought under their sway that these interests
came to be, as it were, forced upon them. Then, indeed
they set themselves with their usual spirit and energy to
turn those interests to their advantage, and reaped a rich
harvest in the act.

The lines of ancient commerce both by land and sea had
by that time changed considerably. The
old supremacy of Babylon and Egypt had   LATER EGYPTIAN
fallen with the Persian and Macedonian   COMMERCE.
conquests, the great trade of the former being mainly transferred to the flourishing Greek colonies in Asia Minor and
Syria, whilst that of the latter had been restored to Egypt
under changed conditions, and was now centred in its new
maritime capital which the genius of Alexander the Great
had called into being.   Alexandria was built designedly
as the successor of Tyre, and after Corinth fell it entered
pretty fully into its projected inheritance.   It retained its
pre-eminence longer too than any of its rivals; and under
every variety of fortune remained a great mart until towards
quite the close of the Middle Ages.   But its period of
greatest prosperity was in the age of the Ptolemies.   These
enlightened monarchs invited colonists from every quarter
of the globe to settle at Alexandria, and the Jews especially
availing themselves of this invitation, came there in great
numbers.   They brought of course their usual keen pursuit
of business, and skill in money-making with them, and the
city was greatly enriched in consequence.   It was in the
reign of Ptolemy II., however, that the later ancient Egyptian commerce made the most rapid strides.   This monarch
greatly encouraged it.   " Ports for the Indian and Arabian
trade were constructed on the Red Sea, at Arsinöe (Suez),
Myos Hormus (Cosseir), and Berenice.   From the two latter
stations caravan roads were made to the Upper Nile, and

the lower river was united to the Red Sea by a canal which was farther continued to the lesser harbour of Alexandria, on the Marœotic lake. The Ethiopian trade was revived with great spirit, and remote countries of central and southern Africa were opened to the enterprise of the Alexandrian merchants."[1]   This prosperity continued, with somewhat diminishing splendour, during the reigns of the succeeding Ptolemies, and was still existent when, after the defeat of Cleopatra by Augustus Cæsar (30 B.C.), the whole country was turned into a Roman province.

From that time for the next three or four centuries the Roman Empire was not only the greatest commercial power in the world but one of the greatest the world has ever seen.   Its commerce extended east and west, by sea and land, in almost sole possession, over a vast and well-governed territory.   It was encouraged by judicious laws and customs and regulated with consummate skill.   An era of general tranquillity had followed a succession of periods of almost uninterrupted warfare.   In the time of Augustus Cæsar, as we know, "all the world was at peace."   This general peace lasted for the greater part of three centuries, being many times broken indeed by expeditions to distant lands, but never during that time by wars of the first magnitude involving the stoppage of commercial relations among the civilised countries of the world.   All these countries vied with one another too during that time in pouring their choicest productions into the lap of Rome.   Here was the final haven for vessels coming from all quarters of the earth where trade had yet been born ; and here the terminus of every land route. The great city stood absolutely without a rival.   The saying that "all roads lead to Rome," if it owed to that time its origin, expressed no more than was literally true.   Not only

IMPERIAL ROME.

---

[1] *Student's Manual of Ancient History*, p. 329.

was the number of ships that approached the capital prodigious, but the latter was connected with every portion
of the empire by magnificent land highways, the marvel
of modern engineers.   These roads, says Gibbon, "were
accurately divided by milestones, and ran in a direct line
from one city to another," and some notion of the extent
of ground they traversed may be formed from the fact
that, "the great chain of communication from the north-
west to the south-east point of the empire was drawn out
to the length of 4080 Roman miles."[1]   A still more vivid
impression perhaps of the extent of imperial Roman commerce, and a good idea meanwhile of the directions taken
by trade routes at this most brilliant period (that of the
Antonines), may be gathered from the following quotation
from the *Student's Manual of Ancient History*, pp. 520-523,
a work to which we have already in this chapter been so much
indebted.   It deals with both the land and sea traffic.   With
a few curtailments the passage is as follows :—" Tadmor, or
Palmyra, the wondrous city of the desert, distant only eighty-
five miles from the Euphrates, and about one hundred and
seventeen from the nearest coast of the Mediterranean, was
the centre of the trade between Europe and southern Persia,
including the countries bordering on the Indus, and the
districts now attached to the Bombay presidency.   In consequence of the great exports that this trade naturally caused
from the harbours of the Levant, great numbers of Syrian
merchants settled in Rome, some of whom attained the
highest honours of the state.   It would appear that some
merchants used a more northern route by the Caspian and
Oxus, for we find the Roman geographers tolerably well
acquainted with the countries that now form the kingdoms
of Khiva and Bokhara.   The great caravan route across
Asia, however, commenced at Byzantium, which was long

[1] *Decline and Fall of the Roman Empire*, vol. i. p. 67, Variorum Edition (Bohn).

the seat of a flourishing commerce before it became the
metropolis of an empire. Having passed the Bosphorus, the
merchant adventurers proceeded through Anatolia, and crossed
the Euphrates near Hierapolis; thence they proceeded to
Ecbatana, the ancient capital of the Medes, and Hecatompylos,
the metropolis of the Parthians. Thence they proceeded
circuitously to Hyrcania and Aria (Herat). Finally they
came to Bactra, long the principal mart of central Asia.
From Bactra there were two caravan routes, one to northern
India, over the western part of the Himalaya . . . the
other towards the frontiers of Serica (China), over the lofty
mountain chain of Imaus." Here we find the ancient
caravan trade between Europe and Asia still in something
like its pristine vigour. Of the maritime trade between Asia
and Africa, and onwards to Europe, we have the following
notice—"The navigation was long confined to circuitous
voyages round the peninsula of Arabia and the coasts of
the Persian Gulf; but about a century after the establishment of the Roman dominion, Harpalus, the commander of
a ship long engaged in the Indian trade, observing the regular
changes of the periodical winds, ventured to steer right across
the Erythæan Sea (or Indian Ocean), and was wafted by
the western monsoon to the Malabar coast. This great
improvement was deservedly regarded as of the highest
importance, and the western monsoon received the name
of Harpalus in memory of the courageous navigator who
had turned it to such good account." The portion of this
trade that now passed by way of Egypt is thus described:
"Cargoes destined for India were carried up the Nile in
boats to Coptos; thence they were transferred by caravans to
Myos Hormus (Cosseir), or Berenice (Hubbesh). The latter,
though the longer, was the more frequented route, because the
Ptolemies had raised excellent stations and watering-places
at convenient distances along the road. From Berenice the

fleet sailed in June or July for Ocelis at the mouth of the Arabian Gulf, and Cané, a promontory and emporium on the south-east coast of Arabia Felix. Thence they steered right across the ocean for the Malabar coast, and usually made Musiris in forty days. They began their voyages homeward early in December, and generally encountered more difficulty on their return on account of the unsteadiness of the winds." Farther north a shifting of trade routes was equally apparent. " The trade of the Black Sea, so flourishing in the age of the Greek republics, appears to have been greatly diminished after the Romans became masters of the countries at both sides of the Ægean ; and it seems probable that little or no commerce passed through the straits of Hercules (Gibraltar) into the Atlantic Ocean. In consequence of this change the amber trade was transferred from the coasts of the Northern Sea to the banks of the Danube, and the barbarous tribes who brought it from the shores of the Baltic are said to have been astonished at the prices they received for what seemed to them so useless a commodity." Furs were at the same time purchased from the Scythian tribes, and tin brought from Britain, but the last apparently not just then to any great extent.

Such was the great commercial prosperity of this age and state, and it was in no small degree from amongst those very sources of prosperity that the impending destruction was prepared. The barbarians—a remote cause of alarm when all knowledge of them was confined to secret voyages to mysterious lands, and barterings on the edges of impenetrable forests,— became a very present and urgent cause of anxiety when they manifested a desire, as they began to do, to follow their customers home, and to give them the benefit of their company as well as of their trade. The merchants, who had consistently pillaged them to the best of their ability, had by no means bargained for this nearer acquaintance, and much resented it. The whole Roman people resented it no less. But they were enervated by luxury, overweighted with their huge sovereignty, and when the contest became really critical it could have but one issue. For a century or so previous to the final catastrophe the intruders were with difficulty kept at bay, and then the effort could be sustained no longer. Rome was taken and sacked; was plundered again and again; its prosperity passed away, the whole old world passed away with it, and the curtain went down for another act in the huge drama of history to be prepared.

The foregoing sketch of Imperial Roman Commerce shows the great trade routes of the world both CONSTANTINOPLE. by sea and land much changed from the time of either Babylonian or Carthaginian supremacy, and still greater changes were impending. For several succeeding centuries, however, it is not easy to discern the course of these. The Roman power in the west had been by that time completely and finally overthrown, and in the east had entered upon that long struggle by which it maintained itself with ever-increasing difficulty for still another thousand years. In the year 330 Constantine transferred the seat of government from Rome to Byzantium, from that time generally called Constantinople, and in another century and a half the western Roman Empire was gone, and the great commerce that had flourished so exceedingly under its wide and stable dominion was gone with it. The new conquerors of Italy were little concerned at this loss. Fresh from the swamps and forests of the north, the Teutonic tribes found too many unaccustomed luxuries in the rich countries that they conquered to think at first of trafficking for more, and were well content instead to settle down to rest in those sunny southern lands, after their long marches and sanguinary fights. A cloud of almost impenetrable darkness invests accordingly the commerce and industry of western Europe for the next few centuries. It is other-

wise with the new capital of the East. Situated on a
point of land where Europe and Asia met, and on the
beautiful waters of the Bosphorus, uniting therefore the
two most important of inland seas, Byzantium seemed from
the first destined by nature for the great fate that awaited
her; and it came in full splendour to her as the successor
of Rome. Acknowledging no doubt some worthy rivals
even then, Alexandria the chief, but also Antioch in Syria,
and Miletus and Ephesus in Asia Minor, Constantinople
was undoubtedly throughout the first half of the Middle
Ages the principal centre of commerce and industry. This
proud position she owed almost wholly, however, to external advantages. Her inhabitants were, and have continued to be for the most part, unenergetic and unenter-
prising, and it is rather as a great mart therefore than as a
great commercial capital that she is celebrated in industrial
history. " When the gates of the Hellespont and Bosphorus
were shut," says Gibbon,[1] " the capital still enjoyed within
their spacious enclosure every production which could supply
the wants or gratify the luxury of its inhabitants. The sea
coasts of Thrace and Bithynia, which languish under the
weight of Turkish oppression, still exhibit a rich prospect of
vineyards, of gardens, and of plentiful harvests; and the
Propontis has ever been renowned for an inexhaustible store
of the most exquisite fish, that are taken in their stated seasons,
without skill and almost without · labour. But when the
passages of the straits were thrown open for trade, they
alternately admitted the natural and artificial riches of the
north and south, of the Euxine and of the Mediterranean.
Whatever rude commodities were collected in the forests of
Germany or Scythia, as far as the sources of the Tanais and
Borysthenes; whatever was manufactured by the skill of
Europe or Asia; the corn of Egypt, and the gems and spices

[1] Vol. ii. chap. xvii. p. 183.

of the farthest India, were brought by the varying winds to
the port of Constantinople." Thus her prosperity and industry came to her as to an eligible site; she did little in return
to spread industry and prosperity amongst others, and her
great inheritances in art and manufacture might almost have
perished had their diffusion depended alone on her initiative.

It was in a very different spirit that the Arab conquerors
of the great sites of ancient commerce
ARABIAN COMMERCE. (Syria, Babylon, and Egypt) conceived their
duty and their destiny; however little they were fated to
carry out their early high ideals. The Koran expressly enjoins
on the followers of Mahomet commerce and industry, as
honourable occupations proper to be spread abroad; and
when the armies of the Caliphs overran in the Middle Ages the
greater part of the known world, they brought those hand-
maids of civilisation in their train, and sedulously laboured
for their dissemination. It was not their fault that the
West did not profit as much by the enlightenment and
prosperity thus proffered it as did the East; though it
could not help but profit somewhat. Even when ignorance
and superstition refused to so great an extent as they
did the gifts offered, yet, when all was done that prejudice
and bigotry could do, still a noble residue was left. It
was possible for Christian merchants to refuse to trade
with Mahometan merchants,[1] and so to discourage their
presence in the western seas, and this was done; but it was
not possible wholly to uproot again the renewed taste for
industry and learning which the strangers propagated there
as faithfully as they did the crude dogmas of their creed.[2]
But the consequences of this policy in Europe were that

---

[1] It was in fact forbidden by the Church. See Lacroix, p. 253.

[2] For a striking account of the comparative civilisation of the Saracens and
the people of western Europe at this time, see *A History of the Intellectual
Development of Europe*, by John William Draper. Vol. ii. chap. 2 (Bell and
Sons, 1875).

Arabian commerce was proscribed, and that the benefits of the Saracen invasion so far as this branch of our subject is concerned were meagre, and generally of an industrial rather than a commercial kind. In Asia, on the other hand, the effects of the Mahometan conquests on commerce were immediate and striking. Bagdad supplanted Alexandria as the great *entrepôt* of the East India trade, Damascus more than renewed its ancient fame, the lines of communication between the East and West were shifted several degrees northwards, and Mesopotamia and Babylonia experienced a brief revival of their former greatness.

One of the most extraordinary series of events that the world has ever seen was now to supervene, and under the guise of a religious move‑

THE CRUSADES.

ment to play a romantic and singular part in shaping the future commerce of the Middle Ages. This was the sudden and almost universal uprising of the West against the East; the facing round of the whole population of Europe, as it were, and its movement *en masse* towards Asia. What was really at the bottom of the enthusiasm of the Crusades it is scarcely our business to inquire here:—whether it were ultimately inspired by a fear of conquest, which the successes of the Saracens had engendered ; whether it were wholly and solely a religious movement; whether there was not some commercial jealousy and curiosity included in the composition of it ; whether it was a reaction against the intolerable dulness and tyranny of the Dark Ages—all of which suggestions have notable authorities on their side—we do not assume to say. Possibly all those motives were separately represented in the minds of Crusaders, and possibly several of them were mixed in the minds of some of them. What is certain is, that their ultimate effect upon European commerce and manufacture was great and lasting ; greater and more lasting than is apparent at first sight. They not merely

opened up a wider knowledge of the world, and introduced
the still semi-barbarous populations of western Europe to the
arts and refinements of the East, but they widened knowledge
itself, then miserably contracted and held bound in the toils
of tyranny and superstition.   The Crusades made the Renaissance possible, and greatly aided in the approaching
general emancipation of mankind.   Even their immediate
effects were far from inconsiderable.   " The conquest of
Palestine by the Crusaders," says Lacroix,[1] " had first opened
all the towns and harbours of this wealthy region to western traders, and many of them were able permanently to
establish themselves there, with all sorts of privileges and
exemptions from taxes, which were gladly offered by the
nobles who had transferred feudal power to Mussulman
territories."   Many of them settled there accordingly, and
entered into the rich trade of the Levant and Black Sea,
finding their principal market as usual at Constantinople, but
also along the coasts of Asia Minor and Africa.   Many more
returned home, bringing with them the knowledge of new
products and processes, which northern Europe had been too
proud to learn from the Mussulman conquerors of Spain,
and which the people of the Greek Empire had been so
backward in communicating.   They brought also extended
ideas of commerce, and a more fearless spirit in the pursuit
of it; and these new ideas spread widely and rapidly.
Gradually the ships of the northern European countries began
to be heard of in the Mediterranean.   " At one time it seemed
as if the navigators of all countries had made a rendezvous
in the eastern waters.   Bremen and Lubeck made the
acquaintance of Genoa and Venice.   The Baltic Sea, a
mysterious retreat of Norman pirates, was discovered and
explored.   The Hanse towns, by putting liberty under the
protection of commerce, prepared in the north a confederation

[1] *Manners, Customs, and Dress during the Middle Ages*, p. 253.

rivalling the Italian republics, which brought, like them, its
tribute of intelligence and wealth to the common centre of
civilisation. Naval architecture increased the size of vessels
for facility in the transport of pilgrims. Fifteen years after
the third Crusade formidable fleets might be seen leaving
the ports of Venice and Genoa such as the Mediterranean
had never before carried. . . . Piracy was repressed.
The regulations for the government of the seas, rigorously
enforced by two or three powers interested in making good
order respected, contributed much to the progress of commerce by giving it a commencement of security. Convoys
of ships followed the coasts of the countries where the
Crusaders were fighting, and became rich by selling them
provisions and munitions of war." Nor was this all, but,
as was to be expected, " manufactures profited no less than
commerce from the impulse given to ideas by the numerous
expeditions to the Holy Land. . . . The Crusaders learned
at Damascus how to work the metals and make cloth
successfully; they found in the East manufactures of camlet,
patterns of which excited the admiration of Queen Marguerite.
Many Greek cities supported silk looms, which gave rise to
the cultivation of the mulberry tree in Italy, and consequently to an immense extension of its graceful products.
The glass-works of Tyre aided in perfecting the fine glass
fabrics of Venice, so justly renowned in the Middle Ages." [1]
Thus the ultimate effects of the Crusades on commerce and
industry were even more important than the immediate
ones, and the former grew out of the latter.

In the meantime, however, a new maritime power had
made its appearance, and began soon to
distance all competitors. This was the power
shared among several young republics of Italy, which

VENICE AND GENOA.

---

[1] *History of Political Economy in Europe*, by Jerome Adolphe Blanqui.
English edition, pp. 131, 132 (Bell and Sons, 1880).

about that time rose to independence and eminence, and exercised a potent influence on commerce and industry. Venice from the first took the lead among these rival powers; Amalfi for a while holding the second place;[1] whilst Genoa, during a brief and brilliant epoch of her history, successfully contested the priority with both. The general disorganisation of the Eastern trade produced by the advance of the Turks was the earliest source of their great prosperity, which was immensely fed and fostered by the Crusades. But these towns had more permanent claims as trading stations than were afforded by these comparatively accidental circumstances. Venice was the natural outlet for the goods of north Italy and Germany tending eastwards; and an admirable *entrepôt* for the luxuries of Asia now coming more and more into demand in the distant north. Similarly Genoa, which had the advantage of a noble harbour, was happily placed for exporting the fruitful products of Piedmont and Lombardy, and affording access to the foreign products destined for Pisa, Lucca, Florence, and Milan, and thence by the overland route to the countries beyond the Alps. The Genoese were also among the boldest and expertest of sailors, and in the zenith of their power had nearly a monopoly of the trade between the Mediterranean and northern Europe. Had they confined themselves more to it, their maritime prosperity would have lasted longer than it did. But the Venetians and Genoese were deadly rivals in the Levant, and after a struggle lasting over a century, the Venetians came out victorious, and other rivals having by this time likewise succumbed or been distanced, they remained the undisputed masters of the commerce of that part. This position they retained till the close of the Middle Ages. At regular intervals thenceforward their fleets were de-

[1] *Middle Ages,* p. 613.

spatched in large companies to their various destinations
filled with the most precious goods; with "silks, satins,
damasks, cottons, and various other costly gear, as well
as spices, saffron, camphor, and a hundred other articles
brought from the east." One fleet went to the Black Sea,
another to Cyprus and Egypt, another to various ports
of the Greek Empire, and so on. One, perhaps the most
important, and to us certainly the most interesting, called
the "Flanders fleet," sailed every year for Bruges. "It
halted and traded at the ports of Greece, Italy, and Spain
as it passed through the Mediterranean, gaily and proudly,
even as Antonio's argosies—

> ' With portly sail,
> Like signors and rich burghers of the flood,
> Or as it were the pageants of the sea,
> Did overpeer the petty traffickers,
> That curtseyed to them reverence,
> As they flew by them with their woven wings,'

and then sailed up the English coast. The Downs being
reached the fleet broke up for a time, some vessels anchor-
ing off Southampton, Sandwich, Rye, and the chief towns
on our southern shore; others going to the principal Flemish
ports; and all making busy trade with the native merchants
who were eagerly awaiting their arrival."[1] Their cargoes
sold or exchanged for other products, the ships met again
off the Dutch coast, and returned after nearly a year's
absence to fit out at once for another venture;—and this
was the ultimate form of that great trade between east
and west, whose origin is lost in fable, before the discovery of another continent across the Atlantic, and of
the passage round the Cape of Good Hope, radically altered
once again the direction of trade routes, and imported
wholly new factors into the calculations of commerce.

[1] *Romance of Trade*, p. 100.

We have now to pass from these familiar homes and
haunts of ancient trade to the distant north,
THE HANSE LEAGUE.
hitherto almost lost in fable and mystery.
The chief rivals of Venice in the Mediterranean during the
Middle Ages were : Genoa, Pisa, and Amalfi; and outside
the Italian trading republics, Constantinople and Marseilles;
with Barcelona in Spain; and the Provençal Roman towns
of Nismes, Narbonne, and Montpelier in the south of France.
The trade to Egypt and Asia Minor was the principal one, ,
and it was shared amongst those ports.   A considerable
independent commerce had been springing up, however, in
the north as well.   " The geographical position of Europe,"
says Hallam,[1] " naturally divides its maritime commerce into
two principal regions : one comprehending those countries
which border on the Baltic, the German, and the Atlantic
oceans; another, those situated around the Mediterranean
Sea."   In the Middle Ages this natural distribution was
more obvious than at present, particularly before the epoch
of the Crusades.   Intercourse by sea between the extremities
of Europe was till that time very rare, owing not only to
the distance and to the difficulties of navigation in the
open ocean, but also to the dangers to be apprehended from
Moorish corsairs who held all the north coast of Africa,
and both sides of the pillars of Hercules.   It was reckoned
impious (as has been said) by the sterner Christians of the
north to traffic with infidels—a superstition which their
more volatile fellow-Christians of the south (the Venetians
particularly) were somewhat more inclined to appraise at
its commercial value, and to ignore or revive as it suited
them.   An undying enmity was consequently aroused
between Christian and Mahometan traders, which tended
to make this division more complete.   The countries lying
beyond the Alps and Rhine became accustomed to supply

[1] *Middle Ages*, chap. ix. part ii.

their distant commercial wants therefore by an overland traffic, and their local ones by an indigenous maritime one; and that traffic, trifling at first, assumed in time larger proportions, and presently developed into a great and lucrative trade. This trade, and the various advantages which the people of the north of Europe derived from it, has been described in a particularly striking manner by Professor Millar, in a tract entitled an "Historical View of the English Government from the Settlement of the Saxons in Britain to the Accession of the House of Stuart;"[1] and we avail ourselves here of that writer's narrative, for it is impossible to state the matter in better terms. "During the barbarous period that succeeded the destruction of the Roman Empire," he says, "the same cause which had formerly promoted the commerce of the Mediterranean gave rise in the northern part of Europe to a small degree of traffic upon the narrow sea of the Baltic. The inhabitants of the southern coast of Scandinavia and the northern parts of Germany, being necessitated in that inhospitable climate to fish for their subsistence, became early acquainted with navigation, and were thereby encouraged to exchange with each other the rude produce of the country. From the convenience of the situation numbers of people were induced to reside in the neighbourhood, and trading towns were formed upon the coast or in the mouths of the adjoining rivers. While they were thus advancing in navigation and commerce they would hardly fail to make some progress in manufactures. By having a vent for the rude produce of that country, they must have had frequent opportunities of observing that by bestowing a little labour upon their native commodities they could draw a much greater profit upon the exchange of them. In this manner they were encouraged to occupy themselves in working up the raw

[1] Quoted in Bischoff's *Woollen and Worsted Manufactures*, pp. 39-50.

materials, to acquire habits of industry, and to make proficiency in mechanical employments." By and by this industrial prosperity developed a spirit of independence, which in practical application necessarily reacted greatly to its advantage. "Having been much oppressed and obstructed in their trade by the barons and military people in their neighbourhood, they were led by degrees into joint measures for their own defence," which resulted, about the twelfth century,[1] in the formation of the famous Hanse League, which from being confined at first to purely local interests, came at length to include "eighty of the most considerable places" in the north of Europe, "divided into four colleges, whereof Lubeck, Cologne, Brunswick, and Dantzig were the leading towns." Of these places Lubeck was the principal, and became, "as it were, the patriarchal see of the league, whose province it was to preside in all general discussions for mercantile, political, or military purposes, and to carry them into execution." The league had "four principal *factories*[2] in foreign parts, at London, Bruges, Bergen, and Novogorod, endowed by the sovereigns of those cities with considerable privileges."[3] Its trade was confined to the north exclusively. The constitution of these factories, or mercantile establishments, was extremely curious, and is full of instruction. The following description of that in London will give a good idea both of the commercial spirit and commercial administrative life of the times, and may be quoted with advantage. This quaint mediæval settlement was located in a place called the Steel Yard,[4] whence the merchants ordinarily obtained the title of "Merchants of the Steel Yard." The description is taken from Mr. Fox

---

[1] Hallam says the thirteenth century, and Macpherson asserts that they were not known as Hanse towns so early. The precise date is unimportant.

[2] *i.e.* mercantile branches.   [3] Hallam, pp. 619-621.

[4] The site is now covered by the Cannon Street railway station.

Bourne's *Romance of Trade*.[1] " Here the *Gilhalda Teutonicorum* was established in very early times as a sort of hotel, in which German merchants could reside and warehouse their goods. In Richard II.'s reign this first building was found too small for its inmates, and a second one adjoining it was added. A third house was found necessary in the time of Edward IV.; and soon afterwards the three buildings, with perhaps some others, were surrounded by strong walls, which often London 'prentices, jealous of the prosperity of the foreigners within, attempted to break through. Within this structure, partitioned in separate cells (says Werdenhagen, the historian of the Hanseatic League) the residents lived under strict regulations. They had a common table, and were probably then, as well as subsequently, divided into companies, each having its master and associates. All were obliged to remain single; any one who married an Englishwoman lost his *hanse*.[2] For the sake of good order, no housekeeper, not even a bedmaker, was allowed. As it was necessary for them to become more united and able to resist the attacks of the London mob, none of the residents, or at least none who belonged to the council of commerce, were allowed to sleep out of the Steel Yard. No less strict was the prohibition against communicating to the English anything which passed in the establishment. The direction was vested in an alderman and two deputies or co-assessors, with nine councilmen, who composed together the chamber of commerce; these persons assembling every Wednesday in summer at seven, in winter at eight o'clock in the morning, to deliberate on general affairs, the authority of the alderman being generally undisputed. He it was who decided what ventures should be undertaken, and how those under him should employ their talents. All negotiations with foreigners were con-

[1] P. 98 *et seq.*   [2] Membership of the League.

14

ducted by him, and it was for him to communicate
with the similar *hanses* in other parts of Europe so as
to bring about a common course of action and secure
the interests of all." The suspicious and exclusive spirit
that characterised mediæval commerce is here admirably
portrayed.

The next most important incident in the commerce of
the Middle Ages northwards, was the rise
THE NETHERLANDS.
and progress of the Netherlands into a great
trading and manufacturing country. The success of the
Hanse League naturally inspired the countries with which
it traded to emulate its achievements on the seas, and aroused
jealousy in many places. In England this jealousy of
foreigners and their monopolies manifested itself in ever-
recurring riots, and much the same was the case elsewhere.
With Denmark, indeed, the League at one time waged an
actual war, and it was engaged in constant quarrels with
Sweden and Norway, excited by matters relating to trade.
Its policy was to blame for much of this ill-feeling, and
for the declining prosperity that at length overtook it, for
while it became careless in cultivating native resources at
home—one of the proper objects of its institution—it grew
greedy and despotic abroad, seeking to crush by absolute
force of arms all opposition, or even rivalry. The consequence
was that one by one its customers, as they found themselves strong enough, turned its own weapons on itself, and
refused to trade with it longer. England, whose maritime
power came rather late in her history, was one of the last
to do this; but already in the reign of Edward VI. the
charters of the Steel Yard merchants had been temporarily
suspended, and in the latter part of that of Elizabeth they
were finally abrogated. The Netherlands had been in active
rivalry earlier; and the Hanseatic League had even gone
to the length of forbidding Flemish ships to navigate the

Baltic. But the Netherlands were far better qualified to support existence out of native resources at that time than Germany was, and opposition only incited their people to fresh efforts. As the Hanse League declined in favour and power, Flanders and Holland continued to grow in both ; adding now a great commercial to the great industrial reputation that they already enjoyed. The same author,[1] to whom we have before been indebted in connection with an earlier trade, gives so happy a description of the progress of this one also, that we cannot do better than avail ourselves again of his bright and philosophical narrative. Of the Netherlands he says : " As the situation of towns upon the coast of a narrow sea was favourable to foreign commerce, a country intersected by many navigable views gave a similar encouragement to inland trade, and thence likewise to manufactures. As inland trade, however, cannot be rendered very extensive without greater expense than is necessary to the trade of a maritime town that all the inhabitants may have the benefit of a market, canals become requisite where the river navigation is cut off; roads must be made where water carriage is impracticable ; machinery must be constructed, and cattle fit for draught must be procured and maintained. It may be expected, therefore, that inland trade will be improved more slowly than that which is carried on along the sea coast; but as the former holds out a market to the inhabitants of a wider country, it is apt at length to produce a more extensive improvement of manufactures. We accordingly find that after the towns of Italy, and those upon the coast of the Baltic, the part of Europe which made the quickest advances in trade was the Netherlands, where the number of navigable rivers, which divide themselves into many different branches, and the general flatness of the country, which made it easy to extend the navigation by

[1] Professor Millar.

canals, encouraged the inhabitants to employ themselves in the manufacture of their natural productions. Besides the facility of water carriage, the inhabitants of the Netherlands appear to have derived another advantage from the nature of their soil. The two most considerable branches of manufacture, which contribute to supply the conveniences or luxuries of many people, are the making of linen and of woollen cloths. With regard to the former of these branches that country seems fitted to produce the raw material in the greatest perfection. As early as the tenth century we accordingly find that the people had, by this peculiar circumstance, been excited to attempt the manufacture of linen, etc." The part of the Netherlands here alluded to is the southern part, or Flanders, now included in the modern kingdom of Belgium. It was as a matter of fact less celebrated at that time for its maritime than its inland commerce, although Bruges, which was its most important town, had been a thriving port[1] and centre of trade for two or three centuries before. Later it became a vast emporium of commerce too. In 1262 it was made one of the four great *staples* (or market towns) of the Hanseatic League, and flourished exceedingly. It continued doing so for about 200 years after, though by that time exposed to the dangerous rivalry of both Antwerp and Amsterdam; but in 1482 the Archduke Maximilian of Germany caused the canal that connected it with the sea to be blocked up at Sluys, and its prosperity passed in a great degree to another part of the Netherlands, most of the merchants of Bruges transferring their business to Antwerp, which then became the greatest centre of trade in Europe. The commerce of Antwerp just at the close of the Middle Ages was in fact immense. "Every nation had here its factory or little

---

[1] Bruges was not during the Middle Ages actually a port, but was connected with the ocean by a wide canal.

colony of merchants." . . . "Two thousand loaded waggons
from France, Germany, and Lorraine passed each day through
its gates, and the merchant ships that bartered their foreign
wares for this inland produce were more than could be
counted." . . . "Often 250 vessels might at the same time be
seen loading or unloading at her quays." Our own share in
this commerce was far from contemptible, and is thus stated by
an Italian historian, Guicciardini: "To England Antwerp sends
jewels, and precious stones, silver bullion, quicksilver, wrought
silks, gold and silver cloth and thread, camlets, grograms,[1]
spices, drugs, sugar, cotton, cummin, galls, linens (fine and
coarse), serges, tapestry, madder, hops in great quantity, glass,
salt, fish, metallic and other mercuries of all sorts, arms of all
kinds, ammunition for war, and household furniture. From
England Antwerp receives vast quantities of fine and coarse
draperies, fringes, and other things of that kind, to a great
value, the finest wool, excellent saffron in small quantities,
much lead and tin, sheep and rabbit skins without number,
and various other sorts of fine peltry and leather, beer,
cheese, and other provisions in great quantities, also malmsey
wines, which the English import from Candia. It is marvellous to think of the vast quantity of drapery imported by
the English into the Netherlands, being undoubtedly, one
year with another, above 200,000 pieces of all kinds, which,
at the most moderate rate of twenty-five crowns per piece,
is 5,000,000 crowns ; so that these and other merchandise
brought by the English to us, or carried from us to them,
may make the annual amount to be more than 12,000,000
crowns, to the great benefit of both countries, neither of
which could possibly, or not without the greatest damage,
dispense with their vast annual commerce." In the sixteenth
century much of the prosperity of Antwerp was transferred

[1] "Camlets," "grograms." These goods were made of Angora wool or
mohair, the fleece of a goat that is a native of Asia Minor.

to Amsterdam. The history of that transfer, and of the
Netherlands in its glorious struggle for independence, does
not concern us here, but it is impossible to pass from even
this brief *résumé* of its brilliant position while still free
without pointing the moral from those elementary principles
which at the commencement of this chapter we instanced
as so greatly affecting commerce ; and the last one in
this case chiefly. Those waste and barren plains, but
lately recovered from the basin of the sea, with no convenient harbours and scarcely any valuable natural productions, yet became, under the impulse of order and by
the love of liberty, the abode of a wealthy, prosperous,
and cultured community, at a time when the greater part
of Europe was plunged in poverty, ignorançe, and chronic
warfare.

In the foregoing remarks mention has often been made
of a mediæval commerce inland, and it will
MEDIÆVAL INLAND   be desirable to say a few words on this sub-
COMMERCE.
ject before concluding a chapter in some
measure extraneous to our proper theme. Such a commerce
would naturally obey the same laws that we have shown to
have governed ancient inland commerce—that is to say, it
would be conducted along the most practicable routes uniting
favoured districts. Some of the most ancient and important
commerce of Europe, as of the East, was conducted accordingly after this fashion. It is certain, for instance, that a
great portion of the tin trade from Britain to the Mediterranean was so conducted from a very early time. The
tin used to be landed in some of the harbours of Brittany
or Normandy, and carried across the country packed on the
backs of mules : either to Lyons, to be transhipped on the
Rhone ; or farther south to Arles, Narbonne, or Marseilles,
thence to be despatched to Greece, Italy, or Asia, as the
case might be. This was clearly the shortest and most

convenient route for the traffic to take across the continent
of Europe, avoiding high mountain ranges, deep rivers, and
the like obstacles, and was consequently the one selected.
Another inland trade route obviously marked out by nature
was that which, passing the Alps and Appenines on the
other side, struck westward into Europe to the north of
those barriers. Starting from the head of the Adriatic Sea
this route first made for the Upper Danube, and continuing
along that valley into Germany passed onward to the Rhine.
Once the Rhine valley was reached further progress was
easy. Augsburg was naturally one of the most important
stations on this route, and a junction for other routes
passing north and east. It was accordingly a city of much
influence and trade in the Middle Ages; Ratisbon and
Nüremberg in the same line were also very eminent ones.
Frankfort, Coblentz, and Cologne were, for the same reason,
rich and powerful cities, and many more might be mentioned
where other routes converged, till the Netherlands were
reached, where the inland traffic ceased, and the ships of the
Hanse League, and later of the Dutch, were in readiness
to distribute the commodities brought overland far and wide
by sea. Within the principal lines of traffic uniting the
extremities of Europe were of course many minor ones, and
these routes were affected of course by political as well as by
physical and industrial causes, avoiding turbulent and ill-
regulated states, and changing sometimes with the changed
conditions of the times. Still, on the whole, it is remarkable how constant inland traffic was throughout all the
commotions of the Middle Ages to the line of least physical
resistance. A hostile state might be passed in safety by
the traders; but a deep river, or a lofty chain of mountains,
were not within the compass of their engineering skill
to overcome.

Fairs played a very conspicuous part in the commerce

of those times.   It was necessary to have a meeting-place
where merchants might come together to
buy and sell, and it was desirable that the
time and place of meeting should be well known and fixed.
Fairs at certain times and places were consequently instituted.   The fairs were generally connected, or supposed
to be connected, with some religious celebration — an
immemorial usage which equally characterised the fairs
of mediæval times, of classical times, and of a still
remoter past.   Thus there were the fairs of St. James at
Munich, St. Denis at Paris, St. Bartholomew at London, and
St. Giles at Winchester, commencing respectively on the
feast days of those saints, and continuing for several days
after.   Sometimes this connection with the Church was
more than a nominal advantage, its protection being
necessary to the safety of the gathering.   It was indeed
greatly on this pretence that the privilege of holding fairs
was originally conferred upon religious corporations at all,
who throve upon the tolls and dues that they exacted in
connection with them.   The privileges thus conferred were
often very extensive, including, in one recorded case, that
of the grant to the church of St. Moritz during the great
Magdeburg Fair, even the right of coining money.[1]   The
facilities offered to traders attending fairs were often also
very great.   Mr. Morley relates how, "in France before a
way was opened for trade by the fair of St. Denis," certain
feudal tolls and rights "absorbed *one-half* of a foreign
merchant's goods upon their first arrival and debarcation."
But to that fair "traders came, exempt not only from
imperial taxation but from many of the ordinary risks of
travel."   It became therefore a great resort of very various
traders : " an emporium for the iron and lead of the Saxons,
for slaves, for the jewelry and perfumes of the Jews, for the

FAIRS.

[1] *Memoirs of Bartholomew Fair*, by Henry Morley, p. 15 (Warne).

oil, wine, and fat of Provence and Spain, for the honey and madder of Neustria and Brittany, for merchandise from Egypt and the east." The right of granting a charter to hold a fair was inherent in the Crown, and a very important source of its revenues. Enlightened monarchs sometimes granted free fairs, for attracting commerce to their dominions. Charlemagne in particular bestirred himself in this direction, and with good results, and the establishment of fairs in Flanders had much to do with the early prosperity of the country.[1] A "free fair" did not mean that goods were exempt from the ordinary dues at the place where the fair was held, but only that they were permitted free passage to and from it; in the absence of which it was in the power of every petty landowner through whose domain they were conveyed to levy what dues on them he thought fit. The extent of business done in these fairs, and their importance in the commercial life of the Middle Ages, can only be realised when we recall such obstacles to transport as these; which are only a few of those that could be mentioned; and the general dearth of shops, which now supply so immediately all our wants. For the more important class of home-made goods in those days the merchant was at once producer and wholesale and retail dealer; and for foreign goods, merchant and retailer in one. Customers did not attempt to supply their needs from day to day, but generally for months at a time. Consequently the fair was the great arena for mercantile activity, and the great local event of the season. Of the fair still held annually at Beaucaire, a little town on the Rhone, not far from Arles, we read: "This fair was once without an equal in Europe. Merchants from Marseilles and other ports of the Mediterranean came hither with rich stores of all the wealth brought from east, west, north, and south by the trading fleets of

[1] See p. 231.

Venice and her rivals. To meet them came traders from all the inland towns, silk mercers from Lyons, wine dealers from Macon and Dijon, and representatives of every mart and factory that had anything to buy or sell."[1] As many as 100,000 persons from a distance used to visit this fair as lately as the middle of the last century, and even at this day more than half that number are said to do so.[2] Of Stourbridge Fair in England, Mr. Thorold Rogers gives an equally striking account.[3] It was held in a field near Cambridge, and was at one time the greatest of all the English fairs, not even excepting St. Bartholomew's, or St. Giles'. Modern representatives of such gatherings continue to exist even at the present day. The annual fair of Nijni Novogorod is still the principal mart for the produce of central Russia; and the great fair at Leipsic remains an event of annual importance in Germany. In India there is a great annual festival, half-commercial, half-religious, as of old, at a place called Hurdwar, one hundred and twenty miles north-east of Delhi, which is attended by multitudes; and there are many others in other parts of Asia. It is only within living memory that Greenwich Fair near London, and Donnybrook Fair near Dublin, were abolished, and their praises are still celebrated in the local ballad literature of those parts. The great facilities of locomotion, and the more perfect organisation of industry have now, however, generally superseded the need of fairs in most civilised countries, and the nearest approach to them with us at the present day are the agricultural shows and exhibitions of various kinds which are held in increasing number.

[1] *Romance of Trade,* p. 66.
[2] *Merchant Enterprise,* by J. H. Fyfe, p. 275 (Nelson).
[3] *Six Centuries of Work and Wages,* pp. 149-152.

CHAPTER VI.

MEDLÆVAL MANUFACTURES

The Dark Ages—The Church—The Greek Empire—Silk—Wool—Flax—
Cotton—Metal Manufacture—Smaller Industries—Locks and Clocks—
Wire drawing—Dyeing—Felting—Paper-making—Pottery—Leather
—Glass—Mediæval System—Trade Societies.

IF it be difficult to follow the movements of commerce
in the early Middle Ages, it is still more
difficult to trace the distribution and progress THE DARK AGES.
of manufacture, and the reason assigned for this by Hallam
is the all-sufficing one, that there was then no manufacture
to trace. " There is not a vestige perhaps to be discovered
for several centuries," writes the historian of the Middle
Ages, "of any considerable manufacture ; I mean of working
up articles of common utility to an extent beyond what the
necessities of an adjacent district required."[1]   The definition
of manufacture in this sentence, it may be noted, is the one
that has been adopted throughout this work, and with so
unexceptionable an authority to rely on, it might have been
held excusable to have omitted a chapter on mediæval
manufacture from it.   Such an arrangement would, however,
have scarcely accorded with the plan laid down at the commencement, of investigating the germs, namely, as well as
the growth and progress of the modern manufacturing system.
Instead then, it is proposed to here pass rapidly in review

[1] *View of the State of Europe during the Middle Ages*, by Henry Hallam,
LL.D., p. 612 (Ward and Lock).

the main facts concerning manufacturing occupations at this
epoch, collected from a few scattered sources, and fitted into
something like the form of a connected narrative. We have
already learned that such rude industry as there was, was
principally local; which means that production had, in
appearance at least, gone back to the prehistoric stage—to
that system of uncombined individual effort which preceded
both the patriarchal and communistic systems of development,
and which has been sketched elsewhere.[1] There was, in
short, just then neither any real industrial nor social system
in modern Europe at all, but only a condition of complete
anarchy. Every one was for himself, either as an oppressor
or as one oppressed, and all were unconsciously looking for
a time when a new order should be evolved out of, and a
new principle infused into, this chaos, that should unite
society again. That new principle of cohesion and progress
was presently to appear in the combined influences of the
Church and feudal system, acting and reacting upon each
other; and to be supplemented by the independent attitude
which the industrious classes assumed later towards the
excessive pretensions of both. But in the Middle Ages and
in the west, up to at all events the reign of Charlemagne :
and after the termination of that reign for some centuries
more : there was little order of any kind, and industrial production for purposes of trade was in many places completely
at a standstill. How indeed could any considerable trade
be profitably conducted ? It was not merely (as we are
assured by Hallam) that, "in the domains of every lord,
a toll was to be paid in passing his bridge, or along his
highway, or at his market," for "it was only the mildest
species of feudal lords who were content with the tribute of
merchants. The more ravenous descended from their fortresses to pillage the wealthy traveller, or share in the spoil of

[1] Chapter ii.

inferior plunderers, whom they both protected and instigated."
Communication itself was difficult to an extent that it is
almost impossible now to realise. The great highways of
the Romans had suffered by nearly a thousand years of
complete neglect, and where they were not there was nothing
else to travel along. There were no inns outside the very
largest towns. There were no conveyances for travelling.
In fine, during this melancholy time, "one has more reason
to wonder at the intrepid thirst of lucre which induced a
very few merchants to exchange the products of different
regions, than to ask why no general spirit of commercial
activity prevailed." [1]

The first ameliorative influence that entered on this dark
scene proceeded from the body of the Church.
The feudal system in its earlier days was but
a temporary expedient, a military organisation set up in the
place of the civil governments which it overturned. The
conquered nations of western Europe still looked from their
alien rulers for some central, all-embracing authority; they
could not immediately, nor for many centuries, shake off the
tradition of that great Roman dominion which had appeared
to them almost as a part of the settled order of nature.
Accordingly, when an all-embracing central authority once
again did present itself, in the ancient capital too, and with
something of the old pretension, the people were predisposed
to acknowledge its claim to sovereignty, and to abide by its
ordinances. Those pretensions, read in the light of past
history and judged by present fruits, did not appear to them
at all so monstrous as the pretensions of a purely spiritual
authority claiming universal temporal jurisdiction might under
other circumstances have done. They accepted them without
much question; they submitted to them for the most part even
joyfully. And the Church's authority at first was true to

THE CHURCH.

[1] *Middle Ages*, chap. ix.

its origin and mission.   It was exercised generally throughout the Dark Ages in the direction of ameliorating the hard
lot of the poor, of curbing the exactions of kings and barons,
and of fostering industry.[1]   The religious houses that
spread over the country became centres of wholesome
effort; the brotherhoods devoting themselves not alone to
religious exercises and missionary labours (which were
welcome to the people too), but to the cultivation of the
soil, and the production of commodities of material use and
value.   In them were preserved the remembrance and
knowledge of processes of art and manufacture which, in the
great confusion and rapine of the times, had otherwise wholly
perished; and by the brotherhoods inhabiting them those
arts and processes were widely taught and practised.   It is
not for us to examine here what other ends the Church had
in view all this while, and with what dexterity and intrepidity
it pursued those ends ; suffice it that its influence on industry
was such as is described.   But it did much more than has
been said.   It made work sacred.   It did more.   By the
establishment of certain periods of tranquillity, under the
name of "the peace of God," it procured for labour occasional intervals of leisure, when it might rest in peace, or
possibly strive to recoup itself for losses sustained at other
times ; and by affording sanctuary to benighted wayfarers
it gave some little help to trade.   It was, moreover, itself
a large employer of labour, and generally a not unfair nor
even ungenerous one, according to the ideas of those times.

Such was the condition of manufacturing industry then
in the west of Europe at the commencement
of the Middle Ages.   In the East, however,
in that portion of it which now comes to be known as the

THE GREEK EMPIRE.

---

[1] "From the third to the thirteenth century," writes Sir Thomas Brassey,
"the Church was the most faithful protector of the labouring man."—*Work
and Wages*, chap. i. (Bell and Sons, 1874).

Greek Empire, its condition was not by any means so bad, and hither, therefore, our attention is first invited.

In the partition of the states that constituted the Roman Empire when the capital was moved to Byzantium, while the greater part of Italy, northern Africa, Spain, Gaul, Germany, and Britain, were assigned to the western division ; Greece (including Thrace, Macedonia, and Illyria), Asia Minor, Syria, Egypt, and Lybia, fell to the eastern part; and over this vast and splendid territory a successor of the Cæsars still reigned. The history of mediæval manufacture and commerce necessarily commences then in this connecting link between the ancient and modern worlds. The preceding chapter showed how the happy situation of Constantinople, its capital, naturally attracted a vast commerce ; and how there, as elsewhere, manufacturing and commercial prosperity went hand in hand. Proceeding now from generalities to details, it will be our endeavour next to sum up a few of the striking facts in the history of that manufacturing progress in the separate histories of some of its principal materials.

The first of these to claim attention is silk. Hitherto we have had little to tell of this material, for its early history is shrouded in great

SILK.

obscurity, and many of the textures which the ancients called silken are believed now to have been woven of quite other things. But from the period that we now reach, silk was to play for some time the most conspicuous part amongst all materials of manufacture in the principal countries of the modern world. The manner in which this result was brought about forms a narrative of singular, and even enthralling interest, in which the centre of action is the Greek Empire. In the whole long history of industry, fruitful as that history has ever been in surprises and romantic episodes, there is perhaps no incident more strange and thrilling, more romantic and interesting, than that of the establishment of the silk culture and manufacture in Europe. From several popular sources of information, easily accessible, we shall endeavour to compile and tell this tale in as brief a way as possible.

In the later days of the western Roman Empire the custom of wearing silk had become pretty general among its wealthier citizens. It was no longer the great rarity that it had been. There was even a little silk weaving done in some of the outlying provinces, especially in Greece, the supply of filament for which was brought from the far east through the ordinary channels of trade. But on the transference of the seat of government to Constantinople a long series of wars which ensued between the Byzantine emperors and the rulers of Persia greatly interfered with this supply of raw material. The Persians cut off the caravans whose route from China lay through their country, and the Greek manufacturers were in consequence unable to keep their looms at work. The emperor Justinian who then reigned, and who was an able monarch, and an economist according to his lights, still further complicated the situation by imposing heavy duties on the importation of rival silken fabrics from Phœnicia, and by the endeavour to treat with the monarchs of Arabia Felix and Abyssinia for obtaining the raw material through them. Neither expedient was successful. The first merely injured the Phœnician manufacturers without at all benefiting the Greeks; and with respect to the second, the Persians it turned out had command of the route by sea as well as by land, and were not to be overreached. The silk manufacture, so lately imported, was on the point of being lost to Europe altogether but for an extraordinary and most unforeseen series of events that then ensued. Two Persian monks, employed as missionaries by some of the Christian churches in Asia, had pursued their evangelical labours so zealously and so far as to have finally reached the mysterious country of the Seres

(China). " There amidst their pious occupations they viewed with a curious eye the common dress of the Chinese, the manufactures of silk, and the myriads of silkworms, whose education either on trees or in houses had once been considered the labour of queens. They soon discovered that it was impracticable to transplant the shortlived insect, but that in the eggs a numerous progeny might be preserved and multiplied in a distant climate."[1] Animated (they declared) by a righteous indignation that so beautiful and lucrative an industry should be the monopoly of infidels, they formed the design to naturalise the silkworm in Christian countries. They devoted themselves accordingly to observing minutely its labours and habits, the mode in which it was fed, tended, and dealt with ; and having made themselves fully acquainted with these particulars they started homeward. But instead of proceeding to Persia, they repaired straight to the court of Justinian, who at that time was at his wit's end to know what to do in this very matter. They related to the astonished emperor how that the beautiful material which had cost him so much thought was not the least what he supposed it to be ; was not either the product of an animal or a tree, but spun from the entrails of an insect, whose habits they had studied, and which they believed could be reared and propagated in his dominions. It may be imagined with what interest Justinian listened to the story. Rewards were liberally promised : and encouraged by the prospect of these, the adventurous monks returned again all the way to the distant Serica, and, eluding with difficulty the vigilance and jealousy of the natives, succeeded in securing a supply of eggs. These they concealed in a hollow cane ; and, a second time successful in retracing their steps in safety, finally arrived with their invaluable burden

[1] Robertson's *Disquisition concerning Ancient India* (Edinburgh : Thomas Nelson, 1839).

15

in excellent condition at Constantinople (552 A.D.). Under
their direction the eggs were hatched in proper season by
the artificial heat of a dunghill, and the insects fed on the
leaves of the wild mulberry tree which grew in the country.
To the intense satisfaction of all concerned they throve and
multiplied, and soon set about employing themselves in their
new home as they had done from time immemorial in that
wherein their useful labours first attracted human notice.
An imperial manufactory and silkworm establishment was
forthwith set up, and skilled weavers brought from Greece
and Phœnicia to work in the former under the supervision
of the monks ; while other persons were instructed in the
management of the worms.   But this monopoly could not
be long sustained.   The discovery that the silkworm con-
ducts its labours as beneficially in Europe as in Asia stimulated other persons to emulate the example of Justinian.
From the imperial manufactory, or from some other
source, more eggs were procured, vast groves of mulberry
trees were planted, and before long myriads of silkworms
were successfully reared throughout the empire, and numerous
manufactories engaged in working up their products.

We have here textile manufactures, and a textile factory
system, already in full operation in eastern Europe as early
at all events as the seventh century.

The sudden cessation of the demand for silk from the
Byzantine empire greatly perplexed the nations of central
Asia.   In the reign of Justin II., the successor of Justinian,
a Sogdian embassy was sent to Constantinople for the
purpose of renewing and extending ancient treaties, with
especial reference to this matter.   To the dismay of the am-
bassadors they found the silkworm already naturalised there,
and their best customers thus rendered independent for the
future of either their good or bad offices (*Gibbon*, chap. xlii.) [1]

---

[1] The other authorities made use of in this account are, *Silk*, *Cotton*, *and*

For several centuries the Byzantine empire exclusively supplied silken fabrics to the rest of Europe; the rivalry of the Saracens, who early established a thriving silk industry in Sicily, being comparatively insignificant in so far as Europe itself was concerned. The chief seat of this silk culture and manufacture, besides Constantinople, continued to be Greece, especially the Peloponnesus, henceforward to be called Morea from the number of mulberry trees which afforded sustenance to the worms. The looms of Thebes, Corinth, and Argos, not merely revived but increased their ancient fame, and a great and lucrative trade sprang up in that land of many memories. These conditions continued practically unaltered till about the middle of the twelfth century. But by that time Sicily had fallen into the hands of Norman pirates, and in 1147 Roger, one of these, calling himself King of Sicily, attacked the Peloponnesus and laid it utterly waste. He also carried away with him many of the industrious inhabitants whom he settled at Palermo; and others escaped into Italy and elsewhere. These last carried the knowledge of the silk manufacture to the now rising towns of Lucca, Milan, Florence, Modena, and some others, which henceforward became famous seats of that industry. At the beginning of the thirteenth century the Morea passed under the dominion of Venice, which now entered also into the silk manufacture, an opportune tumult which occurred at Lucca in 1310 having the effect of placing many already highly skilled workmen at its disposal. From thenceforward for upwards of a century the Venetians were the greatest manufacturers, as they had for some time been the greatest merchants, of silk.

The industrial supremacy of the Greek Empire was by

Woollen Manufactures, chap. v. The volume on "Silk" in Lardner's *Cabinet Cyclopædia*. Sir G. Birdwood's *Industrial Arts of India*, pp. 266-271. The story is also told by Anderson, Macpherson, and others.

this time a thing of the past, and next to Italy in importance ranked Spain. Thither the Saracens had carried the knowledge and manufacture of silk, as they had carried so much other useful knowledge and so many other useful arts ; and towards the end of the Middle Ages, Grenada, Murcia, Almeria, and Cordova were great producers of silken fabrics. The third-named town was especially renowned. A Cordovese historian, one Ash Shakandi, who wrote at the beginning of the thirteenth century, speaks of it as being then " an opulent and magnificent city—the greatest mart in Andalusia ;" while another writer of the same age (Almakkari) gives this further particular description of it :[1]—" But what made Almeria superior to any other city in the world was its various manufactures of silk and other articles of dress, such as the *dîbaj*, a sort of silken stuff surpassing in quality and in durability anything else manufactured in other countries, the *tiraz*, or costly stuff on which the names of sultans, princes, and other wealthy individuals are inscribed, and of which no less than 800 looms existed at one time ; of more inferior articles, such as the *holol* (stripes, silks), and brocades, there were 1000 looms, and the same number were continually employed in weaving the stuffs called *iskalátón* (scarlet). There were also 1000 for weaving robes called Al jorjani (Georgian), and another 1000 for weaving robes called Isbahani (from Ispahan), and a similar number for Atabi." It remains to speak of France and the Netherlands. Italian silk-weavers had crossed the intervening mountains now and then at intervals long before a regular French silk manufacture was established on the other side of them. This we can hardly put before the reign of Louis IX. But that date brings us to the very limit of the period we are now dealing

---

[1] Quoted from *The Industrial Arts of Spain*, p. 250, by J. F. Riano (Chapman and Hall, 1879). Ash Shakandi mentions also Malaga as particularly famous for its textile fabrics.

with, and belongs rather to the history of modern manufacture. Similarly with regard to the Netherlands. It was not until a period even later than this that Antwerp became so celebrated for her silk manufacture as she did become; not in fact until the religious persecution of the sixteenth century had sent the Italian workmen flying across the Alps to seek a land where superstition and intolerance were not yet supreme.

Passing next to the more homely product wool; scarcely any notice at all of its manufacture in eastern or western Europe is to be found

WOOL.

during the early Middle Ages, and it is certain that it suffered a great decay. The barbarous nations that overthrew the Roman Empire in the fifth century felt few of the wants of civilised life, and were rather animated by a brutal hatred of its comforts and refinements. Even agriculture and the care of stock was at first neglected almost wholly by them, and the provision of clothing was left to individual effort. So late as the ninth or tenth centuries, the only mention of anything approaching a woollen manufacture which Hallam can remember to have met with, "is in Schmidt, who says that cloths were exported from Friesland, to England and other parts."[1] But this account is certainly overstated; or perhaps Hallam was not as well informed as usual on this head. Under date 810 A.D., Anderson gives a list of places, quoted from Voltaire's *General History of Europe*, where several manufactures were at that time carried on, which puts a very different complexion on the case. "At Lyons, Arles, and Tours in France," he writes, "and at Rome and Ravenna in Italy, they had *many manufactures of woollen stuffs*, and iron manufactures inlaid with gold and silver, after the manner of Asia. They likewise made glass. But silk was not as yet woven in any

[1] See a note in part i. chap. ix. of *Middle Ages*.

town in the Western Empire, nor till near 400 years
after this period.   Yet about this time the Venetians began
to import wrought silk from Constantinople; but it seems
that linen was very uncommon."[1]   Here then is already a
textile factory system in operation in the west also, at the
very beginning of the ninth century.   The same author
gives the following instance of the rarity of linen (which,
however, he seems to mix oddly with woollen) cloth, namely,
that St. Boniface in a letter to a German bishop about this
time desires him to send cloth with a large nap : " I suppose,
he says, he meant woollen cloth for him to employ in
washing his feet."   Probably, adds Voltaire, this want of
linen " was the cause of all the diseases in the skin known
by the name of leprosy, so common at that time."   In the
next century we have still more certain notice of a woollen
manufacture northwards, where it was soon fated to become
famous.   Under date 960, Anderson writes as follows :[2]—
" About this time, or rather somewhat sooner according to
the great pensionary De Witt, *Interest of Holland*, part i.
chap. ii., the woollen manufacture of Flanders and other
parts of the Netherlands, which make so great a figure for
the six succeeding centuries, took its rise;" and the writer
thus quoted (De Witt) makes the further comments : " that
till now there were scarcely any merchants in all Europe,
excepting a few in the Republic of Italy, who traded with
the Indian caravans of the Levant;" and that, " the
Flemings, lying nearest to France, were the first that began
to earn their living by weaving, and sold the produce of their
labour in that fruitful land (France), where the inhabitants
were not only able to feed themselves, but also, by the
superfluous growth of their country, could put themselves
into good apparel.   Which Baldwin the Young, or the third

---

[1] *History of Commerce*, vol. i. p. 72.
[2] Compare Warden, *Linen Trade, Ancient and Modern*, p. 251.

Earl of Flanders"—he continues—" about the year 960, considerably improved by establishing annual fairs or markets in several places without any toll being demanded for goods either imported or exported."[1] Upon which narrative Anderson observes that "this judicious account from so great a man must naturally carry much conviction along with it, as what may be deemed an authentic, though brief, view of the rise of the famous Netherland woollen manufacture, probably prior to that of linen; the former being in a manner absolutely requisite for preserving men from the inclemency of the weather, the latter rather a species of luxury; many barbarous nations at this day living without any linen at all:"—a quaint old-fashioned fancy which illumines a prosaic theme. The nascent manufacture prospered greatly. "About the tenth century," writes Mr. Warden,[2] "the woollen cloth manufactures of the Flemings had gained a high name in Britain and in Germany, and large quantities of them were exported in exchange for the products of these lands." They were in fact exported far more widely; and in a little while the Netherlands became the principal producer of woollen goods for all the north of Europe, the carrying trade being done by the vessels of the Hanse League. How this great eminence in manufacture produced after a while a corresponding expansion of commerce, even as we have elsewhere seen how expanding commerce promotes increased manufacture, has been already told in the short sketch of the fortunes of that great corporation. This trade continued to flourish and increase for about 400 years, which takes us to about the time that it commenced to settle definitely in England. We shall hereafter have to relate from the English side the history of this transference; the story told from the Flemish side is no less instructive, and should not be omitted. It is given

[1] See p. 217.   [2] *Linen Trade, Ancient and Modern*, p. 291.

in a thoroughly philosophical spirit by Anderson, supplemented by the authority of De Witt, under date 1301, as follows :—" It happened about this time that the halls[1] of those Netherland cities who had at first made restrictive laws, under pretence of preventing deceit by the debasing of those manufactures (exactly answerable to our own mechanical companies in England, Scotland, and Ireland), but which were in reality principally intended for fixing and confining them to the cities alone, forced at length much of this weaving trade out of the cities, where those halls exercised their restraint, into the villages. The wars between France and Flanders drove it back from those villages to Tienen and Louvain in Brabant." But "the Brabanters (says the great pensionary De Witt, in his judicious book), nothing wiser than the Flemings, ran into the like restraining law of the halls of laying imposts on the manufacture ; which imprudent methods had before occasioned many tumults and uproars amongst the weavers in Flanders ; for, in the year 1300, in a tumult at Ghent, two magistrates and eleven other citizens were slain. In the year following the above 1500 persons were slain at Bruges on the same account. And in a similar riot and on the same score all the magistrates of Ypres were killed. Some time after this also, at Louvain, in a great tumult of the cloth-weavers and their adherents, several magistrates were slain in the Council-house, and many of the offenders fled to England, whither they first carried the art of drapery. Many other cloth-weavers with their followers, as well Brabanters as Flemings, dispersed themselves into the countries beyond the Meuse, and into Holland, and amongst other places." Mr. Anderson conjectures that those who took refuge in England at this time were " the same with those mentioned in the *Fœdera* under the year 1351, who had licences from King Edward

---

[1] *i.e.* the Guild halls.

III., and privileges granted by him for settling in England;" scarcely a happy conjecture, as a full half century intervened. However, "these cities of Ghent, Bruges, and Ypres in Flanders; and Brussels, Tienen, and Louvain in Brabant, soon lost much of their trade and manufactures." The importance of the loss thus sustained, and the extent of their woollen manufacture at the period named, may be further gathered from the facts, also mentioned by Anderson (p. 273), that those engaged about it in Louvain alone amounted to "no less than 4000 woollen drapers, clothiers, or master-weavers; and above 150,000 journeymen weavers." Of the prosperity of Bruges at the same time, resulting in a great measure from the same trade, something has already been said; and that the outward symbols of wealth were lavishly displayed is exemplified in the recorded remark of a Queen of France, wife of Phillipe le Bel, who was visiting there: "I thought I was the only queen here, but judging from the apparel of those I see around me, there must be many wives of kings and princes present." Another story told of this city, in company this time with Ghent and Ypres, will suffice to fill up the picture of the pride and power of those mediæval factory towns. It is given thus in Mr. J. Hamilton Fyfe's pleasant and compendious volume entitled *Merchant Enterprise*:[1] "When in 1351 the burgomasters of Bruges, Ghent, and Ypres, went to Paris to pay homage to King John, they were received with much pomp and distinction, but yet found reason to be dissatisfied. Being invited to a grand feast, they observed that their seats at table were not furnished with cushions. In order to make known their displeasure at this want of regard to their dignity, they took off their richly embroidered cloaks, folded them, and sat upon them. On rising from table, they left their cloaks behind them; and being informed of their

[1] Page 148.

apparent forgetfulness, Simon von Eertrycke, burgomaster of Bruges, replied, 'We Flemings are not in the habit of carrying away our cushions after dinner.'" Ghent was in 1400 a city able to furnish 80,000 persons capable of bearing arms, and the weavers alone "provided a formidable contingent of 20,000" (idem). Ypres, Oudenarde, Dendermont, Lille, and several other towns were only in the second rank as compared with these, but were very prosperous centres of manufacture as well. We have no suggestion of factories in connection with this manufacture. It seems to have been wholly of the individualistic handicraft kind.

In the meanwhile the woollen manufacture had been making rapid advances in other parts of Europe. In Italy, more especially at Florence, the weaving and dressing of cloth had become a great business. " In the first half of the fourteenth century there were more than 200 cloth manufacturing and dyeing establishments in Florence. From 70,000 to 80,000 pieces were produced in the year, valued at about 1,200,000 golden florins," and " more than 30,000 persons were engaged in and supported by this manufacture and trade."[1] Into Spain it had been reintroduced by the Moors, and under their skilful supervision had reattained considerable excellence and extent. With their departure it declined. In the sixteenth century Seville possessed upwards of 16,000 looms, which gave employment to 130,000 persons. When Philip V. ascended the throne in 1664, the number had dwindled down to 300 looms. Toledo, in 1550, had upwards of fifty woollen factories, and in 1665 only thirteen: almost the whole trade having been carried away by the Moors, who established it at Tunis. Owing to the same cause the art of manufacturing silk, for which Toledo had been celebrated, was entirely lost, and

[1] History of the Commonwealth of Florence, by T. A. Trollope.

nearly 40,000 persons who depended on it were deprived
of their means of support, and other manufactures shared
the fate.

Next in importance after woollen come linen fabrics.
In his *History of Commerce* (vol. i. p. 96),
Anderson gives the following brief and   FLAX.
comprehensive sketch of the rise and progress of this manufacture in Europe :—" The linen manufacture came first
from Egypt into Greece and Italy, and thence travelled
westward to France and Flanders, next probably into
Germany and England, before it got ground in the more
northern and north-east parts of Europe, where it has since
prospered very much.   Others think that the Carthaginians
first introduced it into Europe." He also says that " the
woollen manufacture in all probability preceded the linen,"
which accords with the opinion of De Witt.   This is, however, scarcely a satisfactory summary of the matter.   It
may, indeed, be allowed without difficulty that the " linen
manufacture came first from Egypt," if by that is meant
that its production on a great scale is first recorded in history
as occurring there ; and also that it found its way from
thence " into Greece and Italy," for that is pretty certain.
But the other suppositions are by no means so well borne
out by well-established facts.   It is known, for instance,
that as the Romans pushed their arms northward through
France and Germany—in other words, when the inhabitants
of those then remote countries were first revealed to the rest
of the world—that a linen manufacture of some kind was
already found established there.   Pliny tells how flax was
grown and woven into sailcloth in many parts of Gaul before
his time, and that in the still remoter regions beyond the
Rhine the women wore linen vestments of native manufacture, and he describes the shape and peculiarities which they
presented.   Tacitus relates the same thing, and adds that the

men also wore linen clothing, except in the coldest districts
where fur and skins were (naturally) preferred. The former
writer even describes the places where these German linens
were woven, namely, in cellars under ground, a statement
full of interest to the prehistoric archæologist and weighty
with suggestion to the practical weaver. Mr. Warden cites
two very ancient authorities to show that the Scandinavian
peoples, with whom the Romans had as yet no intercourse,
were clothed in linen. He relates (p. 200) " how it is
mentioned by Paulus Diaconus, in the history of the Longo-
bards, that the German ancestors of the Anglo-Saxons wore
loose and flowing gowns chiefly made of linen," and that it
is also recorded in Equihart's *Life of Charlemagne* that " the
Anglo-Saxons wore principally linen garments." Gibbon
bears testimony to the same circumstance as regards the
ancient dress of the Lombards (*idem*, p. 201). It is possible,
of course, that this material, or the knowledge of its manufacture, may have originally made its way from Italy, as
suggested, into those remote regions, but it is not very
probable. It is far more likely in our opinion to have made
a way, if a way had to be made for it at all, from the shores
of the Black Sea, travelling northward and westward up the
valleys of the great rivers ; or to have been brought to the
Baltic coast by the early seekers after amber. Most likely
of all, however, it was native to the country from the time
of the Aryan immigration. Spain, indeed, which is a country
not mentioned by Anderson in this catalogue, was celebrated for its linen manufacture long before Italy, France, or
Flanders; and was the country from amongst all others which,
in the disruption of the Roman world, clung to its industrial
character most persistently. The Romans had long possessed
government textile factories there, and even so late as after
the taking of Jerusalem by Titus, namely, in 130 A.D., we
read of the Emperor Adrian transplanting a colony of Jews

thither to be employed in them.[1] The Goths found these factories still established when they occupied the country, and almost certainly continued to work some of them, for they must have been the models on which those mentioned by Voltaire as existing in the south of France were formed; and the Moors established others during their occupation. It appears that the Spanish linen trade was confined then and after principally to the coarser fabrics. It was otherwise with German linen, which early achieved a high reputation both for durability and fineness, second only to the later and still finer textures of Flanders and Brabant. Augsburg was one of the chief mediæval centres of this industry as of so many more. A few other notices of linen in Europe may be cited. It is stated by Macpherson (*Annals of Commerce*) that about 500 A.D. the British and Irish were in the habit of wrapping the bodies of their eminent dead in linen; and Warden mentions that " by the ancient laws of Wales all the officers of the household (of a Welsh king) were appointed to be clothed every year, the king furnishing the woollen and the queen the linen cloth for that purpose."[2] This would seem to argue a pretty extensive native manufacture on a large scale of woollen and linen goods in that quarter of our island at a very early date. At one time linen seems to have been used as a medium of exchange. In 1109, according to Helmoldus, an author quoted by Warden, linen cloth was used as money in the island of Rugen on the coast of Pomerania. It was sixty years after this that the Hanse League was established, one principal object of which undoubtedly was at first the promotion and protection of the linen manufacture of the north of Europe. About the same time France was appearing as a competitor in the linen trade, the principal districts in that country in which it flourished being the Vosges, and

[1] *Romance of Trade*, p. 7. [2] *The Linen Trade*, p. 353.

Brittany. A little later, namely, in 1394, we read how the
French king sent "fine linen of Rheims," to the sultan in
part payment of a ransom. Half a century after we come
upon the name of a celebrated French worthy, Jacques
Cœur, "who had 300 factors, and traded with the Turks
and Persians." He "exported large quantities of linens and
other goods" (presumably of French manufacture). This
great mediæval capitalist lived at Bourges, and had probably
his factories there, or in the neighbourhood. In Italy during
the Middle Ages the manufacture of flax seems never to
have risen to the distinction attained by the manufactures of
silk and wool, notwithstanding the ample supply of the raw
material there. In the later Middle Ages, the Low Countries
and Brabant were, as has been often noted, the principal seats
of both the woollen and linen manufactures. Wherever in
these regions the one throve the other seems to have thriven
too, and for no doubt the same reason—the greater personal
and commercial freedom that was enjoyed in those parts.
Several localities there gave names to fabrics which they
still bear, as Diaper, i.e. drap d'Ypres; Cambric, from the
town Cambray where it was made, etc.

The same causes that ultimately proved fatal to the
Netherlands woollen trade proved fatal to her linen trade
also. It migrated elsewhere, a part passing to England,
Scotland, and Ireland, but by far the greater part going to
France and Germany. At the very end of the Middle Ages
Holland was still pre-eminent for its linens, but the pre-
eminence was not fated to last much longer.

It appears that but little use was made of cotton
COTTON.   by the classical nations, nor anywhere in
Europe up to the breaking up of the Western
Empire (476 A.D.), and for a long time subsequent to that
date. Its early history must be, therefore, sought in Asia.
But scarcely anything satisfactory is to be learned of it even

there. Some cotton pieces were no doubt occasionally sent from India, and possibly from Persia, to Constantinople, for they are named among commodities imported from the former place which were charged with duties in the reign of Justinian ; but they seemed to have excited little remark. "Left to conjecture," says Mr. Baines,[1] "to account for this fact, I can only suppose that the soft texture, glossy surface, and brilliant hues of silk so different from woollen, linen, or cotton, and so much superior, captivated general admiration ; and that muslins and chintzes could not vie with silks as articles of luxury, whilst they were too dear to compete with the manufactures of wool and flax as the materials of ordinary wear." In Arabia, however, in Mesopotamia, and ·in several of the neighbouring countries, cottons were certainly in pretty general use before the era of the Mahometan conquests, which first diffused them widely over the western world. Thus they are found frequently mentioned as an ordinary material for clothing in the history of the early caliphs. Of Omar, the immediate successor of Mahomet, it is noticed that " he preached in a tattered cotton gown, torn in twelve places ;" and of Ali, Omar's contemporary and successor, that, " on the day of his inauguration, he went to the mosque dressed in a thin cotton gown, tied round him with a girdle, a coarse turban on his head, his slippers in one hand, and his bow in the other."[2] This was as early as the latter end of the seventh century. In *The Arabian Nights' Entertainments* (which delightful story-book refers to a period somewhat after this time), *muslins* are mentioned as being in common use, though it has been questioned if these particular muslins were really cotton goods, for Marco Polo, in the thirteenth century, writes of cloths of gold and *silk* . . . " of the manufacture of Mosul,"

[1] *History of the Cotton Manufacture*, p. 26.
[2] Crichton's *History of Arabia*, vol. i. pp. 397, 403.

the town in Mesopotamia from which this fabric takes its
name. This is but another instance of the difficulty of
drawing conclusions from the statements of untrained
observers where industrial technology is concerned. It is
certain, however, that cotton muslins were then, as long
before, and since, made in India, especially in the province
of Bengal ; and they might have easily reached Bagdad from
thence. The same distinguished Venetian, Marco Polo, who
is almost the only authority we possess on the condition
of the Asiatic nations at this time, furnishes several other
interesting particulars of the growth and manufacture of
cotton just previous to its introduction into Europe. They
are thus briefly grouped together by Mr. Baines :[1]—" It
appears that at that period there was a manufacture of very
fine cotton at Arzingam in Armenia Major ; that cotton was
abundantly grown and manufactured in Persia, and all the
provinces bordering on the Indus ; that in all parts of India
this was the staple manufacture ; and that it flourished
particularly at Guzerat, Cambray, Bengal, Masulipatam, and
Malabar."   A note appended to the above statement further
informs us that the fashionable Asiatic ladies of those days
employed artifices for adding to the natural attractions of
the female form, not wholly without a parallel in our time.
The women of Balashan, in Cabul, wore " below their waists,
in the manner of drawers, a kind of garment in the making
of which they employ, according to their means, 100, 80,
or 60 ells of fine cotton cloth, which they also gather and
pleat in order to increase the apparent size of their hips ;
those being accounted the most handsome who are the most
bulky in that part."   Have we not heard something of a
fashion of this kind nearer home, and not so long since ?
Marco Polo mentions one district of China where he says
cotton was woven ; upon which statement Mr. Baines

[1] *History of the Cotton Manufacture*, chap. iii.

remarks that, "as in no other place does he mention cotton
being grown or made into cloth in China," the curious fact
may be inferred, "established too by Chinese annals, that
that early civilised and ingenious and industrious people
remained without the cotton manufacture till the end of the
thirteenth century, when it had flourished among their
Indian neighbours probably 3000 years." In the same
connection the same author quotes another statement from
an Arabic source, to the effect that up to the ninth century
at all events " the inhabitants, from the prince to the peasant,
were clothed in silks." After the conquest of the country
by the Tartars, however,[1] the manufacture of cottons spread
with such rapidity that cotton fabrics were soon, as they
still are, by far the most generally used in clothing. About
the same time it began to spread slowly to the north and
west; its advance being in every case most difficult to trace.
Its principal seat in Europe was Barcelona, renowned during
the later Middle Ages for its manufacture of sailcloth and
fustian; the latter being a coarse cotton cloth deriving its
name from the Spanish word *fuste*—signifying substance.
Mr. Baines has expended much intelligent labour and
research in tracing the rise of the cotton manufacture in
Europe. His conclusion is, that outside the Moorish districts
of Spain it was little known, and that little cotton cloth was
imported. " Descriptions remain of the flourishing manufactures of silk, woollen, and linen in Greece in the tenth
century; of the silk manufactures of Sicily, Lucca, Venice,
and other parts of Italy, in the twelfth, thirteenth, and
fourteenth centuries; of the great extent and perfection of
the woollen manufactures in Flanders, Lombardy, Tuscany,
and Romagna at the same period; and of the extensive
trade carried on by the Italian states, the Hanse towns,
Flanders, and France, on the revival of commerce and the

[1] Compare chap. iii. p. 116.

16

arts. But in the records of all these branches of industry in different parts of Christendom, the manufacture of cotton finds no place."[1] The same writer furnishes, too, what is no doubt the true explanation of this slow spread of so valuable a manufacture northwards,[2] for " between the Mussulmans and the Christians there was as great repugnance as between oil and water " and " reciprocal hatred and scorn, and not less the ignorance and poverty of the Christian nations, formed insurmountable bars to intercourse."

Like the metal manufacture of a still more ancient date, the greatest possible obscurity prevails

METAL MANUFACTURE.

respecting mediæval metal manufacture. Of the *arts* of metal work, the labour of the smith, the armourer, pewterer, cutler, etc., much most interesting information is to be found in a great variety of quarters ; but of the manufacture itself scarce a vestige of information is accessible. Yet this was, undoubtedly, practised on a considerable scale in Europe during the Middle Ages. The production of silver, copper, lead, iron, and tin must have proceeded to some extent there even during the Dark Ages, and with increasing vigour afterwards. Especially must this have been so in the case of iron, the use of which for armour was so general. Where did all the iron come from that was manufactured into swords and suits of mail ? and how was it produced ? It appears probable that the greater part of it came at first from the mountains of north-eastern Germany, and from Scandinavia : the countries which furnished their weapons to the conquerors of western Europe. The arts that had penetrated into those countries in the Roman time remained there afterwards, for they were not overrun at the close of that era by a foreign foe ; and it is therefore likely that they continued to supply their people

[1] Baines, p. 37.   [2] *Idem*, p. 42.

with native metallic products till these had fully settled down
in their new abodes and begun to open mines and to manufacture metals for themselves. Those supplies were supplemented, no doubt, from southern Spain, where the iron manufacture also survived the downfall of the Roman power and
continued to be prosecuted under the rule of the Visigoths ;
and would be increased by whatever trade the new settlers
managed to establish with the Greek Empire, and through
it with the far East, where all forms of metal manufacture
still continued active. Gold would be principally obtained
from Asia ; though the spoils of their luxurious predecessors
must have furnished alone a sufficient store of this metal
for many successive ages of barbarians to draw upon without
exhausting ; and this condition of things continued probably
to the time of Charlemagne, whose efforts in the direction
of promoting all kinds of industry have been often mentioned.
In his reign the division of labour in metal manufacture had
been carried, at all events, as far as to have different orders
of workers in the same metal: as for example a separate
order of shield-makers : and this implies a manufacture of
wrought metal so considerable as to make it almost certain
that the metal itself must have been produced somewhere near
on a large scale. Iron and silver ores existed in plenty
in the eastern portions of Charlemagne's dominions, and it is
thus probable that it was from that quarter that the supplies
of central Europe were thenceforward for some time obtained.
Iron mines were also worked in the Middle Ages in Langue-
doc, Champagne, Lorraine, and Berri, and as early as the
eighth century in Saxony and Nassau. About the same time
the great resources of northern Spain appear to have become
again available to the outer world. Under date 989
Anderson writes : "Towards the close of this century the
people of Biscay, who had with their Christianity preserved
their independence, even when the Moors possessed all the

rest of Spain, being now become more potent by their gain
in ground on the Moors, began to employ themselves in the
manufacturing of their excellent iron, not only for their own
use but for the supply of other nations." This source of
supply was, no doubt, greatly availed of by the neighbouring
countries of France and Italy. For the mode of production
we are dependent upon guess work. In Spain the tradition
of their great ancient metal manufacture would probably
survive, and it is scarcely too rash an assumption that their
methods would be the same as they had practised thousands
of years before. If so, we may even now have a fair idea
of what the primitive appliances were there, for the small
Catalan forge may still be seen at work among the valleys
of the Pyrenees, and for a long time this was the undoubted model of all mediæval bloomeries. Later in the
Middle Ages the interior and east of Germany were still
the principal seats of metal manufacture, both silver and
iron ; and of copper after the discovery of the copper mines
of Hungary and Bohemia. A manufacture of tin and brazen
goods was also established there, particularly at Prague
and Nuremberg, the metal tin being of course an imported
commodity.

Besides the greater industries whose existence has been
thus briefly traced, there was of course an
abundance of smaller ones, many of which
were carried to great perfection in the Middle Ages. It
hardly needs to mention here the beautiful handicraft metal-
work of the Renaissance period, unless it be to point the
moral against the far inferior work produced in our time
under the factory system, and that is not now our theme.
Nor does the not dissimilar subject of wood-carving properly
belong to it. Those smaller industries, particularly such as
were connected with the working of metals, may be found
dealt with, specially or generally, in many popular books

SMALLER INDUSTRIES.

of great repute, and nowhere at once more briefly and better than in M. Lacroix's splendid volumes on the *Arts of the Middle Ages*. In another work of less pretension, *The Technical History of Commerce*, by Dr. Yeats,[1] many curious and instructive particulars are also furnished in a particularly concise manner ; and in the Art Handbooks issued under the auspices of the authorities at the South Kensington Museum (and published by Messrs. Chapman and Hall, London), the study of the subject may be pursued with facility into its more artistic and intricate parts. It is clearly outside the scope of this treatise.

There are two smaller industries connected with metal manufacture, however, which we are loth to pass by unnoticed even in this brief LOCKS AND CLOCKS. summary, on account of both their extrinsic and intrinsic interest in either case. The history of mediæval lock-making is not only in itself a curious and interesting one, but is doubly interesting as recounting the story of a craft that was the parent of much of our modern industrial machinery. "Its complex and ingenious arrangements," says Dr. Yeats, " afforded practical insight into the principles of mechanics," and thus turned many minds to this great source of future power, with such results as we shall see hereafter. Clockmaking undoubtedly arose out of it,[2] and was at first, like it, consecrated to the use of the Church. The locks and keys were not turned out by the gross or bushel as now, but each separate combination was a work of art, and engaged the prolonged attention and ingenuity of the maker.

In Beckman's *History of Inventions*, there is a learned

[1] *The Technical History of Commerce*, by John Yeats, LL.D. (Virtue and Co., 1872).

[2] Richard Arkwright's first patent was taken out in the name of " Richard Arkwright, Clockmaker," and his first models were undoubtedly made for him by the practical clockmakers Kay and Yates.

paper on clocks and watches,[1] from which we extract a few
particulars. The most ancient and obvious way of calcul-
ating time was by noting the progress of the sun. In
classical times, the water-clock, or *clepsydra*, was most in
use; and in the early Middle Ages the sand-glass, which
" was invented in France shortly before the accession of
Charlemagne, by a monk of Chartres, named Luitprand."[2]
These sand-glasses and sand-clocks afterwards became
common throughout Europe. Alfred the Great was the
inventor of candle-clocks, that is of candles placed in
horn lanterns on which the hours of the day were marked.
Mechanical clocks moved by weights and pulleys, however,
were known in Europe during the eleventh century, but
their use was principally confined to the monasteries.[3] In
the thirteenth century they were only beginning to be more
common, and were still very clumsy in construction, but
by the end of the next century great advances in the art
of clockmaking had been made. The first public clock
ever erected was put up at Padua. In 1356 a public clock
was put up at Bologna. Another in 1364 at Genoa. But
one is said to have been erected at Canterbury earlier than
this, namely, in 1292 ; and one at Westminster even earlier,
in 1288. Watches begin to be mentioned towards the end
of the fourteenth century. The principal place of manufacture both of clocks and watches was at first Nuremberg ;
but the manufacture soon spread into other parts of Germany,
and into France and Switzerland, and in time here. In the
present day it seems tending to transfer itself to America.

Another industry of the later Middle Ages, of great
interest for several reasons, is that of wire-
WIRE-DRAWING.
drawing—the reduction of metal in bulk,
that is, to this attenuated condition. This process, which

[1] Vol. i. pp. 340-373.   [2] *Technical History of Commerce*, p. 191.
[3] Beckman, p. 349.

is performed by forcing the metal through successively smaller holes bored in a harder substance, was an invention, according to Beckman, of the fourteenth century, the chief credit of which is due to one Rudolf of Nuremberg. He not only devised a machine for this purpose, but succeeded in working it by water-power.[1] This is one of the circumstances that gives the subject such interest in connection with the present survey. Hitherto the production of metal wire had always been a handicraft operation, and we have elsewhere noted the admirably vivid description of it in the Bible (Exod. xxxix. 3).[2] The application of water-power in this operation was thus one of the very earliest symptoms of that general substitution of other physical forces for manual labour which is the distinguishing characteristic of modern industrial history. Nor does the extrinsic interest in the process end here. After long being a successful manufacture in Germany, wire-drawing was introduced into England about 1565,[3] and became a prosperous trade; and it is said that it was in watching this process, and the somewhat similar one of rolling metal plates, that the first idea of the practicability of spinning by rollers occurred to the mind of Lewis Paul, and led him to attempt with others that extraordinary task.[4] But the manufacture is not without much intrinsic interest as well. Before the invention of wire-drawing, pins and needles[5] were costly luxuries,

[1] *History of Inventions*, vol. i. p. 414.   [2] Chap. iii. p. 92.
[3] Anderson's *History of Commerce*, vol. iv. p. 101.
[4] Compare chap. x. p. 407.
[5] It is said in Felkin's *History of the Hosiery and Lace Manufactures* that "the common sewing needle was brought hither from India after the discovery of the route by the Cape of Good Hope," see chap. x. p. 386. Another account of them is that they first came here from Spain; and they were undoubtedly at first called Spanish needles. "One of our old chroniclers (Stow) states that the making of Spanish needles was 'first taught in England by Elias Crowse, a Germaine, about the eighth yeere of Queene Elizabeth; and in Queene Marie's time there was a negro made fine Spanish needles in Cheap-

toilsomely wrought by hand, and made of bone, ivory, or
such substances. Thousands of millions of them are now
annually made from wire by machinery. In the provision
of suitable ropes for the tremendously heavy and powerful
shipping of modern days again, it has played an important
part; and finally, one of incomparable utility and wonder
in its connection with electricity.

After the fall of the Roman Empire, the art of dyeing
was lost to western Europe for several
centuries, but still flourished in the East,
where great imperial dye-houses continued to exist; and
it was apparently early practised in the North, where the
principal pigments then in use, *woad, weld, and madder*,
were found in profusion. Charlemagne was the first to
revive and encourage this art in the West; he ordered dye-
stuffs to be cultivated on his farms and supplied to the
royal factories, and he encouraged his courtiers to emulate
him in the wearing of handsome and varied apparel. These
efforts were successful, and the process of dyeing thenceforth took its place among other great branches of industry.
" The Frieslanders were the earliest to become distinguished
for their skill in dyeing, and the distinction was long
maintained. The dye-works of Harderwyk, still notable, are
referred to in the twelfth century, especially for the production
of blue and green colours." Flanders was early celebrated
for scarlet cloths, which were so much approved that " the
delivery of 1000 ells, sufficient to clothe 100 knights, was
one of the stipulations made by Count Henry of Schwerin
in 1225, previous to the release from captivity of King

DYEING.

---

side, but would never teach his art to any.' " Another writer states that
" needles were first made in England by a native of India (probably the
negro mentioned by Stow) in 1545, but the art was lost at his death ; it was,
however, recovered in 1650 by Christopher Greening, who settled with his
three children at Long Crendon, in Buckinghamshire."—*Useful Arts and
Manufactures*, Second Series.

Waldemar of Denmark." Scarlet cloths formed an important part of the presents which Henry the Lion, in his Crusades, offered to the Greek emperor. "Flemish dyers carried their art to Vienna where it took root, the artificers always retaining the name of Flemings, by which designation they are referred to in 1208. Ratisbon and Augsburg were, however, the chief places where dyeing was pursued" at this time. In the fifteenth century Italy, and especially Florence, had probably the pre-eminence in that respect. The contact with the East promoted by the Crusades marks an important epoch in the history of dyeing in Europe. "The leaders, leavened with Oriental taste, introduced into their own lands the custom of weaving gay clothing, particularly of yellow and scarlet, striped or. figured." But the rude workmen of those days "could neither understand nor imitate the exquisite harmony which delighted the Arabs, or the felicity of design in which they excelled," and their designs were for the most part either paltry or barbarous. "Nevertheless the colours were permanent, and the weaving and embroidery of very high skill, since many of the robes and tapestries preserved from mediæval times are still fresh and bright and of a fine texture." [1]

Felting is a process of uniting woollen particles without weaving, usually (now almost invariably) employed in the manufacture of hats and caps. FELTING. It was certainly familiar to the Greeks, and probably known from far more ancient times.[2] Saxon writers mention "fellen hats"—worn by their people; and the Tartars had cloaks and tents made of this material. The ancient Gauls

[1] This account of mediæval dyeing, slightly altered, is taken from the *Technical History of Commerce*, by John Yeats, LL.D., pp. 150-154 (Virtue and Co., 1872).

[2] The author of *Textrinum Antiquorum* believes that the knowledge of the process of felting preceded that of weaving. See chap. iii. p. 81.

are also said to have used it for armour. In the early
Middle Ages coverings for the head were little worn except
by persons of dignity, serfs not being allowed to wear them
at all; but gradually, as serfdom was abolished, the custom
of covering the head became more general. Hats and caps
were first made in Europe upon a large scale, about the
middle of the thirteenth century, chiefly in Italy. They
were introduced into France and made popular by Charles
VII., and in the beginning of the sixteenth century the
manufacture was brought over by the Spanish to England,
where it firmly established itself and increased with great
rapidity. In Elizabeth's reign an Act was passed protecting
the manufacture here.

There is a curious book extant in the British Museum, the
production of one Jacob Christian Schaffer
of Ratisbon (1775 A.D.) It describes the
manufacture of paper from different substances, each of the
sixty leaves of the book being made from a different one.
This circumstance will give some idea of the number of experiments in the way of paper-making that have at various
times been tried. There are, in fact, but few vegetable fibres
of a pulpy kind that have not been experimented upon to
this end. The paper now in use, however, is mostly made
of cotton or linen rags, and such was also the case during
the Middle Ages. Previous to paper being manufactured
of those materials, parchment and even papyrus was used
throughout Europe for literary purposes; a bull of Paschal
II. being the latest document known to have been written
on the last-named one. This paper, or papyrus, was principally or exclusively made in Egypt. Linen paper first supplanted parchment, but as it was scarce and dear, cotton paper
began to be purchased from the Arabs about the thirteenth
or fourteenth centuries. The use of cotton paper was derived
from the remote east. It almost certainly originated in

PAPER.

China some centuries before the Christian era, and was first made known to the Saracens when they conquered Samarcand (704 A.D.) Soon afterwards a "paper manufactory is said to have been established at Mecca."[1] The products of this manufactory found their way into Europe as early as the seventh century, and either suggested the possibility of making a similar commodity from flax, or the Arabs carrying the art of paper-making with them to Spain (where large quantities of flax grew) applied it to that material. For reasons already given, the discovery was slow in being brought into use in Christendom, so much so that beyond the bounds of the Moorish dominions in Spain "the first paper-mills appeared in 1340 in the castle of Fabriano, near Ancona, and in 1390 in Augsburg and Nuremberg."[2] The discovery once fully understood and appreciated, however, spread rapidly over Europe, and soon made itself a home in nearly every country of it. It is clear that the production of paper must have been from the first on the large scale, for it is not such an industry as comes naturally within the sphere of handicraft production.

The manufacture of pottery at this period was confined within extremely narrow limits. There was a rude kind of pottery produced in Germany POTTERY. which formed an article of trade, and a greatly improved kind was made long afterwards in Holland, particularly at Delft, from which place it took its name; but it is scarcely too much to say that with these exceptions there was no native earthenware manufactured in Europe. In Asia at the same time beautiful earthenware was being produced; and the Arabs brought into Spain a perfect familiarity with this valuable and useful art; as little availed of in

[1] *The Natural History of Society*, by W. Cooke Taylor, LL.D., vol. ii. p. 257 (Longmans, 1840).
[2] *Technical History of Commerce*, p. 203.

Spain at that time as many other valuable arts and gifts of knowledge which they lavishly offered the superstitious Christians there. The manipulation of terra cotta into graceful forms, and the making of encaustic tiles were among the greatest triumphs of Arab pottery. Italy was the first country outside Spain to profit at length by these opportunities that for centuries had been at her disposal. The knowledge of the Moorish pottery had found its way at some time into the island of Majorca, and it was found there when that island was taken by the Pisans in 1115.[1] Thence it spread to Italy, where a beautiful pottery known since by the name of "Majolica" was the result. The impulse once given continued to spread, and after a while Italy became celebrated for other fine wares. Long afterwards France, under the tuition of the noble Palissy, was taught to rival Italy, and Böttgher, the alchemist, by the discovery and use of native kaolin[2] did almost as much for Germany. But the revival of that industry in which ancient Greece and Italy had once, and possibly for ever, excelled all the world belongs rather to the history of modern than mediæval times.

The skin of beasts either tanned or untanned, whether stripped of fur or not, was a common article of manufacture in the Middle Ages. In the earlier part of that period the centre of Europe was still covered by dense forests, through which innumerable animals roamed, protected by nature in their hairy coverings from the extreme severity of the weather. To remove those coverings from their backs and place them upon human backs was a very obvious artifice for securing comfort to the latter, especially when the stripped carcase could be also utilised for human food. Of the method employed for

LEATHER.

---

[1] *Self Help*, by Samuel Smiles, chap. iii. p. 67 (Murray, 1882).

[2] Compare p. 168.

transforming these skins to leather, and for the preparation
of furs, at that time, not a particle of information rewards
the most sedulous search. The probability is, therefore, as
Dr. Yeats remarks,[1] " that there was nothing new in them,
and that the operations of tanning, from dressing and improving the hides with lime and oak-bark, to the preparing
of leather fit for the saddler, shoemaker, and glover,
as well as the implements used in the manufacture of
the art, had been the same from time immemorial." That
the secrets of those methods were familiarly known from a
remotely ancient past we have already had occasion to note
(*ante*, chap. iv.),[2] and it is an open question to the present
day if, with the experience of all the intervening time, that
primeval manufacture has ever been improved upon.

The three uses of leather just mentioned, *i.e.* for saddlery,
shoes, and gloves, are the principal ones latterly connected in
our minds with the manufacture of this material, but previous
to the development of textile industry complete suits of leather
clothing were common. A well-known passage from Dante,
quoted in Mr. T. A. Trollope's *History of Florence*, illustrates
this fact even in the south of Europe. Speaking of the
great simplicity of Florentine manners before the building
of the second walls, the poet says, "I have seen Bellincion
Berti in the streets with a leather girdle fastened with a
buckle of bone, and his wife coming from the glass with no
paint upon her face. I have seen the De Nervi and Del
Vecchio, content to be clad in plain leather uncovered with
cloth, and their wives busy with the distaff and spindle."
This was in 1078. Leather was in extensive " and almost
exclusive use," says Dr. Yeats, " among the Saxons and the
early English, while the woollen manufactures were as yet
but little developed." The lower orders of the people wore
suits of leather. These complete suits, inclusive of the

---

[1] *Technical History of Commerce*, p. 162.   [2] P. 176.

shoes, were generally of native manufacture; the saddlery
and gloves in use at the same time were principally imported.
The chief seats of these latter manufactures were in the
great towns of central Europe:—Augsburg, Strasburg, Nuremberg, Vienna, etc.—and in Spain. The chief seats of the
glove manufacture were at first almost exclusively in Spain,
and afterwards in France and Italy. The leather workers
of the Middle Ages retained that character for sturdy independence which they had borne from very primitive times;[1]
shoemakers appearing to have been at all times a particularly difficult class of work-people to keep in subjection.
In the later Middle Ages, Flanders became specially celebrated
for its beautiful leather work, and in Flanders particularly
Ghent and Namur.

The great glass factories of ancient Phœnicia had a later
counterpart in the great imperial glass factories of Byzantium, and these again had
their mediæval counterparts in the great glass factories of
Venice. The sandy islands upon which Venice is built
afforded abundant material for this manufacture. It will be
remembered that in an earlier part of this chapter Voltaire
(quoted by Anderson) was cited as saying that as early as
810 A.D. there were manufactures of glass at Rome and
Ravenna, and elsewhere in Italy (see p. 229). So far as
Ravenna is concerned this statement is easily credible, but it
is hardly likely to be true of Rome at that time, though in
the time of Severus (220 A.D.) there were so many glass manufacturers that a special quarter of the city was set apart for
them. Ravenna was then a powerful and prosperous portion
of the Greek Empire, but Rome had been sacked and pillaged
several times over, and was not likely to have many manufactures left.[2] However that may be, it is indubitable that
the manufacture of glass was continued in Europe all through

GLASS.

[1] Compare p. 177.   [2] P. 171.

the Dark Ages, and that it was an article of trade. " Glass melted and passed into plates, is said by St. Jerome to have been used in his day (422 A.D.) to form windows ;" and " about a century later Paulus Silentiarius mentions the windows of the church of St. Sophia, at Constantinople, which were covered with glass."[1] From this period frequent allusions to the similar use of it are met with in various authors. It will be sufficient here to quote but one, that of the venerable Bede, who relates how in 674 Benedict, abbot of the monastery of Wearmouth in Durham, sent abroad for foreign artisans to glaze the windows of his church ; and who says that these were the first instructors of the English in the art of making window-glass. The glass employed on these occasions was stained or coloured glass, for pure white glass was not known in Europe for long afterwards, and from the use of this coloured glass arose glass painting, " the first trace of which is met with in the monastery of Tegernsee in Bavaria (983-1000)." A letter of the abbot of this monastery to Count Arnold is still extant in which he thanks him for providing such decorations for the church. Glass factories appear to have been established at Hildesheim in Germany 1022-1039, and a century later at St. Denis in France, and houses for glass painting at several places.[2] On the substitution of Gothic for Roman architecture, this art spread rapidly throughout Europe, a fresh impetus being given to the staining of glass by the fact that the high pointed windows of the later style afforded much more scope for the development of colouring and ornamentation. But although the windows of churches and cathedrals were thus being glazed by the end of the first half of the Middle Ages, " a thick gloom," says Dr. Yeats, continued " to pervade the apartment, and for a long time

---

[1] " Manufacture of Glass," from Lardner's *Cabinet Cyclopædia*, chap. i.

[2] *Technical History of Commerce*, p. 137.

there were no glass windows in villages, towns, or fortresses. It is supposed," he adds, "that even the castles and palaces of Charlemagne and other German princes were without glass windows. Oiled paper, linen, horn, and any other substance admitting a moderate amount of light, and excluding the winds and rain, were probably used to enhance the comfort of dwelling-houses at that time." Windows of glass were, however, more generally introduced into England in 1180, some of the royal palaces and churches being then provided with them.[1] In the next century cut glass is mentioned as an article of traffic conveyed up the Danube. Glass mirrors, overlaid at the back with lead, are first mentioned in 1279 by Johannes Peccan, an English Franciscan monk who taught at Oxford, Paris, and Rome. In 1363 a corporation of glaziers is met with at Augsburg, and in 1373 one of looking-glass makers at Nuremberg. About this time too white glass was made in Bohemia, as is proved by remnants still remaining in Prague Cathedral and in Karlstein Castle. The use of glass, however, was still very limited, for the Senate-House of Zurich, built in 1402, had cloth windows during the greater part of that century, but fifty years later Æneas Silvius could boast that half the houses of Vienna had glass windows. At about the same time window-glass is said to have been certainly manufactured in England, but glass bottles were still a great rarity.[2]

The mediæval organisation of manufacture was in the early part of the Middle Ages for the most
MEDIÆVAL SYSTEM.
part domestic and individualist; and in the later part generally corporate and municipal. As civilisation spread at that time from the east to the west, its complexion underwent a marked and characteristic change, particularly on the practical side. The Oriental ideals that

---

[1] *Technical History of Commerce*, p. 137.
[2] *Idem*, chap. ii. sec. ii.

influenced European life were principally displayed in the sphere of art; while in those of politics and industry the hardier ideals of the north and west continued supreme. Thus in the particular sphere of labour, the tendency from the Dark Ages down to modern times has been consistently in the direction of more liberty, to the exclusion of caste, ϒ and the abrogation of hereditary succession in trades. Tendencies, however, do not always necessarily, nor still less immediately, fulfil themselves. It is the nature of man that no sooner is he free of all habitual obligations than he must forthwith begin to impose new ones on himself. The better kind of man indeed cannot live without obligations to his fellow-man, and it would be very undesirable if he could. Thus no sooner did labour begin to revolt against early mediæval trammels than it began also to forge new ones. No sooner were the craftsmen generally emancipated from serfdom than they subjected themselves to the tyranny of the municipalities and merchant guilds, and no sooner did they conquer in the struggle with these than they set about devising a new set of prohibitions and regulations in their craft guilds and trade societies. The story of this struggle and of those rules, is the story of the development of the system of mediæval industry; of the victory first of commerce over feudal rights, and next of labour over commercial greed. Nothing but the very briefest sketch of it can be given here.

It is stated by M. Lacroix,[1] that in Germany as late as the tenth century "the ordinary condition of artisans was still serfdom;" but that "two centuries later the greater number of trades in most of the large towns had congregated together in colleges or bodies." According to this testimony then, the eman-

---

[1] *Manners, Customs, and Dress*, p. 274.

cipation of the artisan class over that part of the Continent occurred during the eleventh and twelfth centuries. It may have occurred about the same time in France, but it had certainly commenced earlier in Italy and the Low Countries. The first characteristic form of mediæval labour organisation that resulted from these changes was the Merchant or Town Guild. The members of a merchant guild were invariably freeholders of the town where they resided, but "in addition to the possession of land, many of these freemen carried on trade, some also what in later times were called handicrafts." . . . After a while a change began to pass over them. "As the status and wealth of the people became more diversified, there arose questions of precedence; the old guild was closed to newcomers, and other guilds arose. Then came the higher and the highest guild; and restrictions were introduced as to membership. The oldest guild was no longer equivalent to the whole town or full body of the citizens, and in time the oldest or 'old burgher guild' became the aristocratic guild, assumed the government of the town, and filled the municipal offices of the township." Then another specialisation occurred. "With the increase of wealth and population there also came a greater division of labour; the richer (members) carried on trade, the poorer became craftsmen." Presently a still further specialisation was introduced. Practising handicraftsmen were excluded from membership in the merchant guild, and at length only admitted after having "forsworn their trade for a year and a day."[1] That is to say, the merchant guild about this time was changing from a democratic to an oligarchic institution, and its economic basis shifting from a basis of production to one of exchange. But this was not to be the end. A new kind of association, the Craft Guild, arose in the thirteenth

---

[1] See *The Conflicts of Capital and Labour*, parts iii. and iv.

and fourteenth centuries, in opposition to the elder one, and the contest between the two classes of guilds was practically fought out all over Europe, the victory remaining with the craftsmen. Henceforth the guild system became more an organised system of productive industry, and lost more and more of the patrician and religious character which at other stages it had assumed. The craft guilds were trade societies, composed exclusively of productive members. The constitution, functions, and regulations of these bodies, which were the principal motive power in the industrial labour system of the Middle Ages, are described with ample fulness in Mr. Howell's book, and a statement of them is to be found accompanied by most interesting illustrations in M. Lacroix's. We avail ourselves here of a summary of them from this latter source, as being short enough for quotation. " Generally the members of a trade corporation were divided into three distinct classes—the masters, the paid assistants or companions, and the apprentices. Apprenticeship, from which the sons of masters were often exempted, began between the ages of twelve and fourteen years, and lasted from two to five years. In most of the trades the master could only receive one apprentice in his house besides his own son. Tanners, dyers, and goldsmiths were allowed one of their relatives in addition, or a second apprentice if they had no relation willing to learn their trade ; and although some commoner trades, such as butchers and bakers, were allowed an unlimited number of apprentices, the custom of restriction had become a sort of general law, with the object of limiting the number of masters and workmen to the requirements of the public. The position of paid assistant or companion was required to be held in many trades for a certain length of time before promotion to mastership could be obtained. When apprentices or companions wished to become masters they were called *aspirants*, and were subjected to successive

examinations. They were particularly required to prove
their ability by executing what was termed a *chef d'œuvre*,
which consisted in fabricating a perfect specimen of whatever craft they practised. The execution of the *chef d'œuvre*
gave rise to many technical formalities, which were at times
most frivolous. The aspirant had in certain cases to pass
a technical examination, as, for instance, the barber, in forging
and polishing lancets; the wool-weaver in making and
adjusting the different parts of the loom," etc. . . . The
statutes of some of these corporations had the force of law,
being approved and accepted by royal authority. Others
had only partial authority. They detailed with the greatest
precision the conditions of labour. "They fixed the hour
and day for working; the size of the article to be made;
the quality of the stuffs used in their manufacture; and
even the price at which they were to be sold. Night
work was pretty generally forbidden as likely to produce
imperfect work. . . . In most crafts the masters were
bound to put their trade mark on their goods, or some
particular sign, which was to be a guarantee to the pur-
chaser, and a means of identifying the culprit in the
event of complaint arising on account of the bad quality
or bad workmanship of the article sold. . . . Artisans
exposed themselves to a reprimand, and even to bodily
chastisement, from the corporation for even associating with,
and certainly from working or drinking with those who
had been expelled. Licentiousness and misconduct of any
kind rendered them liable to be deprived of their mastership " (*Manners, Customs, and Dress during the Middle Ages*,
pp. 270-295). Besides the stationary trade societies, there
were wandering bodies of artisans as well, who went about
from place to place hiring out their labour. The confraternity
of " free masons," which still nominally survives, was a fra-
ternity of this kind, and many of the beautiful buildings of

mediæval Europe are the work of wandering members of that craft. The tinker, and village " scissors grinder," of modern life are far off survivals from that time and habit. These societies had their strict rules and obligations like the stationary ones, but it is extremely difficult to learn anything of them.

CHAPTER VII.

ENGLAND BEFORE THE FACTORY SYSTEM TO THE REIGN OF EDWARD III.

The Ancient Britons—Primitive Manufactures—The Roman Period—Roman Manufactures—The Roman System—The Saxons—Saxon Manufactures—The Saxon System—The Normans—Classes at the Conquest—Domesday Book—The Plantagenets—Condition of Trade and Industry—Legislative Restrictions—Social Condition of this Time.

WHO were the original inhabitants of Britain is not, and in all probability cannot be known, any more than it is ever likely to be known who were the original people of the world itself. Here, as elsewhere, the traces of a prehistoric race abound, traces dating from a period so remote as to be related to time only in geologic chronology, and indicating the existence of human inhabitants in an immensely remote past. The islands that now form the kingdom of Great Britain and Ireland are supposed to have been at that time united to the mainland of Europe, and our great rivers flowing eastward, such as the Thames and Humber, to have been tributaries of the Rhine.[1] A race from the plains of central Asia, continually moving westward, and ever urged onward from behind, ultimately reached this most western land of all, and, unable to proceed any farther in its long migration, settled here. They were the people that it is

THE ANCIENT BRITONS.

[1] *Prehistoric Europe*, by James Geikie, LL.D., pp. 507, 509 ; also Appendix, Note C, p. 568, where a map of " Europe in Early Post-Glacial Times " is given (Stanford, 1881).

now usual to call Celts. They either extirpated the original inhabitants or amalgamated with them, thus becoming themselves in time the " Ancient Britons " to later conquerors. A great convulsion of nature severed them at some time from their continental brethren, making of these countries islands : in the interior of which they mostly relapsed into barbarism, retaining a knowledge of the useful arts only in the portions contiguous to the sea coast, which traded with the countries across the narrow seas. In this condition Cæsar found Britain when he first invaded it; from which period it emerges into history for a while, as a valued province of the Roman Empire, to shortly afterwards disappear, and presently reappear again under a new name, and as the home of a new people.

Like most other countries that have of late been carefully explored in the interests of anthropological science, Britain appears to have passed PRIMITIVE MANUFACTURES. through its two stone ages, the "paleolithic" and the "neolithic," or the epochs of rough and polished stone implements. So much the testimony of the ground beneath our feet abundantly reveals. The knowledge of the use of metals appears also to have been early acquired. It is further supposed that this knowledge was imported, not spontaneously developed, for among bronze implements and weapons of foreign shape and great antiquity, are sometimes found what are presumed to be native products of industry in bone, stone, and wicker-work ; and then imitations in metal of these latter occur, importing a new impulse in manufacture.[1] The copper used in this native metal manu-

---

[1] It is impossible to quote separately the authorities made use of here. The materials for this portion of this chapter are principally taken from Wright's *Celt, Roman, and Saxon* (Trübner, 1875) ; *The Early and Middle Ages of England*, by Charles H. Pearson, M.A. (Bell and Daldy, 1861) ; *The Popular History of England* ; Hume's *History of England* ; and Elton's *Origins of English History*.

facture was almost certainly obtained from abroad; the tin
was still more certainly a home product, and was probably smelted on the spot. Antiquarians have discovered
what seem to be the remains of immensely old bloomeries
in the tin regions, and all traditions point in the same direction. The country is first mentioned, though vaguely, as a
tin producing one by Herodotus; and more distinctly by
Aristotle, about 350 B.C. Two centuries later Polybius is
said to have written an entire treatise on this subject, now
unfortunately lost. A subsequent, though still ancient historian, Diodorus Siculus, has left, however (Book V. Cap. 22),
quite a vivid description of the whole process of the ancient
tin production, including even the placing the finished commodity on board the foreign vessels that called for it. "They
that inhabit the British promontory of Belerium" (Cornwall),
he says, "by reason of their converse with merchants, are more
civilised and courteous to strangers than the rest are. These
are the people that make the tin, which with a great deal
of care and labour they dig out of the ground; and that
being rocky, the metal is mixed with some grains of earth,
out of which they melt the metal and then refine it; then
they cast it into square-like pieces, like a die, and carry it
to a British island near at hand called Iktis (commonly but
not universally supposed to be St. Michael's Mount); for at
low tide, all being dry between them and the island, they
convey over an abundance." Diodorus was a contemporary
of the first two Cæsars, but this account may easily in its
essentials be applicable to long anterior times. Where the
copper used in Britain came from it is difficult to say. That
metal is found in many parts of England now, but there is
no evidence of its having been mined until comparatively
recent times.[1] With respect to other metals, Cæsar records

[1] The most ancient record of the extraction of copper ore in England refers
to a grant in the fifteenth year of Edward III., bestowing for a term of fifteen

that in his time iron was produced in Britain, though only
in small quantities. We know also that lead was manufactured either then or immediately after. A plate or "pig"
bearing the name of the Emperor Claudian, and the date
49 A.D., has been found in Yorkshire, and, as this date is
so little later than Cæsar's invasion it is inferred that the
mines, at all events, had been opened by the Britons, even
if the metal had not been manufactured by them.[1] It is
doubtful if native silver was known here then. Cicero
assured his friend Atticus that there was not a scruple of
silver in his day in the whole island ; yet only half a century
later we find Strabo quoting it as one of the mineral products
of the country. The probable explanation is that, as silver
is rarely found in a pure state, the Britons did not become
acquainted with the process of extracting it from its ores
until after the Roman occupation. With respect to textile
fabrics, if the ancient Britons did not bring with them to
our shores, or develop among themselves afterwards, a knowledge of textile manufacture, they must early have acquired
it from the traders with whom they had intercourse.
They were familiar with the arts of dressing, spinning,
and weaving both flax and wool, and seem even to have
been famous for the production of a particular class of
textile goods, similar to the "plaid" or "tartan" of modern
commerce. Upon this curious point Mr. Elton gives some
interesting particulars :—"The British Gauls," he says,
" were expert at making cloth and linen. They wove their
(? linen) stuffs for summer, and rough felts or druggets for
winter wear, which are said to have been prepared with
vinegar, and to have been so tough as to resist the stroke of
a sword. We hear also of a British dress called *guanacum*

years the right of working the copper mines of *Skeldane* in Northumberland,
of Alston Moor in Cumberland, and of those near Richmond in Yorkshire
(see *Technical History of Commerce*, by John Yeats, LL.D., p. 173).

[1] *Early Middle Ages*, p. 7, note.

(by Varro), which was said (Strutt, *Chron.* 275) to be woven of divers colours and making a gaudy show. They had learned the art of using different colours for the warp and woof so as to bring out a pattern of stripes and squares. " The cloth," says Diodorus, " was covered with an infinite number of little squares and lines, as if it had been sprinkled with flowers. The favourite colour was red or a pretty crimson." There is some confusion in this extract between different kinds of cloth, *e.g.* linen and woollen, but it is clear at all events, that both were manufactured with skill, and that the art of dyeing was also in an advanced state. Of the linen cloth found in ancient British barrows, Mr. Warden furnishes some further particulars :—" Some specimens of these were of a reddish colour, the filaments at first appearing like hair. Sir R. C. Hoare," he says, "found in a barrow some bits of cloth so well preserved that the size of the threads could be distinguished, and showed it to be what is now termed a kersey cloth."[1] Considerable controversy has arisen upon the question whether there was a native British manufacture of glass : the common presence of glass beads in tumuli that are opened adding constant fuel to the discussion. Mr. Elton opposes the theory of a native manufacture, and fixes his *ultima ratio* in the circumstance of the British not being acquainted with the manufacture of bronze. He says, " the glass is thought to have been brought from the Alexandrian factories. It is unlikely that it could have been made in Britain because the natives were as yet unable to make bronze (Cæsar, *De Bell. Gall.* v. 12), and glass-making is said to be the concomitant of the manufacture of that metal."[2] Some authorities believe, however, in the manufacture both of bronze and glass by

[1] *The Linen Trade*, p. 354.

[2] Compare Figuier's *Primitive Man*, Tylor's edition, p. 261 :—" The scoriæ from the bronze furnaces are in fact a kind of glass, a silicate of soda, coloured blue or green by the silicate of copper ;" see also chap. iv. p. 169.

the ancient British.[1] Other relics of the primitive inhabitants that have been dug out of mounds and other hiding-
places of the far past, are—the remains of a rude kind of
hand-made pottery, of various form, but most commonly of
that of vases containing the ashes of the dead; and knives,
swords, axes, and arrow-heads of flint, bone, or bronze.
Among the implements of manufacture found, are—circular
stone discs, supposed to have been used as whorls for spinning, and large bone combs or battens for pressing the weft
close up against the woof in weaving. Fishing nets and
hooks are also found, and flint "scrapers" believed to have
been employed in the process of preparing leather. These
with chisels, hammers, saws, pins, and needles, made of
fragments of flint, bone, or horn, may be included in a list
which is still very far from being exhaustive.

Fifty-four years before the commencement of the Christian
era, Julius Cæsar, having completed the subjugation of Gaul, crossed over into Britain
in search of new conquests, but with a force so inadequate
to his purpose that he was quickly compelled to retire,
driven out by the confederated tribes. The next year he
renewed the invasion with a larger army, ravaged part of
the country, and induced or compelled a few of the leading
chieftains to promise tribute, and profess a nominal allegiance
to Rome. The island was not visited again by the Romans
in force for nearly a hundred years, till the reign of the
Emperor Claudius, when an incessant conflict began, which
ended in its practical subjugation by Agricola (78-84 A.D.)
Such is, in brief, the ordinary historical account of the
great events which befell the British people at this time.
It is an obviously meagre and insufficient one. The whole

[1] Mr. Wright believes in, at all events, a Romano-British manufacture of
glass, and even fixes the locality of it, which is the neighbourhood of
Brighton.—*Celt, Roman, and Saxon,* p. 282.

story of the intervening period, certainly one of rapid
development, is left untold. It is said that during that
time the Belgic settlers on the British coast affected much
the Roman manner, and that the other tribes adjoining
them made good progress in civilisation. It is believed
by some that Christianity was preached. It is generally
allowed that a great change took place. But whatever was
the condition of that intervening period, there is no question
of the great and unprecedented prosperity that Britain
enjoyed after the Romans had secured their conquest there.
The next clear view that history gives us of it reveals
a startling transformation. Handsome cities adorned with
theatres, baths, and other public edifices, and connected by
splendid roads traversing a cultivated country, have now
become conspicuous features in a landscape which formerly
consisted principally of marsh and forest, interspersed here
and there with occasional clearings where a tribal settlement had been made, or where a few mud huts claimed to
form a town. Useful arts and manufactures are in a state
of perfection, which they have only lately reattained. The
British workman and British work have already established
a European reputation. In 298 Constantius Chlorus found
that all mechanical arts " were in greater perfection in ·
Britain than in Gaul ; the ruined cities of the latter as well
as the fortresses on the Rhine being for that reason repaired
by British architects and artificers by that emperor's special
direction."[1]   Trade and agriculture flourish exceedingly.
Under Julian (357 A.D.) as many as 800 vessels are
engaged along the English coast in the corn trade alone ;[2]
while numerous other vessels from distant countries frequent
its ports, bringing thither their various products ; and returning laden with tin and lead, with hides and timber, with
pearls from the estuaries of Cumberland and North Wales,

---

[1] Anderson, vol. i. p. 32.   [2] Zosimus, iii. 145.

dogs for the Roman amphitheatre, oysters for the Roman tables, and slaves for the Roman market-place. A period of prolonged peace has supervened on a time of almost constant internecine war. Eumenius, looking over upon it from a distance, is able to panegyrise the country in such terms as these :—" Britannia, fortunate and happier than all other lands, enriched with the choicest blessing of heaven and earth ;" and another orator about the same time to proclaim it " a land so stored with corn, so flourishing in pasture, so rich in variety of mines, so profitable in its tributes, on all its coasts so furnished with convenient harbours, and so immense in its circuit and extent." Yet of that great and memorable time scarcely a record now survives ; no proper monument is left. Saxons, Danes, Jutes, and Norsemen, in the course of another few centuries utterly obliterated them. Deep under heaps of unsuspected rubbish, and in little frequented bypaths, are still found indeed the remains of sumptuous Roman villas, where those luxurious foreigners made their homes; which they adorned with splendid and cultured taste, and tried to live in them the life of the sunny South ; passing from them too as humour prompted for a round of foreign travel, or a season at Cheltenham, Bath, or other of their fashionable watering-places, even as we do yet. But this is all, or nearly all. Such a Britain fifteen hundred years ago it is not easy now to realise ; but such a one undoubtedly there was. A hundred years of pillage and destruction left, perhaps, little of it recognisable ; but five or six hundred years of scarcely intermittent devastation had even then to follow, and how much would be left then ?[1]

---

[1] For an especially vivid and interesting account of the completeness and rapidity with which a country can relapse into barbarism, and a description even of the very processes of decay, see *After London*, by Richard Jefferies, chaps. i. and v. (Cassell and Co., 1885). Consult also Robertson's *View of the State of Europe*, introducing his "History of the Reign of the Emperor Charles V.," *passim*.

Not until this prodigious lapse of time was pretty nearly
spent did anything like reconstruction seriously begin ; by
which time the memory even of that former era had been
all but lost.

Thus it is that of the arts and manufactures which the
Romans introduced into Britain, or finding

ROMAN MANU-
FACTURES.
there improved, so little is actually known.
We may guess at their magnitude by the
few glimpses which history yields us of the general prosperity of the country then, or we may judge of their quality
by the remains of the less perishable kinds that are sometimes still brought to light. But of direct evidence of them,
or of references to any of the processes and operations that
produced them, we have next to none. We know, indeed,
from numerous sources that the Romans greatly developed
the existing textile trades, especially that in woollens,
establishing an imperial manufactory at Winchester, and
others probably in other places. We are told that the
produce of the Winchester factories was so large that it
supplied both the imperial court and the uniforms of the
Roman soldiery (Camden's *Britannia*, quoted by Anderson, vol. i. p. 96), though unless this statement be taken
as only applying to the army in Britain, or at the utmost
as including only the western provinces of the Empire, it
must surely be a great exaggeration. We know that they
were great builders and military engineers. It is believed
that they first set up water-mills for grinding corn,[1] and
possibly for other purposes. It is certain that they established immense potteries, especially in Staffordshire, where
they have since attained such celebrity, and in the valleys
of the Lower Thames and Medway. The sites of many of
these works still remain to attest their judgment and the

---

[1] Macpherson's *Annals of Commerce*, vol. i. p. 223 ; *Pop. Hist. Eng.*, vi.
p. 600. Compare p. 10.

magnitude of their operations. So also, unquestionably, did they greatly develop the mineral resources of the country. It is not only that they continued the mining and smelting of iron, tin, and lead ore that had gone before, but they much improved the processes, obtaining, in the case of the last named, silver from it, and exporting both it and lead in considerable quantity. In the neighbourhood of old mines may still be traced the remains of Roman stations, and sometimes burial-grounds :—places where both in life and death the miserable workers were thus accommodated. That they continued the ancient tin trade we may well believe, though we learn little about it at this epoch, and tin does not seem to have been in much demand in Rome just then. But it was greatly to its vast deposits of iron ore that Britain was even then, as now, indebted for so much of its prosperity. These the Romans worked with energy and great profit. A military forge was established at Bath for the production of manufactured iron on the largest scale; and similar great establishments were formed in other places. Of this great " Fabrica," or military forge at Bath, Mr. Scrivenor (*History of the Iron Trade,* 1841)[1] gives the following graphic account, which conveys too an excellent idea of the Roman system of labour and manufacture. " The *fabrica* of which we are speaking was a college of armourers, where the various military weapons used by the Roman soldiers were manufactured. The business of this society, and the laws which regulated it, are developed by the Theodosian and Justinian codes. It there appears that towards the commencement of the second century the army smiths were created into companies, each governed by its own president or head, denominated the *primicerius.* That the employment of these bodies was to make arms for the use of the

---

[1] Pp. 28, 29.

legion or legions, to ·which it was attached, at public forges
or shops, called *fabricæ*, erected in the camps, cities, towns,
or military stations; that these arms, when forged, were
to be delivered to an officer appointed to receive them, who
laid them up in arsenals for public service; that to prevent
any abuse in this important branch of military economy,
and to ensure its proper and methodical management, no
person was permitted to forge arms for the imperial service
unless he were previously admitted a member of the society
of the Fabri; that to secure the continuance of their labours
after they had been instructed in the art, a certain yearly
stipend was settled on each armourer, who (as well as his
offspring) was prohibited from leaving the employ till he
had attained the office of *primicerius*; and, finally, that
no one might quit his business without detection, a mark
or *stigma* was impressed upon the arm of each as soon as
he became a member of the *fabrica*. These colleges were
of two sorts, the smaller and greater, the latter called by
way of excellence, *fabricæ sacræ*. Not attached to any
particular legion, the *fabricæ sacræ* supplied whole provinces,
and sometimes whole kingdoms, with military weapons.
Of this kind the college at Bath is, with good reason,
supposed to have been, furnishing arms not only to the
garrison of the colony, but to the troops at Cærleon, Chester,
and Ilchester, and to the whole army and line of stations
throughout Britain, and to some bodies of Roman soldiers
on the Continent. An establishment of this nature would
add considerably to the consequence of Bath, which now
became a scene of bustle and business. The road connecting it with the opposite side of the Severn was enlarged
and repaired, as it supplied the forges with the iron manufactured at them, which dug up in the forest of Dean, and
in the hills of Monmouthshire, was transported across the
river at Lydney, landed at Aust, and brought to Bath by

a military way running nearly parallel with the upper Bristol Road. The constant demand for military weapons from all parts of the kingdom gave an additional life and spirit to the city ; its intercourse became general, and the roads which branched from it in every direction were crowded with vehicles that conveyed to different places the various destructive implements of war made at its *fabrica.*" Huge beds of refuse have been discovered here, and in Wales, Derbyshire, Northamptonshire, Yorkshire, Lancashire, and elsewhere, heaps of refuse so vast that 1500 years after their first use many of them have afforded the material for a second great iron industry.[1] This imperial people prosecuted industrial production in the same fashion that they prosecuted military adventure and spread government. The scale was vast, the purpose clear, and the result grand and imposing.

The industrial system of the Romans was, throughout their later history, that municipal system of production whose outlines have been already THE ROMAN SYSTEM.
sketched.[2]   An almost uniform system prevailed in all parts of the empire.   It was the practice to invite skilful artificers of all kinds to Rome, and to colonise conquered countries with the industrial inhabitants of other conquered countries, for the purpose of introducing and spreading useful arts through all its provinces.   These colonists gathered together into companies or " colleges," like that of the *fabrica* at Bath, within the fortified towns, and enjoyed exceptional privileges.   They were subject to strict internal discipline, but were otherwise well used.   Such persons were, however, only the higher kind of artificers: those competent to exercise control over others, and to perform the nicer sorts of workmanship: the mere drudgery of production—the mining and quarrying, the toil at the furnaces and in the

---

[1] Smiles's *Industrial Biography*, p. 16.   [2] Compare chap. ii. p. 67.

potteries, the transportation of heavy burdens, road-making,
and the coarser operations of agriculture—was the work
of slaves. Of this latter class also, we may surmise, were
the persons employed at the great manufactories; which
establishments, too, would probably be not very dissimilar
from the factories of a still remoter past, on which they
were certainly modelled. It is doubtful to what extent
there was an open market for the commodities made at
these places. Some were certainly government manufactories, but others were probably conducted as private
adventures—as we have found reason to believe was the
case with the old Egyptian factories. They were in the
hands of capitalists, and worked with slave labour, the
capitalists being probably protected monopolists:—royal
favourites, successful soldiers, or the younger scions of
patrician houses. But the end of this brilliant epoch was
approaching. From about the close of the fourth century
the Romans began gradually to desert Britain, and the
native population to become more troublesome, and to form
alliances with other tribes. The rich settlers and traders,
left thus without the protection to which they had been
so long accustomed, and harassed by old and new enemies,
were quickly ruined; they either transferred as much of
their possessions as they could elsewhere, or abandoned
them altogether. Some returned to Italy, some passed
to other countries. Many crossed the sea and settled in
Armorica, whence 1000 years after a few of their descendants returned to recolonise portions of their earlier father-
land. Those who remained to continue the struggle fought
long and bravely; but the struggle was vain. Within about
forty years after the dissolution of the Roman government,
the "Saxons," invited into the island as allies, made themselves its masters, and a new era opened.

The name Saxons was applied indifferently by the Romans

to a variety of tribes inhabiting the district between the Rhine and the extremity of Jutland. The principal of these were the Jutes, Saxons, and Engles.

They willingly responded to the invitation of the dominant class in Britain, and having assisted them in defeating the national party, presently set about conquering the country for themselves. In a few vivid sentences Mr. Green has described what followed—the first formal entry of the English into England, and the terrible and memorable fruits thereof.[1] We quote the brilliant passage almost in full :—"Their march led them through a district full of memories of a past which had even then faded from the minds of men ; for hill and hill-slope were the necropolis of a vanished race, and scattered among the boulders that strewed the ground rose the cromlechs and huge barrows of the dead. One such mighty relic survives in the monument now called Kit's Coty House, the close, as it seems, of a great sepulchral avenue which linked the graves around it with the grave-ground of Addington. The view of their first battlefield broke on the English warriors from a steep knoll on which the gray, weather-beaten stones of this monument are reared ; and a lane which still leads down from it, through peaceful homesteads, guided them across the river-valley to a little village named Aylesford, which marked the ford across the Medway. The chronicle of the conquest tells nothing of the rush that must have carried the ford, or of the fight that went struggling up through the village. It tells only that Horsa fell in the moment of victory ; and the flint heap of Horsted, which has long preserved his name, and was held in after time to mark his grave, is thus the earliest of those monuments of English valour of which Westminster is the last and noblest shrine." The victory at Aylesford was but the prelude to the com-

[1] *A Short History of the English People*, chap. i. sec. 2.

plete conquest and transformation that was to ensue. " The
massacre which followed the battle indicated at once the
merciless nature of the struggle which had begun. While
the wealthier Kentish landowners fled in panic over the sea,
the poorer Britons took refuge in hill and forest till hunger
drove them from their lurking-places to be cut down or
enslaved by their conquerors. It was in vain that some
sought shelter within the walls of their churches; for the
rage of the English seems to have burned fiercest against the
clergy. The priests were slain at the altar, the churches
fired, the peasants driven by the flames to fling themselves
on a ring of pitiless steel. It is a picture such as this which
distinguishes the conquest of Britain from that of the other
provinces of Rome. The conquest of Gaul by the Frank, or
of Italy by the Lombard, proved little more than a forcible
settlement of the one conqueror or the other among tribu-
tary subjects who were destined in a long course of ages
to absorb their conquerors. French is the tongue, not
of the Frank, but of the Gaul whom he overcame; and the
fair hair of the Lombard is now all but unknown in Lombardy. But the English conquest was a sheer dispossession
and slaughter of the people whom the English conquered.
In all the world-wide struggle between Rome and the
German invaders, no land was so stubbornly fought for or
so hardly won. The conquest of Britain was, indeed, only
partly wrought out after two centuries of bitter warfare.
But it was just through the long and merciless nature of the
struggle that, of all the German conquests, this proved the
most thorough and complete. At its close Britain had become England—a land, that is, not of Britons, but of Englishmen. It is possible that a few of the vanquished people may
have lingered as slaves round the homesteads of their
English conquerors; and a few of their household words (if
these were not brought in at a later time) mingled oddly

with the English tongue. But doubtful exceptions such as these leave the main facts untouched. When the steady progress of English conquest was stayed for a while by civil wars a century and a half after Aylesford, the Briton had disappeared from the greater part of the land which had been his own; and the tongue, the religion, the laws of his English conquerors reigned without a rival from Essex to the Severn, and from the British Channel to the Frith of Forth " (*idem*).

For about a hundred and fifty years this ruthless slaughter and utter demolition of all the monuments of a previous civilisation continued, after which matters began slowly to mend. During this period Britain once again disappeared almost wholly from history, and we hear of it only in the traditions of other countries, as Ireland and Brittany, the former of which was then by contrast in the enjoyment of a considerable degree of prosperity. Then a slow improvement began. The seventh and eighth centuries saw industry reviving, and the useful arts, though in a much curtailed form, re-establishing themselves. Agriculture and manufactures ceased to be wholly neglected. The rapid spread of Christianity occurring at the same time brought this desolated island once more into relations with other lands, and imported and fostered a new industrial spirit. The missionary monks who settled in England and Scotland founded religious houses in which the practice of useful handicrafts was taught as part of the ordinary discipline, and wherein all industrial processes were assigned an honoured place. One Saxon monarch, Edgar, even passed a law making it compulsory on every priest to learn a trade; and in doing so but turned into positive enactment a common usage. The introduction of stained glass windows into this country (mentioned in the last chapter) dates from this period, and is due to two officers of the Church—Wilfrid, Bishop

of York, and Benedict, Abbot of Wearmouth (674 A.D.) [1]
In the next century the venerable Bede is found writing a
request to a French bishop to send him over workmen experienced in that industry, which would seem to imply that
it had made some sort of settlement in the country.[2]   St.
Dunstan was a skilful smith and bell-founder; and many
more instances of the industrial qualifications of ecclesiastics
might be cited.   Unfortunately, these well-meant efforts
could at the best produce but inconsiderable results; and
the little good they did was in constant jeopardy, owing to
the unsettled state of the country, divided amongst a number
of petty rulers, and exposed to the unremitting and ferocious
ravages of Danes and Norsemen.   Towards the close of the
Saxon period manufacture had indeed made some advance
towards a re-establishment in its former home; but those
repeated invasions, and the accession to sovereign power of
yet two other foreign peoples—the Danes and Normans—
postponed its real return for several centuries more.

The textile arts were familiar to the Saxons before their
arrival in England, and they continued the
practice of them there, after their own methods,
down to the close of the Saxon period.   The
results, however, never reached anything like the excellence
that had been attained in Britain during the Roman occupation; nor was the industry carried on upon anything
approaching the same scale of magnitude.   Their woollen
manufactures were exclusively confined to the production of
coarse cloth, and their linen manufacture—although the flax
plant was indigenous to their own country and linen garments in general use among their upper classes—declined to

*SAXON MANUFAC-
TURES.*

---

[1] Windows were previously protected by lattice-work, or by thin filaments
of horn.   Compare chap. vi. p. 255.

[2] Macpherson says distinctly that a manufactory of glass was established
in Northumberland by Bishop Biscop (*i.e.* the Benedict alluded to above), in
674.—*Annals of Commerce*, vol. i. p. 264.

such an extent, that by the time of the Norman Conquest it is probable that "neither any flax was grown nor any native linen produced."[1] They seem to have been aware of their backwardness in these respects, and one of their early writers, Bishop Aldhelm, offers a sort of indirect apology for the roughness of their work compared with that of other countries. "We do not negligently despise," he writes (in a treatise of about the date 680 A.D.), "the woollen dress of threads worked by the woof and the shuttles, even though the purple robe and silken pomp of emperors shine." Elsewhere he adopts, however, a more triumphant tone, and tells of "the shuttles not filled with purple only but with various colours, moved here and there among the thick spreading of the threads;" and how, "by the embroidery art they adorn the woven work with various groups of images," a passage also proving that embroidery was an industry then practised. This art was indeed not only practised then but carried to great perfection, and seems to have been one peculiarly suited to the genius of the Saxon people, as may be inferred from their elaborately illuminated manuscripts as well as their textile fabrics. It was used in textile industry mostly for tapestry, and was the substitute for those bolder and freer processes of ornamental work which were brought in afterwards by the Normans and other foreign emigrants. The work was laboriously done, either in the monasteries by the monks, or by the Saxon ladies in their long hours of solitude at home. So celebrated did England become at length for this particular kind of manufacture, that towards the close of the Saxon era it was distinctly known as the *Anglicum Opus*, and as such had a large sale abroad. A very notable example of it is still extant in the celebrated Bayeux tapestry; which was worked by the captive Saxon ladies in the retinue of Queen Matilda, wife of William the

[1] Warden, *Linen Trade, Ancient and Modern*, p. 357.

Conqueror, and presented by her to the Cathedral of Bayeux,
where it still remains. The following is a description of
this famous piece of work :—" It is of coarse linen cloth
(canvas) worked with wool, 214 feet long by 20 inches
wide, and divided into 72 compartments representing various
incidents in the Conquest of England." Nothing could
give a better idea of the barbarous condition to which the
western world had come in respect to textile manufacture
than the contemplation of such a work in comparison with
the beautiful fabrics of ancient times, and even of the far
East at that very era. Yet it was probably the best that
that age and country was capable of producing. If we turn
now from clothing industry to metallurgy under the Saxons,
we have to note again the great falling off since Roman
times. Mining operations were almost altogether neglected,
and the consequence was that the production of metals on
a large scale, either for export or for home consumption,
was all but unknown. Iron in small quantities, used
chiefly in the making of arms and armour, was still produced, and is supposed to have been supplied from the
district of the Forest of Dean, for we learn from Camden
that the centre of the trade was at Gloucester; and many
of the Saxons were cunning workmen in metal. The trade
of the smith was indeed one especially valued.[1] But industrial operations were always on the smallest scale, and only
for home consumption. Of their leather manufacture something has been already said.[2] Their pottery was rude and
coarse. With respect to glass, it would appear, from recent
discoveries of " curiously twisted glass goblets " in ancient
Saxon burial-places (mentioned by Mr. Green), and "shown by
their form to be of English workmanship,"[3] that its manufac-

---

[1] For instances of the high value set upon smith's work by the Saxons, see
Smiles's *Industrial Biography*, chap. i.

[2] Chap. vi. p. 254.

[3] *The Making of England*, by John Richard Green, p. 161 (Macmillan, 1881).

ture continued; and in some other materials, such as wood and
horn, a good deal of manual dexterity was displayed. But the
Saxon genius was not industrial. The life of the people was
for the most part spent in agriculture, and the horizon of their
wishes and exploits is pretty well defined by that limit.

These facts may possibly tend to modify a very pre-
valent belief that the Englishmen of to-
day have received the greater share of their   THE SAXON SYSTEM.
industrial qualities as an inheritance from their Saxon forefathers. Such is far from being the case. That rude people
brought no increase of knowledge to their adopted land, and
during their long tenure of power there developed no new
skill. On the other hand, they visited with undiscrim-
inating destruction the mighty fabric of industry that their
predecessors had laboriously raised. What they did bring
with them, to our eternal obligation, were qualities quite
other than these, certain political and racial characteristics
in which were the germs of our present political and social
life. They brought the patient plodding spirit that makes
up now so much of the national character; the love of
home, and the reverence for home ties and duties, which are
still happily ours. They brought, or rather restored, the
principles of individual responsibility and local self-government which the Roman domination had all but crushed out;
and the hardy self-reliance that is born of those principles.
But for every increase of industrial knowledge, and every
improvement in the processes of manufacture during the
earlier history of England, we are indebted not to Saxons,
but to immigrants from almost any other part of Europe,
from France, Flanders, Italy, and Germany. The Saxon
system was, indeed, quite incompetent to develop improvement in industry. It was purely domestic, and had no
relation to national resources at all. Textile manufacture,
except in the religious houses, was exclusively a feminine

occupation, and all kinds of manufacture were at all times subordinate to the pursuits of agriculture, war, and the chase. The Saxon titles " spinster " and " wife,"[1] with their obvious derivations, are the best proof how thoroughly this conception was engrained in the Saxon mind,[2] nor did the practice lack encouragement in the highest places. The most aristocratic Saxon ladies did not disdain the labours of the distaff, loom, and needle. The four daughters of King Edward the elder were regularly instructed in spinning and weaving—" which was so far from spoiling the fortunes of these royal spinsters," remarks Mr. Warden (p. 356), " that it procured them the addresses and the hands of the greatest princes then in Europe." Alfred, in his last will, specifically describes the female portion of his family as " the spindle side," and we have already noted to whose cunning fingers we are indebted for the Bayeux tapestry. With regard to their general labour system, it was, like the Roman, a system of slavery, and probably of even a more rigid kind, for it had not the variety and elasticity of the wide-spreading Roman method. The land was the great source of wealth, and to it all institutions were made subservient. Every considerable household had an independent existence within a definite area, and round it the serfs and slaves of the landowner were grouped. Where no chief householder exercised prime authority, his place was taken, and local government administered, by little congeries of freemen, also with slaves under them, who practically made their own laws and saw after their enforcement; and these little communities were for the most part self-supporting, supplying to themselves all the actual necessaries of life.

Thus when the Normans completed their conquest of

---

[1] From the *woof* in weaving.
[2] Compare *The Making of England*, chap. iv.

England, it was in a state very different in an industrial
point of view from that in which its Saxon
invaders had found it 600 years before. THE NORMANS.
Then, the country was a rich and favoured province of a
powerful empire, under which it had long enjoyed prosperity; they found it, on the contrary, an obscure and but
partially civilised kingdom, torn by intestine feuds, and
stagnant in industry. The new invaders quickly perceived the inferior acquirements of the conquered race, and
treated it accordingly. England became a mere appanage
of the Norman dukedom. The Saxon aristocracy were
generally despoiled of their estates, and the common
people carried off to fight in foreign wars. The artificers
were reduced to penury by the competition of imported
craftsmen, and the peasantry were evicted from their
little holdings to enlarge the hunting-grounds of the newcomers. Yet even in this time of gloom and misfor-
tune, the seeds of future progress, both industrial and
commercial, were being sown, in the manner too that for
long continued the most familiar one in English history.
One of the earliest results of the Conquest was a great
immigration of the industrial and trading classes from
abroad, for "every Norman noble as he quartered himself
upon English lands, every Norman abbot as he entered
his English cloister, gathered French artists or French
domestics around his new castle or his new church."[1]
Nor was this movement confined to the followers of the
Conqueror alone. During the reigns of the first three
Norman kings, several bands of Flemings, driven from their
country by successive inundations of the sea, crossed also
over to England, and were hospitably received: William
I., with excellent judgment, settling most of those who
came in his reign in the north (chiefly in the neighbour-

---

[1] Green's *Short History*, chap. ii. sec. 6, p. 88.

hood of Carlisle), where they might serve as a bulwark against
the Scotch, as well as be a source of wealth to one of the
poorest parts of his dominions. Unfortunately this particular colony did not get on well with its Cumbrian
fellow-subjects, and Henry I. (with no less policy) transplanted it bodily to the Welsh frontier, to a district named
Rhos (Ross) in Pembrokeshire and Herefordshire, where the
colonists maintained themselves with valour and address,
and laid the foundation of the great west of England fine
woollen manufacture so long and so justly celebrated. Others
which followed were settled in the eastern counties, especially about Norwich; some at Kendal on the border of the
Lake District; some in the southern counties; and some,
it is thought, in parts of Lancashire. These immigrants
and refugees brought with them the possibilities and promise
of new industrial prosperity, and were also our pioneers
in commerce. Before that promise and those possibilities
could be realised, however, great changes in the political and
social life of the nation had to occur, and to a consideration
of these we must now very briefly address ourselves.

    The English people up to the time of the Conquest had
been, speaking broadly, divided into the
three political classes of *corl*, or landed
proprietor, *ceorl*, or half-free cultivator,
and *theow*, or absolute slave; but these separate classes had
latterly tended to intermix and pass into each other in a
variety of ways, and this tendency was, in the case of the
last two classes, pretty nearly completed by the full establishment of the feudal system, under which, by a process
of degradation, the second class became merged in the
third under the common title of *villeins*. We have already
had something to say of the nature of feudalism, and its
place in social evolution.[1] It did not run precisely the

CLASSES AT THE
CONQUEST.

---

[1] P. 71.

same course in England as abroad, nor was it actually
introduced here by the Normans, for already in Saxon times,
and especially after the conquests of the Danes, an approach
to feudalism may be noticed in English society. But it
was under the Norman dominion that it finally supplanted
all previous systems, and its main characteristics were
everywhere the same. Those characteristics were primarily
the substitution of personal for communal or imperial obligations, and the supercession of custom by law. The *villeins*
under it lost their semi-independent position and became
mere slaves. Status faded more and more, and was succeeded, now by contract, now by mere brute force: the
law that is of the strongest. There were no longer in
the State several classes approaching and often touching each
other, but only two elementary ones—the masters and the
men. It is probable that the after effects of this change
were politically useful through the constitutional results of
the antagonisms it aroused; and it is certain that the
system had its virtues as well as its vices. The industrial
results, however, which are our chief concern, were of the
worst kind. The producing classes, whether agriculturists
or artificers, were completely separated from the ruling
classes; innumerable disabilities were imposed on them,
and the right to live itself barely conceded. The haughty
barons regarded them as an inferior kind of persons, to
be pillaged at home, or carried off abroad on foreign
adventures at their whim and pleasure; as a sort of unwholesome excrescence on that military form of society
which was their ideal.

A most valuable source of information concerning the
classification and status of labourers, and
the condition and distribution of industrial $\qquad$ DOMESDAY BOOK.
operations at this period, is Domesday Book, prepared by
order of William I. near the close of his reign; and from

this great national record many useful particulars concerning land tenure and the position of the agriculturists
may be learned, which are more or less relevant to this
subject. A summary of them is given in Mr. Cunningham's
interesting work, *The Growth of English Industry and Commerce*,[1] pp. 95-100, from which we will take the liberty
to quote it pretty nearly in full, as it does not seem possible
to usefully condense the matter there given, or to present
it in a more attractive form. "The land was divided into
three distinct parts : first, the lord's domain ; second, the
holdings of different classes of tenants ; and third, the waste
which belonged to the lord, except in so far as many of the
tenants had definite rights in regard to it, for he might not
use it so as to prejudice these rights. The socmen of the
village, who were associated with the lord of the manor in
his jurisdiction, were in some cases quite independent ; in
others they had become attached to the soil, and were thus
assimilated to the position of the humbler tenants. The
necessary work on the domain was done by the various
tenants without actual wages, but the lord of the manor
provided their food while they worked for him ; the workers
may be classified in three divisions according to the amount
of labour which they were bound to render. Those who
were best off only worked at times of special pressure, *e.g.*
a day or two in harvest, and gave assistance in conveyances.
Others were bound to work at these times of special stress,
and also one or two days a week all the year round. The
lowest class, whose service does not seem to have been so
limited, and whose holdings were mere gardens in all probability, are not specified as a class ; but individuals like
the beeherd would constitute a group corresponding to the
servi of Domesday and *nativi* of a later period ; on this

[1] *The Growth of English Industry and Commerce*, by W. Cunningham,
M.A. (Cambridge University Press, 1882).

class the lord relied for the necessary industries such as spinning, weaving, and for household duties. The villain would have his whole time to work on his own holding except at special times, the boor would have four days for himself, and the serf might have little if any time he could call his own. But the holdings and the domain were cultivated together; the lord almost always supplying part, if not the whole, of the teams for ploughing; the seed was found by the labourers even for the domain lands. The *ballivus* was entrusted with the management of the estate and exaction of the services due from each labourer; the *præpositus* was a sort of foreman, selected annually by the labourers, and freed for the time from service himself, who was the representative of the labourers' interests from day to day."

"The duty of the bailiff was more complicated; he had not only to superintend the labour, but to keep a reckoning of the stock, especially of the seed, and to see that the respective portions of the collective stock belonging to the lord and the labourers were not confused. Anything of the lord's that was used on the labourer's holding must be accounted for, and, if necessary, replaced. Such was the general character of the system by which the agricultural produce was raised; but it was open to disadvantages. The forced labour was unwilling and inefficient; the seed supplied was not always of the best quality, and it was soon found to answer better if the services were compounded for. A portion of the lord's land was cut off and cultivated by the villain as an additional holding on his own account, while he paid dues for the labour of which the lord was thus deprived; the lord no longer received the produce, but he no longer provided the labourer's food; he was glad to accept a composition which represented the difference between his outlay and the annual produce, and which freed him from the

trouble of exacting so much service. If a villain succeeded
in commuting all his services, both regular and occasional,
for an annual payment, the bailiff would only have to keep
an account of the amount of the lord's stock which was lent
him, while the labourer became more entirely his own master,
and was better able to enjoy the fruits of his own labour.
The benefit was a double one, and, as a consequence, the
system was generally introduced before the time of our
earliest records. The land thus assigned might either be
cut out of the waste—so long as no prejudice was done to
common rights, *terra essarta,*—or cut out of the domain, when
it was called *terra assisa;* in any case it was the sign of a
well-managed estate to have large portions thus assigned,
and yielding an annual value instead of tardy services and
varying crops. But this return, too, was liable to fluctua-
tions; if a villain died without heirs, his holding would
escheat to the lord—it might not be possible to find a successor who had time and stock enough to work an additional
holding; the lord would then be forced to rely on the
services for which no composition was made; his annual dues
would be less, but he would have a larger produce for the
time from the unassigned domain. The annual returns, as
estimated in money, of each estate varied according as more
or less of the estate was assigned to labourers who had compounded for their services; and variations have no relation
either to the gross produce or market price of the estate.
These labour dues are spoken of as rents, but they were quite
different in character from rents as understood in England
in the present day. They were payments made in lieu of
work, and they may be described as analogous to *profit,*
which economists tell us is the difference between the whole
outlay and the produce; but the analogy is not very close,
as—(1) the lord had not supplied the labourer's entire
requirements as wages do; (2) the labourer provided part

of the capital; (3) the payments included a share of the taxes due from the land which the labourer held. Indirectly, however, the labour dues probably came to have some relation to definite quantities of land, as modern rents have. If a labourer paid fourpence to be quit of the obligation to serve two days a week, he could not, however, afford to be idle, and would wish for as much land as he could cultivate in these two days a week; while the landlord would not assign a portion that yielded a greater profit than fourpence. One might describe such a tenant as living at a *fixed rent*, but the rent was not fixed by a direct reference to the quantity of land held, still less to its productiveness; the labourer paid for freedom to work on his own account, and he had assigned to him such a portion of land as could be worked in the time; thus set free, his rent is called a *quit rent*, because he is quit of service (*quietus est*)." Referring to occupations more nearly approaching the industrial, we find mention made in Domesday Book of carpenters, smiths, goldsmiths, farriers, potters, armourers, fishermen, millers, bakers, salters, and tailors. There are signs, too, of a growing town population. There was, however, no great industrial specialisation as yet into urban and rural occupations; the towns were small, and most of the dwellers in them continued to find at least partial employment on the land. Of definite places of production, there are named: vineyards, corn-mills, salt-works—both marine and inland, and mines of iron, tin, and lead. The mineral industries appear to have been in a state of extreme depression. Lead-works existed only on the king's domains in Derbyshire; and "it was not until a century and a half after the Conquest that the Norman monarchs received a revenue from the Cornish tin mines. The times were characterised by cruel oppression and exactions; famines were frequent, and farms and monasteries were alike exposed to the pillage of crowds

19

of foreign mercenaries" (*Pop. Hist. of England*, chap. xviii. p. 267). In such a condition of things manufacture was necessarily carried on merely for the supply of local needs, and under circumstances of great discouragement.

Feudalism reached its climax in England under the Norman kings. The reign of Stephen is described by Sir James Mackintosh as " the most perfect condensation of all the ills of feudality to be found in history." With the opening of the Plantagenet era, however, in the reign of the second Henry (1154), affairs began to show improvement, though wasteful foreign wars and bitter domestic struggles continued to oppress the nation. The old race feud was dying out; Saxons and Normans were slowly drawing together, and feeling a common impulse towards a national life. Magna Charta stands in our history in this relation, as the sign of a new epoch, though in itself it represents a class struggle and a class victory only. The barons won it for themselves without any great thought for the people at large, who were described in it merely as " things," and were, under it, as much " chattels " as the stock and implements used on the lands; and it was thus no charter of liberty to the working classes, as we now understand those words.[1] But although it did not enfranchise the people, it extended to them privileges of which they were not formerly in possession, and so far raised them in the scale of manhood. The 12th clause especially provided some defence against the inordinate tyranny and spoliation that had previously prevailed. It enacted that " A freeman shall not be amerced for a small fault, but according to the degree of the fault; and for a great crime in proportion according to its magnitude, saving always to the freeman his tenement, and after the same manner saving to a merchant his merchandise. And a

THE PLANTAGENETS.

[1] *Short History of the English People*, chap. iii. sec. 3.

villein shall be amerced after the same manner, saving to him his wainage (*i.e.* carts, plough, tools, etc.), if they fall under our mercy; and none of the aforesaid amercements shall be imposed except by the good men of the neighbourhood." Here we have several classes of the industrial community distinctly recognised and legally protected, even the unfreeman, for the first time in our history, being secured in the possession of his fixed capital, and accorded a status in the courts of law. We notice, too, the concern beginning to be shown by the State in production and trade, and the rise of a merchant class. The *artisan* does not yet, however, find any separate mention; showing the continued insignificance of this order of persons as a *class* at that time, though they undoubtedly existed as individuals. Some skilled workers were perhaps included in the merchant class as members of corporate trade bodies; and the rest were probably counted still among the villeins.

The results of this evolution of a new middle or merchant class are soon apparent. During the earlier Plantagenet epoch signs of progress both in the commercial and industrial life of the people begin to show themselves in various directions. The export trade of the country was still very small, but the import trade was of an increasing character. The effect of the Crusades was beginning to be distinctly felt in commerce, and articles of Oriental luxury were finding their way into the English markets. The whole trade of the country had been hitherto in the hands of foreigners. About the reign of Henry III., however, a native trade guild, the Merchants of the Staple, was established, and this was succeeded shortly after by another association, that of the Merchant Adventurers, formed upon a still wider basis. As no national mercantile marine was yet in existence,

however, this commerce was still carried on in foreign
ships, and London and Bristol were the chief ports and
emporiums of foreign trade; while numerous inland towns,
as ´Chester,[1] Winchester, Beverley, Lincoln, York, and Norwich, boasted of important fairs and markets where the
foreign luxuries were distributed. By far the greater part
of the inland commerce of the country was carried on at
such fairs. Native manufactures were pursued only to a
very limited and extremely localised extent, but were
improving. Amongst others, the iron trade in the south
showed at this time some signs of revival; and Newcastle had already furnished a supply of coal to London,
for the use of brewers and dyers. In 1301 Manchester
first appears in industrial history in connection with the
mention of a fulling mill on the banks of the Irk, given
by one Robert Grelle to the monks of Swinehead in
Lincolnshire, on 14th May of that year.[2] This is the
fulling mill mentioned in Baines's *History of the Cotton
Manufacture* under date 1322, and quoted in chap. i.[3] The
woollen manufacture, soon to be of such supreme importance in the story of English industrial life, was in operation
too at London, Oxford, York, Nottingham, Huntingdon,
Lincoln, and Winchester (Madox's *History of the Exchequer*,
vol. x.). The colonies of Flemish weavers which William
I. and Henry I. had established in various parts of the
country practised this industry on the system of individual
production at those places; and it appears that there were
also dealers, who were not manufacturers, as their licenses
gave permission only " to buy and sell," in Bedford ;
in Beverley, and other towns in Yorkshire; in Norwich,

---

[1] In the time of the Romans Chester was a port, but already in the Middle
Ages it had practically lost its maritime character, to be presently succeeded
by Liverpool.
[2] *Antiquities of Manchester*, by James Butterworth, 1822, p. 16.
[3] Page 11.

Huntingdon, Northampton, Newcastle-upon-Tyne, Lincoln, Grimsby, Barton, St. Albans, Baldock, Berkhampstead, and Chesterfield. This enumeration would go to show the specialisation already of an important class of middlemen at this time. We read further of regular establishments, and even a system of factory labour as having now sprung up,[1] but the reference is insufficient. Bartholomew Fair was the great market for woollens. This celebrated fair originated in a grant from Henry I. to one Ranger, a jester who had turned monk.[2] Its great fame, however, as a place of trade dates from the reign of Henry II. It was held annually in the grounds of Bartholomew Priory, just outside London, lasted three days, and was frequented by clothiers from all parts of England. In time it became the great market for both coarse and fine woollen stuffs, as Winchester had been previously; though the fair at the latter place continued to be held long after then, and the town to retain its position as a great centre of the woollen trade. The linen manufacture began about this time too to creep into the country again, and many of the processes of handicraft employed in it are said to have been greatly improved. It is related in Madox's *History of the Exchequer*, says Warden,[3] "that fine linen was first made in Wilts and Sussex in 1253, and in order to patronise the infant manufacture, Henry III. ordered the sheriffs of each of these counties to buy for him 1000 ells of fine linen, and to send it to his wardrobe at Westminster." But the woollen manufacture was still the one that made the most rapid strides, aided as it was by the great production of wool in England, and by the constant immigration of skilled workmen from the Con-

---

[1] In Mr. Fox Bourne's *Romance of Trade*, p. 103, who speaks of "factories of a rude kind" . . . "set up in various parts of the country" about this period.

[2] Morley's *Memoirs of Bartholomew Fair*.

[3] *Linen Trade*, p. 358.

tinent, so that it already promised to become the staple[1] industry of the country. Unfortunately the progress that was made was mostly lost during the wasteful internecine struggles that occurred in the reigns of John and Henry III. and their immediate successors, one of the darkest epochs in the industrial annals of the country. Lord Chief Justice Hale, alluding to these reigns, bears this conclusive testimony as to the effect of those troubles upon the woollen manufacture:—"That in the time of Henry II. and Richard I. this kingdom greatly flourished in that art. But by the troublesome wars in the time of John and Henry III., and also in the times of Edward I. and Edward II., this manufacture was wholly lost, and all our trade ran out in wools, wool-fells and leather carried out in specie; and that manufacture during those warlike times had its course in France and the Netherlands, and the Hans towns." It was about the same time that Matthew of Westminster wrote of it, with a touch of bitterness that gave point to the exaggeration, that "all the nations of the world were kept warm by the wool of England made into cloth by the men of Flanders."

The taunt of Matthew of Westminster recorded above was far from being a wholly undeserved one. LEGISLATIVE RESTRICTIONS. Commerce and industry were plagued at this time by numerous exactions and restraints; some of them the work of private persons or corporations, but others the work of Parliament and the king, and all injurious to manufacture. Every kind of productive industry was subjected to these inflictions. No sooner did there seem a

[1] This word "staple" is of much significance in the history of English commerce in the Middle Ages. It is a Saxon word, meaning originally *prop* or *post*; hence anything settled, as a settled market; hence "staple town." In the commercial economy of this time commodities chargeable with duties to the king or public had to be brought to staple towns to have the duty levied; they thus came to be called staple commodities.

prospect of the woollen manufacture making a home in England than every ingenious artifice was devised (of course with the best intentions) to drive it away again. A detailed account of these interferences would expand this chapter and this book far beyond the proportions it is intended to assume, and would be somewhat beside its general intent as well. Confining our attention to the one principal commodity wool, and omitting all reference to earlier and feebler attempts at restraint, it will be enough to refer to a Statute passed in 1261 which forbade all exportation of raw material, and also the use of any apparel made out of the country, or made at home from foreign wool; thus absolutely prohibiting all foreign trade in it. Such a law, if it could have been carried out, would have inflicted great hardships on the wool-dealers without benefiting the manufacturers. But in point of fact it could not be carried out and soon fell into abeyance, being almost immediately remitted in favour of France and Normandy, while it was only nominally enforced against the Flemings, and was thus at once objectionable and inoperative. It was found that while the statute hampered trade, it was really powerless to prevent it, smuggling merely taking the place of open traffic, and the law-abiding merchant being sacrificed to the law-breaker.

In the reign of Edward I. attempts were made to remove some of these evils afflicting commerce and industry, by abating or abolishing such local and imperial exactions, and establishing more uniform laws for all home and foreign produce. The celebrated Statutes of Merchants, passed respectively in 1283, 1285, and 1303, were intended to have effect in this direction, to give greater security in the collection of debts, and to sanction and protect foreign trade. The first of them (11° Edward I.) ordains as follows: —" Forasmuch as merchants which heretofore have let (sold) their goods to divers persons be greatly impoverished because

there is no speedy law provided for them to have recovery
of their debts at the day of payment assigned; and by
reason hereof many merchants do refrain to come into this
realm with their merchandise to the damage as well of the
merchants as of the whole realm," etc., therefore certain
penalties and regulations were enacted against these flagitious
practices in future; and the last statute, besides repealing
the Act of 1261, has the following most important provision:
—" The merchants of Germany, France, Spain, Portugal,
Navarre, Lombardy, Florence, Provence, Catalonia, Aquitaine,
Toulouse, Flanders, Brabant, and of *all other foreign parts*,
who shall come to traffic in England, shall and may safely
come with their merchandise into all cities, towns, and ports,
and sell the same by wholesale only, as well to natives as
to foreigners.   And the merchandise called merceries, as
also spices, they may likewise sell by retail.   They may
also upon payment of the usual customs carry beyond sea
whatever goods they buy in England excepting wines . . . .
Wherefore all officers in cities, towns, and fairs are commanded to do sure and speedy justice to all foreign merchants according to the law merchant or merchant's custom,
etc. etc."   These were valuable and enlightened measures,
and had they been maintained in their efficiency and fairly
obeyed they would in fact have established free trade in England at this early epoch.   Unfortunately, they were evaded,
and soon repealed in obedience to public clamour, and the
legislation in respect to trade that for a long while after
took their place was of a much more retrograde character.

In the meanwhile the country had undoubtedly been
making progress in other directions under
the able rule of this monarch.   Edward
I. devoted a large portion of the time that
he could spare from warlike operations to the restoration of
public order, and the improvement of the administration of

SOCIAL CONDITION
OF THIS TIME.

the law. He added to his famous Statutes of Merchants
his scarcely less famous Statute of Winchester (13°
Edward I.), for securing the safety of the public highways,
and establishing a better system of local government in the
towns. The substance of one principal provision of this
Act will afford a better insight into the condition of the
times, especially in relation to the insecurity of life and
property, than any lengthened description would do. It
is to the effect that (clause 5) "highways leading from one
market town to another shall be enlarged, so that there
be no dyke, tree, nor bush whereby a man may lurk to do
hurt, within two hundred foot of the one side, and two
hundred foot on the other side of the way. And if percase
a park be near to the highway, it is ordered that it be set
back two hundred foot from the highway as beforesaid, or
that a wall, dyke, or hedge be made, that offenders may not
pass to do evil." Another clause exhorts people to keep
arms in readiness to protect themselves from violence; and
yet another commands "that in great towns, being walled,
the gates shall be closed from the sun setting until the
sun rising, lest they be entered and plundered during
the night." These efforts were not fruitless. Robberies,
murders, and other outrages became somewhat less frequent,
and the authors of them more amenable to justice. A
circuit of judges was established to enforce the laws locally,
and those laws themselves were rendered more clear and
definite. In still another direction a no less important
advance was made. The representative element in Parliament was widely increased by the admission of burgesses
and knights of the shire; and thus that form given to the
fabric of our Constitution that it has ever since, through
many modifications, retained.

Still the social condition of all classes was low in the
extreme; even that of the rich being such as would be con-

sidered utterly despicable now by the sorriest pauper. The gloomy stone castles in which they lived, and that over-spread the land to terrorise the native population, were the most uncomfortable dwellings inside that it is almost possible to conceive; foul, bare, and squalid : without windows, without chimneys, almost without furniture ; the unplastered walls hung with tapestry to keep out the cutting winds that entered by every chink and cranny. The life led in these dreadful places was sombre as the places themselves, when not wholly consumed in action. There was then but little stir of mental life anywhere outside the monasteries. There were scarcely any books; there was little or no interchange of hospitalities; none except on very rare and very grand occasions. Even the rude revelry that we read of in the stories of novelists must be greatly exaggerated, for little wine, or other strong drink, was drunk, and foreign luxuries of all kinds were very limited and difficult to obtain. Occasionally some great fête would be held, or a royal progress would be made through the country; and as this last was the great opportunity for the display of all feudal magnificence, it will be well to give a description of what one was like, which we shall do in the words of a historian dealing specially with the social condition of the English people. "The most squalid wretchedness, and vice in its most revolting form were rudely blended, and, as it were, incorporated," says Sir George Nicholls,[1] "with the pomp and pageantry of the royal processions. These processions were, in fact, little better than organised mobs, perambulating the country, and levying contributions, without stint or mercy, upon all who unhappily came within their reach. Estates were then held on the condition of furnishing straw for the royal beds, and litter for the royal apartments. The rush-strewer was a

[1] *A History of the English Poor Law*, by Sir George Nicholls, K.C.B., vol. i. p. 18 (Murray, 1854).

recognised officer in the royal household, and it was considered an act of unusual magnificence to cover the floor of the great dining-hall with clean rushes or clean straw daily, so that those who could not find room at the common table might sit on the floor without soiling their clothes." Needless to say there were no such implements as knives or forks in use at those repasts, and we learn from many other sources how filthy the rush-strewn floors became when these epochs of " unusual magnificence " were over.

When such was the condition of the higher classes, it is easy to imagine how pitiable was that of the lower. These, in fact, were not *housed* at all, but *stabled*, in the outbuildings of the lord whom they served. Even the residents in towns were, up to the fourteenth century, accommodated in dwellings built only of mud held together by beams of wood (as are sometimes seen still), for stone houses were hardly known up to that time, and the art of brickmaking had been completely lost since the departure of the Romans, and was only just then being reintroduced from abroad. The majority of the nation was still in bondage to the minority : and the whole nation in bondage to ignorance, sloth, and dirt. The reigns of the first two Edwards are to some extent the turning-point of this drear time ; for partly through the efforts of the former, and partly owing to other influences, more or less glanced at as we have proceeded, a better time was in store, as the next chapter will disclose.

CHAPTER VIII.

ENGLAND BEFORE THE FACTORY SYSTEM——FROM
EDWARD III. TO WILLIAM III.

Edward III. : Establishment of the English Woollen Manufacture—John
Kempe—The Black Death—The Statutes of Labourers—Wat Tyler—
Emancipation of the People—The Wars of the Roses—Political Economy
of this Period—Wages—Sumptuary Laws—The Tudors—Elizabeth—The
Poor Laws—Apprenticeship—The Iron Industry—The Stuarts.

WE enter upon a new era in the history of English industry
from the accession to the throne of Edward

EDWARD III. ; ESTAB-
LISHMENT OF THE III. During the long reign of that mon-
ENGLISH WOOLLEN arch, lasting just fifty years (from 1327 to
MANUFACTURE.
1377), England became again a manufac-
turing country, clothing not merely her own people at home,
but exporting home-made cloth to other countries. Unfortunately this prosperity was scarcely established before
many things occurred to check it, but the impetus then
given was never afterwards quite lost. In a variety of
ways—some little noticeable, others more or less manifest,
with now a step forward here, now a retrogression there—
our country began to advance from that time forward to the
great industrial destiny that awaited her. Once again, too,
it was to the foreigner that she was indebted for this new
impulse. Edward had married a Flemish princess, Philippa
of Hainault, and to that union is immediately owing—indeed,
to the queen's personal efforts and influence, it is said [1]—

[1] Strickland's *Lives of the Queens of England*, vol. i. ; *Philippa of
Hainault* (George Bell and Sons, 1880).

that great event in English history, the re-establishment of a native woollen manufacture. The story is told with much quaintness of detail by Fuller (*Church History*, Book III.), whose animated narrative supplies not only a history of what occurred, but an intelligible and coherent description of the motives and the means that were engaged in bringing the end about. Writing under date 1336, this old writer says:—" The King and State began now to grow sensible of the great gain the Netherlands got by our English wool; in memory whereof the Duke of Burgundy not long after instituted the Order of the Golden Fleece, wherein—indeed, the *fleece* was ours, the *golden* theirs—so vast their emolument by the trade of clothing. Our king therefore resolved, if possible, to reduce the trade to his own country, who as yet were ignorant of that art, as knowing no more what to do with their wool than the sheep that wear it, as to any artificial and curious drapery; their best clothes then being no better than friezes, such their coarseness for want of skill in their making. But soon after followed a great alteration, and we shall enlarge ourselves in the manner thereof"— which accordingly he proceeds to do in the following words: —" The intercourse now being great betwixt the English and the Netherlands (increased of late since King Edward married the daughter of the Earl of Hainault), unsuspected emissaries were employed by our king into those countries, who wrought themselves into familiarity with such Dutchmen as were absolute masters of their trade, but not masters of themselves, as either journeymen or apprentices. These bemoaned the slavishness of these poor servants, whom their masters used rather like heathens than Christians; yea, rather like horses than men. Early up and late in bed, and all day hard work and harder fare (a few herrings and mouldy cheese), and all to enrich the churls their masters, without any profit unto themselves. But oh, how happy should they

be if they would but come over into England, bringing their
mystery with them, which would provide their welcome in
all places.   Here they should feed on fat beef and mutton,
till nothing but their fulness should stint their stomachs;
yea, they should feed on the labours of their own hands,
enjoying a proportionable profit of their pains to themselves.
Their beds should be good, and their bedfellows better, seeing the richest yeomen in England would not disdain to
marry their daughters unto them; and such the English
beauties were, that the most envious foreigners could not
but commend them.   Liberty is a lesson quickly conned by
heart, men having a principle within themselves to prompt
them, in case they forget it.   Persuaded with the promises,
many Dutch servants leave their masters and make over for
England.   Their departure thence (being picked here and
there) made no sensible vacuity, but their meeting here
altogether amounted to a considerable fulness.   With themselves they brought over their trade and their tools, namely,
such which could not as yet be so conveniently made in
England.   Happy the yeoman's house into which one of these
Dutchmen did enter, bringing industry and wealth along with
them.   Such who came in as strangers within their doors soon
after went out bridegrooms, and returned sons-in-law, having
married the daughter of their landlords who first entertained
them.   Yea, those yeomen in whose houses they harboured
soon proceeded gentlemen, gaining great estates to themselves, arms and worship to their estates."   He then proceeds to mention various places of settlement allotted to
these strangers by the king, who, continuing the able policy
of his predecessor Henry I., " bestowed them through all the
parts of the land, that clothing thereby might be the better
dispersed."   These places, with the special manufactures pursued there, were as follows :—" *East*—(1) Norfolk, Norwich
fustians; (2) Suffolk, Sudbury baize; (3) Essex, Colchester

sayes and serges; (4) Kent, Kentish broadcloths. *West*—
(1) Devonshire, kerseys; (2) Gloucestershire, cloth; (3)
Worcestershire, cloth; (4) Wales, Welsh friezes. *North*—
(1) Westmoreland, Kendal cloth; (2) Lancashire, Manchester
cotton;[1] (3) Yorkshire, Halifax cloths. *South*—(1) Somer-
setshire, Taunton serges; (2) Hampshire, cloth; (3) Berk-
shire, cloth; (4) Sussex, cloth."

Our author adds :—" Observe we here, that Mid-England
—Northamptonshire, Lincolnshire, and Cambridge—having
most of wool have least of clothing therein," a peculiarity of
those counties that practically continues still. The effect
of this great influx of industrious foreigners, of the example
they set, and the assistance that they required in their undertakings, told rapidly in two important directions also noticed
by Fuller. First, a more considerable division of labour
was now introduced into English manufacture; the wool
" passing through so many hands, every one having a fleece
of the fleece—sorters, combers, carders, spinsters, weavers,
fullers, dyers, pressers, packers." Second, there was a greater
diffusion of the means of livelihood among the masses; inasmuch as "many poor people, both young and old, formerly
charging the parishes (as appeared by the accounts of the
church officers), were hereby enabled to maintain themselves."
Thus was the great English woollen manufacture established.
Thus, too, were the seeds of the new economical order of
things sown. The purely domestic and individualistic system
of production, natural to a people like the Saxons, could no
longer suffice for a people looking for subsistence to other
sources than the mere cultivation of the soil, and emulous of
entering into the competitions of trade. That agricultural
conformation of society had, accordingly, first to find a place
within itself for a separately industrial element, and next,
to make room alongside itself for a new producing system.

[1] *i.e.* coatings.

The spirit of industry, imported from abroad, made its way
at the same time among the English poor, infusing into
them new ideals, and rousing them from their deep lethargy.
It took possession of the middle classes.   It made converts
even in the higher and highest class.   The time had now
arrived when the condition of our manufacture was no longer
to be a subject of indifference politically, but a matter of
high state concern, and when the Lord Chancellor of England,
presiding in the legislature, took his seat upon a *woolsack*
in full testimony thereof.   Meanwhile wealth was obviously
increasing.   The earlier part of this reign was certainly a
time of greater prosperity than had been enjoyed in England
since the coming of the Normans, and for long before.
Provisions were abundant, employment was plenty, society
—under still a feudal organisation—fairly stable.   The
policy of the young king was yet a liberal one to all interests,
and commerce flourished in consequence.   The towns were
everywhere increasing in power and importance, and securing themselves in their municipal privileges.   The country
was better cultivated than it had ever been before.

The patriarch of the woollen manufacture in England was
one John Kempe, a Flemish weaver, whom,
JOHN KEMPE.
as early as 1331, Edward invited to establish
his business here.[1]   Four years later he appears to have done
so, first settling with a small colony of his fellow-country-
men at Norwich, where he is said to have been occasionally
visited by the queen.[2]   He afterwards removed to Kendal,
where it is probable other Flemings had settled before, and
which thenceforth became celebrated for its cloth manufacture, especially for a particular class of goods called " Kendal
Green."   An interesting article in *Household Words* of
15th November 1851 gives the following reasons for this
change of residence, and contains also some other interesting

---

[1] Strickland's *Lives*, vol. i. p. 382.   [2] *Idem.*

particulars about John Kempe. "The sheep were one reason, and another was no doubt the abundance of the broom, called by the country people 'woodass,' which grew on the neighbouring wilds. . . . Indigo was not then known as a dye, and woad was the only blue. Now blue is one-half of green, and in the broom which grew near Kendal Mr. John Kempe and his successors had the other half, the yellow; hence arose the famous Kendal Green, which was renowned for centuries, even to within a hundred years, when it was driven out by the Saxon green. This Kendal green was the first celebrated English colour."[1] The colony of Flemish weavers at Kendal prospered exceedingly; whilst that left behind at Norwich acquired still greater fortune and celebrity. All processes of manufacture for the production of fine cloth were carried on at these two centres, where, likewise, a very large number of workmen came soon to be employed. The memory of John Kempe does not now probably count for much in Norwich, which has passed through so many and such great vicissitudes; but it is still held in reverence in Kendal, where the manufacture that he introduced continues.

Two most calamitous occurrences now supervened, inflicting a serious blow, not alone on the nascent woollen manufacture, but on the THE BLACK DEATH. whole national economy. The first of these was the breaking out of those long and wasting wars with France which, commencing early in the reign of Edward III., were continued almost without intermission for a hundred years; the second was the arrival in England of the terrible pestilence known as the Black Death. This frightful epidemic had originated somewhere in the interior of Asia about

---

[1] See also Nicholson's *Annals of Kendal*, p. 238. But there seems to have been a green cloth earlier celebrated, viz. "Lincoln green," familiar to us through the Ballads of Robin Hood.

the year 1346, and reached the south of Europe two years
later. Early in 1348 Italy was in its clutches, and
Boccaccio has recorded in the introduction to his well-known
book (*The Decameron*) the appalling results that ensued.
In the winter of the same year, and again in the following
(1348) it visited England, its destructiveness increasing each
time. Of the 4,000,000 people, or thereabouts, who then
constituted the population of this country [1] quite *one-half*
perished. In Norwich alone, the number of victims has been
set down at 60,000 ; and in Bristol it was said "the living
were hardly able to bury their dead." [2] In London, mention
is made of one burial-ground in which *alone* 50,000 corpses
are said to have been interred ; but there is probably exaggeration in these estimates. The towns and villages were
deserted, the land all thrown out of cultivation, and the cattle
roamed wild about the country with no one to look after them.
All functions of government, and most of the ordinary offices
and arrangements of society were suspended. A complete
paralysis fell, of course, upon industry. Of what use was it
to work when there would be presently no one left to consume the product, and when life itself from day to day had
become all but unbearable ? The majority of the labouring
population probably died. Those who were left found themselves, consequently, when confidence began to revive, in
a very unusual position, for from this universal wreck a
new prosperity had to be evolved, and so few labourers
surviving they were in unprecedented demand. The price
of labour rose enormously, while the means of paying it
were accessible only in an inverse proportion. The command of the market for once was on the side of the worker.
The free artisans naturally used this advantage to the utmost ;
whilst the serf, who had either lost his master by death, or

---

[1] These details are taken from Green's *Short History of the English People*,
pp. 241, 242.   [2] *Idem.*

had taken advantage of the general confusion to run away from him, assumed the status of a freeman, and also offered his services to the highest bidder. An economical problem of unexampled difficulty was thus suddenly presented to the rulers of the country, and was the immediate cause of a very remarkable body of laws that arose out of it.

For it was the endeavour to grapple with this economical difficulty that produced the celebrated Statutes of Labourers, which in industrial THE STATUTES OF LABOURERS. history have made the reign of Edward III. almost as famous as the re-establishment of the woollen manufacture itself; and whose principles, says a popular writer, "however gradually mitigated, pervaded the relations of employer and servant long after the days of feudal despotism, and still cling to our institutions."[1] Of these very arbitrary enactments it will not be necessary here to give more than a brief résumé, though that much is indispensable to fill in the outlines of the industrial picture of those times. The preamble to the first of them (23° Edward III.) enunciates very clearly the true economic law of wages, against which it then proceeds with equal precision to legislate. "Because," it states, "a great part of the people and especially of workmen and servants, late died of the pestilence, many seeing the necessity of masters and great scarcity of servants, will not serve unless they may receive excessive wages. . . . Be it therefore enacted . . . that every man or woman, of whatsoever condition, free or bond, able in body and within the age of threescore years; . . . and not having of his own whereof he may live, nor land of his own about the tillage of which he may occupy himself, and not serving any other, shall be bound to serve the employer who shall require him to do so, and shall take only the wages which were accustomed

[1] *Pop. Hist. of England*, vol. i. p. 470.

to be taken in the neighbourhood where he is bound to
serve . . . in the twentieth year of the king, and in five
or six common years next before." If they would not do
this, whether bond or free, they were to be committed to
prison. Of course they would not do it, and indeed could
not do it; and accordingly a second Statute of Labourers
was passed the year after (1350), enacting still sterner
and more stringent regulations. In this one the country
is informed how " it is given the king to understand that
the said servants have no regard to the said ordinances,
but to their ease and singular covertise do withdraw themselves to serve great men and others, unless they have
livery and wages to the double and treble of what they
were wont to take before," and it is declared that, therefore,
this " ease and singular covertise " must be put a stop to.
An elaborate scale of wages is accordingly set forth at
length, and rendered obligatory under heavy penalties; and
the principle of confining labourers to their native districts
(the principle that is of " settlement") is more firmly
established. The labourer was not to quit the parish where
he resided, in search of better paid employment elsewhere, nor
" go out of the town where he dwelleth in the winter to
serve the summer, if he may serve in the same town;"
nor indeed do anything at all to better his position. If he did
so he was to be severely punished. This law was not more
successful than its predecessor, and the reasons for its failure,
together with instances of some of the cruelties practised
in its enforcement, are thus concisely summarised by Mr.
Green:[1]—" To enforce such a law must have been impossible, for corn had risen to so high a price that a day's
labour at the old wages would not have purchased wheat
enough for a man's support. But the landowners did not
flinch from the attempt. The repeated re-enactments of

[1] *Short History*, p. 242.

the law shows the difficulty of applying it, and the stubborn-
ness of the struggle which it brought about. The fines
and forfeitures which were levied for infractions of its
provisions formed a large source of royal revenues, but so
ineffectual were the original penalties that the runaway
labourer was at last ordered to be branded with a hot iron
on the forehead, while the harbouring of serfs in towns was
vigorously put down. Nor was it merely the existing class
of free labourers which was attacked by this reactionary
movement. Not only was the process of manumission
suddenly checked, but the ingenuity of the lawyers who
were employed as stewards of each manor was recklessly
exercised in cancelling on grounds of informality, manumission, and exemptions which had passed without question,
and in bringing back the villein and the serf into a bondage
from which they held themselves freed." In so unfair a
fashion was this inconsiderate legislation attempted to be
enforced. Such oppressions roused a fierce spirit of resistance among the people. The lower class of free craftsmen
in the towns, and the peasants in the country districts,
began to combine together for mutual protection, and were
joined by those serfs and villeins who were discontented
with the hardships of their lot or had been left without
masters after the plague. Various political, economical,
and religious motives added to the strength of the movement. The expenses of the French war had from the
first borne heavily on the poor, but when to meet them the
expedient of a debased coinage was resorted to, the burden
became all but intolerable. One of those religious "revivals," —
which from time to time seems to sweep over the English
masses, exciting in their minds new doubts and arousing
new enthusiasms, had for some time been in operation, and
fundamental questions in ethics were being asked and
answered among them in a spirit that boded no good to

their rulers. A local leader was found in the person of one John Ball, and nothing but an appropriate occasion was now wanting to set the whole mingled mass in motion. It was presently found.

Edward III. was dead, and his grandson Richard II. sat upon the throne. The French war still continued, its cost weighing ever heavier on an impoverished nation. To raise funds for prosecuting it a poll-tax was ordered to be levied on every one over sixteen years of age, and the great efforts made to collect this tax fanned the rising flame of discontent into a conflagration. The immediate cause of the insurrection that ensued is said to have been an insult offered by a tax collector in the discharge of his duties, to the daughter of one Walter or Wat, a tiler, of Dartford in Kent. The story has been disputed, but anyhow such a person put himself at the head of the rebels in his own neighbourhood and marched straight for London. The event is familiar to all readers of history. Wat Tyler was treacherously slain during an interview with the king, at the very moment that the latter was promising the people redress of their grievances, and the rebellion was rapidly and completely quelled. Other risings in other parts of the country suffered the same fate. Nevertheless, the victory in the long run was with the people. The spirit of dissatisfaction that found expression in those risings, and the habits of organisation which they fostered, were the infallible prelude of an end now coming into view, the real end at which they aimed. That end was the general emancipation both from slavery and serfdom of the whole nation. The full story belongs more to constitutional than industrial history, but is too closely connected with the latter to be altogether passed over. We shall endeavour to supply accordingly an intelligible account of what occurred.

WAT TYLER.

It has been already noted into what classes the population of the country was divided at the Norman Conquest, at which time the agricultural population was so much in excess of the industrial, and the middle artisan and farming class was swamped by feudalism. With respect to the first of these classes, we must confine ourselves in this chapter to few observations, for it occupied considerable space in the last, and the farm labourer is, after all, but indirectly connected with our theme. The process of emancipation in his case was in all countries slower and less obvious than in the case of other workmen. It was, moreover, a process very generally evolved by more violent means. In England it required a series of peasant revolts to give the required impetus; and in France the horrors of the Jacquerie, and ultimately of the French Revolution, were necessary to bring it to a prosperous conclusion. In other countries like conditions commonly prevailed; while, alongside of all this convulsion, the old processes of enfranchisement went quietly on, and new economical developments appeared. The manorial system declined; the position and rights of the feudal tenants improved; and lastly, the villein began to receive a competitive price for his labour, *i.e.* to be remunerated in *wages*—a fact prophetic of so many changes for good or ill yet to come. But with respect to the petty trader, the skilled and unskilled artisan, and the operative labourer, the tale is somewhat different. The process in each of these cases was commonly of a more peaceful kind. The first great movement in their favour, both at home and abroad, was the advance to wealth and power of the towns. In England, under the Saxon regime, this movement had been scarcely noticeable; for the economy of Saxon government was altogether rural in its character, and when it began to develop other tendencies it was already far on its way to extinction. But no sooner had the Normans settled here than the towns commenced to increase in consequence, and to seek for, and gradually to obtain, an existence apart from the rest of the community. Two influences greatly favoured them in this enterprise. The first was the essentially military character of the despotism which the Normans established—a depotism scorning trade, yet forced to make use of it for the wealth that it brought for the prosecution of military adventure : the second was the character of those military adventures themselves, which, with a few exceptions, were carried on away from home, leaving time and opportunity for the development of another type of life in the unmilitary residue of the population that remained behind. The townsfolk were thus thrown more and more upon their own resources. At first, clustering under the sheltering walls of some feudal castle or abbey, they had looked to it for defence ; but afterwards, building walls of their own, and organising their own forces, they became independent of such protection, purchased liberty of their feudatories, and resolutely set themselves to maintain it. The lords, for their parts, were often glad to be rid of their responsibilities on these terms. Feudal obligations required them to live among and protect the vassals over whom they were placed, while their inclinations drew them more towards their native France, or the glory to be won in the far East. How happy a solution of the difficulty was it, then, to receive a good round sum of ready money, enabling them to follow their inclinations, in return for conceding privileges that relieved them of all trouble ! Thus many towns acquired their liberties. Others—and these were the first enfranchised—purchased them direct from the king in much the same way, and owing to the operation of very similar causes. The king, when not fighting with some one abroad, was generally fighting with his barons at home, and was thus invariably in want of funds. A judicious advance on the security of a forfeiture of rights if the loan were not repaid, was generally too tempting an offer to be refused. It seldom was refused; the loan was not repaid, and the rights were forfeited accordingly. So, silently, and unnoticed for the most part in history, were the towns enfranchised, and the burgher class raised up; and so were the traditions of self-government, of free organisation, and equal justice preserved to the English race in their keeping. What part the actual artisan and labourer had in this development of municipal life is exceedingly obscure; but whatever it was, the influence was probably exerted through the medium of the craft guilds. It is certain, too, that the spread of manufacturing industry added largely to the populousness of the towns, and greatly nurtured this rising spirit of independence within them. It did so, both under the impulse of the law that would naturally induce industrious persons to seek the company and protection of other industrious persons, and also as a result of express encouragement. It was provided that any operative and any person in a servile condition, who could prove residence in a free town for a year and a day, should be thenceforth free; and it is easy to believe that that endeavour would, under such circumstances, be pretty often made. We have presumptive proof, indeed, that it was so made in a statute (34° Edward III.), passed in 1300, by which a fine of £10, payable to the king, was imposed on the officials of any town "who refused to deliver up a labourer, servant, or artificer" who had fled thither from his master's service, on being duly required to do so. The king and the towns probably made something out of this arrangement between them, while the people profited most. By the time that the Statutes of Labourers were passed, the English towns and townsmen were mostly free; and by the end of another century they were all so.

Scarcely were the great calamities of the Black Death and the French War well over, when another calamity fell upon the nation in the form of a civil war among the barons, in respect to a disputed succession to the throne. This monstrous conflict raged through the country for several years : certain powerful nobles, with trains of dissolute followers, attacking each other whenever they could meet, ravaging each other's territories that had been assigned to them in trust for the nation, and changing sides as inclination prompted. Since the evil days of Stephen had not been seen so wicked and wasteful a war, notwithstanding the pretty popular title under which its memory is preserved. At its close the first Tudor ascended the throne, and a new epoch in our history commenced.

THE WARS OF THE ROSES.

The Wars of the Roses, inadequate as they were in their motives and results, and shocking in their sacrifice of human life, were not in the end an unmixed evil to industry, for they aided, by the wholesale destruction of the feudal aristocracy, in the emancipation of the people. They were, however, while they lasted, very destructive to trade and manufacture. Scarcely any notice at all of these is to be found accordingly throughout the history of the period that they occupied. Of the progress of the newly established woollen manufacture, in particular, we search in vain for any recognition, and can only conjecture of it, either that that progress was altogether stayed for a while, or that it was confined to remote and obscure parts of the country, where the foreign settlers sought refuge from internecine struggles in which they had no patriotic or other interest.[1] The linen manufacture seems to have nearly, if not completely, died out. Mr. Warden gathers " from the roll of the king's wardrobe in 1415, that the

---

[1] It is exceedingly probable that it was at this period that the foreign immigrants began to settle definitely in Lancashire and Yorkshire with the

greatest part of the linen then used in England . . . was imported," and quotes the testimony of Strutt to the same effect.[1]   Anderson (*History of Commerce*, vol. i. p. 450) has nothing encouraging to say of English manufacture of any kind then, but also mentions that in 1430 " fine cloth of Ypres and of Courtray, of all colours, much fustian, and also linen cloth," were imported in Spanish ships from Flanders ; while he tells, later, of the " staining of linen cloth," which had been " an old trade in England, whereof some excellent cloths yet remain, but the art is now lost in this realm "—doubtless during the commotions of this time.   The silk industry had not yet made that settlement that was impending, though some indications of its approach had even before now shown themselves.   The great mineral resources of the kingdom remained practically unused.   At the termination of this senseless conflict the productive energies of the country were nearly wholly prostrate.

Paradoxical, and almost unaccountable as it may at first sight appear, it is nevertheless just this period of English history that some recent POLITICAL ECONOMY
OF THIS PERIOD. and most competent authorities have fixed upon as opening the brightest era throughout the whole of our country's long and troubled annals : as being in fact the " Golden Age " of England.   The paradox is only an apparent one, and that view of things not so unaccountable as it seems ; though the difficulty at first sight of reconciling such apparently contradictory facts is not to be denied. The seeming contradiction is in the aspect in which we choose to regard the political-economical conditions of these times : that is, whether from above or from below ; whether

view of carrying on their industries there, for these counties, by reason of their difficulty of access, were comparatively exempt from the evils of the time.   [1] *Linen Trade*, p. 360.

in the interests of the ruling or of the working classes.
Regarded purely in the former light, England was indeed
in a bad way just then; the succession to the throne
unsettled, the country involved in a cruel civil war, commerce nearly non-existent, population failing, wages high,
profit small, and the lower orders ever trenching upon the
traditional privileges of the higher. Regarded from the
other point of view, that of those lower orders themselves,
these very elements of political dissatisfaction wore the
aspect of bright promise, and were the just foundations of
their rising hope. The very lowness of profits and sparsity
of population—political-economical evils to the employing
and trading classes—were sources of wealth, and therefore
of unaccustomed comfort to labourers, whose general condition
was greatly raised in consequence. But further, when the political turmoils ceased at length, the popular advancement thus
fostered began to tell with redoubled effect in face of the more
happy position of things attained, and the impetus to spread
to higher strata of society. All classes commenced then to
feel it. The rate of wages was still unprecedently high, but
the rate of profit began to rise with it. Our exports, particularly of wool, were greatly increased. The nation made
wealth rapidly. Even the destruction of property caused by
the Wars of the Roses was not able, it would seem, to prevent
the English people at their close from being in the enjoyment of a condition of wellbeing which made them the envy
of their neighbours, and to which the working classes long
looked back with affectionate regret. Our country was
then " Merrie England," a title conferred upon her by rival
nations, which she accepted and felt that she deserved. It
is only necessary to compare this estimate of us with that
of any foreigner of to-day, to add to the astonishment with
which we must regard this fact. If there is one thing
that invariably strikes every intelligent visitor here now, it

is the exceeding gloom of our life, the absolute incapacity for joyousness which the national character displays. Merriment is the very quality of which the modern Englishman seems to know least. Wealth has vastly increased since then; the standard of comfort has been immensely raised, political freedom is general, and yet at the end of a century of enormous prosperity, the country which once—at the conclusion of a time too all the reverse of that—was "Merrie England," is now the gloomiest, weariest, least enjoying on the face of the earth. Here is a fact and a problem surely of singular interest. Something towards the solution of it we may perhaps be able to evolve as this narrative proceeds.

That the picture itself is not overcoloured, so far, at least, as the payment of labour is concerned, has been abundantly proved by Mr. Froude, whose assertions have been confirmed by the careful researches of Professor Rogers and others. Applying the test of wages, a crucial one if we include the consideration of their real and nominal value as well as their amount, the first-named writer says of a period somewhat later indeed than this, but sufficiently near for the purpose of comparison:[1]—" For a penny, at the time of which I write, the labourer could buy as much bread, beef, beer, and wine—he could do as much towards finding lodging for himself and his family— as the labourer of the nineteenth century can for a shilling. I do not see that this admits of question. Turning then to the table of wages, it is easy to ascertain his position. By the 3rd of the 6th of Henry VIII. it was enacted that master carpenters, masons, bricklayers, tilers, plumbers, glaziers, joiners, and other employers of such skilled workmen, should give to each of their journeymen, if no meat

WAGES.

---

[1] *History of England*, from the Fall of Wolsey to the Defeat of the Spanish Armada, by James Anthony Froude, vol. i. pp. 26-29 (Longmans, 1870).

or drink was allowed, sixpence a day[1] for the half-year,
fivepence a day for the other half, or fivepence halfpenny
for the yearly average. The common labourers were to
receive fourpence a day for half the year, for the remaining
half threepence. In the harvest months they were allowed to
work by the piece and might earn considerably more (mowers,
for instance, were paid eightpence a day), so that in fact
(and this was the rate at which their wages were usually
estimated) the day labourer, if in full employment, received
on an average fourpence a day for the whole year. Allowing a deduction of one day in a fortnight for a Saint's day
or a holiday, he received therefore steadily and regularly,
if well conducted, an equivalent of something near to twenty
shillings a week, the wages at present paid in English
Colonies." But even this is far from being a full account
of his advantages. "Except in rare instances the agricultural labourer held land in connection with his house; while
in most parishes, if not in all, there were large ranges of
common and unenclosed forest land, which furnished his
fuel to him gratis, where pigs might range and ducks and
geese; where if he could afford a cow he was in no danger
of being unable to feed it; and so important was this
privilege considered that, when the commons began to be
largely enclosed, Parliament insisted that the working man
should not be without some piece of ground on which he
could employ his own and his family's industry. By the
7th of 31st of Elizabeth it was ordered that no cottage
should be built for residence without four acres of land at
lowest being attached to it for the sole use of the occupants
of such cottage." On the same subject, see Mr. Thorold
Rogers's *Six Centuries of Work and Wages*, chap. vi. *passim*.[2]

[1] Professor Rogers has shown that the working day was a day of eight hours.— *Work and Wages*, p. 180.

[2] I have not quoted more fully from this work, simply because I have not room to do so, and if one commenced quotation it would be impossible

If, however, further confirmation of the prosperity of this
period were required, it could be furnished
abundantly by a full recital of the provisions
of the Sumptuary Laws, passed by successive Parliaments
then and after.   When we find the legislature finding grave
cause to enact that "grooms and servants of lords, as well
as they of mysteries, and artificers, are to wear nothing of
silk or of gold or of silver embroidered; and their wives
and children are to be of like condition of like clothing and
apparel," etc., we recognise that wages must have been at all
events so far above the margin of subsistence that a handsome
surplus for the gratification of personal extravagance was
left.   But the above law [1] goes on with even greater exacti-
tude to state what people *are* to wear, as well as what they
are not, prescribing the particular apparel to be worn by
"handicraftsmen and yeomen, and by esquires and gentlemen, and by merchants and citizens, and by knights and by
the clergy;" and lastly, "by carters, ploughmen, drivers of
the plough, oxherds, cowherds, shepherds, swineherds, and
other keepers of beasts, threshers of corn, and all manner of
people attending to husbandry, and all other people that
have not forty shillings of goods and chattels;" so that this
legislation was not for the working classes only.   To come to
details :—the last-named persons, from the carter downwards,
are prohibited from wearing any manner of cloth "but
blanket and russet of twelvepence a yard, with girdles of
linen according to their estate;" and they are "to eat and
drink in the manner as pertaineth to them, and not exces-
sively."   And finally, "to the intent that this ordinance
may be maintained and kept in all points without blemish,
it is ordained that all makers of cloth within the realm

to know where to cease.   It is throughout a rich mine of information on
everything of an industrial kind pertaining to this period.
[1] 37° Edward III. Cap. 14.

shall conform them to make their cloths according to the price limited by this ordinance," which fixes minimum prices accordingly.[1] There can be little doubt of the prosperity of a period when such laws were considered necessary.

These astonishing minute provisions were of course disregarded, as were also some others enacted in the reign of Richard II., and re-enacted with severer penalties in that of Henry IV., which need not be quoted, for they were all of the same kind. The reigns of Henry V. and Henry VI. witnessed some feeble efforts to renew them, likewise not worth quoting, and all culminated in two very important statutes in the reign of Edward IV., called the "Ordinances of Clothing" (3° Edward IV. Cap. 5 ; and 22° Edward IV. Cap. 1), wherein a penalty was attached to the *making*, as well as the wearing, of unlawful garments, in continuation of the attempt to regulate the manufacture itself, as in the Acts of Edward III. But these laws were not without their wise and liberal provisions as well. The good name of the country was not to be imperilled abroad by any deceitful trade artifices. In 1464 an Act (4° Edward IV. Cap. 1) was passed, setting forth "that wherever the workmanship of cloths and other woollen goods was become to be of such fraud and deceit as to be had in small reputation in other countries," etc. . . . for remedy thereof it was now enacted that "broadcloth, fully watered, should be twenty-four yards and one inch in length, and two yards, or at least seven quarters, in breadth, and that no cloth of any region but Wales or Ireland shall be imported, except cloth taken at sea." The different processes of "carding, spinning, weaving, shearing, fulling, curling, and dyeing" were also regulated, and the measuring and sealing of the *aulneger*[2] made

[1] Sir George Nicholls's *History of the English Poor Law*, vol. i. p. 43.

[2] The *aulnager* was the officer appointed by government to certify to the cloth being of the legalised kind.

more effective. The same reign witnessed a prohibition even
more closely related to our subject, and which will afford
further matter for consideration hereafter. A complaint`
had, it appears, been made to Edward IV. "that hats, caps,
etc., hitherto made in the wonted manner, with hands and
feet, were now made in an inferior manner by the use of
mills, *i.e.* tucking mills;" and "the use of such mills was
forbidden in 1482."[1] Here we perceive the first symptom
of that jealousy of machinery which was afterwards to be a
conspicuous feature in the development of English industry. -
It is as well to finish with this subject of Sumptuary Laws
at once, though it may lead us to anticipate. Henry VIII.,
extravagant enough in his own person, repeated the follies
of his predecessors in endeavouring to ordain for others what
they should wear, and of course with the usual result ; and
other monarchs long continued the same policy, without distinguishing between what was defensible and indefensible in
it. In the reign of Edward VI. a very important Act (5°
and 6° Edward VI. Cap. 22) was passed (1557), "for the
putting down of gigge mills," in which, alongside the osten-
sible purpose, it is easy to recognise the purpose of the Act
of 1482. It states in the preamble that certain mills,
called "gigge mills," are newly devised, erected, and used in
many parts of the country for the perching and burling of
cloth, "by reason whereof the true draperie of this realm is
wonderfully impaired, and the cloth thereof deceitfully
made." It is therefore directed, that such mills shall not
be used, under a penalty of £5 "for every cloth wrought
in or by any of the said mills called gigge mills."[2] In 1571,
in the reign of Elizabeth, an Act was passed providing that
all persons above the age of six years, except the nobility
and other persons of degree, should on Sabbath days and

---

[1] Draper's *Dictionary*, Article, "Fulling" (*Warehousemen and Drapers'
Journal* Office). [2] Sir George Nicholls, vol. i. p. 139 ; compare p. 11.

holidays wear caps of wool of English make, and no other
sort of headgear; and eight years later (in 1579) this was
followed by a most comprehensive and elaborate statute on
the whole subject of the social position, clothing, and general
domestic concerns of Her Majesty's subjects. It remains to
mention the last and oddest of all the Sumptuary Laws,
namely, the Act passed in 1666 (under the Commonwealth),
forbidding burial in any other but a woollen garment, renewed
in the reign of Charles II. (1678), and not repealed till
1815. Long before the last of the Sumptuary Laws was
passed, however, the necessity for legislating against the
inordinate extravagance of the labouring class had ceased to
form even the pretence for action.

The "golden age" of the English worker had passed its
zenith when the second sovereign of the
Tudor race ascended the throne. The
Tudors had come into possession of the kingdom for the
most part against the will of the old feudal aristocracy, and
amid the indifference of the people, and they felt the necessity
of leaning upon the middle class—then fast becoming an
important factor in social and political life—as a support
against the rapidly-decaying power of the former and the
rising power of the latter, and they found also this class ready
to accept their overtures and to recompense royal patronage by
subservience to the royal will. An alliance was consequently
formed between the Crown and the mercantile community,
which, in spite of many errors of policy and acts not always
defensible, resulted in a great increase of commercial prosperity. The power of the Crown at this time was further
strengthened, too, by the decay of the large towns. The passing
away of feudalism, and the better organisation of government,
had removed the need for seeking the protection of their
walls, while the industrial disabilities imposed upon their
inhabitants were now far in excess of any advantages

THE TUDORS.

conferred by residence there. The consequence was that manufactures were leaving them and seeking open villages instead, where they should have space to develop their full capabilities in independence of the cramping and vexatious rules of old-fashioned corporations. Laws were vainly passed to check this tendency.[1] Thus it was forbidden (14° and 15° Henry VIII. Cap. 1) to any one in the county of Norfolk "to dye, shear, or calendar cloth" anywhere but in Norwich alone; and in the northern counties to make "worsted coverlets" except in the city of York (33° and 34°. Henry VIII. Cap. 10). By an Act passed in 1530, ropemaking was to be exclusively confined to Bridport in Dorsetshire; and in 1534 the inhabitants of Worcester, Evesham, Droitwich, Kidderminster, and Bromsgrove, the only towns then in Worcestershire, having represented that their former prosperity was being destroyed because "divers persons dwelling in the hamlets, thorps, and villages of the county made all manner of cloths, and exercised weaving, fulling, and shearing within their own houses," Parliament enacted that none but the inhabitants of the petitioning towns should be allowed to carry on that trade, "except solely for their own and their families' wearing." It was all to no purpose. The corporate privileges had become as oppressive as the old feudal services, and could no longer either profitably or patiently be borne. The only result of the interference of Parliament was, to ruin the places legislated for, by more surely transferring their industry elsewhere. It is to the credit of Henry VII. that he saw more clearly than his successor the true cause of this change in the localisation of industry, and attempted to prevent it by more reasonable means, namely, by limiting the arbitrary dealings of the corporations themselves. But the movement once begun was not to be checked by that or any other

[1] See p. 74.

artifice, and progressed in spite of every effort to stay it.
The hardly-won freedom of the mediaeval towns could offer
no inducement to industry commensurate with the still
greater freedom that was now to be had outside them—in
the country, and in the new towns of the modern type fast
springing up. From this period is commonly dated the rise of
Manchester, Sheffield, Bolton, Halifax, Leeds, Bury, and many
of the other great Lancashire and Yorkshire factory towns,
which, commencing then as mere villages, have developed
since into the great hives of production with which we are
familiar. A notable change was, in fact, coming over the
manufacturing system of the country as well as over the
localisation of its manufactures. A sort of incipient modern
factory system was being established in several industries.
Master manufacturers, delivered from the fears of open
violence, and weary of municipal fetters, were migrating into
remote districts, in little communities organised wholly for
industry, and graduated so as to afford ever greater scope
to the division and combination of labour. The system of
apprenticeship introduced from the Continent about the same
time was a potent factor in this system, and filled the place
in it that slavery had done in ancient factory systems. The
selling of goods was conducted on a larger scale, and ever
more on the competitive plan. Instead of localities looking
chiefly to supply their own needs, they rather aimed now at
supplying the requirements of the country generally, and were
indifferent to local traffic. Production was for profit, not
use. This was a very different system from that of the cotton
cottage industry which immediately preceded the introduction of the modern factory system in the north of England,
and which will be described hereafter.[1] It was, in fact, not
a domestic industry at all, but one of congregated labour,
organised on a capitalistic basis, just as ours is, only that

[1] Chap. x.

the masters then were not quite so far off from their
workmen as they became afterwards. The "cash nexus"
was not the whole bond between them. Something of
the spirit of feudal times, the spirit of personal sympathy
and obligation, still characterised and permeated it. Such
of these masters as were engaged in the woollen manufacture were called clothiers, and we read of some famous ones
already established in the north. Among them were Cuthbert
of Kendal, Hodgkins of Halifax, and Martin Brian or Byron
of Manchester. Each of these, says Anderson,[1] "kept a
great number of servants at work—carders, spinners, weavers,
dyers, shearers, etc." There were others in the south, and
in London. Of one John Winchcombe, or Jack of Newbury,
we read (*Romance of Trade*, p. 216), that he was "the first
great English clothier on record," and "perhaps his was the
first woollen factory in England." . . . "A hundred looms,
it is said, always worked in his house, and he was rich
enough to put a hundred of his journeymen in armour and
send them to Flodden Field. His kerseys were famous all
over Europe." Of a similar class of masters in other manufactures we as yet learn nothing, but are soon to meet with
them in connection with another branch of native industry
equally characteristic of our country from the earliest times.[2]

Under the vigorous government of Henry VII. and
Henry VIII., England had been advancing
rapidly in power, and in all the external
symbols of prosperity; and the weak reign of Mary failed
to greatly undermine the position thus won. During the
long one of Elizabeth this appearance of prosperity was more
than maintained, and when it was over, the country occupied
a place in the comity of European nations greater than it
had ever done before. It is true that that splendid position
was purchased at a high price, but it was boldly obtained

ELIZABETH.

---

[1] Vol. ii. p. 400. [2] See p. 333.

and brilliantly held.   The English spirit, both industrial
and political, was just then unusually strong and aspiring.
The English court was graced by the presence of some of
the greatest men of any time.   The production of wealth
was proceeding on a scale that had never been known before.
The naval and military resources of the country were unprecedented.   The price that on the other hand was paid for
this great appearance of prosperity is typified by the many
stern measures for the repression of discontent that were
enacted in this reign, and by the extraordinary expedients
that had to be resorted to to provide sustenance for large
masses of the population.   These last are the portions of the
story with which we are most concerned.   With the external
position of England we have less concern, though that too is
not without a distinct bearing on our subject, and may be
briefly alluded to.   The two great political factors of the time
were :—the preponderating influence of Spain at the head
of the Roman Catholic Church, and the rising power of the
reformed churches in France, Germany, and the Netherlands.
Elizabeth was probably a sincere Protestant, and was certainly
a cruel persecutor of adverse sects.   She was also probably
herself a really capable diplomatist, and she assuredly had
very capable diplomatists about her.   She refrained from
committing herself in the European quarrel for a while,
watching how things were going among the contending
parties, and then at the proper time threw in the whole
weight of her influence on the ultimately successful side.
It is true that the doing so was at the cost of a formal
invasion of her dominions by the greatest military power
then extant; but even in this her invariable luck adhered
to her.   The "Invincible Armada" was scattered by the
friendly winds and waves, while the efforts made to repel
it evoked a spirit of patriotism and self-reliance that greatly
benefited her rule, and had a lasting influence for good on

the character of her people. As a result of this policy England became the hope of the Protestant connection, and the home of hordes of industrious artisans who fled thither for protection from the persecutions of their native lands. Its maritime power received an impulse that carried it onward far beyond any point that it had yet attained; and the foundations of its future great colonial empire were first laid. At home the problems that faced her were of a different, though scarcely less difficult, kind; but she addressed herself to them with the same spirit, and with a somewhat similar success. The overthrow of the barons, succeeded by the entire suppression of the religious houses, and the confiscation of their estates in both cases, had greatly altered the social and industrial organisation of the country. The influence of the Church as a social and industrial power within it was gone. " The vagrants and mendicants were at once deprived of their accustomed doles; and their ranks were at the same time swelled not only by the persons discharged from the numerous religious institutions, but also by the many who were heretofore occupied with the forms and ceremonies of the Romish religion, for whom there was no place under the more simple ritual by which it was superseded."[1] To these categories should be added the many industrious workmen, formerly in the employment of the wealthy corporations, now looking about on their own account for work, and the refugees flocking into England, bringing with them, indeed, many useful qualities and talents, but generally wholly without any present means of support. " When to these immediate consequences of the Reformation is added the fact that serfage and villeinage had at no very remote period been abolished, and that by such abolition the people had acquired the right of independent action, and severally taken upon themselves

---

[1] *History of the Poor Law*, by Sir George Nicholls, vol. i. p. 199.

the duty of providing for their wants, we cannot wonder
if mendicancy and vagrancy were for a time increased "
(Nicholls). Certainly not; and the great problem how to
provide for those persons in a new way was now for the first
time attempted to be solved. As there is nothing in our
history more intimately related to the industry of the people
and the legislation affecting it than this attempt, it will be
necessary to state in a few words the course that it took.

The immediately preceding pages have suggested some
of the causes of that social change which
became the occasion of a series of enactments—the Poor Laws—unexampled in the history of
any other European people. This legislation had two
distinctly marked stages: the first almost purely repres-
sive, the second—in intention, at least—remedial. The
first stage dates from the passage of an Act (23° Edward
III. Cap. 7) prohibiting the giving of alms to "valiant
beggars," thus showing incidentally how early that species
of gentry had begun to make themselves unpleasantly
prominent; and this continued to be the principal object of
the Poor Laws up to the enactment of the 43° Elizabeth,
which famous statute marked the second stage of the
legislation. This Act was far more humane and more
carefully considered than any of its predecessors. Its chief
provisions were as follows:—It directs that in every parish
" substantial householders shall . . . be yearly nominated
in Easter week," and that these, with the churchwardens,
shall be overseers of the poor, who are, with consent of the
justices, to carry out the provisions of the Act. They are
to raise " in every parish, by taxation of every inhabitant,
. . . such competent sum and sums of money as they shall
think fit," in order to set to work, and to apprentice, children
whose parents are unable to maintain them; they are to
provide work for all indigent persons without employment,

THE POOR LAW.

and to buy "stock of flax, hemp, wool, thread, iron, and
other ware and stuff to set the poor on work," as also " for
the necessary relief of the lame, impotent, old, blind, and
such other among them being poor as are not able to work."
Thus work in some form or other is to be provided for
the idle, and relief for the infirm. The overseers are to
meet together at least monthly, and are yearly to render
an account of their expenditure. These are the principal
provisions. The liability of parents to maintain their
children, and of children to maintain their parents (established by the 39° Elizabeth), is extended to grandparents.
The possibility of an excess of poverty in any district, and
of a deficiency of means to relieve it is provided against
by giving power to extend the area of taxation to adjoining
parishes, and, if necessary, to the county.

The main principles of this Act have been followed in
all subsequent legislation ; the changes made prior to the
beginning of the present century being so unimportant as
not to require detailed mention here, and those made after
then not being within the purview of the present work. It
recognised as binding two mediæval principles, communal
in their character, namely, that every person has a definite
place in the commonwealth, and so long as he remains in
his place and does his duty there he is entitled to be
maintained in it ; and that the commonwealth is responsible
for seeing that he does his duty, and for keeping him
in his place. Such was the old Saxon doctrine ; and the
Poor Law was but a reaffirmation of it under changed
conditions. It was of a piece with all other legislation of
the *customary* era, before the advent of competition ; and
still remains, though greatly altered in scope and method, as
a monument of that tone of thought in a competitive time.
But the confining of indigent persons, willing to seek work
elsewhere, to their districts, became after a while a cruel

anomaly; and the finding employment for them in the
districts, or compelling them to work there, degenerated into
the "workhouse test:"—labour imposed, that is, merely as
a deterrent from idleness or imposture, and not organised
and made remunerative as was intended. The former principle has accordingly been in time abandoned; and what of
reality still lingers about the latter is found only in the system,
still partially pursued, of apprenticing out young persons to
work under these and other Acts. The general scope of the
legislation in modern days has become, with that exception,
but a gigantic system of eleemosynary relief. The special Acts
dealing with apprentices have generally suffered a like
eclipse, but were, while they lasted, something so much
worse than this, and had moreover so considerable a bearing on some portions of our subject as to require separate
notice.

The Poor Laws, we have seen, had from the first
a close relation to labour, as well as to
APPRENTICESHIP.
their more immediate concern of poverty;
the theory being that it was a criminal offence for a poor
person to be an idler. This theory had in itself much to
recommend it, but it was inevitable that its realisation
being placed in the hands where it was should often lead
to abuse. A like result followed the far more tyrannical
law that was passed in this same reign having reference to
apprenticeship. Apprenticeship is a system of industrial
employment peculiar to modern times. It had its origin in
the mediæval guilds, and represents (according to some)
the triumph of the craft guilds over the rival merchant
guilds. It was general throughout Europe from the twelfth
century, but is first incidentally mentioned in the English
statute book in the year 1388 (12° Richard II. Cap. 3); and
the custom after that appears to have rapidly spread. From
the 7° Henry IV. Cap. 17 (1405, 1406), we learn that

apprenticeship had already become a common practice, and
it has appeared to a diligent student of those times [1] " that
this law was intended to prevent children from going into
trades, and to retain them as agricultural labourers." In
a subsequent statute (8° Henry VI. Cap. 11), the taking of
apprentices is stated to have been at that time " a custom
of London time out of mind," but this is a vague generality.
The whole law of the subject was at any rate consolidated
under Elizabeth in the Statute of Apprentices (5° Elizabeth
Cap. 4), of which the second half (sections 25-48) is almost
exclusively occupied in defining the terms of apprenticeship
in various trades. The general result is, that apprentices
must be under twenty-one years old when taken into
employment; must serve seven years at least; that in
manual occupations their apprenticeship must not cease
before they are twenty-four, or in agriculture twenty-one
years old. Under section 31, the law only applied to
occupations *then usual*, a restriction which had important
results afterwards. Masters are given very extensive powers
in dealing with refractory apprentices; and the justices
of the peace retain the power of fixing all rates of wages.
This system, which was variously availed of, and parts of
which still prevail as a custom in some trades, is of
peculiar interest in relation to later developments of the
factory system. It was repealed in 1809 (49° George III.
Cap. 109). On its principles as a labour regulating system,
Mr. Jevons writes:—" The general theory of the Act is
that every servant or artificer shall be compelled to work
in the trade to which he was brought up. Any workman
departing from his city, town, or parish without a testimonial from his previous employer or some officer, was to
be imprisoned until he procured a testimonial; or, if he

---

[1] *The State in Relation to Labour*, by W. Stanley Jevons, p. 76, the
English Citizen Series (Macmillan and Co., 1882).

could not do so within the space of one-and-twenty days, he
was to be whipped and used as a vagabond. The hours of
labour were prescribed, not, as in our Factory Act, by way
of limitation, but by imposition. Thus, from the middle of
the month of March to the middle of September, all
artificers and labourers hired by time were to be and
continue at their work at or before five o'clock in the
morning, and continue at work and not depart until betwixt
seven and eight of the clock at night—two and a half
hours in the course of the day being allowed for meals and
drinking, thus the legal day's work was to be about twelve
hours at the least." [1]   Mr. Jevons rightly characterises this
this statute as " a monstrous law." . . . " From beginning to
end it aimed at industrial slavery." [2]   It will be noticed
too that it deals, as all restrictive legislation up to this
period had dealt, both with adults and young people. The
clauses relating to the former class of persons, however,
were soon suffered to fall into abeyance ; but those relating
to the apprenticeship of young men were for long acted
on. It may be doubted if those more particularly dealing
with young women were equally enforced, for these were
perhaps the most monstrous provisions of all. Thus the
24th section enacts that any two justices of the peace,
or other competent magistrates, shall " appoint any such
woman as is of the age of twelve years and under the age
of forty years and unmarried, and forth of service as they
shall think meet to serve, to be retained or serve by the
year, or by the week or day, for such wages and in such
reasonable sort and manner as they shall think meet, and
if any such woman shall refuse so to serve, then it shall be
lawful for the said justices of peace, mayor, or head officers, to

[1] The State in Relation to Labour, pp. 34, 35. Compare this with Mr.
Thorold Rogers's estimate of a day of eight hours' work, a century earlier.
See p. 318, note.   [2] Idem, p. 34.

commit such woman to ward until she shall be bounden to
serve as is aforesaid." By such an enactment young women
were simply placed at the orders of the magistrates.[1]

The moral of these laws is clear; they were efforts to
substitute some other principles of social order in the
place of the feudal system that had gone, and of ancient
customs fast fading away, and to do so by suppressing the
aspirations of the lower class, which at the decline of the
feudal period had been so high. The age of reciprocal
obligation had passed, the age of wage payment in full for
all services had not yet arrived, and in the transition time
it was desirable for the ruling classes to keep the new,
which were the industrial, elements in social progress down,
in part by bribery in part by force.

During this reign (Elizabeth's) our country once again
became the seat of a considerable iron
industry; a position which it maintained   THE IRON INDUSTRY.
for about a century, and then lost, to be reoccupied presently on an infinitely greater scale than ever. From the
time of the conquest to the Plantagenet era, there was little
or no iron made in England, the general paralysis that
had fallen upon all industry particularly affecting the
manufacture of metals, and from the time of John to that of
Edward III., iron was worked in the southern counties only,
the centre of the iron trade being Gloucester.[2] But in the
twenty-eighth year of this latter reign there is proof of at all
events a sufficient production of iron to make it worth while
to pass an Act of Parliament (1354) forbidding its export,
either wrought or unwrought, under heavy penalties; after
which all trace of it is again lost for a while. During the

---

[1] It is curious to compare with this enactment an earlier statute (37°
Edward III. Cap. 6), which appears to give women greater freedom than
men; for it is "the intention of the king . . . that women . . . shall
work freely as before without hindrance or restraint from this ordinance."

[2] Scrivenor's *History of the Iron Trade*, p. 31.

fifteenth century some new impetus appears to have been
received, for an Act was passed (in 1483) against the importation of a great variety of those goods that have since become
familiar in English commerce under the name of "hardware,"
and into which iron enters as a principal ingredient.   It
was about this time too that Sheffield began to be recognised
as the centre of a native hardware trade, and Camden
mentions "much iron digged up in these parts."   The great
production was still, however, in the southern counties,
especially in Sussex.   In Mr. Smiles's *Industrial Biography*[1]
(chap. ii.), a very graphic and interesting account is given
of this early English iron manufacture, and of some of
the early manufacturers and their methods :—" Their works
were established near to the beds of ore, and in places
where water power existed or could be provided by artificial
means.   Hence the numerous artificial ponds which are
still to be found all over the Sussex iron district.   Dams
of earth called "pond bays" were thrown across water
courses, with convenient outlets built of masonry, wherein
was set the great wheel which worked the hammer and
blew the furnace.   Portions of the adjoining forest land
were granted or leased to the iron smelters ; and the many
places still known by the name of 'Chart' in the weald,
probably mark the lands chartered for the purpose of supplying the iron-works with their necessary fuel."   When
cannon came to be employed in war, the nearness of Sussex
to London and the Cinque Ports, which were the centres
respectively of the military and naval life of the kingdom,
gave it a great advantage over the remoter iron-producing
districts in the north and west of England; and for a long
time the iron-works of that county enjoyed in consequence
almost a monopoly of the manufacture.   The metal was
still too precious, however, to be used for cannon balls,

---

[1] *Industrial Biography*, by Samuel Smiles (Murray 1879).

"which were hewn of stone from quarries on Maidstone Heath. Iron was only available, and that in limited quantities, for the fabrication of the cannon themselves, and wrought iron was chiefly used for that purpose." . . . Many representatives of noble families prosecuted this iron manufacture in the sixteenth century "with all the apparent ardour of Birmingham and Wolverhampton men in modern times," and the ranks of the operatives were constantly recruited, as in other branches of skilled industry at that time, from industrious immigrants, Flemish and French principally, who had taken refuge in this country from the religious persecutions abroad. The iron manufacture of Sussex reached its height about the beginning of the reign of James I. So active was it then that "it is supposed one-half of the whole quantity of iron produced in England was made there," and "Simon Sturtevant in his *Treatise of Metallica*, published in 1612, estimates the whole number of iron mills in England and Wales at 800, of which he says 'there are foure hundred milnes in Surry, Kent, and Sussex,'" an estimate which another authority (Norden) considers exaggerated so far only as Sussex is concerned, and which proves at all events the great prosperity of the industry at that time. Wood was exclusively used as fuel in this manufacture, and the consumption of it was accordingly enormous ; "the making of every ton of pig-iron required four loads of timber converted into charcoal fuel, and the making of every ton of bar-iron required three additional loads."[1] We have no estimate of the number of persons employed, but it must necessarily have been very large.

This material prosperity continued to grow under the Stuart kings, in spite of civil strife and the political complications of the time ; and the brief interval of the Commonwealth had little effect on

THE STUARTS.

[1] *Industrial Biography*, p. 40.

industry, or the little it had was probably in its favour,
owing to the more democratic cast of public opinion at that
time.   During the Civil Wars certain parts of the country,
no doubt, suffered : some more than others : and in one
particular instance, that of the South Wales iron trade, a
promising industry was wholly extinguished at the hands
of the Parliamentary forces.[1]   But it is curious on the
whole how little interruption to industry was caused.   The
woollen trade still continued the predominant one,[2] though
that great predominance was not long to be maintained.[3]   As
the commerce of the country expanded, the character of its
manufactures became more various.   A succession of new
recruits to industry were constantly arriving in the persons
of the foreign refugees, bringing with them new trades, new
devices, and a happy unconcern in our domestic quarrels.
In Mr. Smiles's *Huguenots in England and Ireland* (Murray,
1884), chap. vi., are to be found very full particulars of this
immigration, from which work, before concluding this already
too long chapter, we will venture to quote only a few details as
to the number, occupations, and location of these persons, the
arrival of whom was certainly the most important industrial
event of this epoch.   In 1621 " there were 10,000 strangers
in the city of London alone (besides still larger numbers in
the suburbs), carrying on 121 different trades."   Of 1343
such persons, whose occupations are specified in a census
taken at that time, " there were found to be 11 preachers,
16 schoolmasters, 349 weavers, 183 merchants, 148 tailors,
64 sleeve-makers, 43 shoemakers, 39 dyers, 37 brewers,
35 jewellers, 25 diamond cutters, 22 cutlers, 20 goldsmiths,
20 joiners, 15 clockmakers, 12 silk throwsters, 10 glass-
makers, besides hempdressers, threadmakers, buttonmakers,

[1] *Industrial Biography*, p. 41.
[2] *Silk, Cotton, and Woollen Manufactures*, p. 51.
[3] The progress of the woollen manufacture will be considered in the next
Chapter.

coopers, engravers, gunmakers, painters, smiths, watch-
makers, and other skilled craftsmen." Nor did these and
others like them, confine themselves by any means to
London and its neighbourhood, but rather spread themselves very widely over the country. They re-established
the city of Norwich in more than its former prosperity,[1]
and performed something like an equal service for Colchester.
In the west "they settled at Worcester, Evesham, Droitwich,
Kidderminster, Stroud, and Glastonbury; . . . in the
north at Manchester, Bolton, and Halifax, where they made
coatings; and at Kendal, where they made cloth, caps, and
woollen stockings. . . . Another important settlement of
the Flemings was at Bow, where they established dye-works
on a large scale. . . . Another body of the refugees settled
at Wandsworth and began several branches of industry,
such as the manufacture of felts, and the making of brass
plates for culinary utensils. . . . Another body of Flemings
established a glass-work at Newcastle-on-Tyne," and "manufactories for the better kinds of glass were in like manner
established in London by Venetians, assisted by Flemish
and French refugee workmen." Others settled both in
Ireland and Scotland. Many of the above had come over
in Elizabeth's reign, particularly after the massacre of St.
Bartholomew, and the wise policy inaugurated by that
monarch of affording them shelter and sympathy was continued by the Stuarts to the lasting benefit of the country.

[1] Although Norwich had been originally indebted mainly to foreign
artisans for its commercial and manufacturing importance, the natives of
the city were among the first to turn upon their benefactors. The local
guilds in their usual narrow spirit passed stringent regulations directed
against the foreign artisans who had originally taught them their trade.
The jealousy of the native workmen was also roused, and riots were stirred
up against the Flemings, many of whom left Norwich for Leeds and Wakefield,
where they prosecuted the woollen manufacture free from the restrictions of
the trades unions; whilst others left the country for Holland, to carry on
their trades in the free towns of that country.—*Huguenots*, p. 104.

It was during the Stuart era indeed, otherwise distinguished
by so much political and domestic tyranny, that these aliens
became a regular part of the population, to be presently
incorporated into that widely mixed amalgam, the English
people.

The exterior industrial legislation of the country proceeded all this while pretty much along the same lines as
formerly, the interior legislation being still generally directed
to keeping down the working classes and aggrandising employers.   Free from the control of actual slavery, rescued
from the toils of feudalism, and from the self-imposed fetters
of the guilds and mediæval towns, the former were now
to experience what direct legislation at the instance of the
landholding and commercial classes meant, when acting in
harmony with, rather than in opposition to, crude economic
forces—so destructive to humanity in their action when not
properly comprehended and restrained.   From this time
forth *competition* makes its appearance as a prime motive
power in the history of English industry : a figure of portentous import, extending to growing millions the open
hand of plenty, or crushing them under its iron heel, according as it is viewed, as it is availed of, as it is understood.
The continued growth of population and of a capitalistic
class was already affording this principle the opportunity
of displaying its characteristic features in its two most
characteristic ways : in promoting the accumulation of
wealth, and the depreciation of labour.   The ballads of the
day, hitherto filled with quite other subjects of exultation
or complaint, begin now to deal with this one.   One of
them, chanted about the streets of Leeds and Norwich in
the time of Charles II., is preserved in the British Museum,
and may still be read on the original broadside.   "It is
the vehement and bitter cry of labour against capital.   It
describes the good old times when every artisan employed

in the woollen manufacture lived as well as a farmer. But those times were past. Sixpence a day was now all that could be earned by hard labour at the loom. If the poor complained that they could not live on such a pittance, they were told that they were free to take it or leave it. For so miserable a recompense were the producers of wealth compelled to toil, rising early and lying down late; while the master-clothier, eating, sleeping, and idling, became rich by their exertions."[1]   There is a familiar ring about these complaints the significance of which cannot be missed.   y

[1] *The History of England from the Accession of James the Second*, by Lord Macaulay, vol. i. p. 204 (Longmans, 1880).

CHAPTER IX.

THE MODERN FACTORY SYSTEM

William III.—Social Condition of the Time—Commerce—Manufacture—
Birth of the Modern Factory System—English Silk Industry—John
Lombe—The First Factory—Successful Result—Woollen Manufacture
— *The Fleece* — Linen Manufacture — Decline of the Iron Industry —
Pottery—Paper—Smaller Metal Industries : Sheffield and Birmingham
—General Increase of Production.

THE accession of William III. marks the close of a civil
strife in England which had for its object
WILLIAM III.
the political emancipation of the landed and
high commercial interests from the thraldom into which
they were sought to be led by the Stuart sovereigns.
With the final dismissal of the legitimate monarch, and the
substitution of a foreigner in his place, the English upper
classes secured that constitutional ascendency in the government of the nation which remained with them for just one
hundred and fifty years ; which devolved upon the middle
class for just another fifty years in 1832 ; and has now
been transferred—with what results it is yet too early even
to attempt to forecast—to the labouring population. The
British Constitution had already assumed the form with
which we are to-day familiar; but its sphere and purpose
were then more accurately defined, and its machinery and
method were perfected. The religion of the country was
finally established as Protestant, and the succession to the
throne determined. The national economic ideal became

thenceforth almost wholly commercial. In the great diorama of English history which we may imagine to have been before us in the two preceding chapters, mediæval England had vanished, Tudor England was fading away; and in their places there is seen appearing modern England— a faint and blurred likeness as yet, but looming immense and wonderful in the now obviously contracted space which the other pictures filled so easily. We can with difficulty go back in thought to Tudor times, and place ourselves in the position of citizens who devoutly burned their fellows with whom they differed on recondite points of dogmatic theology, partly as a duty, partly as a pastime ; who sincerely believed that the world was a limited plain, and the sky a superincumbent abode of the blessed; who might have conversed with Bacon and Burleigh, and seen Shakespeare act. But even more difficult is it to reproduce in thought the earlier England, of knight and squire, abbot and crusader, lord and serf; the England of Cedric, and Gurth, and Front de Bœuf. The difficulty in this latter case is, in fact, so great that to most persons it is insuperable. Not even the fiery energy and earnest moral purpose of Carlyle[1] has sufficed to bring home to the apprehension of ordinary Englishmen the "age and body" of that time, the truth of it, the historical evolution of it, the high motive forces that displayed themselves within and sufficed to continue it. We read about those times usually as if they were but part of a pleasant romance, in which, indeed, the actions of the characters are facts with which we are in sympathy, but all the surroundings of which strike us as not only strange but fanciful. Yet those epochs were the well-marked stages in the progress of the

---

[1] In *Past and Present.* The student who is anxious to know something of the *spirit* not less than the *form* of Middle Age society should often read this book.

nation to what it has since become; those varying conditions were the most *real* things of anything in history. The most real and the most lasting. The story of national life properly told is a history, not of catastrophe, but of continuity—of the sum of all just such circumstances.

On the other hand, it would doubtless be a great mistake to picture the country which William came to rule over as resembling in any very close degree the England of to-day.

SOCIAL CONDITION.

The superficial resemblances were few enough. The connecting links were below the surface —in the obscure workings of the minds of men, and in the imperceptible tendencies of the time. " Could the England of 1685," says Macaulay,[1] "be, by some magical process, set before our eyes, we should not know one landscape in a hundred, or one building in ten thousand. The country gentleman would not recognise his own fields. The inhabitant of the town would not recognise his own street." With the exception of the "great features of nature" (mountains, rivers, and lakes), and "a few massive and durable works of human art," everything would be strange. "Many thousands of square miles which are now rich corn land and meadows, intersected by green hedgerows and dotted with villages and pleasant country seats, would appear as moors overgrown with furze, or fens abandoned to wild ducks. We should see straggling huts built of wood and covered with thatch, where we now see manufacturing towns and seaports renowned to the farthest ends of the world." The population of the country at this time is estimated by the same writer at five millions and a half. At the commencement of the century it has been reckoned by another at about five millions;[2] so that, notwithstanding all adverse influences, it had increased by about half a million under the

---

[1] *History of England*, vol. i. chap. iii.
[2] *Pictorial History of England*, vol. iv. pp. 540-542.

Stuarts. There was yet no standing army. There was no police. The navy was a half-public, half-private, mostly piratical kind of service, and naval administration "a prodigy of wastefulness, corruption, ignorance, and indolence." The general administration of justice and of the country's affairs, both at home and abroad, was equally extravagant and corrupt. The penal code was savagely severe. Malefactors were hanged in batches for what would be considered now comparatively trivial offences. Others, guilty of greater crimes, escaped with scarcely any punishment— owing, not merely to the uncertainty of the law, but to the impossibility of executing in every case its frightfully severe decrees.[1] The prisoners during confinement, whether guilty or not, were pillaged by the gaol-keepers if they had anything to give, and shamefully ill-used if they had not. The difficulty of travelling at that time is almost inconceivable to any one living at the present day and remembering that the period in question is only two centuries ago. It was probably much greater than it had been twelve or fifteen hundred years before. "On the best lines of communication the ruts were deep, the descents precipitous, and the way often such as it was hardly possible to distinguish in the dusk from the unenclosed heath and fen which lay on both sides. . . . It was only in fine weather that the whole breadth of the road was available for wheeled vehicles. Often the mud lay deep on the right and the left, and only a narrow track of firm ground rose above the quagmire. At such times obstructions and quarrels were frequent, and the path was sometimes blocked up during a long time by carriers, neither of whom would break the way. It happened almost every day that coaches stuck fast until a team of cattle could be procured from some neighbouring farm to tug

[1] *The Punishment and Prevention of Crime*, by Sir Edmund F. Ducane, chaps. ii. and iii.—English Citizen Series (Macmillan and Co., 1885).

them out of the slough. But in bad seasons the traveller
had to encounter inconveniences still more serious." . . . A
" coach-and-six " in those days meant something more than
a mere display of ostentation : it meant a reasonable supply
of power for bringing the coach to the end of its journey
within a reasonable time. The postal facilities were ridicu-
lously incommensurate with our modern notions on this subject. In the most favoured districts " the bags were carried
on horseback day and night at the rate of about five miles
an hour." In less favoured districts " letters were received
only once a week." Education was at a deplorably low
level, and confined to a mere fraction of the population.
There were almost no native professors of the fine or other
arts. Four-fifths of the common people were still employed
in agriculture ; their wages, calculated in the necessities and
comforts of life, being much lower than they had been in
the fifteenth century.[1] Of the remaining fifth an increasing
number found employment now in mines and factories.
The mineral wealth of the kingdom was, however, only
beginning to be again developed. Tin ore was extracted
from the ancient mines of Cornwall, though the rich veins
of copper which lie in the same regions were unaccountably
neglected.[2] Coal was coming into more general use, especially in London ; and the salt of Cheshire, known to the
Romans but long left untouched, was again being worked in
a small way. The production of lead was confined to a few
obscure places, and was on the very smallest scale. Taxation
was high, luxuries were dear, and " the great majority of
the nation lived almost entirely on rye, barley, and oats."[3]

Foreign products were, however, beginning to make their
way into England in a greater volume than
formerly, and from more distant places
than had been known before. The first mention made of

COMMERCE.

[1] Macaulay's *England*, vol. i. chap. iii.   [2] *Idem.*   [3] *Idem.*

tea and chocolate as articles of diet is about the year 1660. Coffee had been introduced earlier by the Turkey Company; by whom also sugar was imported in small quantities and at a high price; and tobacco was brought from America even earlier. The first great extension of English commerce had occurred under the reign of Elizabeth, since when its sphere had been almost continuously enlarged. In the half century prior to her accession, Columbus had discovered America; Cabot, Newfoundland; Vasco di Gama had rounded the Cape of Good Hope; and Mexico and Peru had been desolated by the soldiers of Spain. The tidings of new worlds to conquer, and of the riches that filled them, fired the imaginations of restless adventurers in all parts of Europe, and the desire for maritime exploration spread. But in England especially, and more particularly after the defeat of the Spanish Armada, this desire became a passion. Its fulfilment became also then to some extent a necessity. The great fleet that had been called into existence for the defence of the country could not be easily and at once disbanded; and what more happy destination for it than to intercept the richly-laden Spanish galleons returning from the western continent? or to follow in the wake of Dutch and French cruisers proceeding there, and plant the English flag alongside of theirs? With all these adventures, and with the complex spirit that animated them, Elizabeth keenly sympathised. She was proud of her country and its great deeds, after the manner of her race, ambitious and avaricious at the same time, like a genuine Tudor. She encouraged the spirit of colonisation and naval enterprise, partly for its own sake, partly as a means of strengthening and widening the national power and resources, and partly for the immediate profit which it brought to her realm, and even sometimes, it is said, to herself personally. The name Virginia appearing on American maps remains to remind us at what time it was that the great colonising movement from this country began. Previous to then there had been no overflowing of population from England : the colonising was all to us. From that time she gradually advanced to the position of the greatest colonising nation that ever was ; she began to grow from an insignificant kingdom into a great empire. James I. was just the kind of monarch to appreciate and continue this policy. He even ventured on some not very successful experiments of his own in connection with it ;[1] and the other Stuart monarchs were, generally speaking, well, though not so strongly affected toward it; while the Commonwealth, occurring near the middle of this period, acknowledged the same impulse. There had arisen by this time in England a new colonising motive. The work of the Reformation had not been wholly confined to the robbing of monasteries ; it had inculcated besides, in some minds, a love of simplicity and sincerity in religious worship, which no after-compulsion of prelate, priest, or king could eradicate. A small band of devoted men and women who had left England for Holland to escape from the tyranny of James, a few years previously, departed also from that country in 1620 for America, and in the winter of the same year made the first British settlement in the New England States. They were followed after a while by others, and have been followed thither by increasing multitudes ever since. When the puritans in England triumphed in their turn, many of the cavaliers acted in a similar way, taking generally, however, a more southerly route, and making for the fertile plains of Carolina and Virginia. No longer wholly then for the mere love of gain, but for the love of liberty, in the holy name of religion, and under the sacred guise of principle, did

[1] In 1608 he commenced his attempts to compel the raising of silkworms in England, and it required fourteen years of costly failures to persuade him of the uselessness of the effort. Then he tried to make the colonists in Virginia substitute this industry for the cultivation of tobacco, which scheme failed too.

the colonisation from the "mother country" now proceed. This great movement could not long go on without immensely benefiting commerce. The early colonists were at first almost exclusively dependent on the supplies from the old world for many of the actual necessaries of life, such as clothing; and for most of its more skilled products, such as tools and weapons. At first this commerce was mostly in the hands of the French and Dutch, so far as North America was concerned, and the South American mostly in those of the Spanish and Portuguese; but by William's time a great part of both was already passing into the hands of English merchants. At the same time a great East Indian trade was going forward. The East India Company had been established in the reign of Elizabeth, and had been reorganised and reconstituted under the Stuarts. In 1651 the first of the great Navigation Acts was passed, to secure the carrying trade for the ships of this and other companies, one of the earliest and best results of which was to largely conduce to the improvement of shipbuilding. Unfortunately, much of this natural expansion of trade was checked in the reigns of the later Stuarts by the ordaining of unwise privileges and restrictions; but nothing could withstand, in the long run, the spirit that now animated the people, nor deprive them of the opportunities that were thus presented to them. By the beginning of the next century the commerce of the country had vastly increased, and before the middle was well abreast of that of any nation. Long before the end it surpassed all others. The result of this commercial activity was a great increase of wealth in England, especially of wealth in the form of money.[1] The precious metals, flowing into the country at a rapid rate, were

---

[1] Hume, quoting from Sir Josiah Child, says, "that in 1688 there were on the 'Change more men worth £10,000 than there were in 1650 worth £1000; that £500 with a daughter was, in the latter period, deemed a larger portion than £2000 in the former; that gentlewomen in those earlier times thought

immediately coined and put in circulation. The real value
of commodities fell, while the nominal value rose ; and labour,
considered with other things as a commodity, was worse
and worse remunerated notwithstanding a general plenty.
At the same time, the power and consideration attached
to the possession of money increased, and the popular
sentiment towards it underwent a change. To buy in the
cheapest and sell in the dearest market was esteemed a
proof of wisdom, not a crime. Usury ceased to be regarded
as a practice against the interests of the common weal,
but, on the contrary, as a most legitimate and useful one.
Banks,[1] and trading companies of various kinds, entered into
business as dealers in money, or as shippers and intermediaries in the distribution of the productions of this and
other countries. The younger sons of noble houses, who in
another age would have been trained to arms or transformed
into high church dignitaries, took to trading as an outlet
for their energies—otherwise fated to lie dormant ; and on
the other hand some successful traders were ennobled. The
opportunities for accumulating riches were thus greatly
increased, while the possession of them was held in ever
more esteem.

While the trader was thus busy, the manufacturer was
upon the whole active and prosperous too,
MANUFACTURES.
notwithstanding the difficulties which bad
legislation was constantly throwing in his way. The expanding markets, afforded by the new possessions and the
extending commerce of the country, were a constant spur
to his productive energy. The foreign manufacturers, princi-

themselves well clothed in a serge gown, which a chambermaid would, in
1688, be ashamed to be seen in ; and that, besides the great increase of rich
clothes, plate, jewels, and household furniture, coaches were in that time
augmented a hundredfold."—*History of England*, by David Hume, reprint of
the edition of 1786, vol. iii. p. 778 (Ward and Lock).

[1] The Bank of England was first established in 1693.

pally Dutch and Flemish, had hitherto maintained a decided superiority over the English in quantity and quality of goods made, but we learn that in both respects the latter were now coming up with them. It was not until 1668, according to M'Culloch,[1] that the clothiers here succeeded in making the finest cloths; but they were never surpassed in the manufacture of them afterwards. Their production too was carried on in establishments of far greater size than formerly. It is stated by Sir George Nicholls that "some clothiers at that time employed as many as 500 hands,"[2] and other authorities bear a like testimony. We must not imagine these workers all congregated together in the same building: though many of them doubtless were so: but rather spread over a considerable area, in adjacent buildings or open sheds, working separately at various processes. Of these buildings, the only one where power other than manual would be used, would still be the "tucking" or *walk* mill,[3] though more frequently this would be a separate establishment on the banks of a stream at some distance, and not necessarily in the occupation of the same master. The other labour would be all handicraft. It is a remarkable circumstance, however (brought to light by Mr. Thorold Rogers), that as early as 1610, one Vaughan, a Herefordshire gentleman, published a project for relieving the poor persons engaged in isolated hand spinning and weaving in the district where he resided by employing water-power in those branches of manufacture. "He tells us that stretching for a mile and a half on either side of his house are 500 poor cottagers, who are entirely engaged in spinning flax and hurds. . . . He proposes that to relieve the poor and unemployed population water-power should be employed for manufactures, and that some thirty looms

---

[1] *Statistical Account of the British Empire*, vol. ii. p. 45.
[2] *History of the English Poor Law*, vol. i. p. 282.   [3] See chap. x. p. 387.

moved by the abundant stream should be set up for spinning
and weaving woollen, flaxen, and hempen fabrics, and even
silk, promising that in this way a market would be found
for a far larger amount of agricultural produce than could be
profitably raised or grown at present."[1]   The worthy squire
does not describe the mechanical appliances that were to be
substituted for human fingers in manipulating the textures,
nor how the power was to be communicated to them, but it
is certainly a proof of great prescience to have foreseen by
more than a hundred years the future course of English
industry.   The work people employed in both isolated and
congregated manufacture at this time were free, that is to
say, they were neither slaves nor serfs, nor members of a
caste or guild.   Their persons and their labour belonged
to themselves, not to others, as long as they obeyed the
laws.   Those laws (in the making of which they had no
voice) were often hard on them, and to some, and in some
cases (as for instance in the cases of apprenticeship and
of settlement), amounted to a practical legislative slavery,
and their maximum wages were still regulated by statute.
Still it was not slavery, and principally in this respect the
factories of that age differed from those of more ancient
times.   In other respects the labour system was very
similar to that of ancient Egypt or Assyria, or later Greece
and Rome.   There also, both isolated and congregated labour
were known, as we have seen,[2] and the latter variety was
of the capitalistic kind.   The isolated type was in former
times, however, chiefly hereditary (equally in Egypt, where
a factory system prevailed as well, and in India, where that
particular form of labour organisation does not ever seem
to have been adopted), while elsewhere it was sometimes
communistic in character, as in Peru (chap. ii.)[3]   But in

---

[1] *Six Centuries of Work and Wages*, pp. 454, 455.   [2] Chap. iii.
[3] Page 127.

England, at the epoch of which we are now treating, there
was no political slavery and no communism; the guild
system and the mediæval municipal system had both broken
down; the labour provisions of the sumptuary enactments
had long been disregarded,[1] those of the poor law only
applied in particular instances, and labour as labour was
under no exterior control.   There is even beginning to be
visible now on the other hand some legislative effort in
favour of labour; in favour of securing it in the enjoyment
of its fruits, such as they were allowed to be, and of protecting it from the greed of employers.   An Act was passed
in the first year of Anne's reign (1° Anne, Statute 2, Cap.
22), and renewed in that of George I. (12° Geo. I. Cap. 34),
against the principle of *truck*, or the payment of workmen's
wages in commodities supplied by their masters.   The first
declares that in order to "prevent the oppression of the
labourers and workmen" employed in the woollen, linen,
cotton, and iron manufactures, all payments for work done
by them shall be in lawful coin of the realm, and not by
any commodities in lieu thereof, on pain of forfeiting double
the value of what was due for such work.   The second
reiterates and confirms these enactments.   It is well known
that similar provisions were inserted later in the Factory
Acts; so that already, and before the modern factory system
was introduced, we find ourselves approaching that era of
the protection of the producer which is the fundamental
principle of that remarkable body of laws.   In other and
equally characteristic directions at this time we begin to
notice too how the evils of unregulated employment were
approaching an excess which was a grave scandal to the
country.   Acts of Parliament, tables of wages, and the
like, show female labour ever more and more in rivalry with

[1] The Sumptuary Laws became practically obsolete under James I., but
were not finally and formally repealed until 1856.

male labour, and in rivalry with it in some of the hardest
and least feminine occupations. The practice of setting
children prematurely to work also—a practice, says Macaulay, " which the State, the legitimate protector of those
who cannot protect themselves, has in our time wisely
and humanely interdicted,"[1]—prevailed in the seventeenth
century to an extent which (compared with the extent of the
manufacturing system) seems almost incredible. "At Norwich, the chief seat of the clothing trade, a little creature
of six years old was thought fit for labour. Several writers
of that time, and among them some who were considered
as eminently benevolent, mention with exultation the fact
that in that single city boys and girls of very tender
age created wealth exceeding what was necessary for their
own subsistence by twelve thousand pounds a year." Lord
Macaulay gives in a note the names of the chief of these
writers, and the titles of their works, which we cannot do
better than insert. They are, Chamberlayne's *State of
England;* Petty's *Political Arithmetic,* chap. viii.; Dunning's
Plain and Easy Method; and Firmin's *Proposition for the
Employing of the Poor.* "It ought to be observed," he adds
with a touch of pardonable bitterness, " that Firmin was
an eminent philanthropist." The same distinguished writer
points the moral from these facts in nearly the direction
that we should wish to point it here : " The more carefully
we examine the history of the past," he says, "the more
reason shall we find to dissent from those who imagine
that our age has been fruitful of new social evils. The
truth is that the evils are, with scarcely an exception, old.
That which is new is the intelligence which discerns, and
the humanity which remedies them." That is true in a
high degree ; but it is also true that the social evils of one
age are not necessarily social evils in another; that the

---

[1] *History of England,* p. 205.

evolution of society to be harmonious and successful should be in conformity with its environment, and that the environment assuredly does change from age to age. But a new factor was now to make its appearance in English industry; to completely revolutionise labour; supplant all previous methods of production; and enormously to stimulate both the good and evil qualities of the current system. That factor was the application of new motive forces to manufacture combined with the successive inventions of great mechanical appliances for them to operate with and upon.

The birthplace of the modern factory system was nevertheless not England, notwithstanding that all the conditions of labour were favourable at the time to its generation here; notwithstanding that it was the land of its greatest after-triumphs; in spite even of the strong hint of it given by Squire Vaughan more than a century before. This country is but the country of its adoption. Like so much more that has made our industrial history so imposing that great element of prosperity came to us from abroad. Far away, in a very different land, among very different customs, traditions, and surroundings, the germ was brought to life that, transplanted to a hardier clime, and subjected to novel treatment, developed a product so portentous. The great mountain chain of the Alps interposes between us and that country; a period of at least two centuries [1] between our succession to it and those crude beginnings of the new industrial era. Under the clear skies of Italy the seemingly uncongenial seed was sown; there first took root and bore

BIRTH OF THE MODERN FACTORY SYSTEM.

[1] Mr. Smiles says that "until the *beginning of the sixteenth century* Bologna was the only city that possessed proper throwing mills," namely, of the kind that are afterwards mentioned (see *Invention and Industry*, p. 110). Clearly, then, Bologna did possess them before the beginning of the sixteenth century, and other places soon after. This, in a measure, fixes the date of their invention. They were not known in England till the eighteenth century.

its earliest fruit. Over no part of our subject, obscure in
so many of its parts, does more obscurity prevail than over
this one ; and in relation to no more unlikely product of
English manufacture than the one actually concerned, might
an investigator, unacquainted with the facts beforehand,
look to trace the origin of the English factory system. The
staple manufacture of this country had long been wool. It
was one with which the prosperity of the English people,
and the very greatness of the English name, was often
held to be bound up ; in which the greatest advances
in the division and combination of labour had undoubtedly
been made, and on which the impulse to continually increased production acted with by far the greatest force. Next
to it, the iron manufacture had lately risen into a prominence
and importance which recalled the old Roman time ; while
other native industries—the mining of tin and coal, the
production of earthenware, the leather manufacture, ship-
building, and lately the ingenious lace and stocking trades
of the midland counties—were equally awaiting the stimulus
which a new system of production might bring ; and the
hitherto unfamiliar cotton fibre was supplanting flax in the
textile industries of the north. But it was in connection
with none of these materials, with no ancient industry, and
no native product, that the amazing change in the productive
powers and industrial organisation of the country that
ensued was to be introduced. A foreign material was to be
the subject of the earliest experiment ; an industry recent
in comparison with the great native industries was to
have the honour of leading the way. For about three
centuries previously a primarily struggling, though lately
much increasing, silk manufacture had settled itself in the
neighbourhood of London, and a few other places ; and once
again in the history of industry this beautiful fibre was to
contribute a story of profound and romantic interest to

that profoundly interesting and constantly romantic recital. Before proceeding to relate what is known of that strange story—the story of the introduction of the factory system into England—a brief survey of the origin and progress of this industry there will be desirable.

The manufacture of silk may have been introduced at any time after the Crusades, but at first in probably too trifling and obscure a form to attract notice. It is first mentioned by statute in the thirty-seventh year of Edward III., and again in 1455 in the reign of Henry VI., when an Act (33° Henry VI. Cap. 5) was passed "upon the heavy complaint of the women of the mystery and trade of silk and thread workers in London . . . that divers Lombards and other foreigners enriched themselves by ruining the said mystery, and all such kinds of industrious occupations of the women of our kingdom"[1]—to the effect that "no wrought silk belonging to the mystery of silk-women should be brought into England by way of merchandise during five years to come." It is of the silk works here alluded to that Anderson remarks[2] that they must have been "only needle works of silk and thread, since only women are said to have been concerned in them," a conclusion which does not exactly follow from the premises, especially as we know from the same author[3] that as soon, at all events, as twenty-five years later, articles of haberdashery—"ribbands, laces, corses, callisilk and colleinsilk[4] twined,"—were the subjects of legislation. However, it is still improbable that the manufacture of broad silk had yet reached us. The process of "throwing" silk was certainly practised in England as early as Edward IV., and in the year 1562 the silk throwsters

---

[1] Madox's *Firma Burgi*, chap. i. sec. 10, p. 33.

[2] *Idem*, vol. i. p. 478. [3] *Idem*, vol. i. p. 572.

[4] That is Calais silk and Cologne silk. See Draper's *Dictionary*, Article "Silk."

of London were united into a fellowship, though they were
not regularly incorporated into a chartered company till
1629, by which time, too, woven silk fabrics were certainly
produced in considerable quantities by the refugees who had
come over from the persecutions in the Low Countries.   It
was in the year immediately preceding the first of these
dates, namely, in 1561, that occurred that interesting event
of a presentation to Queen Elizabeth of a pair of silk
stockings.   The facts are given by Dr. Howell in his
History of the World, vol. ii. p. 222, thus :[1] " Queen Elizabeth, in this third year of her reign, was presented with
a pair of black knit stockings by her silk-woman, Mrs.
Montague, and thenceforth she never wore cloth any more."
The author adds, that even " King Henry VIII., that magnificent and expensive prince, wore ordinary cloth hose, except
there came from Spain by great chance a pair of silk
stockings ; " . . . while " his son King Edward VI. was
presented with a pair of long Spanish silk stockings by
his merchant, Sir Thomas Gresham, and the present was
then much taken notice of," showing the continued rarity
of the fabric.   During Elizabeth's long and prosperous
reign, however, the silk manufacture obtained a firm footing
here, being much fostered by her wise policy in encouraging
the immigration of foreign artisans.   The same policy was
pursued with even greater success by James I., who also
made vigorous though unsuccessful efforts to introduce the
culture of silkworms into England, as had been done so
successfully in France ;[2] and a like course was pursued by
his unfortunate son, Charles I.   It was in the reign of
the last-named monarch that the throwsters were formally
incorporated as above ; and so greatly had they prospered
a short time afterwards, that the preamble to an Act of
Parliament of Charles II.'s reign (13° and 14° Charles II.

[1] Quoted from Anderson (vol. ii. p. 116).   [2] See p. 346.

Cap. 15) declares, that "the said Company of silk throwsters employ above 40,000 men, women, and children therein." The industry received still further accessions of strength after the revocation of the Edict of Nantes in 1685, large numbers of refugee silk weavers settling in London, Norwich, Coventry, and elsewhere; and the fabrics then woven being considered to "equal, if not exceed, any foreign silk whatever." The looms of Spitalfields became celebrated all over the world, and a new and valuable source of wealth was thus added to those already at the disposal of the English people. The usual legislative consequences followed. The manufacturers clamoured for protection, and in 1697 received it in an Act prohibiting the importation of French and all other European silk goods, followed by another one in 1701, extending the prohibition to the productions of Asia as well. In 1721 almost the last device of the protective system was resorted to, in granting a bounty upon exported home-made stuffs, to be limited, however, to four years; and in 1765 a general law forbidding the importation of silk goods manufactured in all other countries was enacted, and continued in force for a long series of years, not being wholly repealed until 1845.

Notwithstanding these precautions, however, and many more of the same kind, foreign silk continued to be smuggled into England, often JOHN LOMBE. in great quantities, and chiefly in the form of thrown silk or "organzine." This came principally from France and Italy, and at so low a price was it offered on the market as to completely undersell the home dealers, and render its production by them no longer lucrative. The English trade in silk, thus interfered with, went more and more into weaving; and the large and important body of throwsters were at their wits' end to account for the phenomenon, and to know what to do. It began to be rumoured that the

French or Italians, or both of them, had some way of producing this organzine on a larger scale than was known of here, and that the greater production was connected with improved machinery. A person called Crochet had indeed about this time[1] set up a silk machine of a novel kind at Derby, but the adventure had failed. The matter was much talked about, but owing to the distances to be traversed, and to the careful manner in which the secret of the foreigners was guarded, little more than grumbling and vain speculation came of it for a while. At length the rumours began to attain more consistency. It was said that something like to in appearance the machinery of a great water mill (*i.e.* water-driven corn mill), was used to perform the delicate operation of unwinding the cocoons, and that thus assisted it was possible for human labour to produce almost any required quantity of organzine. No wonder, it was argued, that exposed to such competition, the English throwster produced at a loss; no wonder that, with the cheapening of the product thus effected, no prohibitions were strong enough to keep a foreign supply off the market. Persons were found who had seen others who had met others who had actually *been employed* about these great machines, and who vouched for their being something more than a fantastic dream. Still the incredulous were not to be convinced. Whatever use, they argued, such great machines might be for the heavier kinds of industry, how could they possibly deal with the slender filament here in question? The notion was absurd! Amongst those who had heard these rumours, and to whom they were moreover matter of great personal concern, were three brothers of the name of Lombe, carrying on the business of silk throwsters in London, but the youngest of whom, John, had been apprenticed to, and worked as a mechanic for that Mr. Crochet whose silk

[1] It was in 1702.

machines at Derby had failed so signally. Finding himself, when that event occurred, without employment, a bold idea struck him, which he hastened to communicate to his brothers. He would utilise his leisure, and the technical knowledge of machinery he had acquired, in piercing this great secret. The brothers highly approved of the idea. The rest of the story is told very graphically in Mr. Knight's *Old England*,[1] Book VII. chap. ii., from which we copy it verbatim:—"They had been previously manufacturers at Norwich. These gentlemen were deeply impressed with the disadvantage England laboured under through its being compelled to receive all its silk thread from Italy, where machinery of a very superior kind had been applied to the manufacture with such success that the English manufacturers were totally unable to compete with the Italians. How could the nature of this machinery be discovered? Would it be possible to send any one to Italy who might succeed in fathoming the secret? But then the hazard of doing so! We are informed in a document subsequently issued by one of the brothers that the Italians by the most severe laws preserved the mystery among themselves for a great number of years to their inestimable advantage. As for instance, the punishment prescribed by one of their laws for those who discover or attempt to discover anything relating to this art is death, with the forfeiture of all their goods, and to be afterwards painted on the outside of the prison walls hanging by the gallows by one foot, with an inscription denoting the name and crime of the person, there to be continued for a mark of perpetual infamy. Not the less, however, was one of the brothers Lombe determined to risk this frightful punishment, and the only point of consideration was how the attempt might be best and most safely

[1] *Old England. A Pictorial Museum of Regal, Ecclesiastical, Baronial, Municipal, and Popular Antiquities* (Charles Knight, 1845).

made.   The firm had an establishment at Leghorn for the
purchase of the raw silk sold by the Italian peasantry at
the markets and fairs ; and, of course, there were scattered
about among the Italian ports and chief towns many other
English mercantile houses.   Now it was a custom among
the English merchants engaged in this trade to send their
sons and apprentices to the houses of their agents or corre-
spondents in Italy, in order to obtain a complete knowledge
on the spot of the transactions between the two countries
with which they were to be afterwards so intimately connected.   The idea of the brothers was to take advantage
of this custom, and send the youngest of the three to attempt
the discovery of the Italian process of silk throwing.   But
the circumstance that it was necessary to send a very young
man made the danger greater, the chances of success less.
But there are young men whose youth consists only in
their age, such a man was John Lombe.   He set out for
Leghorn in 1715.   One of his first movements was to go
as a visitor to see the silk works ; for they were occasionally
shown under very rigid limitations, such as that they could
be seen only when in motion—the multiplicity and rapidity
of the machinery making it impossible then to comprehend
them—and the spectator was also hurried very rapidly
through the place.   At first young Lombe thought he
could have accomplished his object in this way by going
again and again under different disguises.   One time he was
a lady, another a priest.   He was as generous too with his
money as he could be without exciting suspicion.   But it
was all in vain.   He could make nothing of the hurried
glimpses he thus obtained, and every effort to see the
machinery put in motion, or at rest, failed.   He now tried
another course.   He began to associate with the clergy, and
being a well-educated man and of liberal tastes, he succeeded
in ingratiating himself with the priest who acted as con-

fessor to the proprietor of the works. And, however revolting it is to our notions of patriotism to see a man who
should be of more than ordinary moral elevation playing
the traitor both to his country and to his friends, there can
be no doubt of the fact that this priest's assistance was
obtained by Lombe. Neither do we think there can be any
doubt of the means by which that assistance was won.
Hardly any bribe could be too great that enabled the young
adventurer to succeed in his object. A plan was now
devised and put in execution for Lombe's admission to the
works. He disguised himself as a poor youth out of
employment, and went to the directors with a recommenda-
tion from the priest, praising his honesty and diligence,
and remarking he had been inured to greater hardships
than might be supposed from his appearance. Lombe was
engaged as a boy to attend a spinning engine called a filatoe.
He had now evidence afforded of the sufficiency of his
disguise, or rather perhaps of the fulness of the confidence
the directors placed in the priest who had sent him; he
was accommodated with a sleeping-place in the mill. In a
word, his success was as it were at once secured. But even
then he had an arduous and most hazardous task to perform.
After he had done his thorough day's work the secret work
of the night had to begin; and if discovered in that
employment! The young man must have felt many a cold
shudder pass over him as he contemplated such a possibility.
Even the few appliances he required were an additional
source of danger; their discovery would have opened the
eyes of the directors to what was going on. It appears
there was a dark hole under the stairs where he slept, and
there he hid his dark lantern, tinder-box, candles, and
mathematical instruments. And now the work went rapidly
on. Drawing after drawing was made from different parts
of the machinery and handed over to the priest, who called

occasionally to inquire how the poor boy got on that he had recommended. The priest handed the drawing over to the agents of the Messrs. Lombe, who transmitted them to England piecemeal in bales of silk. And thus at last every portion of the machinery from beginning to end was accurately drawn, and the all-important secret a secret no longer."

The conclusion of this history is no less strange and exciting than the rest of it.

"It would have been suspicious to have left the works until a ship was ready to place the suspected out of reach, so Lombe stayed in the mill. And this, as well as the other circumstances we have narrated, may show how shrewd a head was placed upon these young shoulders. But the ship came, Lombe immediately went on board and was off. And instantly—so quick did the suspicion he had anticipated arise—instantly was there an Italian brig despatched in pursuit. And the English merchant would have been more than one of the Knights of Commercial chivalry—he would have been a martyr to the cause—had not the English vessel been the better sailer."

The author of the above sketch adds, that the fate of the priest who played so prominent a part in this great matter is not accurately known, some saying that he was "tortured," no doubt to extract information from him of what had occurred; but others, "that after Mr. Lombe's return to England an Italian priest was much in his company," presumably the guilty one in question. Nor is the fate of the hero himself removed from as dark, or a still darker, suspicion. "He died at the age of twenty-nine, and there is a tragical story told of his death which is likely enough to be true. It is said the Italians, when they heard of the whole affair, sent over a female to England commissioned to poison him. Lombe had brought with him from Italy two natives of that country who were accustomed to the manufacture for which he risked so much. The woman obtained the ear of one of these, and succeeded through his means in administering a deadly poison." And so—if we are to believe this story—was poetical justice fulfilled at the expense of one who for good or evil gave the first opportunity to the modern factory system to become a really great power on earth.

Howsoever that be, what is certain is, that immediately on his return to England Mr.
THE FIRST FACTORY.
Lombe set about erecting on the banks of the Derwent, near Derby, a large silk mill on the model of this Italian one, and that a patent, taken out in 1718, granted to his brother Sir Thomas Lombe the exclusive right in the new invention for a period of fourteen years. "This amazingly grand machine," as Anderson calls it,[1] was propelled " by mills which work three capital engines," and contained " twenty-six thousand five hundred and eighty-six wheels, and ninety-seven thousand seven hundred and forty-six movements, which work seventy-three thousand seven hundred and twenty-six yards of organzine silk thread every time the water-wheel goes round, being thrice in one minute, and three hundred and eighteen million five hundred and four thousand nine hundred and sixty yards in one day and night. . . . One water-wheel gives motion to all the other movements, of which any one may be stopped separately without obstructing the rest," and " one fire-engine conveys warm air to every individual part of this vast machine, containing in all its buildings half a quarter of a mile in length." In Knight's *Old England* a picture of this establishment (Fig. 2390) is given, which corresponds with this description. The plate shows a building five stories high, resembling in its essentials many others which may

[1] *History of Commerce*, vol. iii. p. 91.

be seen at the present day in the factory districts. There
are even two tall chimneys at either end of it, which imply,
either that the sketch of the original building was taken at
a date subsequent to the introduction into it of steam power
as a motor (if this ever occurred), or that they were connected with the appliance for conveying "warm air to every
individual part" of the fabric which Anderson mentions.
At the expiration of Sir Thomas Lombe's patent (in 1732),
so highly was his enterprise approved, that by an Act of Parliament (5° George II. Cap. 8) "fourteen thousand pounds was
granted to him from the public as a consideration for the
eminent services he has done the nation in discovering, introducing, and bringing to full perfection at his own expense
a work so beneficial to this kingdom," and it is further
provided, "that his Majesty may and shall direct proper
persons to view the said engines, and to take an exact
model thereof to be deposited in such place as he shall
appoint, to secure and perpetuate the said art for the
advantage of the kingdom." Thus then was the first factory
established in England, and secured as a model for ever
to the people of this country. A few more details, taken
from a recent work of not much pretension, called *All about
Derby*, by Mr. Edward Bradbury (London : Simpkin and
Marshall, 1884), may be added with advantage, in a matter
of so much interest. The mill was erected in 1718, on an
"island swamp in the Derwent, 500 feet long and 32 feet
broad," near where Crochet's former experiment had been
made, and was held "to rent on a long lease for £8 a year."
It cost £30,000 in building. It contained "eight large
rooms lighted by 468 windows." "The foundation was
formed in oaken piles 16 to 20 feet long, driven close to
each other. Over this consolidated mass of timber was
laid a bed of stone from which were turned stone arches to
support the walls;" and while it was building John Lombe

"hired rooms at the Town Hall, where he erected temporary machines." According to this account, too, John was succeeded in the management of the mill by his brother William, whose "end was a tragic suicide;" and it was not until 1726 that Sir Thomas Lombe became the owner of the factory.[1] It has quite lately been demolished.

The success of Lombe's experiment—he is said to have made "the modest little sum of £120,000 out of the undertaking" (Bradbury), independently of his gift from Government — quickly induced SUCCESSFUL RESULT. others to follow in his footsteps. Several silk mills on the same principle were immediately erected in this neighbourhood, and at Congleton in Cheshire, at Stockport, and in other places. Nor was the impulse long in communicating itself to other branches of textile industry. The woollen manufacture soon began to accommodate itself to the new order of things; that of linen was not far behind; whilst that of cotton, from having been an almost quite inconsiderable one, came now rapidly to the front, and first entered on that amazing career of prosperity which was to distinguish it above all others during the next century. To this last great manufacture, hitherto little more than an obscure novelty in England, it will presently be our duty to devote much attention. We shall therefore, before doing so, take a brief and final glance round at the remaining great ones of the country, previous to the introduction of the new factory system.

The woollen manufacture, which had attained such considerable dimensions under the Tudors and earlier Stuarts, continued to flourish under the Commonwealth, owing in no slight degree to the democratic tendencies of that time, opposed WOOLLEN MANUFACTURE.

---

[1] These last particulars, which are found originally in Hutton's *History of Derby*, are, however, stigmatised by Mr. Smiles as "a romance."—*Invention and Industry*, chap. iv.

alike to the exclusive privileges of corporations and to
unnecessary legislative meddling with the concerns of individuals. Protective enactments in the old style continued indeed to be passed, but they had ceased to be
useful, and in one way or another were evaded. It had
long been the custom to grant to certain favoured persons
the privilege of ignoring them ; just as other favoured
persons were given monopolies of trade in certain commodities ; and at this time such licenses were granted so
freely as almost to render the original statutes nugatory, while
even where that was not the case, pretty much the same
result was obtained by the usual resource of smuggling, now
almost openly practised. Scarcely was Charles II. seated
on the throne, however, when protection in its more stringent moods was again restored, and measures of new and
exceptional rigour resorted to for enforcing the mandates
of the law.[1] Acts of Parliament were passed prohibiting
absolutely, and under penalty of death, all exportation of
wool, and of fuller's earth, imposing heavy duties on imported stuffs, regulating exactly the length and breadth of
all home-made woollen goods, enforcing particular methods
for their making and dyeing, and requiring (after the
manner of the ancient Egyptians in the similar instance of
their national linen manufacture) the interment of every
British corpse in none other than a woollen shroud.[2] The
general effect of all these devices was detrimental to the
woollen industry, which began now to be passed in prosperity by other industries comparatively new to the
country and not so much hampered. Several woollen
manufacturers, in consequence, set about transferring their
business to other countries. In 1665, 2000 workmen

---

[1] For the legislation of this period and its effects, see Bischoff's *History
of the Woollen and Worsted Manufactures*, vol. i. See also Smith's *Memoirs
of Wool*, etc. etc.   [2] See p. 87.

from Warwickshire, under the leadership of one Thomas
Tillham, emigrated to the Palatinate, to engage in the woollen
manufacture there; and they were soon followed by others
from the neighbouring county of Hertfordshire.[1] Shortly
after this, one Courteau led another body of cloth manufacturers to Portugal;[2] and at the same time the competition
of Scotland and Ireland in woollens began to be first
seriously felt in England. The Scotch manufacturers had
just at that time made a considerable step forward, owing, it
is said, to the direct encouragement of the Duke of York;[3]
and the Irish woollen manufacture, which had been rising in
importance for some time, was then increased by the erection
of "several manufactories; among others, a company at
London, with a joint-stock of £100,000; and artisans from
the west of England, set up one near Clonmel for cloths
and stuffs."[4] Under William and Mary, in whose reign, as
we have seen, the general conditions of industry were
prosperous, some attempts were made at relieving the
English woollen trade from these onerous burdens, but they
were half-hearted and wavering, while on the other hand
an unequivocal effort was made at the instance of the
English growers and manufacturers of wool to destroy the
Irish trade.[5] A law was passed (10° and 11° William
III., Cap. 10) to wholly prevent the exportation of English
wool, and the importation of Irish woollens. It was pre-
tended that the linen manufacture was more suitable to the
circumstances of that country than the woollen; and it
was accordingly proposed that the former, which was not
much valued in England at that time, should be encouraged
there at the expense of the latter, which, it was assumed

---

[1] *Woollen and Worsted Manufactures*, p. 72.
[2] Smith's *Memoirs*, quoted by Bischoff, p. 83.   [3] *Idem*.   [4] *Idem*, p. 80.
[5] See *The English in Ireland*, by James Anthony Froude, vol. i. book ii.
sec. 5 (Longmans, 1872); *A History of England in the Eighteenth Century*,
by W. E. H. Lecky, vol. ii. pp. 206-216 (Longmans, 1878), etc. etc.

belonged to England of right.　Some steps were even taken,
and continued to be taken for long afterwards, to put this
notable design into execution.　But it failed in its principal
object, that of securing a monopoly to the English clothiers,
though it succeeded only too well in inflicting permanent
injury on the rising woollen manufactures of Ireland.　A
few masters transported their industry from there to other
countries, and the rest kept up a contraband trade with
them, productive of results no less injurious to the political
than the economical relations of the kingdoms.　The linen
manufacture, artificially fostered, made but little real way,
nor ever became a staple industry in Ireland till government
encouragement of it was discontinued.　In spite of these and
other efforts to advance it, to so poor a pass had the woollen
manufacture come in the latter half of the seventeenth
century that, while in the year 1662 "the Company of
Merchant Adventurers declared in a public memorial that
the white clothing (i.e. undressed cloth) trade had abated
from 100,000 pieces to 11,000," it was the opinion of many
well-informed persons that in the course of the next century
there was a probability of its perishing altogether.[1]　Yet it
was at this very time that the country was on the eve of
making that extraordinary advance in productive industry of
every kind that distinguished the close of the century.　It
was in 1730 that John Kay, a native of Bury, took out his
patent for "the making, twisting, and carding mohairs and
worsted, and for the twisting and dressing of thread," and
three years later his still more famous one for the "fly-
shuttle," the first of the "great mechanical inventions."　Just
about this time too was published the poem of *The Fleece*, cele-
brating the glories of a manufacture thus apparently hastening
to decay; in the pleasant lines of which there is more to
be learned concerning it, the manner of it, and the im-

---

[1] *Silk, Cotton, and Woollen Manufacture*, p. 52.

plements used in it, than from almost all other contemporary records. It is no small advantage to be able to supplement our rough and bald summary of the past great English woollen trade with this picturesque description of what it was during that transition period: ere yet the old methods had quite given place to the new, but while the new already had begun to make some encroachment on the old. Independently of the intrinsic charm of the verse, it is for this purpose worth quoting pretty freely here, and is so quoted accordingly.

The Fleece was written by John Dyer, LL.B.; it was published in 1757, and purports to give an account of the wool, woollen manufacture, and woollen trade of that time. The author divides the subject into four books. The first book relates to the growth of wool; it points out the necessity of the pastures being adapted to the different breeds of sheep, and celebrates the excellences of the English pastures above others. The second relates to the process of sorting wool, and the illicit trade in it at that time. The following stanzas deal elegantly with both these subjects, mentioning besides several prominent English industries in which wool was then used:—

THE FLEECE.

> " In the same fleece, diversity of wool
> Grows intermingled, and excites the care
> Of curious skill, to sort the several kinds."
>
> .   .   .   .   .
>
> " Nimbly with habitual speed
> They sever lock from lock, and long and short,
> And soft and rigid, pile in several heaps.
> This the dusk hatter asks ; another shines
> Tempting the clothiers ; that the hosier seeks ;
> The long bright lock is apt for airy stuffs.
> If any wool peculiar to our isle
> Is given by nature, 'tis the comber's locks,
> The soft, the snow white, and the long grown flake.

24

Hither be turned the public's watchful eye,
This golden fleece to guard with strictest watch,
From the dark hand of pilfering avarice,
Who, like a spectre, haunts the midnight hour,
When nature wide around him lies supine
And silent, in the tangles soft involved
Of deathlike sleep ; he then the moment marks,
While the pale moon illumines the trembling tide,
Speedy to lift the canvas, bend the oar,
And waft his thefts to the perfidious foe.
Happy the patriot who can teach the means
To check his frauds, and yet untroubled leave
Trade's open channels !"

The third book describes the several processes of manufacture known at that period, and is deserving of close
attention. We have here exhibited, first, the purely manual
domestic kind ; and afterwards other kinds, thus :—

"Come village nymphs, ye matrons, and ye maids,
Receive the soft material : with light step,
Whether ye turn around the spacious wheel,
Or, patient sitting, that revolves which forms
A narrow circle. On the brittle work
Point your quick eye, and let the hand assist
To guide and stretch the gently lessening thread.
There are to speed their labours, who prefer
Wheels double spol'd, which yield to either hand
A several line ; and many yet adhere
To the ancient distaff, at the bosom fixed,
Casting the whirling spindle as they walk ;
At home, or in the sheepfold, or the mart,
Alike the work proceeds."

There are three kinds of hand wheels mentioned in this
quotation (besides the "ancient distaff") as instruments
used in spinning. There is first, the "spacious wheel,"
which seems to have required a standing posture in use, as
it is named in opposition to "that which forms a narrower
circle," and was utilised in "patient sitting ;" and there

are the "wheels double spol'd." The first and second were probably greater or less varieties of ordinary spinning wheels; the third must have been an improvement on them, as it yielded "*either hand a several line.*" The passage is unfortunately obscure, and even defective; not having escaped the fate that seems to pursue every composition that deals with this subject. But the implements so far are still clearly all of the domestic kind. In the following passage recent mechanical improvements come into view :—

> "But patient art,
> That on experience works from hour to hour,
> Sagacious, has a spiral engine form'd,
> Which on an hundred spoles, an hundred threads,
> With one huge wheel, by lapse of water, twines ;
> Few hands requiring ; easy tended work,
> That copiously supplies the greedy loom."

The machine here described is obviously a new invention, and is supposed to have been that for which Lewis Paul took out a patent in 1738.[1] These machines will be severally described in the next chapter, where also the appropriateness of this description of them may be seen. It is clear that the author had studied the subject. He held just views also on the question of machinery, and its influence on the labour market; and thus eloquently displays them—

> "Nor hence, ye nymphs, let anger cloud your brows,
> ' *The more is wrought, the more is still required.*'
> Blithe o'er your toils with wonted song proceed ;
> Fear not surcharge ; your hands will ever find
> Ample employment. In the strife of trade,
> These curious instruments of speed obtain
> Various advantage, and the diligent
> Supply with exercise, as the fountain sure,
> Which, ever gliding, feeds the flow'ry lawn."

[1] See p. 408.

From spinning the poem proceeds to a description of weaving—

> " From hand to hand
> The thready shuttle glides along the lines,
> Which open to the woof, and shut alternate ;
> And ever and anon, to firm the work,
> Against the web is driven the noisy frame,
> And o'er the level rushes like a surge,
> Which, often dashing on the sandy beach,
> Contracts the trav'ller's road.   From hand to hand
> Again, across the lines oft op'ning, glides
> The thready shuttle, while the web apace
> Increases."

Then to other processes—

> " Next from the slackened beam, the woof unroll'd,
> Near some clear sliding river, Aire or Stroud,
> Is by the noisy fulling-mill received,
> Where tumbling waters turn enormous wheels ;
> Where hammers, rising and descending, learn
> To imitate the industry of man.
> Oft the wet web is steep'd, and often rais'd,
> Fast dripping, to the river's grassy banks ;
> And sinewy arms of men, with full strain'd strength,
> Wring out the latent water : then up hung
> On rugged tenters, to the fervid sun
> Its level surface reeking, it expands ;
> Still bright'ning in each rigid discipline,
> And gath'ring worth ; as human life in pains,
> Conflicts, and troubles.   Soon the clothiers' shears
> And burlers' thistle skim the surface skeen."

" It would appear," says Bischoff, from whose work these lines are quoted,[1] " that Dyer next proceeds to describe a factory, and probably the first in which the different processes of the woollen manufacture, or rather those of slubbing, scribbling, and spinning were brought into one building ;" and that factory appears to have been, says he,

[1] Chap. iii.

" raised for a parish workhouse in the vale of Calder in Yorkshire." The passage is as follows—

" Behold in Calder's vale, where wide around
Unnumbered villas creep the shrubby hills,
A spacious dome for this fair purpose rise
High o'er the open gates, with gracious air,
Eliza's image stands. By gentle steps
Upraised from room to room we slowly walk,
And view with wonder and with silent joy
The sprightly scene ; where many of busy hand,
Where spoles, cards, wheels, and looms, with motion quick,
And ever murm'ring sound, th' unwonted sense
Wrap in surprise. To see them all employ'd,
All blithe, it gives the spreading heart delight
As neither meats nor drinks, nor aught of joy
Corporeal can bestow.
                    With equal scale
Some deal abroad the well assorted fleece,
These card the short, those comb the longer flake ;
Others the harsh and clotted locks receive,
Yet sever and refine with patient toil,
And bring to proper use. Flax too, and hemp,
Excites their diligence. The younger hands
Ply at the easy work of winding yarn
On swiftly-circling engines, and their notes
Warble together, as a choir of larks :
Such joy arises in the mind employed.
Another scene displays the more robust
Rasping or grinding tough Brazilian woods,
And what Campeachy's disputable shore
Copious affords, to tinge the thirsty web ;
And the Caribbean isles, whose dulcet canes
Equal the honeycomb. We next are shown
A circular machine of new design
In conic shape ; it draws and spins a thread
Without the tedious toil of needless hands.
A wheel invisible, beneath the floor,
To ev'ry member of the harmonious frame
Gives necessary motion. One intent
O'erlooks the work ; the carded wool he sees

> Is smoothly lapp'd around the cylinders,
> Which, gently turning, yield it to yon cirque
> Of upright spindles, which, with rapid whirl
> Spin out, in long extent, an even twine."

The fourth book deals exclusively with the *trade* in wool. Here is a woollen factory already then in full operation as early as 1750-57, not twenty years after the expiry of Sir Thomas Lombe's patent—a factory in all respects in the modern sense. The expression "one intent o'erlooks the work" goes to the very heart of the matter, and exactly describes the fundamental principle of factory labour; while the description of the machinery, and the use of water-power as a motor, shows it to be a factory of the modern kind. Let us now turn to another fibre.

The linen manufacture was at the end of the seventeenth century so depressed, that it was offered, as

LINEN MANUFACTURE.

we have seen in an earlier part of this chapter, by the English to their Irish neighbours as a gift. It is impossible to go beyond this for an instance of the little value set upon it. This declension had been going on for a long time, and was probably coincident, if not also connected, with the rise of the woollen manufacture. In 1477 it had dwindled to such small proportions that an Act of Parliament of that year, dealing with the foreign trade of the country, scarcely mentions it as an article of native commerce then at all. In 1531 the legislature seems to have felt bound to do something to encourage it, and a statute was accordingly enacted providing that "for every sixty acres of land fit for tillage one rood should be sown with flax and hemp seed;" and "in the register of Pulham, St. Mary, fines paid for the non-fulfilment of this law are recorded."[1] In 1622, to such a pass had matters come that a special commission was appointed to "consider also that whereas our Eastland mer-

---

[1] *The Linen Trade, Ancient and Modern*, p. 361.

chants did formerly load their ships with undressed hemp and flax in great quantities, which set great numbers of our people to work in dressing the same, and converting them into linen cloth, which kind of trade, we understand, is of late almost given over by bringing in hemp and flax ready, and that for the most part by strangers. How may this be redressed?" In 1643, and again in 1663, laws were passed imposing heavy duties on the importation of linens; notwithstanding which, says Mr. Warden, "in 1668 England was almost wholly supplied with linens from France."[1] In 1677 Andrew Yarranton, a Worcestershire ironmaster, and a man of remarkable energy and industrial foresight, published his celebrated pamphlet, " England's Improvement by Land and Sea," in which he deals largely with the conditions and prospects of the linen manufacture both at home and abroad, and propounds an elaborate scheme for its re-crudescence in England. This was to be done by introducing here, especially into the counties of Warwick, Leicester, Northampton, and Oxford (each of which counties was to raise money to start the manufacture at first), the system pursued in Germany. " In all the towns in Germany there were schools for little girls from six years old and upwards, where they were taught to spin, and by this early training they were enabled to produce a very fine thread more easily than if they had learned when older. The wheels were moved by the foot and went easily, with a delightful motion, and the mode of teaching the children was as follows :— Around a large room a number of benches were placed, in which sat perhaps 200 children spinning. In the centre stood a pulpit, in which the mistress sat with a long white wand in her hand, watching the spinners. When any one was seen idle she was tapped with the wand, but if that did not do a small bell was rung, which brought out a woman,

[1] *Linen Trade, Ancient and Modern,* p. 363.

to whom the offender was pointed out, and who took her
into another room, where she was chastised.   All this was
done without speaking a word ; and this training, the author
thought, would do good in England, where the young women
were so given to chatting.   In an adjoining room a woman
prepared and put the flax on the distaffs, and when a maid
had spun off the flax the bell was rung, the rod pointed to
her, another distaff given, and the bobbin with the threads
removed, and put into a box with others of the same kind
to make cloth.   As the children learned to spin finer they
were raised to higher benches, and great care was taken to
sort the thread and keep it uniform, and so to make regular
cloth."[1]   The yarn thus spun was floated down the Elbe
or Rhine in flats to Holland and Flanders, where it was
woven, bleached, and then sent abroad.   This is a very
curious and interesting account of these German spinning
schools, which, however, were *not* introduced into England
at Yarranton's instance.   The linen trade went instead from
bad to worse, till at length that supreme stage of badness was
reached that urged the English manufacturers to memorialise
William III. " to induce the people of Ireland to *cultivate
the joint interests of both nations*," by depriving themselves
of their thriving woollen business and applying themselves
to flax ; and that impelled the monarch of "glorious, pious,
and immortal memory" to do his best to bring that con-
summation about.[2]   A similar policy was pursued towards

[1] *Linen Trade*, p. 365.
[2] It is but fair to state, however, that the Irish legislature were a consent-
ing party to the contract, and that the British government strove at first to
carry out their part of it by subsidising the Irish linen trade, though they
also imposed disqualifications on it afterwards. A Board of Trustees was
appointed for the purpose of fostering the manufacture, and a sum varying
from £6000 to £20,000 a year was at different times placed at their disposal with
this object ; and other privileges were granted. This Board was in existence
up to 1828, when it ceased to exist ; and from that time the real rise of the
great Irish fine linen manufacture may be dated.

Scotland, after the Union (in 1707), and with like results. At the time of the introduction of the factory system, the linen, like the woollen manufacture had reached throughout the three kingdoms a very low ebb indeed. This statement applies, however, only to the linen manufacture pure and simple. There was a mixed manufacture of cotton and linen that was just then very successful in England, and had been increasingly so for some time, and of this there will be something more to say hereafter. But it will be better said in connection with the general review of the cotton manufacture and of the industrial condition of these times, which will follow in the next chapter.

In the meanwhile the manufacture of iron, which had become so considerable a one under the later Tudors and the earlier Stuarts, had been **DECLINE OF THE IRON INDUSTRY.** showing evident signs of giving way: the great destruction of timber that was involved in it alarming the country ever more and more as the forests in the southern districts disappeared before the insatiate demands for fuel. Up to a certain point this clearing of the land had been an advantage for agricultural purposes, but now the inhabitants of the large towns, and especially London, began to complain of the increased cost of wood for domestic purposes, and to foresee a time when their native supplies might be altogether exhausted. It took but a short time to cut down a forest; but it took a very long time indeed to replace it. An Act was passed accordingly, in 1581, prohibiting the employment of wood for fuel in making iron, forbidding the erection of new iron-works within twenty-two miles of London, and restricting the number of those erected beyond the above limits, in Kent, Surrey, and Sussex.[1] Similar enactments followed in future Parliaments, and the Sussex iron industry received a check from

[1] *Industrial Biography*, p. 41.

which it never recovered. Several of the ironmasters gave up the business altogether; and others removed their works to other places, especially to South Wales, where, during the civil wars, they suffered severely at the hands of the parliamentary troops; and the manufacture of iron everywhere throughout the country continued to be discouraged in all possible ways. After the Restoration the same policy was pursued, till in 1740 there were only fifty-nine furnaces in all England, of which ten were in Sussex; and in 1788 there were but two![1]

On the other hand the manufacture of earthenware, which had been during so many centuries in so degraded a condition in England, began about this time, and principally owing to the exertions of one man, to assume the importance of a national industry. There had been a manufactory of fine earthenware at Stratford-le-Bow, probably as early as the reign of Elizabeth, but the records of those times give little information concerning it. There had been one at Norwich perhaps earlier, for in 1570, according to Stow, Jasper Andries and Jacob Janson, potters, in a petition which they addressed to her, set forth that "they were the first that brought in and exercised the said science in this realm." There was also a manufactory of fine ware at Fulham, which was celebrated about a century later, but its operations seem to have been upon a small scale.[2] The great centre of the native pottery manufacture was then, as it is now—and had long been—Staffordshire, and from thence the new impetus was to come. But up to the beginning of the eighteenth century the manufacture even there was of the coarsest and commonest kind, and the organisation of labour, both for consumption and

POTTERY.

---

[1] *Industrial Biography*, p. 42.
[2] *The Ceramic Art of Great Britain*, by Llewellynn Jewitt, pp. 75, 88-92 (Virtue and Co.)

distribution, altogether primitive. A few objects of mere utility were made by individual potters in scattered villages, and were hawked about for sale by the workmen themselves, or by travelling pedlars, who conveyed them in baskets on their backs through the adjoining counties,[1] while the better articles of earthenware for domestic purposes were procured principally from Delft in Holland; and ornamented ware from France, Germany, and (of course) China. About the year 1690, however, two brothers named Elers, natives of Nuremberg, settled in Staffordshire, and introduced into the rude work of the district some improvements, especially a new method of glazing. Every precaution was used to keep their processes secret, but no precautions sufficed. The new glaze was discovered by one Astbury, who had feigned idiocy for the purpose of getting employment in their works and studying it there; and, yielding to the disgust which this mishap inspired, and to the persecution to which as strangers they had been from the first subjected, the Elers brothers removed to Chelsea, which afterwards became so famous for its ornamental earthenware.[2] The way was now clear for some one competent to take up this imperfect and struggling industry at this point and carry it forward to prosperity and success, and the required man was not long in appearing in the person of Josiah Wedgewood, born in 1730, at Burslem, in the heart of the pottery district. Apprenticed while still a child to his brother, who had a small pottery, he gave up that business at the close of his apprenticeship, and did not resume it till 1759, when he commenced on his own account. From this time he applied himself with the utmost diligence to his calling. He studied

---

[1] Lardner's *Cabinet Cyclopædia*, "Porcelain," p. 13.
[2] This is Mr. Smiles's account.—*Self-Help*, p. 88. Mr. Jewitt connects the early Chelsea manufacture with the name of John Dwight,,who established the Fulham Works.

the productions of other potters, now entering the country from several directions, and meditated long and anxiously on the principles and history of the fictile art. He made himself acquainted with the elements of chemistry, experimenting unceasingly with materials; and these efforts were crowned with success. He produced in time a hard white earthenware superior to any that had been made before; that ware in fact which is now in most extensive use all over the world. Turning his attention next to works of beauty, he became equally distinguished in that department of his trade, imitating and even rivalling the pottery of the ancient Etruscans : which had always an especial charm for him :[1] and leaving to posterity many beautiful specimens of this kind of work still identified with his name. His business increased enormously, while its great success stimulated others to emulate his example. The district became completely metamorphosed. From being in a half-populated, half-civilised state when Wedgewood's career began, it was by the end of it a populous and busy centre of industry, where the rickety potteries of the past were rapidly giving way to commodious buildings, in which all advantages, mechanical and industrial, of the modern factory system were found. Nor has its progress since been much less remarkable. Just at the time then that textile industry was entering in England on its great career of conquest; at that very time the ancient English art of pottery was entering upon a new and brilliant era of development as well, and they have gone forward together ever since.

It was long believed that at Dartford in Kent paper was first made in England, in 1588; but it is now proved that a paper-mill had existed in this country quite a century before then. This earlier

PAPER.

---

[1] He even called the place where his works were situated Etruria, and this has now become a considerable town in the pottery district.

paper-mill belonged to one John Tate, and was situated at Stevenage, in Hertfordshire. In a little book called *Historic Ninepins*, by John Timbs, F.S.A.H.,[1] some curious particulars of dealings between the proprietor of this paper-mill and Henry VII. are given (p. 135). The mill at Dartford is said to have been in the occupation of John Spillman or Speilman, who was afterwards knighted by Queen Elizabeth. He had previously been court jeweller, and Her Majesty was pleased to give him a license "for the sole gathering for ten years of all rags, etc., necessary for the making of such paper." But a paper-mill is mentioned also by Shakespeare as being in existence quite a century before this time. In *Henry VI.*, Jack Cade winds up his series of accusations against Lord Say with the terrible climax "contrary to the king, his crown and dignity, *thou hast built a paper-mill*" (2d Part *Henry VI.*, Scene VII.) It is a question if this is but an instance of the great Bard's notorious contempt for mere chronological accuracy, or if it alludes to a real establishment. The paper made at any of these mills was, however, of only a very common kind, and it was not until 1770 that the making of fine paper was introduced from the Continent; or until later that paper-making became an important industry.

We must hasten to an end of this period. In no department of industry was more progress made in the time between the accession of William III. and the introduction of the modern factory system, than in that of the smaller trades engaged about making objects of ordinary utility out of metals. It was to these, along with one or two others, that the growing prosperity of the country was chiefly due when the woollen manufacture began seriously to fail. It is to them that the great hardware centres, Sheffield and Bir-

SMALLER METAL INDUSTRIES: SHEFFIELD AND BIRMINGHAM.

---

[1] Lockwood and Co., 1869.

mingham, owe in an especial degree their rise. Sheffield had
been famous for its cutlery long before then—as early, in
fact, as Chaucer, who alludes to it;[1] but its distance from
the sea, and the difficulties of transport inland, had for long
kept it back. Similarly with Birmingham, which, "lying
as it does a little out of the line of the ancient Watling
Street, the original North-Western line from London to
Chester,"[2] was comparatively little noticed by the travellers
of old times, and gave no premonition of its great future.
The first authentic reference to it occurs in the *Itinerary*
of Leland (1538): "I came through a pretty street as ever
I entered, into Bermingham towne. . . . There be many
smithes in the towne that used to make knives and all
manner of cutlery tooles, and many lorimers that make
bittes, and a great many naylors, so that a great part of the
towne is maintained by smithes, who have their iron and
sea-cole out of Staffordshire." In the latter part of the
sixteenth century references to its industrial prosperity continually increase, till, " during the seventeenth and eighteenth
centuries the progress of Birmingham manufactures was
simply marvellous."[3] It is obviously impossible in a work
like this to even enumerate the infinite variety of industries
carried on at these, and other such places, at the epoch we
have now reached, or to attempt to deal with their developments. Such endeavours are best confined to the local
histories of the places, and to the technical works which treat
of the several industries. Many of them have been but little
altered by the introduction of the modern factory system : the
addition of an exterior motive power being a comparatively
trivial matter when so much of the labour still continues of

---

[1] In the case of the miller of Trompington :—

    " A Shefeld thwytel (*i.e.* whittle) bare he in his hose."

[2] *Industrial History of Birmingham*, by Samuel Timmins, p. 209 (Hard-
wocke, 1866 .   [3] *Idem*, p. 211.

the handicraft kind.   The older factory system may therefore to a great extent be still seen in operation in these
districts, and may often be studied there with advantage ;
and they are in this respect a connecting link, as it were,
between the present and the past.   But the link is ever
becoming a weaker one as new processes and motors are
invented, and applied, for supplanting hand labour, and as
the other characteristics of the factory system come into
play.

The position of these industries was that of many at this
time.   Long before the astonishing series
of inventions to be described in the next GENERAL INCREASE
OF PRODUCTION.
chapter occurred, the industrial development
of this country was progressing enormously, and with it
was progressing the complexity of all industrial relations.
Improvements in the processes of textile manufacture, and
their results, first brought the social and economic consequences of this progression to a head, and first enlisted
public sympathy in them ; but (as was proved afterwards
by the course of legislation) those results were confined
to the production of no particular class of commodities,
and to no novel method of producing them.   They were
the natural economic consequences of a great increase of
production itself, to which these details were but auxiliary.
That general increase of production was the distinguishing
industrial characteristic of the period just before the introduction of the factory system, which accordingly had to deal
with no new, but with old and familiar problems, already
awaiting, and even urgently demanding, solution.

CHAPTER X.

BEFORE proceeding to trace in this chapter the course of those
great mechanical inventions which made
the industrial history of the eighteenth EARLY APPLIANCES.
century so memorable in England, it will be desirable to take
a rapid glance backwards at the earlier appliances in use.
There is a great absence of reliable information on this
head; the ordinary course being to close the investigation
summarily with the remark, that "all labour was manual."
This is certainly not the case; though it is the case that,
up to the time of Elizabeth, at all events, the mechanical
appliances used in production were few and of a rude kind.
There were water-mills, as we have elsewhere remarked,[1]
from the time of the Romans, and windmills from the period
of the Crusades. The fulling-mill on the bank of the Irk,
existent in 1280, has been more than once mentioned; and
there is an old record showing that in 1323 Edward II.
granted to Nicholas le Lystere (*i.e. dyester* or *dyer*) of Ripon,
the use of his mills under the castle of York for a term of

[1] Page 10.

six years, at the end of which time the sheriff of that city is
ordered to repair the weir that diverted the water supply to
them. Other like instances at or about the same period
might be quoted. Attention has been already drawn to the
statutes directed against " tucking " mills and " gigge " mills
respectively, in later times : interesting not only in connection
with their professed objects, but also as showing how early
the jealousy of machinery showed itself in the domain of
textile manufacture. But of the precise character of the
processes performed at these places, and the extent and
nature of the labour-saving appliances which they contained,
there is scarcely any information accessible. Upon this
point, then, we are glad to avail ourselves of a list given in
Mr. Felkin's *History of the Hosiery and Lace Manufactures*,[1]
which professes to be fairly exhaustive. According to this
authority, previous to the reign of Elizabeth, " water-power
and windmills had been employed for ages in grinding corn,
also in later times in fulling, milling, and dressing cloth.
The latter processes were as yet so imperfectly performed,
however, that those cloths which were exported were sent
away in the unfinished state in which they issued from
the looms. . . . Even the spinning wheel was as yet but
little employed, the spole and distaff being commonly used.
The looms for woollen and cotton weaving were very
numerous and universally spread, but were constructed in
almost their primitive simplicity, only varied in width and
gearing to suit the materials and the articles to be produced,
such as broad and narrow cloth, blankets, linsey-wolseys,
and linens or flannels. At Norwich calendering machines
were used. Mills for scribbling cloth had been devised, but
their use was prohibited for fear of injuring the texture of
the article, and taysells (teazles) were re-employed for that

---

[1] *A History of the Machine Wrought Hosiery and Lace Manufactures*, by
William Felkin, p. 20 (Longmans, 1867).

purpose by order of Parliament. In like manner cotton
fustians might not have their nap raised by iron instruments
or machines, because of injuring their wear. Iron-wire drawing was used for chain armour, as also wire of the precious
metals for the use of gold and silver lacemakers, and for
figured weaving purposes. This was early practised to
supply the demand for garments made from cloth of gold
and silver. There were simple machines for plaiting stay-
laces, and making silk or cotton fancy braids to be wrought
into needleworks. The turning-lathe was very much used.
Casting of hollow cannon, having been preceded by forged
ordnance, was long practised; till about 1730 it was
followed by well constructed machinery for boring them.
Metal pins were introduced from France in 1543. Within
but a very short time after, machines had been constructed
to be used in making pins. Hitherto they had been filed to
a point, and the head had been soldered on by hand.
Great opposition was made to this novelty, but utility
and cheapness prevailed in its favour. The common sewing
needle was brought hither from India, after the discovery of
the route by the Cape of Good Hope. Before that time
sewing was performed in the method still used by shoemakers. A man discovered the method of punching the eye
in steel needles; and having kept his secret he realised a
large profit by it."[1] In addition to these appliances there
was much heavy machinery in use about the mines and iron-
works of the south of England, already rising into prominence;
and machinery was also used in making paper.[2] In Camden's
Britannia there is a specially vivid account of the machinery
employed about the early Sussex ironworks. This county,
we are told, "is full of iron mines everywhere, for the casting of which there are furnaces up and down the country,
and abundance of wood is yearly spent; many streams of

[1] Compare p. 247 and *note* 5.   [2] *Supra*, pp. 334, 331.

water are drawn into one channel, and a great deal of
meadow ground is turned into pools for the driving of mills
by the flashes, which, beating with hammers upon the iron,
fill the neighbourhood night and day with their noise."[1] To
this graphic description Mr. Smiles[2] adds the following
particulars :—" The hammer shaft was usually of ash, about
nine feet long, clamped at intervals with iron hoops. It was
worked by the revolutions of the water wheel, furnished with
projecting arms or knobs to raise the hammer, which fell as
each knob passed, the rapidity of its action, of course,
depending on the velocity with which the water wheel
revolved. The forge blast was also worked for the most
part by the water power. Where the furnaces were small,
the blast was produced by leather bellows worked by hand,
or by a horse walking in a gin. The foot blasts of the
earlier iron-smelters were so imperfect that but a small proportion of the ore was reduced, so that the iron makers of
the later times (*i.e.* of these times), more particularly in
the Forest of Dean, instead of digging for ironstone resorted
to the beds of ancient scoriæ for their principal supply of
this metal ; this was, of course, a great saving of labour."
In Lardner's *Cabinet Cyclopædia* (" Manufactures in Metals,"
vol. i. p. 289) we read of metal-grinding mills driven by
water, which existed in the neighbourhood of Sheffield long
before this time,[3] and which were used in the production of
many small useful articles of steel and iron. They were of
great " simplicity of structure and arrangement." Reference
is often made in old documents to what are called *walk*, or
walck mills, and the name is still found in use in remote
country places, though apparently without any knowledge of
its meaning. These *walk* mills were undoubtedly fulling-

---

[1] Quoted from Scrivenor's *History of the Iron Trade*, p. 34.
[2] *Industrial Biography*, p. 39.
[3] The author says, " probably seven or eight hundred years ago.".

mills, and the term *walk* is derived in two ways. The most obvious derivation is, that the fulling of cloth was then done by the fullers absolutely walking on it, and the common name Walker is cited in support of this view.[1] But another explanation is, that the term comes from the Flemish verb *walcken*, to full, and this seems a probable derivation. Possibly, however, the two explanations are not irreconcilable. A few other labour-saving appliances of a humble kind were likewise in use for various small operations of industry, previous to the invention of that most remarkable one to which we now pass.

The invention in question, one of the most ingenious ever made, and known by the name of the Stocking Loom or Frame, is that by which the manual process of knitting was so largely

WILLIAM LEE :
THE STOCKING FRAME.

superseded. There is, as so often happens in such cases, some controversy as to both the personality and history of the inventor of this wonderful contrivance, but there is none as to the period when the invention became known. This was in the latter years of Elizabeth's reign. The details of the controversy may be studied in Mr. Felkin's exhaustive history of the whole subject, in Beckman's *History of Inventions*, in Miss Aiken's *Elizabeth*, Mr. Knight's *Old England*, in several local histories of Nottingham and Leicester, and elsewhere. Summarising the most authoritative conclusions from these various sources, it seems proved beyond all reasonable doubt that one William Lee, a graduate of St. John's College, Cambridge, was the inventor of the stocking frame. As often happens too in industrial history (so often and so unjustly reckoned dull), there is a pleasant romance, of which he is the hero, connected with this apparently prosaic matter, that suffers from a

[1] See *Gentleman's Magazine*, March 1884; "Art, Trades, Crafts, and Callings," by E. Whitaker.

similar confusion of facts. According to one story, Lee, having married contrary to the regulations of the university, was expelled therefrom and subsisted for a time upon his wife's earnings at knitting, having then no other means of livelihood, when he contrived in conjunction with her this machine.[1] " But the following," says Dr. Ure, " is probably a more correct account of the origin of this contrivance. According to an ancient tradition in the neighbourhood of Lee's birthplace (Woodborough, near Nottingham), the stocking frame was meditated under the inspiration of love, and constructed in consequence of its disappointment. Lee is said to have been in early youth enamoured of a fair mistress of the knitting craft, who had become rich by employing a number of young women at this highly prized and lucrative industry. The young scholar, after studying fondly the dexterous movements of the lady's hand, had become himself not only an adept in the art, but had imagined a scheme of making artificial fingers for knitting many loops at once. Whether this feminine accomplishment excited jealousy or detracted from his manly attractions is not said; but his suit was received with coldness, and then rejected with scorn. Revenge now prompted him to realise the ideas which love had first inspired. He devoted his days and nights to the construction of the stocking frame, and brought it ere long to such perfection that it has remained nearly as he left it without receiving any essential improvement. Having taught its use to his brother and the rest of his relations, he established his frame at Culveston, near Nottingham, as a formidable competitor of female handiwork, teaching his mistress by the insignificance to which he reduced the implement of her pride, that the love of a man of genius was not to be slighted with impunity." We cannot relate

[1] This is obviously the version accepted by Mr. Elmore, R.A., in the composition of his celebrated picture, "Origin of the Stocking Loom" (first exhibited in 1847).

the issue better than in the words of the same lively writer, which we shall therefore still continue to quote : " After practising this business during five years, he had become aware of its importance in a national point of view, and brought his invention to London to seek protection and encouragement from the Court, by whom his fabrics were much admired. The period of his visit was not propitious. Elizabeth, the patroness of whatever ministered to her vanity as a woman and her state as a princess, was in the last stage of her decline. Her successor was too deeply engrossed with political intrigues for securing the stability of his throne to be able to afford any leisure for cherishing an infant manufacture. Nay, though Lee and his brother made a pair of stockings in the presence of the king, it is said that he viewed their frame rather as a dangerous innovation, likely to deprive the poor of labour and bread, than as a means of multiplying the resources of national industry, and of giving profitable employment to many thousand people." The encouragement refused in England was offered in France, where Henry IV. was at that time king, and Sully first minister. Both these eminent men saw at once the advantage of the invention, and invited Lee to cross the water, which he accordingly did, and settled at Rouen. But bad times were in store for France just then, and soon overtook her ; and after Henry's tragic death, Lee, proscribed as a Protestant, had to fly to Paris for concealment, where in sorrow and obscurity he died. Some of his workmen returned to England, and, bringing back their frames with them, settled in London. William Lee's brother James was among them. After some wavering he fixed his permanent abode in Nottinghamshire, where in conjunction with others he brought out machines of an improved construction, and the trade ultimately remained established principally in that neighbourhood.

Though it was by various modifications of the stocking frame that lace was first made by machinery, the ingenious process of pillow lacemaking LACE MANUFACTURE. was an independent invention of about the period of which we are now treating. "It has been almost universally attributed to Barbara, the wife of Christopher Uttman," a native of Saxony, and will be found fully described in Mr. Felkin's work (chap. viii.) The manufacture traversed Flanders, France, and Spain before it reached this country, where it is said to have been introduced by refugees about the beginning of the seventeenth century.[1] It settled at first principally in Bedfordshire and Buckinghamshire, where lace schools were established for teaching the delicate process to children, generally to children of very tender years. These "schools" were similar to those German flax-spinning schools described in the last chapter, for the introduction of which into England Andrew Yarranton was so much concerned, and it is to be feared that great cruelties were sometimes practised in them. Workshops, where this process of manufacture is carried on, retain the name of "schools" still. It can scarcely be doubted that the spread of these ingenious industries throughout England acted as an incentive to other portions of the population to seek for other labour-saving appliances, and assisted in particular in concentrating attention on the immense field offered to inventors by the great textile industries. The special course of the inventions that supervened will presently occupy our full attention, and, in the meanwhile, a few words may be advantageously said respecting the history in this country of that staple with which they were most immediately concerned, and on the industrial characteristics of this period.

The first unequivocal mention of anything approaching

---

[1] *Hosiery and Lace Manufactures*, p. 130.

a cotton *manufacture* in England occurs in a work called *The Treasure of Traffic*, published by one

COTTON MANU-
FACTURE. Lewis Roberts in 1664. The reference is as follows :—" The town of Manchester in Lancashire must be also herein remembered, and worthily for their encouragement commended, who buy the yarn of the Irish (*i.e.* linen yarn) in great quantity, and, weaving it, returne the same again into Ireland to sell. Neither doth their industry rest here, for they buy cotton wool in London, that comes first from Cyprus and Smyrna, and at home worke the same, and perfect it into fustians, vermillions, dimities, and other such stuffs, and then return it to London, where the same is vented and sold, and not seldom sent into forrain parts, who have means, at far easier termes, to provide themselves of the said first materials." The same author tells of the trade in English woollens to the East, that, "The Levant or Turkey Company bring in return thereof great quantities of cotton and cotton yarne, Grogram[1] yarne, and raw silke into England ; for here the said cloth is first shipped out and exported in its full perfection, dyed and dressed, and thereby the prime native commoditie of this kingdom (wool) is increased, improved, and vented, and the cotton yarn and raw silk obtained." Cotton wool in small quantities and for obscure uses had no doubt been imported into this country long before that time. Mr. Baines, quoting from the books of Bolton Abbey in Yorkshire, shows that it had been used there for candle wicks as early as 1298 ;[2] and mention of it is also found in the old poem, "The Processe of the Libel of English Policie," first published in 1430, and republished in Hakluyt's collection of early voyages a century and a half or so later.

---

[1] *i.e. gros-grain*, of a coarse grain or texture ; "a kind of cloth made of silk and mohair."—See Draper's *Dictionary*, "Grogram."

[2] Baines, p. 96.

From the same source too we obtain the following information respecting it, viz. that "in the yeeres of our Lord 1511, 1512, etc., till the year 1534, divers tall ships of London with certaine other ships of Southampton and Bristow, had an ordinary and usual trade to Sicilia, Candia, Chio, and somewhiles to Cyprus, as also to Tripolis and Barulti, in Syria. The commodities which they carried thither were fine kersies of divers colours, coarse kersies, white Westerne dozens, cottons (really woollen goods), certain clothes called statutes, and others called cardinal-whites, and calneskins, which were well sold in Sicilia, etc. The commodities which they brought backe were silks, chamlets, rubarbe, malmesies, muskudels, and other wines, sweete oyles, *cotton wool.* . . ."[1] Thus cotton was long used in England for trivial purposes before its use attained the dignity of a manufacture, and Mr. Baines inclines to think that it was first put to this nobler use by some of the Flemish refugees flying here from the Spanish devastations in the Netherlands. There is the stronger reason, he believes, "to suppose that the manufacture of cotton would then be commenced here, as there were restrictions and burdens on foreigners setting up business as masters in the trades then carried on in this country, whilst foreigners commencing a *new* art would be exempt from those restrictions."[2] At any rate it appears that it was in Manchester and the neighbourhood that the early cotton manufacture located itself, and that this was probably towards the close of the sixteenth century; and from "A Description of the Towns of Manchester and Salford" about the year 1650, quoted by the same author from Aikin's *History of Manchester*, p. 154, we gather the further information, of special interest to us here, that child labour was

---

[1] Hakluyt, vol. ii. p. 206. Quoted by Baines.

[2] Baines, p. 99. Compare Macpherson's *Annals of Commerce*, vol. ii. p. 176.

from the first made available in it. "The trade is not
inferior," says the author of this sketch, "to that of many
cities in the kingdom, chiefly consisting in woollen frizes,
fustians, sackcloths, mingled stuffs, inkles, tapes, points,
etc., whereby not only the better sort of men are employed,
but also the very children, by their own labour can maintain
themselves." We also learn that Bolton was at first the
principal market for the coarser class of goods, while the
finer sorts found a ready sale in Manchester. Preston
was principally engaged in making linens; Rochdale and
Bury woollens; whilst Blackburn and Oldham were still
unimportant villages. The cotton manufacture thus established was at first, as has been noted, mostly of a hybrid kind,
the cotton being mixed with some other material, generally
flax. The spinning appliances in use were not capable of
producing a cotton yarn strong enough for warp. Accordingly the cotton textures woven in Lancashire, and elsewhere
in England, previous to the middle of the eighteenth century,
were of linen warp and cotton weft, and scarcely ever of
cotton wholly. In this they differed of course from those
imported from the East, especially from India, which were
all of cotton; and some important consequences resulted from
this difference. We have already[1] had occasion to mention
the legislation of William III.'s reign, prohibiting in the
interests of the woollen manufacturers the importation of
foreign calicoes. There can be little doubt that that legislation had other results than were anticipated, and that it
gave a stimulus to home production of a kind that had not
been foreseen. The Lancashire manufacturers at once availed
themselves of the opening, and increased their production
of mixed flax and cotton fabrics, imitating in manufacture,
printing, and dyeing, the prohibited goods, and continually
imitating them more successfully and with a still increasing

[1] Chap. ix.

sale, till the woollen masters found too late that they had not secured the monopoly they had desired, but had only transferred the competition nearer home. They loudly protested in consequence, and at length obtained an Act of Parliament in their favour (7° Geo. III. Cap. 7), imposing a fine of £5 on any person found wearing any kind of printed or stained calico, *whether manufactured at home or abroad*, by which means they hoped to do for the nascent cotton manufacture what they had already done for the ancient linen manufacture—to procure its banishment, that is—whether to Ireland or elsewhere was immaterial. But the foreign artisans that had settled in Lancashire and mixed with the native population there, had already begun to develop that spirit of enterprise and dogged determination that has since characterised them. Instead of allowing their industry to be suppressed by so unjust and tyrannical a law, they sought by every ingenious means to evade it, while keeping up a continual protest all the while against the injury that it was calculated to do them. They were successful in both respects. Certain qualities of goods had been exempted from the operations of the Act from the first, and under their names they continued to furnish the public with what they required, in spite of all restraints, till Parliament, yielding at length to their clamours, passed (in 1736) another statute known as the Manchester Act, permitting the free sale of their commodities. From that time forward the cotton manufacture was firmly established in this country. A writer in the *Daily Advertiser* of 5th September 1739, whose account was copied into an after number of the *Gentleman's Magazine*, could say of it without exaggeration: " The manufacture of cotton, mixed and plain, has arrived at so great perfection within these twenty years, that we not only make enough for our own consumption, but supply our colonies, and many

of the nations of Europe;" adding, with an evident pride
which seems strangely disproportionate now, "the benefits
arising from this branch are such as enable the manufacturers of Manchester alone to lay out above thirty
thousand pounds a year for many years past, on additional
buildings. 'Tis computed that two thousand new houses
have been built in that industrious town within these
twenty years."

The characteristics of this industrial period are of exceeding interest, and are best studied in con-
INDUSTRIAL CHARAC-
TERISTICS OF THIS
PERIOD.
nection with the great event which we
have last discussed. The establishment of
the cotton manufacture forms an epoch in
English history of at least as great importance as the
establishment (or re-establishment) of the woollen manufacture under Edward III., which was long looked upon as
the most important commercial fact in our national annals.
Moreover, it is nearly exclusively in connection with this
new industry that the few industrial details of that period
that are accessible have been preserved to us. The other
textile industries (with the exception of silk) were at this
time much depressed ; and we are sadly short of information
respecting the condition of the workers in all other branches
of production ; but the sudden and wonderful rise of the
cotton trade, and the fact that it was undoubtedly in this
department that the factory system first exhibited its full
strength as a productive agent, has ever conspired to concen-
trate attention upon it. Taking then about the middle of the
eighteenth century as the climax of this transition period,
we propose to compile from some well-known sources as
vivid a picture as is consistent with great brevity of the
industrial life of the time. "At the period" (i.e. previous
to 1700), writes Mr. Baines,[1] "the extent of mercantile

[1] Page 105.

establishments, and the modes of doing business were extremely different from what they are at present. Though a few individuals are found who made fortunes by trade, it is probable that the capital of merchants was generally very small until the end of the seventeenth century, and all their concerns were managed with extreme frugality. Masters commonly participated in the labours of their servants. Commercial enterprise was exceedingly limited. Owing to the bad state of the roads and the entire absence of inland navigation, goods could only be conveyed on pack-horses, with a gang of which the Manchester chapmen used occasionally to make the circuits to the principal towns, and sell their goods to the shopkeepers, bringing back with them sheep's wool, which was disposed of to the makers of worsted yarn at Manchester, or to the clothiers of Rochdale, Saddleworth, and the West Riding of Yorkshire." . . . "It is probable," says Dr. Aikin, "that few or no capitals of £3000 or £4000 acquired by trade existed here before 1690. However, towards the latter end of the last (seventeenth) century and the beginning of the present (eighteenth), the traders had certainly got money beforehand, and began to build modern brick houses in place of those of wood and plaster. For the first thirty years of the present century the old established houses confined their trade to the wholesale dealers in London, Bristol, Norwich, Newcastle, and those who frequented Chester Fair. The profits were thus divided between the manufacturer, the wholesale, and the retail dealer; and those of the manufacturer were probably (though this is contrary to the received opinion) less per cent upon the business they did than in the present times. The improvement of their fortunes was chiefly owing to their economy in living, the expense of which was much below the interest of the capital employed. Apprentices at that time were now and then taken from families which could pay a moderate fee. By an indenture dated 1695, the fee paid appears to have been sixty pounds, the young man serving seven years. But all apprentices were obliged to undergo a vast deal of laborious work, such as turning warping mills, carrying goods on their shoulders through the streets, and the like. An eminent manufacturer in that age used to be in his warehouse before six in the morning, accompanied by his children and apprentices. At seven they all came in to breakfast, which consisted of one large dish of water porridge, made of oatmeal, water, and a little salt, boiled thick, and poured into a dish. At the side was a pan or basin of milk, and the master and apprentices, each with a wooden spoon in his hand, without loss of time dipped into the same dish and thence into the milk pan ; and as soon as it was finished they all returned to their work. In George I.'s reign many country gentlemen began to send their sons apprentices to the Manchester manufacturers ; but though the little country gentry did not then live in the luxurious manner they have done since, the young men found it so different from home that they could not brook this treatment, and either got away before their time, or, if they stayed till the expiration of their indentures, they then for the most part entered into the army or went to sea. The little attention paid to rendering the evenings of apprentices agreeable at home, where they were considered rather as servants than pupils, drove many of them to taverns, where they acquired habits of drinking that frequently proved injurious in after life." The state of society, and the mode of conducting business by the merchant, manufacturer, and apprentice alike, described in these extracts, were probably the same as had prevailed at any time since the Elizabethan era ; and as yet we have no glimpse of the actual operative. His lot was no doubt much the same, however, so far as the staple manufactures of the kingdom were concerned. But with the extension of the cotton industry in Lancashire, and the increasing location of industries of all kinds beyond the limits of the large towns, another condition of things had arisen in these districts. This was the establishment of an exclusively domestic manufacture, undertaken often in conjunction with, sometimes in subordination to, agricultural operations. Such a combination seems natural enough in the flax or woollen industry, where the raw material is found on the spot, but did not seem so in the case of a manufacture like that of cotton, where the raw material was imported from abroad. Yet just previous to the introduction of the factory system it was common to the manufactures of cotton, flax, and wool alike, and it is very curious to note this return to an absolutely primeval system at this time. The best description of that domestic manufacture we know of is in Mr. Espinasse's *Lancashire Worthies* (chap. xii.),[1] from whose bright pages other particulars in this chapter have been freely borrowed. "There had arisen at this time," he says, "in Lancashire a primitive manufacture, into which cotton entered as an element, and all the operations of which, weaving included, could be performed by the same household. It was for the most part carried on in combination with small farming by whole families at home, and to it the factory system presents a very striking contrast. In some households the manufacturing was subsidiary to the farming operations; in others, it was the principal employment of the family. Of both kinds we have sketches; one of them by the late Samuel Bamford, writing chiefly from tradition; the other by William Radcliffe, the improver of the power loom, and embodying the results of his personal experience." Then follow the extracts in question, from

---

[1] *Lancashire Worthies*, Francis Espinasse (London : Simpkin and Marshall, 1874).

which we abbreviate the most pertinent parts. "Farms,"·
says Samuel Bamford,[1] speaking of the district and time
in question, "were mostly cultivated for the production of
milk, butter, and cheese. . . . The farming was generally
of that kind which was soonest and most easily performed,
and it was done by the husband and other males of the
family, whilst the wife and daughters and maid-servants, if
there were any of the latter, attended to the churning,
cheese-making, and household work, and when that was
finished they busied themselves in carding, slubbing, and
spinning of wool or cotton, as well as forming it into warps
for the loom. The husband and sons would next, at times
when farm labour did not call them abroad, size the warp,
dry it, and beam it in the loom, and either they or the
females, whichever happened to be least otherwise occupied,
would weave the warp down. A farmer would generally
have three or four looms in his house, and then, what with
the farming, easily and leisurely though it was performed,
what with the housework, and what with the carding,
spinning, and weaving, there was ample employment for
the family. If the rent was raised from the farm so much
the better; if not, the deficiency was made up from the
manufacturing profits." Here the agricultural element is the
more prominent; in the next extract, "Radcliffe's description
of his own parish of Mellor, fourteen miles [from Manchester," the manufacturing element is the more so. "In
the year 1770," this writer says,[2] "the land in our township was occupied by between fifty to sixty farmers; rents
to the best of my recollection did not exceed ten shillings
per statute acre; and out of these fifty or sixty farmers
there were only six or seven who raised their rents directly
from the produce of their farms; all the rest got their rents

[1] *Dialect of South Lancashire*, Introduction, p. 4.
[2] *Origin of Power Loom Weaving*, pp. 59-66.

partly in some branch of trade, such as spinning or weaving woollen, linen, or cotton. The cottagers were employed entirely in this manner, except for a few weeks in the harvest. Being one of these cottagers, and intimately acquainted with all the rest, as well as every farmer, I am better able to relate particularly how the change from the old system of hand labour to the new one of machinery operated in raising the price of land. Cottage rents at that time, with a convenient loom shop and a small garden attached, were from one and a half to two guineas per annum. The father of a family would earn from eight shillings to half a guinea at his loom; and his sons, if he had one, two, or three alongside of him, six or eight shillings per week; but the great sheet-anchor of all cottages and small farms was the labour attached to the hand-wheel; and when it is considered that it required six or eight hands to prepare and spin yarn, of any of the three materials I have mentioned, sufficient for the consumption of one weaver, this shows clearly the inexhaustible source there was for labour for every person, from the age of seven to eighty years (who retained their sight and could move their hands), to earn their bread, say from one to three shillings per week, without going to the parish." Mr. Espinasse calls this "the idyllic period of Lancashire manufacturing, gone never to return," and in its externals it certainly presents many features of an unsophisticated and attractive character. There are, however, some dark suspicions in connection with it, which later observations among other industries somewhat similarly circumstanced have not tended to remove. It is said that under the stimulus of sordid motives aroused by an unusual demand, great cruelties were sometimes practised in the background of those idyllic scenes : that spinning was occasionally so profitable that every child in the cottage was called on to bear some part in the process, often at an age

26

and to an extent far beyond their strength to bear. "We
have conversed," says Dr. Cooke Taylor, "with very old
persons, who remember when the weavers, or their factors,
travelled about from cottage to cottage with their pack-
horses, to collect yarn from the spinsters, often paying a
most exorbitant price for it, which absorbed the profits of
weaving. This was the commencement of the system of
infant labour, which *was at its worst and greatest height
before anybody thought of a factory.*"[1] Some of the facts with
respect to other "cottage industries," brought to light long
after this, and made public in the several reports of the
Children's Employment Commissions, give a colour of probability even to this strong statement. How it came
about that the great pressure thus put upon spinning came
subsequently to be put also upon weaving, will be seen as
we proceed, for both results flowed from the same causes
acting in kindred spheres, and were produced by the invention of labour-saving machinery, and by the particular—by
in fact the inevitable—course which the inventions took.

The popular saying that "Necessity is the mother of
invention" is a concise summary of the
PHILOSOPHY OF IN-   philosophy of the whole subject. If men
VENTION.   had no necessities there would be no inventions; for it is the purpose of these to supply those.
Generally, too, the greater or less urgency of a necessity
concerned about different branches of even the same thing
determines the direction which an invention will take. If
the requirement is very much more in one direction than
another, it is probably along that line of usefulness that
human ingenuity will travel. This tendency is by no means
necessarily the same with discoveries, which in all branches

---

[1] *Silk, Cotton, and Woollen Manufactures*, p. 105. See also Report on the
Factory System of the United States, by Carroll D. Wright; *The Factory and
the Domestic Systems of Industry Contrasted*, p. 18 (Washington, 1884).

of human affairs are often made at most unlikely times, and under no sort of utilitarian impulse, and which may lie dormant accordingly, or remain unused, for an indefinite time, or (if already made and forgotten) until rediscovered. But as soon as they at length are turned to practical account —if that time ever comes—it is probable then that a pressing occasion for an invention in connection with them has arisen : that there has ensued a demand for something which a utilising of the precedent discovery will supply: and that the invention will then follow the line of most immediate need, and be the offspring of this demand. This general statement has nowhere met with more signal illustration than in the history of textile manufacturing industry ; and it is both curious and instructive to notice how persistently the principle has clung about it. ´ We have seen how at the dawn of the textile arts weaving preceded spinning,[1] and how the distaff and spindle were themselves, in fact, first called into existence for the purpose of providing material for the loom. So in the case of the great mechanical inventions that accompanied the introduction of the modern factory system :—they followed a precisely similar routine, under the influence of quite similar causes. It was the superior producing power of the loom to that of the old spinning appliances that set people thinking how the producing power of the latter could be increased, and which led to the invention of an entirely new method of spinning after the lapse of so many thousands of years. The weavers under the domestic system of production had often more orders than they could execute, owing to the scarcity of weft, and were sometimes even at length stopped altogether from the impossibility of obtaining certain and adequate supplies. It was, Mr. Guest informs us,[2] at that time " no uncommon

---

[1] Chap. iii. pp. 80-83.
[2] *A Compendious History of the Cotton Manufacture, with a Disproval of*

thing for a weaver to walk three or four miles in a morning,
and call on five or six spinners, before he could collect
weft to serve him for the remainder of the day; and when
he wished to weave a piece in a shorter time than usual,
a new ribbon or a gown was necessary to quicken the
exertions of the spinner." Local traditions contain many
references to these allurements to redoubled industry, held
forth on occasions by the weavers, or their representatives,
not always with the happiest results of either a moral or
industrial kind. It became evident that a crisis for English
textile manufacture was impending. " It must either receive
an extraordinary impulse, or, like most other human affairs,
after enjoying a partial prosperity, retrograde. The spinners
could not supply weft enough for the weavers. The first
consequence of this would be to raise the price of spinning.
In the then state of manners and prejudices, when the
facilities of communication between places were less, and the
population generally possessed with much greater antipathy
to leaving their native place than at present, this inducement
would have failed to bring together a sufficient number of
hand-spinners, and a further rise in the price of spinning
must have been the consequence. This would have rendered
the price of the manufactured cloth too great to have been
purchased for home or foreign consumption, for which its
cheapness must of course have been the principal inducement."

Such was the position of things then in the earlier years
of the eighteenth century, and the difficulty
pointed out was aggravated as the century
advanced by a very simple contrivance, first
introduced into woollen manufacture, but gradually adopted
in others, for facilitating the weaving process. This was
the invention of John Kay, a native of Bury, then a seat

JOHN KAY: THE FLY-SHUTTLE.

the Claims of Sir Richard Arkwright to the Invention of its Ingenious Machinery,
by Richard Guest, p. 12 (Manchester, 1823).

of that industry.[1] Kay's father had removed to Colchester
some time before, also at that time a seat of the woollen manufacture, and it was whilst employed in his father's mill there
that his inventive genius began to display itself. "He introduced improvements into the looms which his father had
brought from abroad, as well as into the contrivances then
in use for 'dressing, batting, and carding wool.' . . . He
also effected a great improvement in reeds for looms, by
making the dents of thin polished blades of metal instead
of cane (the only material then in use), whereby they were
rendered more durable, and became adapted to weave fabrics
of a much finer, or of a much stronger and more even,
texture than was practicable by cane reeds. . . . They were
a new manufacture, and from their great superiority became
universally adopted." In 1730 Kay took out a patent for
an engine for both spinning and carding worsted, which is
supposed by some to be that referred to in the poem of *The
Fleece*,[2] though this appears unlikely; and three years later,
one for "an improved mode in weaving," that with which his
name is indelibly associated. This invention was a way of
communicating motion to the shuttle which enabled the weaver
to make more than double the quantity of cloth in a day that
he could before, and for that reason it was called the "Fly-
Shuttle." It consisted in substituting for the actual throwing
of the implement from hand to hand at either end of the loom
"the picking or throwing peg," an arrangement by means of
which strings worked from a central point did this. The
shuttle thus impelled was thrown oftener, with greater force,
and at a far less expenditure of physical effort. The consequence was a still more rapid production of cloth, and a
consequently still greater demand for yarn. Invention so
far had but aggravated existing difficulties. A son of John
Kay's, Mr. Robert Kay, afterwards added another ingenious

---

[1] *Lancashire Worthies*, pp. 310-312.   [2] Compare p. 371.

appliance—the "drop box"—by means of which a weaver could at pleasure use any one of several kinds of yarn to form a variegated pattern, an invention still in use. The spinners were put more than ever on their mettle by these repeated improvements in weaving, and the accumulating calls that they made on their industry. Every nerve was strained to work up to the required demand, spinning became still more a general occupation, and the families of industrious cottagers enjoyed large profits. About the same time Lombe's silk mill at Derby was a subject of wondering speculation and remark. "Would it not be possible," it began to be asked, "to do with other materials something like what was done there for silk with such great results? Could not a machine be devised which would produce a thread suitable for weaving, from cotton, flax, and wool?"

This was the problem presented, and it is certain that it exercised many thoughtful minds at that time, many more than posterity has ever heard of as being employed upon it. To properly understand it, however, and to appreciate even partially the difficulties that had to be overcome, it will be necessary to perceive with some fulness what was actually involved. In the case of silk there is no such process as spinning requisite; this filament comes already in a continuous line from the bowels of the worm. But in the case of other materials for the manufacture of textile fabrics— flax, cotton, wool, and the rest—the fibres are all short, bent, and contorted more or less, and not susceptible in their natural state of being easily twisted together. One of the least difficult to treat in this way is worsted (which is the long staple of wool), and we have seen how, accordingly, it was the earliest that is known to have been thus dealt with, or attempted to be dealt with, by Kay. But Kay's spinning inventions did not come to much, and were almost certainly

SPINNING BY MACHINERY.

not the models upon which those great after ones were formed which were soon to astonish the world. On the other hand, cotton is perhaps the most difficult of all fibres to spin, for its staple is short, and it has not the cohesive properties of animal staples. Hitherto, from the beginning of time, that operation had been invariably performed by twisting the cotton between the fingers and thumb of the human hand : and instances have been adduced, and might continue to be adduced even in our own day, of the astonishing perfection to which such hand-spinning can be brought under the influence of long practice and inherited aptitude. But it was ever a slow one at best, and liable, when not at its best, to many drawbacks as well :—to the drawbacks of uneven and inter-mittent work and individual caprice, not to do more than mention the obvious one of variety of tactile perception in the spinners. What was wanted was a machine that would pro-duce yarn with rapidity and certainty, while it would imi-tate or supply the place of human fingers in drawing out the fibres and working them together. Nor was this quite all that was wanted. The crucial difficulty was not so much the even twisting of the yarn, as the obtaining from the raw material a body that could possibly become yarn :—the procuring by machinery a sufficiently attenuated length of evenly laid fibres (technically called a "roving") to bear a twist at all.[1] To this end the ingenuity of the earliest and of all succeeding inventors was directed.

The first really great advance towards successfully imitat-ing in a machine the motion of the hand in spinning is undoubtedly due to either of WYATT AND PAUL. two persons, John Wyatt or Lewis Paul, both of Birmingham.[2]

---

[1] Compare Ure's *Cotton Manufacture*, vol. i. p. 219.

[2] The claims of Wyatt are advocated by Baines and some of the earlier writers on the subject, but Mr. Smiles has, we think, succeeded in establish-ing the title of Paul to the invention.

The patent that describes their joint invention was taken out
on the 20th of July 1738, in the name of the latter person,
and it is given in full in Mr. Baines's *History of the Cotton
Manufacture* (pp. 122, 123). Omitting the preliminaries,
and all unessential parts, we shall quote from thence the
inventor's own description of this so celebrated machine :—
"The said Machine, Engine, or Invention, will spin Wool
or Cotton into Thread, yarn, or worsted, which, before it
is placed therein, must be first prepared in manner following—(to wit), all those sorts of Wooll or Cotton which
it is necessary to card must have each Cardful, Batt, or Roll
joyned together so as to make the mass become a kind of a
Rope or Thread of Raw Wooll ; In that sort of Wooll which
it is necessary to combe, commonly called jarsey, a strict
regard must be had to make the Sliver of an equal thickness
from end to end : The Wooll or Cotton being thus prepared,
one end of the *Mass*, Rope, Thread, or Sliver, is *put betwixt
a pair of* Rollers, Cillinders, or Cones, or some such movements, *which being twined round by their motion, draws in
the Raw Mass of Wooll or Cotton to be spun*, in proportion to
the velocity given to such Rowlers, Cillinders, or Cones : as
the prepared Mass passes regularly through or betwixt these
Rollers, Cillinders, or Cones, a succession of OTHER ROLLERS,
Cillinders, or Cones, MOVEING PROPORTIONABLY FASTER THAN
THE FIRST, draw the Rope, Thread, or Sliver, *into any degree
of fineness that may be required :* sometimes these successive
Rowlers, Cillinders, or Cones (but not the first), have another
Rotation besides that which *diminishes the Thread*, yarn, or
worsted (viz.), that they give it a small degree of Twist
betwixt each pair, by means of the Thread itself passing
through the axis and center of that Rotation.   In some
other cases only the first pair of Rowlers, Cillinders, or
Cones are used, and then the *Bobbyn, spole, or quill, upon
which the Thread,* Yarn, or Worsted, is *spun*, is so contrived

as to *draw faster than* the first Rowlers, Cillinders, or Cones
give, and *in such proportion as the first Mass, Rope, or Sliver,
is proposed to be diminished."* There can be no question
that this description contains the germ of the afterwards
completed system of spinning by rollers : that which most
nearly imitates the motion of the human fingers in performing this feat. The inventors set up a mill at Birmingham to put their appliances to the test of practice,
but the machinery was still too clumsy, and the venture
did not result successfully. The motive power, supplied
by two asses, was also assuredly of a more suggestive than
imposing kind. Ten girls only were employed in tending
the machines. Another experiment, with the same machinery,
was, however, made upon a larger scale at Northampton
under the direction of a Mr. Yeoman, a gentleman skilled
in textile manufacture, but was likewise unsuccessful. The
motive power in this case was water; the machines contained 250 spindles, and employed 50 pairs of hands.[1]
Apparently something was still wanting to complete the
efficiency of the invention ; and where the deficiency lay
seems to be implied in another patent also taken out in Paul's
name, and directed to the process of *carding,* the object of
which is to procure a better *sliver* or *roving* suitable for being
spun. Presumably this was obtained. But even with that
improvement, and others that were subsequently introduced,
this machinery proved a failure. Wyatt, who was the salesman,
never succeeded in disposing profitably of his machine spun
yarn in competition with that produced by the old methods ;
after a hard fight he gave up the contest (about 1764); and in
the opinion of the majority of the practical men of that day
the idea of spinning by machinery was finally disposed of.

[1] These particulars are taken from a letter by Mr. Charles Wyatt on his
father's claims as the inventor of the spinning machine, quoted by Baines,
p. 133.

Such was far, however, from being really the case. The idea had on the contrary taken firm root, both in the factory districts and elsewhere.

JAMES HARGREAVES.

In 1761 the Society of Arts published an advertisement offering a reward of fifty pounds, and twenty-five pounds, for the best and second best " invention of a machine that will spin six threads of wool, flax, hemp, or cotton at one time, and that will require but one person to work and attend it ;" and the records of that society show that several spinning machines were in response submitted for its approval.   It is thus clear that public attention had been aroused to the possibility of some such device succeeding at length ; and that the failures of Paul and Wyatt were not universally regarded as final.   Nevertheless, it was not, after all, in response to those inducements, nor owing to any advance in the anticipated direction, that the next great improvement in spinning machinery was due.   It proceeded from quite another source.   There lived about that time in the neighbourhood of Blackburn a hand-loom weaver, " illiterate and humble,"[1] named James Hargreaves.   That he was always a man of some mechanical skill seems to follow from the fact that we first hear of him (about the year 1760) as aiding in the construction of a carding machine for Mr. Robert Peel,[2] a manufacturer of that district, and the founder of the illustrious family of that name.   Hargreaves had a wife and a large family, and, like other weavers of the time, was often sorely pressed for weft, his loom remaining idle for want of material to go on with notwithstanding the utmost efforts of his household to keep it supplied.   It happened one day, when possibly he was revolving this position of affairs in his mind, that he observed a one-thread wheel of the kind then in use overturned on the floor, when the wheel and spindle still continued to spin

[1] Baines, p. 156.   [2] *Lancashire Worthies*, p. 321.

round. An idea struck him. What would be the effect of placing several spindles in this position, *i.e.* perpendicularly instead of horizontally, all to be set in motion by the same wheel? He resolved to make the experiment. He did so; and the "Spinning Jenny" was the result—Jenny being, according to one account, the cant name in that neighbourhood for the old wheel; according to another, being that of one of his children; and according to another, of one of Highs's.[1] "He contrived a frame, in one part of which he placed eight rovings in a row, and in another part a row of eight spindles. The rovings, when extended to the spindles passed between two horizontal bars of wood, forming a clasp, which opened and shut somewhat like a parallel ruler; when pressed together this clasp held the threads fast. A certain portion of the roving being extended from the spindles to the wooden clasp, the clasp was closed, and was then drawn along the horizontal frame to a considerable distance from the spindles, by which the threads were lengthened out and reduced to the proper tenuity; this was done by the spinner's left hand, and his right hand at the same time turned a wheel, which caused the spindles to revolve rapidly, and thus the roving was spun into yarn. By returning the clasp to its first situation, and letting down a presser wire, the yarn was wound upon the spindle."[2] It is obvious from this description that the spinning jenny was a mere multiple of the hand wheel, and only applicable to the last stage in spinning: the conversion of roving into yarn. The roving itself had still to be made separately. For cotton spinning it was especially defective, and never indeed got beyond spinning weft, being incapable of forming yarn hard enough for warp. Nevertheless, as it was just then weft that was most wanted, it may be said to have answered its purpose even for cotton, while in its appli-

[1] See next page. [2] Baines, p. 157.

cation to wool and other fibres its success was still more
decisive. Its ultimate teaching was immeasurable. From
the hour of its conception hand-spinning was obviously
doomed. "All, and more than all, that Kay's shuttle
had done for the weaver," says Mr. Espinasse,[1] "the jenny
did for the spinner. If the fly-shuttle doubled the productive power of the weaver, the jenny at once octupled
the spinner's." But this was only the beginning. The
number of spindles in the jenny had increased from eight
to sixteen by the time Hargreaves obtained his patent
(1770); they soon rose to twenty, thirty, and many more.
Moreover the jennies could be worked by children as readily
as by adults, nay better. "The awkward posture required
to spin on them was discouraging to grown-up people, who
saw with surprise children from nine to twelve years
of age manage them with dexterity, whereby plenty was
brought into families overburdened by children, and the
poor weavers were delivered from the bondage in which
they had lain from the insolence of spinners."[2] The motives
that impel to the employment of juvenile labour received
thus a new and most powerful impulse.

We have now to pass to another great invention in
spinning, the history of which is of a far
THOMAS HIGHS.   more difficult and complex kind. While
Hargreaves was improving his machinery and trying to
secure it by patent, many ingenious minds were travelling in the same direction, and in a neighbouring village
in particular a series of independent experiments were being
made at the instance of one Thomas Highs or Hayes, a
reedmaker, which were destined to eventuate in an even
more important invention than that of the spinning jenny.
It is in connection with this last invention that the great

---

[1] *Lancashire Worthies*, p. 322.
[2] Aikin's *Description of the Country round Manchester*, p. 167.

name of Arkwright first appears in industrial history, and as the connection between him and Highs (although it was afterwards the subject of judicial investigation) has been treated by many writers as of a very mysterious character, we shall give details at some length here concerning it, which seem to have escaped the notice, or not to have been within the knowledge, of the writers in question. They are principally taken from a small local history entitled *Leigh in the Eighteenth Century*, by Mr. Josiah Rose, published at the *Journal* Office, Leigh (1882), and from Guest's *Compendious History of the Cotton Manufacture* (1823), which is principally an arraignment of Arkwright, and a championship of Highs. Leigh is a manufacturing village in the neighbourhood of Bolton, not far from Manchester and Warrington, and the question at issue is, to what extent Arkwright was indebted to Highs for the great name and fame that he afterwards achieved. It is not stated if Highs was born there, but in 1763 he and a clockmaker, John Kay—not to be confounded with Kay the inventor of the fly-shuttle—resided in a street called the Walk in that town. "Kay had lived in Warrington previously to 1763, and he again went to reside there when he left Leigh in 1767." It was while resident in Leigh, and under the following circumstances, that both Highs and Kay became acquainted with Arkwright. "In March 1761 Richard Arkwright, barber and hairdresser of Bolton, married Margaret Biggins, who then lived with her father Mr. Biggins, in the Market Place in Leigh, at a house, now a public-house, and known as the sign of the Mill Stone.[1] After his marriage Mr. Arkwright was frequently at Leigh ; he came thither in the way of his business, and got orders for wigs, through the influence of his father-in-law, Mr.

---

[1] This was his second wife. His first was Patience, daughter of Robert Holt of Bolton, schoolmaster.

Biggins, who was a respectable inhabitant, and lived many years in the town. It thus appears that Highs, Kay, and Arkwright were together in Leigh, and may be considered in the light of fellow-townsmen there about the year 1763, and for some years subsequently." Now in 1769 Arkwright took out his first patent for a new system of spinning by rollers, and in 1781 and 1785 instituted legal proceedings to protect this and other patents from infringement. At both these trials Highs appeared as a witness against him, and at the latter trial, under cross-examination, declared that he invented two years previously the very machine patented by Arkwright in 1769. "Highs swore that he had invented the mode of spinning by rollers in the year 1767, and employed Kay to make models for him. Kay corroborated the evidence of Highs as to the invention, and swore that in the latter part of the year 1767 he resided in Warrington (having left Leigh in the course of that year), and that Mr. Arkwright (who then resided at Bolton) came to him and requested his assistance in getting some pieces of brass turned. Kay recommended some person to do it for him, but finally did it himself. On subsequent days Mr. Arkwright came again, gave him some other jobs to do, and invited him to an inn where they had wine together. Some conversation then took place between them on the subject of spinning by rollers, when Kay said he thought he could make it answer. On the following morning Mr. Arkwright came to him and prevailed upon him to make a model of a machine for spinning by rollers, which he did, on the principle of that which he had made under the direction of Highs," and this model Arkwright took away with him. He subsequently induced Kay to enter his service altogether, nominally employing him at first in clockmaking, and in his supposed experiments in search of perpetual motion, but, after a while, undisguisedly in constructing spinning machines of the kind he had made for Highs. Ultimately, he dismissed him from his service on a charge of felony that was never pressed. Kay's wife corroborated this testimony as to the facts, and two other testimonies by Thomas Leather and Thomas Wilkinson respectively in written statements, and one by Robert Blackstone in an oral one, were afterwards adduced in support of them. The first-named declared that in the years 1763, 1764, and 1765, Highs and Kay lived next door but one to each other, he occupying the house between them, and that they were at that time much employed in making machines for spinning. The second deposed that when between twelve and fourteen years of age, and then living in the Walk, Leigh, Thomas Highs, " who then lived in the same street, made a spinning-wheel with twenty spindles for his father," and that " he *saw* Thomas Highs set up this spinning-wheel in his father's house." Robert Blackstone stated orally that Highs had made such a machine for him. They agreed generally that the machines had had no great success.[1] There is a singular tale, too, which forms a melancholy pendant to these quasi love visits of Arkwright, and relates how afterwards, when already on the high road to fortune, he quarrelled with the wife that he had found at Leigh, and that they thereafter lived apart. It is said she did not believe in the ultimate success of his machinery, and would not sell some small property that she owned to assist in perfecting it. But this misunderstanding coincides strangely with the time when Arkwright finally got rid of Kay, and did not occur by any means, it is to be noted, when he was most in need of money. Is it not at least possible that Mrs. Arkwright, concerned for the honour of

---

[1] These statements are appended to Mr. Guest's *Compendious History*, and also to a later work, the *British Cotton Manufacture*, where they can be read in full.

her native town, may have advocated Highs's claims, and so brought down upon herself her husband's displeasure? Highs stated in evidence that after Arkwright's machinery had been some time in operation he met him by chance in Manchester, and reproaching him with having appropriated his idea without acknowledgment, Arkwright did not deny the imputation. It was ever an article of faith, too, about the neighbourhood of Leigh, that Arkwright had behaved badly to his early friends. On the whole we conclude, then, and it is now pretty generally allowed, that Arkwright was *not* the inventor, but only the adapter of the machinery which he acquired through Kay from Highs; and which, finding almost a barren thing, he turned to such excellent account. To him belong, indeed, many honours in connection with the establishment of the modern factory system, but not this one.[1]

It is time, however, that we should come to Arkwright

RICHARD ARK-WRIGHT: THE WATER FRAME.

himself, who was the perfecter, at all events, of the early methods of spinning by machinery; and to the numerous contrivances that he set in motion to that end. He was born in Preston on the 23d of December 1732, being the youngest of thirteen children.[2] His education was of the scantiest kind: his "Uncle Richard taught him to read, and he gathered some little further instruction at a school during

---

[1] Mr. Guest goes a step farther than we have gone in the text, and claims Hargreaves as being an imitator of Highs as well (*Compendious History*, pp. 13, 14 *et seq.*) His reasoning on this point, however, is not conclusive, and the arguments in favour of the two inventions being quite independently made, are weightier. Mr. Baines points out (*Cotton Manufacture*, pp. 145, 146) how "a machine, on the same principle as that which was unfinished in the hands of Highs, had beyond all question been completed, made the subject of a patent, and set to work thirty years before by Wyatt," which might, therefore, he thinks, be the common parent of both. We do not share this view. The controversy is still a favourite one among industrial writers on this period, and may be studied in many well-known works.

[2] *Lancashire Worthies*, p. 370.

winter evenings;"[1] but "it is doubtful if he ever learnt to read with ease."[2] He was early apprenticed to a barber at Kirkham, and when his apprenticeship was out appears to have migrated to Bolton, where he married, and carried on that business there. Many stories, more or less genuine, are told of him at this period. It is evident, at all events, that he was no ordinary barber, or did not long continue so, for we presently hear of him as the possessor of a " valuable chemical secret" for dyeing hair, and that "one part of his business was to attend the hiring fairs frequented by young girls seeking service, for the purpose of buying their long hair to be worked up into perukes, and he is said to have been unusually expert in such negotiations " (Quarterly Review, No. 213, p. 58, quoted by Mr. Espinasse). When Arkwright was about twenty-eight years old his first wife died ; and, as we have already seen, he was fortunate enough to find a second at Leigh, one of the towns which no doubt he was in the habit of visiting pretty frequently. She accompanied him to live at Bolton, which is but seven or eight miles from Leigh, where Arkwright became from that time more than ever a frequent visitor, taking also a journeyman from there, one Dean, who afterwards succeeded to his Bolton business. These were the fateful visits to which reference has been made in connection with the inventions of Highs. Arkwright was said to be at this time engaged in investigating the problem of perpetual motion: a highly suspicious story, which appears, however, to have received very general credence. It is far more likely that he was engaged all the while in investigating the subject with which his name became afterwards so closely associated. That subject— the possibility of spinning by machinery—would probably be a good deal discussed in the district through which he

---

[1] *History of the Borough of Preston*, by Charles Hardwick, p. 650 (Preston, 1857).   [2] *Lancashire Worthies*, p. 370.

travelled, and in the town where he lived. An acute, pushing, thoughtful man, like Arkwright, would not fail to have many opportunities of listening to such discussions, and would doubtless ponder them. He had heard, too, of Wyatt's and Paul's invention, for he confessed years afterwards, in the "case" presented to Parliament asking compensation for alleged infringements of his patent rights, that he was aware how, "about forty or fifty years ago, one Paul and others, of London, invented an engine for the spinning of cotton, and obtained a patent for such invention," and how (he was careful to say) "they spent many years and much money in the undertaking without success; and many families who were engaged with them were reduced to poverty and distress."[1] It is more than probable, too, that he knew of Hargreaves's invention, which was then in use. Putting these probabilities together then, and connecting them with his knowledge of the work Highs and Kay were engaged upon at Leigh, and his taking the latter into his service afterwards, it is not a very far-fetched inference that Arkwright's studies of perpetual motion bore about the same relation to what was really in his mind, that his setting Kay to make a clock when he first engaged him did to what he really engaged Kay for. Anyhow, the undoubted result was, that in 1768 Arkwright succeeded in constructing, with the help of Kay and others, a machine for spinning better cotton yarn than had yet been produced; and that it was set up and tried in the same year in his native town Preston, owing to the influence and by the assistance of a friend, John Smalley, "a liquor merchant and painter . . . in the parlour of the house belonging to the Free Grammar School, which was lent by the head-master to Mr. Smalley for the purpose."[2] Mr. Smalley thenceforth entered heartily into

[1] Hardwick's *History of Preston*, p. 363.
[2] This is Baines's account (*Cotton Manufacture*, p. 150). Hardwick (*History*

Arkwright's hopes and projects in relation to his spinning machines. Being convinced by this trial of their utility, they resolved to get others constructed on a still greater scale, "but aware of the riots which had recently occurred at Blackburn against the spinning jenny—the contemporaneous contrivance of James Hargreaves—they resolved to abandon their native county, then under violent fermentation, and set them up elsewhere."[1]   They removed accordingly to Nottingham, already the seat of a flourishing industry engaged in the production of silk and worsted stockings; whither Hargreaves had previously gone.   There they erected some machines, and with the assistance of Messrs. Wright, bankers of that town, fairly started on their enterprise. The Messrs. Wright after a little time, however, "finding that the results of the machinery were not so advantageous or promising as they had expected, took alarm, having the disasters of Northampton (*i.e.* the failure of Paul and Wyatt's machines) before their eyes, and withdrew from the concern," previously "introducing Arkwright to Mr. Samuel Need, a considerable manufacturing hosier of Nottingham, who had for a partner that eminent mechanician and excellent man, Mr. Jedediah Strutt of Derby, the inventor of the only capital improvement ever made on Lee's stocking frame." Mr. Strutt discerned at once the sound principles of Arkwright's machines, and frankly declared his conviction that

---

of Preston, p. 364) tells the story somewhat differently.   Speaking of Smalley he says : "This gentleman allowed Arkwright the use of a room in his own house for the prosecution of his labours.   In this room the first complete machine constructed, and afterwards patented, by Arkwright was fitted up. The house is situated at the bottom of Stoneygate.   It was afterwards for a long period the residence of the Rev. Robert Harris, D.D., head-master of the Grammar School."   To Baines's account a note is appended that " these facts are stated on the authority of Nicholas Grimshaw, Esq., several times Mayor of Preston, who has personal knowledge of them."   This is the authority generally followed.

[1] Ure's *Cotton Manufacture of Great Britain*, pp. 226, 227 *et seq.*

with some slight alterations they would spin excellent hosiery yarn:—a great desideratum in the cotton manufacture of that day, since both the hand-wheel yarn and the jenny yarn of Hargreaves was too soft and loose for making good stockings.   The sequel to these anxious transactions is given thus in the words of Dr. Ure: " Being now associated with capitalists of probity and enterprise, Arkwright tasked his faculties of mind and body to their utmost stretch to organise more completely the factory at Nottingham, which, with the aid of Smalley and Messrs. Wright, he had mounted so early as 1768, and driven by horse power.   On the 3d July 1769 his first patent is dated—a year ever memorable also in the annals of industry for the patent invention of James Watt.   In the following year, 1770, he was joined by Messrs. Need and Strutt.   In 1771 this admirable triumvirate selected an excellent factory site at Cromford on the Derwent, where they erected the first water-spinning mill—the nursing place of the factory opulence and power of Great Britain."

The placing it in the first cotton mill of which the motive power was water, procured for Arkwright's spinning machinery the name of the Water Frame, which it long retained, and which still survives in the term *water twist* as applied to a certain quality of yarn.   The specifications annexed to the patent show that this machinery included in its principles both the modern *drawing frame* and the *throstle*, that is appliances both for the conversion of rovings into yarn, and for the formation of the rovings themselves. The original purpose of it (the idea that he probably took from Highs) was confined, it is believed, to the first process, but it was so evidently applicable to the latter one that this soon grew out of it.   What part Strutt had in introducing that or other improvements is not known.

Meanwhile invention had been active in the direction of

a process which in textile manufacture precedes either of the above, the process namely of Carding, or reducing the raw material from a crowded mass into a condition where its fibres become straightened, and lie parallel to each other: as is obviously necessary to be done before it can be spun. This process derives its name from the old method of performing it, which was by means of two implements shaped like hand-brushes, the backs of which were made of stout card and the fronts fitted with wire teeth. In the period of cottage industry it was usually performed by women, who placing one of the cards on the knee and holding it firm with the left hand, then spread the cotton or wool in small quantities over the wire and drew the other card repeatedly over it with the right hand, until the fibres were deemed sufficiently straight. That accomplished, the cardings were taken off in a roll and laid so as to be united into a continuous roving by the spinning wheel. Hemp and flax are still sometimes treated in much the same way. The first obvious improvement on this process was to fix one of the cards to a bench or table, and the next to attach the other one to some beam or projection over it, so that they should merely require to be brought into contact in the desired manner, not to be held in position as well. Such new contrivances were called "stock cards;" and could be made double as large, and could perform double as much work as the old ones. But "the grand improvement in carding" was the application of rotary motion; and this improvement, says Mr. Baines,[1] "singular as it may seem, is traced back to Lewis Paul, the patentee of spinning by rollers." That remarkable man had taken out a patent for a machine for carding cotton as early as 1748, which seems to have included the principle of the revolving cylinder, still in use, and it is

CARDING BY MACHINERY.

[1] *History of the Cotton Manufacture,* p. 172.

believed to have been used at the factory at Northampton which ended so disastrously. After the breaking up of that establishment, "it was purchased by a hat manufacturer from Leominster, and by him applied to the carding of wool for hats; and about 1760 it was introduced into Lancashire, and reapplied to the carding of cotton by a gentleman of the name of Morris, in the neighbourhood of Wigan,"[1] and also by the first Sir Robert Peel, with whom it did not answer.[2] The chief difficulty to be surmounted was the feeding and stripping the machines; and, without plunging into another controversy as to who first found a remedy for their defects, it will be enough to say that a successful method of supplying the wool was at length devised by John Lees of Manchester in 1772, while the most effective method of withdrawing it (i.e. by means of the "crank and comb") was patented by Arkwright in the following year. "By these several inventions and improvements," says Mr. Baines,[3] "the carding engine was perfected;" and, the same distinguished writer adds, "the factory system of England takes its rise from this period. Hitherto the cotton manufacture had been carried on almost entirely in the houses of the workmen; the hand or stock cards, the spinning wheel, and the loom, required no larger apartment than that of a cottage. A spinning jenny of small size might also be used in a cottage, and in many instances was so used: and when the number of spindles was considerably increased adjacent workshops were used. But the water frame, the carding engine, and the other machines which Arkwright brought out in a finished state, required both more space than could be found in a cottage, and more power than could be applied by the human arm.

See *Memoirs of the Literary and Philosophical Society of Manchester*, vol. v. of the second series, p. 326. Quoted by Baines, p. 175.
    [2] Compare p. 410.   [3] Page 179.

Their weight also rendered it necessary to place them in strongly-built mills, and they also could not be advantageously turned by any power then known but that of water."[1] Further, the use of machinery was accompanied by a greater division of labour, and therefore a greater co-operation was requisite to bring all the processes of production into harmony and under a central superintendence. Accordingly, " all these considerations drove the cotton-spinners to that important change in the economy of English manufactures, the introduction of the factory system; and when that system had once been adopted, such were its pecuniary advantages that mercantile competition would have rendered it impossible, even had it been desirable, to abandon it." Even the final glory of being a subject of inspiration to the poet was not denied it either, and Dr. Darwin in the *Botanic Garden*, taking Arkwright's establishment at Cromford for his theme, produced these graceful lines on the new system in its application to Cotton manufacture, as it had already been celebrated by Dr. Dyer in its application to Wool.[2]

> " Where Derwent guides his dusky floods
> Through vaulted mountains and a night of woods,
> The nymph Gossypia treads the velvet sod,
> And warms with rosy smiles the wat'ry god ;
> His pond'rous oars to slender spindles turns,
> And pours o'er massy wheels his foaming urns ;
> With playful charms her hoary lover wins,
> And wields his trident while the monarch spins.
> First, with nice eye, emerging Naiads cull
> From leathery pods the vegetable wool ;
> With wiry teeth *revolving cards* release
> The tangled knots, and smooth the ravell'd fleece :
> Next moves the *iron hand* with fingers fine,
> Combs the wide card, and forms th' eternal line.

---

[1] Pp. 184, 185.   [2] *Supra*, page 369.

> Slow with soft lips the *whirling can* acquires
> The tender skeins, and wraps in rising spires ;
> With quicken'd pace *successive rollers* move,
> And these retain, and those extend, the *rove :*
> Then fly the spokes, the rapid axles glow,
> While slowly circumvolves the labouring wheel below."[1]

While these great triumphs over physical and mechanical difficulties were being won, it should be no OPPOSITION TO THE GREAT INVENTIONS. matter of surprise that they were not universally appreciated.   They were in fact very far from that.   It was well enough for statesmen, for poets (who are in their nature seers), and for a few very enlightened persons, to perceive the value and detect the real significance of such great conquests over Nature :—to those who stand upon an elevation the inequalities or even sterility of a landscape are but reckoned among its picturesque and inevitable features.   But to those who have to level the inequalities, and to wring subsistence from the sterile parts, the effect is somewhat different.   There is little room in their lives for poetry or prescience: and it was thus with the workers—both masters and men—whom the new system displaced.   It was inevitable that they should suffer inconvenience, and should resent both that present inconvenience and any prospect of its increase ; and they did both.   We have seen how very early in the history of English industry protests had been raised against the rough inventions of the times—the " gigge mills " and " tucking mills " of that era,—and they continued to be made long after.   Nor were those protests by any means confined to the less instructed of the population.   Even the wide and astute mind of Elizabeth was not proof against so common a prepossession in the supposed interest of the working classes.   When Lord Hunsdon claimed from her a reward

---

[1] The *Botanic Garden* was published in 1781.

for William Lee, on account of his great invention of
the stocking frame, she replied:—"My Lord, I have too
much love for my poor people who obtain their bread by
the employment of knitting, to give my money to forward
an invention that will tend to their ruin by depriving
them of employment, and thus make them beggars," and
the invention itself was a fertile source of riot and
disorder in the midland counties for more than two centuries after.[1]   Similarly, when those appliances for superseding hand labour in the cotton and other industries,
which we have described, were coming into vogue, they
excited a great deal both of unfavourable comment and of
open animosity.   The weavers of Colchester resented Kay's
invention of the fly-shuttle so vehemently that he removed
from there to Leeds in the hope of escaping persecution.   A
vain hope.   "At Leeds both masters and men were banded
against him."[2]   The former, indeed, adopted his invention,
"but most of them refused to pay for its use ;" and "Kay
became involved in so many law and chancery suits that,
although they were decided in his favour, he was nearly
ruined."   The latter did their best to suppress it ; and
probably did succeed in preventing other useful inventions of his from being popularised.[3]   Ultimately, when he
returned to his native town, Bury, it was not to experience
either gratitude or peace.   "In 1753 a mob broke into
Kay's house, destroying everything they found, and no doubt
would have killed him had he not been conveyed to a place
of safety by his friends in a wool-sheet."   An ignominious
exit indeed for so great a benefactor.   The case of poor
Hargreaves is even still better known, but will bear repeti-
tion.   "Hargreaves is supposed to have invented the 'jenny'

[1] For a full account of these riots, under the name of "Luddism," see
Felkin's *History of the Hosiery and Lace Manufactures*, chap. xvi.
[2] *Lancashire Worthies*, p. 313.   [3] *Idem*, p. 313.

about 1764, and certainly by 1767 he had so far perfected
it that a child could work with it eight spindles at once.
When first invented it was doubtless a rude machine, and
Hargreaves is said to have kept it a secret, and to have
used it merely in his own family and his own business, to
supply himself with weft for his looms.   It was, of course,
a secret which could not long be kept, and, when it was
discovered, the fate of the inventor of the fly-shuttle befell
the putative inventor of the spinning jenny.   If the jenny
came into general use, the weaver would no longer be at
the mercy of the spinner; the production of yarn would be
multiplied, and its price would fall.   The spinsters of
Blackburn, their fathers, brothers, sweethearts, were not
students of political economy, and did not reflect that
increased supply at a lower price would produce an increased
demand.   They looked only to the probable immediate
effects of the jenny on the number of the persons employed in spinning, and on the price of yarn.   The very
weavers were dissatisfied, being afraid, it seems, lest
the manufacturers should demand finer weft woven at
the former prices.   The Blackburners rose upon Hargreaves, broke into his house, destroyed the jenny or
jennies, and made the town and neighbourhood too hot for
him."[1]   Another story, but not so well authenticated, is, that
the secret of the unusual production of yarn by Hargreaves's
family was disclosed by his wife, either to gratify some feminine
whim or as a means of procuring an immediate supply of
necessaries; and Hargreaves and his invention had to betake
themselves elsewhere.   In Arkwright's case, and equally in
Paul's, the opposition took another form, that of a combination among the merchants and manufacturers against
buying their products, and to what extent this opposition was

[1] *Lancashire Worthies*, p. 324. See also *British Cotton Manufacture*,
p. 147.

responsible for Paul's and Wyatt's conjoint failure we have
no means of ascertaining, though it had probably more to do
with it than has usually been allowed. Arkwright, however,
was a man of a different calibre from any of these; or
indeed from most of his contemporaries and antagonists.
The greater the opposition to him the more industriously
did he devote himself to perfecting his machines, and the
higher rewards did he claim for them. By indomitable
energy and perseverance he prevailed against all obstacles,
forced his goods upon the market, and himself into a position
of dignity and opulence. The merchants and manufacturers
who had banded against his yarn were only too glad
eventually to accept it, and only too eager to follow in the
paths that he had marked out.

To what extent, we may ask at this point, was this
conduct, and were the feelings that prompted
it, justifiable? Or were they wholly inex-
cusable? These are questions that should
not be shirked. So far as employers were concerned in
adopting the courses above described, it is perhaps the
best excuse for them to plead simple ignorance, and that innate
opposition to change which naturally characterises dull and
unimaginative minds; and it is curious to notice in this
connection how few of the great inventors of mechanical
appliances sprang from the employers' class. Many of them
would be impelled by self-interest to resist changes which were
in advance of the little stock of knowledge and experience
they possessed, or had amassed; some would be envious of
the greater facilities of production that the new inventions
placed at the disposal of others; some, we may even believe,
or hope, would be genuinely influenced by the kindly but
mistaken views of the great Elizabeth. But for the working
classes, so far as their experience of the situation was concerned, no excuse is needed; though it is, of course, melancholy .

that their bitter experiences should sometimes have led them into the excesses that they sometimes did. They believed that machinery deprived them of much that they valued, and machinery *did so*. It deprived them of some of the most precious parts of the poor inheritance that might ever be theirs. It deprived them of the freer, more hopeful, more personal existence that was the lot of the handicraft worker; of the individual utilities acquired or the aptitudes inherited which distinguished this or that particular man from this or that other, and from the general mass. It sapped, or threatened to sap, as they saw it then, that feeling of separate identity, of self-sufficingness, of pride (in its better sense), that is the proper glory of very manhood. But it did even more. Coming upon the country, as the new system of production came, at a time when the means of communication were under any circumstances few and rude, and when every further obstacle which could be imposed upon change of place and work was imposed —by custom, by education, and even by positive law—it deprived (in transferring it elsewhere) large numbers of the population of the means of earning their living; it planted famine in their midst. This is what they *saw*, just as the former conditions were what they *felt*. They saw the labour that they had been accustomed to do with their hands, and that was intimately related to every action and passion of their lives, performed, and far better performed, by a passionless indefatigable machine: a mere combination of wood and metal : without a heart to feel, a stomach to be fed, or tender ties and sympathies to be accounted for. There were counterbalancing advantages of course. At some future time those machines were to cause more persons to be employed than they had ever thrown out of employment; they would from the first supply the operatives with the goods they had been used to make themselves, cheaper than they had ever made them. But what was that to them? They did not want to buy the goods but sell them. They could not wait for this new era, for they must exist meanwhile. The due fulfilment of economical laws did most assuredly, in the absence of any exterior impulse to the contrary, involve their present destruction; and that they knew, and for the moment it was all they cared to know. Thus gloomily, amid tumult, fear, and suffering, was the modern factory system introduced.

It is time, however, to end with the great mechanical contrivances which were instrumental in bringing that issue about, and to close this SAMUEL CROMPTON : THE MULE. chapter and this book. The invention of the " Mule " by Samuel Crompton (with the improvements which were afterwards introduced into its action)[1] brought the modern appliances for spinning up to the highest point of perfection. The water frame of Arkwright had been of the greatest use in spinning warp, but had failed in weft, which required more delicate treatment; the jenny was not capable of giving the requisite twist and consistency to warp yarns. Mr. Crompton, " a weaver of respectable character and circumstances," who lived in the neighbourhood of Bolton, devised a machine which was equally capable of either part, and united the better qualities of both, and it was from this mixed origin that it received its name. He tried for a while to keep the invention secret; but it soon became known, and was quickly pirated; for he had not guarded it by patent. It superseded at once the other machines for almost all kinds of manufacture, though after improvements in the water frame have since restored that appliance to

---

[1] Improvements were made by Mr. William Strutt of Derby and Mr. Kelly of Lanark ; but the great improvement, that of making the Mule self-acting, is the invention of Mr. William Roberts, who took out a patent for it in 1825.

some of its former popularity. Poor Crompton shared the fate of most great inventors and died in comparative poverty, notwithstanding the substantial but inadequate reward of £5000 which was voted him by Parliament in 1812. His death occurred in 1827.

For fifty years the tide of invention had thus set entirely in one direction, that of perfecting the operation of spinning, and a wondrous success had been achieved. It was the other department of production, the textile proper, or that of weaving, that now lagged behind. Those were halcyon days for weavers: however the poor spinsters suffered. The demand for their labour was unprecedented: its remuneration proportionally high. Hand looms were set up almost everywhere in the manufacturing districts; whole villages of weavers congregating in the neighbourhoods of the now fast rising factory towns, and every available space being utilised for putting up a loom. We have briefly glanced at the industrial characteristics of this period, and, a little more at length, at those of the period which immediately preceded it. Both were presently to pass wholly away;—to vanish as completely from English life as those other earlier industrial epochs which we have also endeavoured elsewhere to portray briefly, and this further great revolution was to be accomplished by the successful application of powers other than human to the action of the loom itself; by causing weaving, like spinning, to be performed " by machinery." Such a design had no doubt been often entertained in that era of great mechanical enterprise, and we have seen how the idea had even occurred to an English squire long before spinning by machinery had been attempted.[1] The effort had also been actually made. " A loom moved by water had been contrived by M. de Gennes so far back as the seventeenth

THE POWER LOOM.

----

[1] Page 349.

century. . . . About the middle of the eighteenth century a swivel-loom was invented by M. Vanconson; and in 1765 a weaving factory, probably filled with those looms, was erected by Mr. Gartside at Manchester; but no advantage was realised, as a man was required to superintend each loom."[1] But it was reserved for an English clergyman, and for the year 1785, to render this project practically feasible, and to see it successfully put in operation. The gentleman in question was the Rev. Dr. Edmund Cartwright, brother of the celebrated Major Cartwright, the well-known advocate of radical reform a century ago; and the circumstances that led to his invention are detailed by himself in an article on the " Cotton Manufacture," contributed to the first edition of the *Encyclopædia Britannica*, and repeated in the present (the ninth) edition. "Happening to be at Matlock in the summer of 1784 (he says), I fell in company with some gentlemen from Manchester, when the conversation turned on Arkwright's spinning machinery. One of the company observed that as soon as Arkwright's patent expired so many mills would be erected and so much cotton spun that hands never could be found to weave it. To this observation I replied that Arkwright must then set his wits to work to invent a weaving machine or mill. This brought on a conversation on the subject, in which the Manchester gentlemen unanimously agreed that the thing was impracticable; and in defence of their opinion they adduced arguments which I certainly was incompetent to answer, or even to comprehend, being totally ignorant of the subject, having never at that time seen a person weave. I controverted, however, the impracticability of the thing by remarking that there had lately been exhibited in London an automaton figure which played at chess. Now, you will not assert, gentlemen, said I, that it is more difficult to construct a machine that shall weave than one which shall make all

[1] *History of the Cotton Manufacture*, pp. 228, 229.

the variety of moves which are required in that complicated game. Some little time afterwards, a particular circumstance recalling this conversation to my mind, it struck me that, as in plain weaving—according to the conception I then had of the business—there could only be three movements which were to follow each other in succession, there would be little difficulty in producing and repeating them. Full of these ideas I immediately employed a carpenter and smith to carry them into effect. As soon as the machine was finished I got a weaver to put in the warp, which was of such materials as sail-cloth is usually made of. To my great delight a piece of cloth, such as it was, was the produce. As I had never before turned my thoughts to anything mechanical, either in theory or practice, nor had ever seen a loom at work, or knew anything of its construction, you will readily suppose that my first loom was a most rude piece of machinery. The warp was placed perpendicularly, the reed fell with the weight of at least half a hundredweight, and the springs which threw the shuttle were strong enough to have thrown a Congreve rocket. In short, it required the strength of two powerful men to work the machine at a slow rate, and only for a short time. Conceiving, in my great simplicity, that I had accomplished all that was required, I then secured what I thought a most valuable property by a patent, 4th April 1785. This being done, I then condescended to see how other people wove; and you will guess my astonishment when I compared their early methods of operation with mine. Availing myself, however, of what I then saw, I made a loom in its general principles nearly as they are now. But it was not till the year 1787 that I completed my invention, when I took out my last weaving patent, August 1 of that year." There is little to add to this simple and profoundly interesting description. Dr. Cartwright entered into business and failed; and the progress of the power-loom in general use was slow and painful, while its final triumph was, of course, inevitable. The history of that progress, and of the circumstances that accompanied and surrounded it, does not concern us here, but belongs to the history of the modern factory system, which this—the last of the great mechanical inventions of that age in the domain of textile industry—finally started, for good or evil, on its way.

INDEX

THE END.

J. D. & Co. Printed by R. & R. CLARK, Edinburgh.